P9-EDK-531

THE NEVER-ENDING WAR

THE NEVER-ENDING WAR

Terrorism in the 80's

CHRISTOPHER DOBSON
AND
RONALD PAYNE

Facts On File Publications
New York, New York • Oxford, England

THE NEVER-ENDING WAR: Terrorism in the 80s

Published by Facts On File, Inc.
460 Park Avenue South, New York, N.Y. 10016

Library of Congress Cataloging-in-Publication Data

Dobson, Christopher
  The never-ending war.

  Bibliography: p.
  Includes index.
  1. Terrorism. 2. Terrorists. I. Payne, Ronald.
II. Title.
HV6431.D615 1987 303.6'25 86-24093
ISBN 0-8160-1537-6

Printed in the United States of America
10 9 8 7 6 5 4 3 2 1

Contents

Preface

The aim of this book is to take a fresh look at international terrorism by examining the activities, tactics and techniques of the most active groups. Terror in this fin de siècle period has become such a staple in the daily news diet for millions of people that newspaper readers and television watchers cannot fail to be aware of its dramatic manifestations. Despite the detailed coverage of the big events it is difficult for nonspecialists to comprehend what it all means. Our purpose is to beat a path through the jungle of sects, communiqués and appalling deeds to help such people in their attempts to follow the complicated moves and to master the significance of big events as they develop. Even among police, army and intelligence officers whose task it is to fight against the perpetrators of violence in their national territory and who are experts about their own opponents, there is ignorance about other people's terrorists. Yet only too frequently other people's terrorists choose to bring their war to your territory.

Nearly 200 years ago Edmund Burke, writing of the French revolutionary feeders of the guillotine, referred to "thousands of those hell hounds called terrorists." What we have attempted to do in *The Never-Ending War* is to sort out their twentieth-century descendents into categories according to the declared aims of their violence. The purpose is to get to know them, not in a caring way but the better to destroy them.

As we completed research there was an upsurge of terror, state-sponsored by Libya, Syria and Iran and masterminded by their intelligence officers and diplomats. One form it took was a revival of the medieval practice of hostage taking. Sometimes individuals were seized in the streets of Beirut; on other occasions armed men took prisoner all the passengers aboard an aircraft or a liner. Here was the starting point; the acts of the most ferocious of the newcomers, religious terrorists for the faith of the Shi'ite branch of Islam, claiming to be sponsored by Allah as well as by Arab governments. The Shi'ite offensive spawned an alliance of state-run terrorists, mostly from the many-headed Palestinian movement. Colonel Gaddafi of Libya became its vociferous spokesman. Aided and abetted by his co-patron, President Hafez Assad, he went too far and the military might of America was deployed against him. All these events are examined in detail. Finally we shed new light on the complications and subtleties of the Soviet connection.

The story continues with an analysis of the actions and motives of the new European left-wing doctrinal terrorists. There is a close look at the old established bands in Spain and Ireland with nationalist/separatist objectives as their excuse for murder. The phenomenon of the many-headed Palestinian nationalist terrorists in competition with the Shi'ites is the other main theme. That section precedes a brief survey of the newer manifestations of low-intensity warfare in Latin America and the Far East.

There is some comfort to be found in the fact that the Western response to terror is increasingly vigorous and that terrorism, even in its most extreme form, is remarkably ineffective. Despite all the bloodshed, despite all the murderous ventures of the last 20 years, it can be seen that fighters in scores of forlorn causes have failed to achieve their aims. The Palestinians have not gained one inch of Palestinian territory; the Armenians are no closer to their homeland. In Europe ideological raiders have failed miserably in their hope of destabilizing the old democracies.

Even so, this is no time for smugness and much remains to be done to make life harder still for the terrorists and their masters. The book concludes by using examples from the narrative to provide some helpful clues for further measures to protect the West.

For the title we are indebted to Colonel Muammar Gaddafi. In a hectoring and belligerent mood after President Reagan's denunciation of Libya for its part in the hijack of an Egyptair flight to Malta, he threatened to make never-ending war. It seemed appropriate to borrow the words of such an undoubted expert in terror to categorize a form of warfare which once started goes pointlessly on and on. Terrorists become so tied up in the intricacies of plotting and planning that they are apt to lose sight of the original aims. It often seems that terrorist activity is interminable and that for the rest of our lives we shall have to put up with all the tiresome humiliations of security, so necessary to protect citizens from its ravages. We in the West even have to sacrifice a morsel of the freedom we fought so hard to attain.

The trouble with writing a book about terrorism is that the action never stops for very long and so the most critical task is to decide when to put a period at the end of the last paragraph. Despite that difficulty the authors believe that it is a worthwhile enterprise to set down the truth as they see it about the most dangerous groups operating in the world today.

We would like to acknowledge with gratitude the help and guidance received from our many friends in the Middle East, none of whom, things being what they are in that part of the world, would like to have their names set down here. The German section could not have been researched without the help of Bernt von Waldorf, counsellor at the embassy of the Federal Republic in London, who took great trouble to arrange for us to meet senior people in the BKA, the Ministry of the Interior, the Public Prosecutor's office and to visit Colonel Dee of GSG 9. Beppe Severgnine, London correspondent of *Il Giornale*, with the help of the archivist at his newspaper, placed at our disposal a great deal of information about Italian terrorism. Annaloa Copps was invaluable as a charmingly enthusiastic researcher and Italian translator. U.S. diplomats and other officials gave a hand with the intricacies of American politics and reactions. Members of President Mitterrand's special staff at the Elysée kindly brought us up to date with developments in France. The world's most experienced antiterrorist police officers, at New Scotland Yard and at the headquarters of the Royal Ulster Constabulary in Belfast, were generous with their time and help.

Introduction:
The Unexpected

After the explosion, the only recognizable part of the body of Raad Ajeel was a severed hand. Only because in life he had been fingerprinted was it possible to discover the identity of this Arab who deliberately crashed his General Motors truck through the gates of the United States embassy in Kuwait and, knowing that he would die, detonated its cargo of hexogen and butane.

This was not the first human bomb in the Middle East; other Shi'ite Moslems had already destroyed the American embassy in Beirut. They had killed 241 American servicemen and 58 French soldiers of the international force in that tormented city. Nor was it to be the last such attack. But there was a particular horror about the events that took place on December 12, 1983 in Kuwait because the suicide terrorist was actually named and traced, and can be seen as a real human being.

Raad Meftel Ajeel was just 25 years old, shown in his identity photograph as an otherwise insignificant Iraqi Arab with bushy eyebrows, a little moustache and puzzled eyes. Both he and his brother, Saad, were sincere Moslems, much affected by the religious revival which led to the persecution of fellow Shi'ites in Iraq. To strike back against the persecutor of their sect, President Saddam Hussein, they threw grenades at Baghdad police stations. Both brothers were sentenced to death; Saad was executed and Raad escaped to Iran, where true to the teachings of Al Dawa (The Call—for religious reawakening) he offered his services to exiled Iraqi guerrillas. They trained him as a bomber in the holy city of Qom and, for the faith, he was ready to sacrifice his life to destroy an American lair in Arabia for, through the confusions of geopolitics, the United States was regarded as the root of all evil.

Then they sent him to Kuwait just across the Gulf and fixed him up with a job as a driver with Sultan, a local trading company in Kuwait. Early one December morning he drove steadily through the streets of the modern Gulf city, thinking God knows what thoughts, and pressed the button which destroyed himself.

Acts like this deeply shocked the Western world which continues, even after all our wars, to regard individual human life as sacred. The very idea of the self-directed human bomb, the bomber as a detonator of himself, deeply shocked Americans and Europeans, though they were already accustomed to living with modern forms of ancient violence in all their strange manifestations. To surrender life deliberately to make just one more pointless terrorist gesture seemed horrendous.

It was the feelings evoked by such actions and the scale of the casualties which first brought home to public opinion in the United States that Americans and their way of life were a prime target for the powerful forces of theocratically inspired terror emanating from the Middle East. The natural response of such a vigorous country as America was that something urgently needed to be done, not just by taking defensive measures but by striking back at those responsible for it. Lebanon was the cockpit and the no-man's land for the first countermeasures. The battleship USS *New Jersey* offshore fired its 16-inch guns at the shadowy men in the mountains. Warplanes from the fleet made their attacks, but two were shot down and the surviving crews became hostages of the terrorists and their Syrian backers.

Though it was satisfying to strike back, it had to be admitted that the tactical results were less than satisfactory. The debate began about how best to fight the elusive killers.

It brought realization that the suicide attackers were only the point men for interested states which backed them. Behind the Shi'ites stood the power of revolutionary Iran and already the Carter administration had received an object lesson in the dangers of military operations against that country. Nor was Iran the only state patron of terror. On the border of Lebanon was Syria, an aggressive tyranny armed to the teeth with Soviet military hardware, more than 4,000 tanks including 1,000 T-72s and 500 combat aircraft. The terrorists, Shi'ite and Palestinian, were offered safe refuge to plot and prepare under the guns and antiaircraft missiles of this state. The United States had the power to take military action there, but to do so would involve Israel and quite likely lead to a general Middle East war with the USSR as the protector of the Syrians.

Even the Israeli airforce, the most experienced and battle-hardened in the world, had trouble in dealing with targets in the great terrorist haven of the Bekaa valley on the Syrian border. It needed a major air assault to destroy the SAMs provided by the Soviets complete with 12,000 instructors and Red Army officer helpers. The Israeli jet strikes during their invasion of Lebanon led to a full-scale air battle. To hit the guerrilla bands they first had to destroy a chunk of the Syrian MiG force.

The dilemma for President Reagan was there. Tempting though it was to bring the weight of American military power to bear on the regional state sponsors of terror, such action would involve the probability of a large-scale confrontation, with incalculable consequences in a region which is, moreover, close to the backyard of the Soviet Union. Would the results justify the effort and the dangers?

There was, however, another possibility. The remaining and junior partner in the triumvirate of terror-backing states was Colonel Muammar Gaddafi's Libya. Iran supplied Islamic religious and revolutionary fervor supported by American-made weapons of war sold previously to the Shah. Syria provided the real muscle and the big battalions guarding the terrorist's lair. Colonel Gaddafi was the financial provider.

Here then were the three pillars of the unholy alliance of terror sponsorship. In June 1985 members of that alliance agreed at secret meetings to activate the groups under their respective control. Iran would manipulate Islamic Jihad and Hizbollah (Party of God), all of which had bases in the Bekaa valley under Syrian control. Syria itself was to use the so-called "Palestine Salvation Front," the dissidents from the Arafat PLO, including the Abu Nidal faction. These bands all had headquarters both in Damascus and in Libya.

Muammar Gaddafi, being the most garrulous and reckless

of the three heads of the terror-backing states, took it upon himself to become the spokesman. Determined to be the star of the show he used his oil millions to further his vaunting ambition to become the new leader of the Arab world on the backs of gunmen and bombers of his own Middle East equivalent of the Foreign Legion. For all that he was the weakest link in the chain, and therefore on any rational assessment the best choice as a target.

Libya, which looks so big on the map, is a relatively small state consisting of three or four principal cities, a coastal strip and a great deal of sand. Its population of only three million not very martial people is barely able to sustain its small armed forces, grotesquely oversupplied with Soviet tanks, missiles and aircraft. With its long Mediterranean coastline the country, which has for years provided funds, weapons and training to almost every known terrorist and guerrilla group on earth, lay wide open to sea and air attack.

The factor which further singled out Libya as a country ready-made for attack was the fact that Colonel Gaddafi is such a publicity-conscious braggart and loudmouth. He had the effrontery to say that he intended to declare war on the United States. His technique was first to boast about what he would do to launch international terrorists, then to deny that he approved of terrorism, using a weasel argument that there was a great difference between a terrorist and a "freedom fighter." Although even Gaddafi cannot be held responsible for every single act of terrorism committed by Arabs, his increasingly provocative and boastful language gave the impression that he was.

Certainly it was one of his *protégé* organizations, the Abu Nidal faction, which killed 16 people, including five Americans, at Rome and Vienna airports just after Christmas 1985. The gunmen used Tunisian passports obtained courtesy of the Libyan government. That was the act which brought the terror crisis to a head. A day later planning began in Washington for a confrontation with the manic-depressive colonel from Tripoli as the administration began considering what it might do. Already the Sixth Fleet was being reinforced, ready for a naval demonstration of strength.

On March 24, 1986, the overconfident Muammar Gaddafi provided a good reason for action when his missile batteries fired two SAM 5s at U.S. naval aircraft flying lawfully over the Gulf of Sirte (or Sidra). The Libyans were in a minority of one in claiming that the waters below were Libyan south of

32° 30' north latitude, dramatically called by Gaddafi the "line of death." After four more missiles had been fired the Navy went into action, hitting four Libyan patrol boats and twice attacking missile sites onshore.

Until then President Reagan had held back because of anxiety about the fate of the thousand and more Americans still in Libya. Early in January while announcing a trade embargo, he gave a clear warning to Colonel Gaddafi by ordering all American residents to leave. Their departure would "untie our hands" for further measures.

Meanwhile the Libyan leader too busy with forward planning. In early February 1986 he gathered under his auspices in Tripoli the bosses of 20 of the most active groups of Middle East terrorists, including those masterminded by Syria and Iran. In secret conference they prepared a campaign of murder, hijack and bombing "to escalate the armed struggle" against Israel, Europe and against Americans in Europe and the Mediterranean area. They also set up what they called "revolutionary suicide forces." Among those present at the secret meeting were the operations chief of the Abu Nidal faction and heads of the Popular Front for the Liberation of Palestine (PFLP). The Israelis made a spirited attempt to catch some of these notorious terror masters by forcing down a Libyan executive jet on route from Tripoli to Damascus. They chose the wrong plane, for when the passengers were identified, they turned out to be Syrian leaders of the Baath party.

It was not long before the results of the Tripoli terror plan were demonstrated. In quick succession a bomb aboard a TWA flight from Rome to Cairo blasted a hole in the airliner through which three adults and a baby were sucked to their death over the Gulf of Corinth on April 12, 1986. The number-one suspect was the Abu Nidal faction. Three days later another device planted in La Belle, a crowded Berlin discotheque patronized by U.S. servicemen, killed an American army sergeant and a Turkish woman.

This time, speaking of the involvement of Libyan diplomats from East Berlin and of state intelligence men in planning and organizing the disco raid, the President was confident enough to declare: "Our evidence is direct, it is precise, it is irrefutable."

Muammar Gaddafi was firmly in the dock. The Reagan administration with the backing of the intelligence community felt convinced that their information, obtained by communications intercepts, proved his complicity no matter how he wriggled. Action was called for. The time was right and so was the target. Already a fleet of warships led by the carriers *Coral Sea* and *Saratoga* were on station within range of Libya. Aircraft from the Sixth Fleet were briefed for a strike on Benghazi and a flying tanker force was mustered to fuel British-based F-111s for the attack on Gaddafi's Revolutionary Headquarters and other terrorist centers in Tripoli. At last retribution was to be delivered. "We are going to defend ourselves, and we are certainly going to take action in the face of specific terrorist threats," warned President Reagan.

There can be no doubt about the efficacy of the air strike when it came. It destroyed terrorist centers and communications and the effect upon Colonel Gaddafi himself was dramatic. For the first time in living memory he disappeared and went silent for several days, leaving public duties to the remaining quartet of fellow revolutionary officers who came to power with him. He was plain frightened, as well he might have been. Several factors nonetheless marred the success of the air strike. An F-111 was shot down and its crew perished. Either because of this, or for other reasons, a number of bombs damaged nonmilitary buildings including those of European embassies. There were between 50 and 100 civilian casualties, including Gaddafi's small adopted daughter.

The death rate was not enormous for an operation on this scale, but enough to raise public outcry and indignation, exploited by Libyan propagandists and by other Arab states. Once again it was the television images of death and destruction caused by bombing which hit the outside world first. Libyan news management carefully fostered the impression of suffering civilians and took good care to prevent any pictures of military target damage from appearing. Yet most bombs did strike their targets, for example in the sprawling fortress of the Azzizia barracks where Gaddafi has his home and his headquarters. His electronic war room was destroyed, even though he and the famous tent survived. In Europe and in the Arab world there was indignation, and yet again the caricatures of President Reagan as the wild shooting cowboy made their appearance.

The secondary wave of what can only be described as anti-Americanism arose out of the fact that the F-111 jets used in the strike were based, under a long-standing treaty arrangement, at British airfields. Prime Minister Margaret Thatcher agreed to the use of those airfields on certain conditions, namely that every effort should be made to ensure that the air strikes were surgical, and that everything possible should be done to ensure accuracy. The other European allies in NATO refused even to allow the aircraft to overfly their airspace, thus forcing the mission to detour around the Atlantic coast to Gibraltar and then over the Mediterranean to the North African shore. This greatly increased the complexity of the operation.

Although the British government had given its blessings to an old friend, the opposition Labour party used the affair to its own advantage and Mrs. Thatcher lost points in the public opinion polls. Because she won the admiration and thanks of the administration she was unkindly described in Parliament as "Reagan's poodle."

What seems even more extraordinary is that, on the one hand, the Europeans and many in Britain, in sympathizing with Libya, seemed to forget that it was Gaddafi, by sponsoring terrorism, who had caused the trouble in the first place. On the other hand, after the raids they put themselves in a panic about the terrible reprisals in their countries which they were convinced that the Libyan leader would order. To read again some of the commentaries made at the time, it might be imagined that the old continent was in for a positive bloodbath of a summer. In fact nothing of the kind happened, though of course there were incidents starting with a thwarted attempt to blow up an El Al flight at London airport by getting a pregnant woman to try and carry explosives aboard. The chances are that long before that American raid this operation had been planned to coincide with the Jewish Passover.

The reason for the panic goes back to the earlier wave of suicide bombings in the Middle East. They created an enormously strong impression that there were thousands of such men and women available to bring the new form of warfare to the West. The triple alliance of terror played upon this fear by constantly referring to perfectly ordinary hit teams as "suicide squads."

In their alarm the Westerners sought refuge in clichés to explain such strange events. The bombers were put down as "ruthless fanatics," "zealots," "kamikazes" of a strange and mysterious religion. But none of these words managed to exorcise the fears. For what is a religious fanatic but a firm and righteous believer in the faith. Nor was it easy to explain the nature of the new enemy in this clash between two worlds. The beliefs of men and women keen and anxious to kill and destroy even at the certain price of their own life do not fit neatly into TV commentaries and electronic reportage. It did not help to look back into Arab history and explain that centuries ago the *hashishin*, assassins, were persuaded to kill while under the influence of hashish. The world is upside down and we are the drug smokers and injectors now, and they are the ones who do not need to be drugged to die, or to kill.

While the comfortable outside world began doubting that there was any defense possible against such religious terrorists, the suicide technique was copied by other Lebanese, and, it must be remembered, the citizens of Lebanon are among the most civilized and intelligent in the Arab world. The new suicide attacks, a score or so within a year, and mostly against Israeli forces and their local auxiliaries, were not made by people primarily inspired by religion. The attackers were mixed ethnically and divided in religion. Some were Shi'ites, but others were Greek Orthodox Christians, Druzes, Palestinians and Sunni Moslems. Their inspiration was nationalist and political, for in the main they were members of a curious survival of a leftover party of the 1930s which began life under the inspiration of Benito Mussolini, the Italian dictator. It was called the Syrian National Socialist party, nazi for short, though its modern members preferred to forget that by inverting the title to socialist national.

These new suicide bombers, death volunteers driving the explosive trucks and parlor cars, added a horrible refinement of technique by calling in the power of television. Before setting out on a mission they recorded on video a message about themselves and what they were about to do. Sana Mahaidali, the first woman to blow herself up to kill Israeli soldiers, announced her reasons on videotape before setting out. In the posthumous transmission she made only a polite nod towards religion.

"I am very relaxed as I go to do this operation. I am from a group that decided on self-sacrifice and martyrdom for the sake of the liberation of land and people."

Sixteen, with long hair and dark eyes, she had told her parents she was going out to buy some lipstick. She looked and talked more like a heroine of the French resistance than an Iranian woman swathed in a *chador*. Miss. Ibtissam Harb, the next woman suicide, in her video appearance before death by bomb, wore lipstick, eye shadow, a combat jacket and a red beret with the SNSP party badge. She looked a thoroughly nice Lebanese girl, but she said she hoped to kill as many Jews as possible. She was followed on the screen by a sad young man with the same beret, who later preceded her to his death ride in a Peugeot which exploded at a road block killing him and 15 others.

So the young people made their appearance to smile for the cameras and then to die on forlorn missions for which they had been chosen, as though by some evil casting director, because they looked right. They were watched on screens in comfortable living rooms in faraway Western places, evoking wonder, even sympathy, and bewilderment. They were not wild-looking, rag-headed fanatics like followers of the Mahdi, but nice kids in Western clothes who looked like people's brothers and sisters, sons and daughters. It was not their words which struck such deep chords, but their appearance and subsequent deeds.

Theirs was a new brand of terrorism, alien in philosophy, but familiar in personnel. How could these people bring themselves to do it? That is one of the questions this book attempts to answer. It was not only the feeling of incomprehension that such agreeable, well-brought-up kids could kill themselves, but fear about the impossibility of defense against what seemed a mass willingness to die, not in battle, but simply to make gestures of hatred against both Israel and its friends. Bearded ayatollahs and faction leaders exploited their death to boast that thousands more were ready and willing to follow the example.

Jeane Kirkpatrick, the former U.S. ambassador to the United Nations, spoke for many, when in a *Newsweek* interview about specifically Shi'ite bombers, she said: "It's very hard for us to believe that they are suicidal, that they are really basically indifferent to their own survival, and also that they are indifferent to what we think of as rational self-interest."

The new Middle East terrorists, and a score or so of suicide bombs, shook the world. Their emergence and its effect on public opinion was a factor in forcing the Israeli army out of Lebanon, for even the iron fist of Israel was attached to the limp wrist of public opinion. The attacks persuaded the international force of Americans, British, French and Italians in

Lebanon to quit the field. Alarm caused by the new terrorists, and fear that they would operate also in Western homelands, led to the creation of tank-trap defenses around the White House itself and outside government offices in Whitehall. Millions were spent on defending diplomatic missions around the world. Because it had been so successful in the eyes of those who launched human bombs, every imitative terror group in the Middle East underworld began at least to pretend that its politically motivated killers were in fact suicide teams.

The threat came when the Western world was just beginning to believe that it was getting terrorism under control after the litany of names and dates which are markers in the long war, from Munich to Entebbe, from Belfast to Brighton, from OPEC in Vienna, to Tehran and Beirut. All the techniques available to the assorted red armies, national liberation fronts and commandos named after martyrs, seemed to have been explored. Kidnap, assassination, hijack, bombs and machine-gun raids had all be cataloged, analyzed and guarded against. There had been preemptive alarms ·about terrorists and nuclear bombs, poisoned water supplies and germ warfare. Then came the unexpected horror shock of the suicide bomb. It was a terrible reminder of the shudder caused when the first Japanese kamikaze pilot aimed his flying bomb at an American warship in the Pacific. There seemed no limit to human ingenuity and determination to find new and horrible ways to destroy each other.

When the first Shi'ite Moslem drove his truck bomb into the compound of the U.S. embassy in Beirut it announced the beginning of a new era in the wars of nastiness. It was not simply the act but the philosophy behind it which caused alarm and indignation. In the Western world, where despite all wars and brutalities and the paganization of society enough of the old Christian ways still exist to make human life appear to be still sacred, it seemed unthinkable for a man deliberately to take his own life in order to blow up others, no matter what the cause.

In our part of the world ineluctable self-slaughter, no matter what the cause, seems wrong. In the materialist society, life is something to be held on to at all costs. Even when the flame burns low in old age, doctors still employ every skill to fan the embers. Our humanist way of life is dedicated to staying alive as long as possible. It was not always so; for while the overwhelming Christian majority still believed in life after death, the time of a human being in this vale of sin and woe did not seem so important.

Our forbears would have understood better the attitude of the Islamic terrorists who remain staunch believers that if they die in a good cause they will be rewarded in heaven. Death is the final and feared enemy of agnostics and the doubters; to the believers its terrors are soothed. Modern Western man was terrified by the terrorists of Islam because of his greater fear of the last enemy. Seeing the rise of the suicide bomber, he began to despair. The cry was that nothing could be done against these people, strange and alien as creatures from outer space, who willingly threw away their lives.

As further evidence of the impossiblity of coming to terms with such people, commentators drew attention to the war between Iran and Iraq in which human waves of young Iranians seeking martyrdom advanced hopelessly through the minefields, simply to explode the devices so that others behind them might succeed in the attack. But that was different. The Iranians were not the only young men to have made hopeless assaults on enemy positions. There was never a shortage of volunteers in the Duke of Wellington's army in Spain to join the "forlorn hope," a first small unit to launch the attack upon a besieged fortress. On the Somme in the First World War, the Barnsley Pals, a volunteer regiment from northern England, was torn to pieces in hopeless advances across no-man's-land. They were not called human wave fanatics, but heroes. United States Marines fighting their way up the beaches at Iwo Jima did not rate their chances of survival very high, but they were not crazy zealots, simply brave men fighting for a cause.

We should remember our own history when observing the wars and terror campaigns in the Middle East. Nor should it be forgotten that the suicide bombs and the human wave fighters are nonetheless human beings like ourselves. The mass of them may well be devout believers. But they are still people with the same bodies and minds as those whom they terrify. This fact in itself is a pretty sure indication that among them are doubters and backsliders. In their ranks, too, are those who wonder whether there really is a paradise waiting, and reason that the life they know here on earth may yet be preferable, because of its familiarity, to anything awaiting when it ends. The supply of death volunteers never has been, and is unlikely to become, inexhaustable.

Not every Iranian longs for martyrdom, not every terrorist is ready to volunteer to blow himself up with his target. Long lines of people in search of visas form outside almost every foreign embassy in Tehran. They are the ones attempting to vote with their feet against suicidal war and the probability of death-and-paradise missions. Neither the ranting clergy, who themselves show little disposition to achieve the martyrdom they urge upon others, nor the political brainwashers are capable of psyching up all of the people all the time. Religious revivals do not last forever.

By and large the new terrorists in the world of Islam are those inspired by religion. But the Palestinians who resorted to the weapons of terror in a hitherto unsuccessful struggle to establish their own state will not allow us to forget that *their* motivation is nationalist. Although their powerful Arab allies have three times been defeated in the field by the Israeli enemy, the Palestine exiles, now divided into many factions, and having lost their base in Lebanon, still fight on. Old leaders perish, usually through illness. For it is noticeable on this front too in the terror wars that the leaders are of the "go on" variety, rather than the "come on" sort. Abu Nidal for a while pretended that he was dead, the better to conceal his plots. Then he reemerged in the winter of 1985, sponsored by Colonel Gaddafi of Libya, to send his team to hijack an Egyptian airliner and take it to Malta. New groups come to prominence with new men at the top, running their terror bands under the sponsorship of friendly states for whom they do favors. Arab leaders like Muammar Gaddafi, and President Hafez al-Assad of Syria, whenever it suits their purposes, cynically pick up such groups like cards from a pack and use them to plant bombs here, or to machine and murder there. With even greater cynicism they then piously denounce terrorism and blame the West for failing to recognize "freedom fighters."

Even Yassir Arafat, while negotiating diplomatically, found time to create a new raiding group called Force 17 in 1984 from the ruins of Fatah. Its murder of three Israelis aboard a yacht moored at Larnaca in Cyprus brought the traditional Israeli response of an air attack upon the PLO's headquarters-in-exile in distant Tunis. The Larnaca act itself was a warning that the divided island of Cyprus only a few miles from the Arab mainland was in danger of "Beirutalization."

From the Larnaca affair emerged another example of the

changing face of terrorists. The Palestinian hit squad there was led by a young Englishman, a carpenter named Ian Davison, who was happy to boast about killing Israelis. Partly under the influence of revolutionary socialists in his hometown of South Shields, but largely, he explained, because he had been so shocked by a television film about the massacres in Lebanon, he joined a PLO hit squad. After being sentenced to life imprisonment in Cyprus he declared that he was content with what he had done, no doubt believing that before long his group comrades would get him free. Sure enough, a few months later they kidnapped two Cypriots in Lebanon and offered their lives against his release.

In 1985 the new terrorists were at large almost everywhere. After a period of relative calm in West Germany and in Italy the groups of the ideological young rampagers were on the march again. They chose as their targets the installations of NATO, the North Atlantic Treaty alliance, set up to protect Europe and the United States from Soviet military ambitions. The Red Army Faction and the Revolutionary Cells across the Rhine, and Direct Action in France, announced their combined conspiracy to strike at the alliance and at the defense industry, its managers and controllers. In this campaign they were helped by CCC, the acronym for Cellules Combattantes Communistes, a new Belgian group, responsible for 28 attacks in 14 months, and by the reviving Red Brigades in Italy.

The only Western countries still relatively immune from the plague of terrorism, at least from that carried out by their own citizens, are Britain and the United States. Yet it has been estimated that two-thirds of all victims of terror are Americans, almost all of them people living abroad. It is one of the paradoxes of the terror conflict that although more Americans have been attacked and killed than nationals of any other single country, very few of them have come to harm within their own country. But overseas, soldiers, diplomats and government officials at work in many parts of the world have been murdered. Business executives do not escape terrorist attentions. They are obvious murder, kidnap and ransom targets for those waging war upon capitalism and its multinational business outposts.

By 1985 there had been well over 3,000 terrorist attacks upon Americans and American property. Including casualties caused by the Lebanese suicide bomb attacks, more than 350 have been assassinated. Yet within the United

States many more people die as victims of criminal attacks than at the hands of terror groups.

Such bands as do operate from time to time within the country are imported international ones, like Armenians and Croatians or Latin Americans, rather than domestic ones. Of the 31 domestic incidents reported in 1983, two-thirds were the work of groups with interests in the Caribbean or in Latin America. They included such groups as Omega 7, an anti-Castro outfit, the Macheteros and FALN, armed forces of national liberation from Puerto Rico. The only domestic groups were the Revolutionary Fighting Group and the Armed Resistance Unit, both protesting U.S. involvement in Latin America. But the following year the homegrown groups tended to be more active against defense contractors. They also began choosing as targets companies and people doing business with South Africa. The aim was to display their disapproval of racial discrimination in that country and to attack those branded as supporters of it.

The crisis in South Africa became the focus of attention in 1986 as America and the Europeans became ever more outspoken in challenging the ugly system of apartheid and its white apologists. Although this is not the place to examine in detail the complicated scenario unfolding there, it must be observed that the movements of protest against South Africa were beginning to provide a cause comparable to that of the Vietnam War. More violent elements in the West will undoubtedly seek to exploit genuine public indignation. Mass demonstrations, be they political or ecological, tend to draw to themselves all those anarchist and fringe movements of the left and right which always seek to enroll mass support to justify their attempts to overthrow a hated system through terror and violence.

In South Africa itself all the symptoms appeared presaging a large-scale terrorist conflict. Within a few weeks of the South African government's imposing a draconian state of emergency, a dozen bombs exploded in the big cities, a sure sign that the ANC (African National Congress) was treading a dangerous path of terrorism.

The only terrorist movements in America and Britain to compare with the European ones now reactivated made their appearance 20 years ago. The Americans had their Weathermen, the student radicals nourished by the campus causes of the 1960s, and the British had their Angry Brigade. But, although they were busy on both sides of the Atlantic for a while, both perished, and they failed in attempts to restart later. In 1981 the May 19 Communist Organization, a Weathermen spin-off, was involved in an attempt upon a Brink's armored car in which two police officers and a guard were killed at Nyack, New York. It is an interesting phenomenon that in neither of the Anglo-Saxon countries does native terrorism easily catch on. The kind of open democracy practiced in these old, established and stable societies discourages that form of violence. Dissatisfied people can make their views known in other and less violent ways and the terror tradition is absent. Perhaps too, the self-confidence of such parliamentary states makes it difficult for the worst kinds of violence to take root.

But such defenses are less efficacious in protecting the two countries against imported new terrorism from the outside world. Britain has suffered more than most countries from a many-pronged foreign assault. The Provos of the IRA are on the doorstep, always tempted by the prospect of a big coup in England by their active service units. Their most ambitious attempt so far came in 1984 when they almost succeeded in blowing up Mrs. Thatcher and her ministers in a conference hotel at Brighton. A triumphant statement from the IRA boasted that the blast would make the British prime minister realize "that she cannot occupy our country . . . and get away with it." The Provo command ended with a warning: "Today we were unlucky, but remember we only have to be lucky once." In that remark there is a certain truth about terrorism; those who need to defend themselves against the bombers and killers do need to be lucky all the time. There was no doubt that the IRA would try again. Indeed the announcement late in 1985 of an agreement between the British government and that of the Irish Republic intended to restore peace in the troubled island was the signal for a new campaign of terror by the Provisionals. The Irish zealots will no doubt strike again. But they are not the only ones active in London, which as a surrogate capital of the Middle East pulls in the assassins and bombers from every part of the world of Islam anxious to use it as killing ground in their own quarrels.

Most European capitals suffer the same fate. So too, do Americans, though they have been fortunate so far to escape the worst of Islamic terror on home territory. Attempts have been made to enroll the support of American black Moslem groups to work with infiltrators from the Middle East. But the Federal Bureau of Investigation, the lead organization in protecting the United States against terrorism, has displayed skill and diligence in fending off the attackers, by infiltrating their cells and by a policy of controlled surveillance. Even so, Senator Jeremiah Denton, (Rep. Ala.), chairman of the Subcommittee on Security and Terrorism, has pointed out that responsibility for dealing with terrorism remains divided among at least 18 different agencies. America remains in an exposed position to new terrorist threats. Despite work done on establishing and training the Delta Force, it has still not proved itself in action, and the Beirut hijack in 1985 and that in Malta demonstrated, yet again, not only the need for special forces, but also the great difficulties of employing them in hostile regions of the world.

A terrorist threat continues to hang over almost every country. Even the Russians are not immune. Four of their diplomats in Beirut were seized as hostages. One of them was murdered and impossible Moslem demands were made that the Soviet Union should force their client state, Syria, to stop a factional battle in Tripoli. Suddenly the Russians were confronted by exactly the same dilemma that embarrassed the United States when the Islamic hijacker of the TWA flight insisted that Washington must compel its client state, Israel, to release prisoners in exchange for lives.

So the unlikely drama of world terrorism continues. The scriptwriters always have another paradox at hand, a fresh twist for the plot, and a few new terrorist movements waiting in the wings—the Sikh nationalists from India, the Tamil Tigers from Sri Lanka, or the Shining Path from Peru.

There is some consolation to be found in the fact that not all terror movements go on forever, some just fade away. The alpine valleys of the Tyrol no longer echo to bombs planted by discontented Germans incorporated in Italy. Quebec separatists, once considered such a threat, are no longer operational. Cyprus now independent for 25 years was once a terror center as EOKA (*Ethniki Organosis Kyprion Agoniston*, National Organization of Cypriot Fighters) Greeks battled with the British. Although nearly half the island has been seized by the Turks, the Cypriot Greeks have never shown any sign that they intend to form terrorist bands to fight against people they call oppressors. And, whatever became of the Tupamaros of Latin America?

Terrorism is the art of the unexpected.

Part One

HOLY WAR

1.

Terror
From
Tehran

The new Islamic forces of murder, mayhem and brutality sprang fully armed from the Iranian Revolution of 1979. This began in a form which would have been entirely familiar to Robespierre and the French revolutionaries of the eighteenth century. The newly created Revolutionary Guards persecuted and massacred supporters of the Shah's overthrown regime in general, and in particular members of the old state security organization, Savak. Then they turned to smelling out heresy and hunting down any Iranian who faltered in enthusiasm for the regime of Ayatollah Khomeini. The search for traitors involved the new regime's intelligence organization in active service abroad. Their task was to seek out, and to liquidate, opponents who had taken refuge in foreign countries.

Revolutionary fervor turned upon foreign countries condemned by the Ayatollah Khomeini because of their support for the Shah. It was inevitable that at the top of this list stood the United States, a country which in the eyes of the new Iranian zealots must now be punished for its sins. The first punishment took the form of the seizure by an armed mob of the U.S. embassy in Tehran. The Iranians held 52 American diplomats and staff as hostages for 444 long days. When President Jimmy Carter's rescue mission failed in the wreckage of the helicopters and aircraft which had carried Colonel Charles Beckwith's Delta force to Iran, America was

3

again branded as enemy number one and marked down for further scourging when the time became ripe.

So a new form of terror came into being. Its instruments were, first the Tehran mob; then the Revolutionary Guards and the state security apparatus, both directed by Shi'ite fundamentalist clergymen. In 1982 the regime dispatched 2,000 Iranians to Baalbek in the Bekaa valley, ostensibly to fight the Israeli invaders, but in fact to spread revolution to Lebanon. With the cooperation of the Syrian army which in general controlled that part of the country close to the Syrian border, they transformed that region into an Iranian stronghold.

Lebanon is a place of arms. Already it had suffered the misfortune of having a large part of its territory dominated by the Palestine Liberation Organization and all its many factions. In 1982 the Palestinian forces were being driven out by the invading Israeli army, but they were speedily replaced by the new Shi'ite terrorists and militia based upon the Baalbek redoubt of Iranian revolutionaries.

In Lebanon there already existed a strong Shi'ite community relieved to see the departure of domineering Palestinians, and even ready to welcome the Israelis, who won temporary favor by driving out a mutual enemy. The Shi'ites were particularly strong in the south of Lebanon, and they also controlled the southern suburbs of Beirut, especially when the population there was strengthened by the arrival of thousands of refugees from the war zone farther south. If they were pleased by the discomfort of the Palestinians, they rejoiced even more at the arrival in the Bekaa valley of coreligionists from Iran bringing with them the enthusiasm of a triumphant Shi'ite revolution.

Lebanon was already a place of many armies—private ones, at that. From this reservoir of partly trained men, smaller groups of multinational Islamic terrorists—later known as suicide bombers—were recruited, and this small country in the Mediterranean had the misfortune to become the cradle of new terrorism.

Terrorist groups are the "special forces" of guerrilla warfare. They exist to take the opponent by surprise, to shock and create alarm and apprehension in his ranks with the aim of promoting their cause. Before the word Shi'ite had ever figured in newspaper headlines, both the Israelis and then their enemies the Palestinians turned to this form of subversive warfare. The new factor in Middle East terrorism of the 1980s was that fresh groups in the Middle East, although obviously influenced by political considerations, were motivated by religion.

The Islamic terror movement had its deeper roots in the great resurgence of the Moslem faith during the latter half of the twentieth century. Burning religious zeal inspired the young Shi'ites who replaced the Palestinians as the most formidable terrorist group of the eighties. Although the religious reawakening affected the whole of the world of Islam with its teeming millions, the warlike consequences of it were most remarkable in the Shia sect, with its 87 million adherents scattered throughout the minaret world from Morocco to Afghanistan and Pakistan. The Moslem population of the Soviet republic of Azerbaidjan, formerly Iranian, is overwhelmingly Shi'ite.

The theological-political quarrel with the orthodox Sunni Moslems (of whom there are 650 million), goes back in history to the seventh century A.D. Shortly after the death of the Prophet Mohammed in A.D. 632 Shi'ite rebels broke with the Sunnis on the question of who should succeed him. It was important to them for Mohammed had established not only a new religion but a new community of which he was also the guide and sovereign. Although there could be no other Prophet, they believed that leadership of Islam should pass to Ali, husband of Mohammed's daughter, Fatima. Instead Abu Bakr was appointed caliph. In the civil wars which followed the rebels came to be known as the Shia—the Shiat Ali, or party of Ali—and also the party of dissent. When Hussein, son of Ali, was killed fighting the Sunnis in the great battle at Kerbela (A.D. 680) in what is now Iraq, he became the inspiration for that spirit of martyrdom which has dominated the Shi'ite tradition ever since. Shi'ites are the followers of Ali, and believe that the spiritual and secular leadership of Islam remained in his family. It is an article of their faith that an Imam will one day return to begin the reign of perfect justice on earth. But until recent times the Party of Ali could boast of no more recent political success than the takeover of Iran in the sixteenth century.

In no Arab country was the word preached more fervently than among the Shi'ite communities in Iran and in Iraq. Even so, it was religious enthusiasm among followers of this sect in Lebanon which produced spectacular events. The terrorist movements which were fueled from there may be considered not only state-sponsored but in fact "God-sponsored" as well.

In Lebanon the Shi'ites, downtrodden by Sunni Moslems and by Lebanese Christians, were to be found among the most wretched and impoverished part of the population. It is not surprising, therefore, that the new forces which emerged to provide cohesion and leadership to restore the faith, and also community pride of an underdog group, had no difficulty in recruiting young people to fight for their cause.

The Shi'ite revival which transformed Middle East politics by inspiring the overthrow of the Shah and revolutionizing Iran began not in that country but in Iraq, in the holy city of Najaf. This center of Shi'ite theological scholarship and debate in the 1960s was in a ferment of intellectual and religious activity. A young philosopher and writer named Sayid Mohammed Baquir Sadr was the founder of a new movement which he spoke of as "The Call of Islam." He preached that the call was for a return to God's dispensation, and that the way to achieve it was through a social revolution against injustice, based not upon class like the Marxist revolution, but upon universality. In his revolution "the virtuous rich and the virtuous poor stand shoulder to shoulder."

This call led to the foundation of Al Dawa, which began to draw powerful popular support as a revolutionary party of protest against the ruling powers in Iraq. Demonstrations and riots, especially in the slums of Baghdad, attracted the attention of President Saddam Hussein's regime, whose natural response was repression. The religious revivalists at Najaf were persecuted, and a number of them fled the country. Among those who went into exile was Sheikh Mohammed Fadlallah (later to become deeply involved in terrorism), who returned to Beirut.

After the Iranian revolution in 1979 Tehran radio began speaking of Baquir Sadr as the "Iraqi Khomeini." That was too much for President Saddam, who saw The Call and its leaders as a threat to his own Baathist, Arab socialist regime. Baquir Sadr and his sister were arrested and executed in 1980, together with a number of other Islamic theologians from Najaf. Rank-and-file supporters of the Islamic revolutionary movement accused of terrorist attacks on police stations and other government buildings were arrested in thousands; some were publicly hanged. The survivors fled to

Iran as refugees. Many came under the influence of what was called the supreme council of the Iraqi Islamic Revolution, established to aid men anxious to fight back against Iraq and to spread the revolution. Supreme council groups came under the orders of Sayid Mohammed Bakr al-Hakim. The most active was Iraqi Dawa, held responsible for later bombings in Kuwait, which was controlled by Mohammed Taki al-Mudarrissi. Another similar body which drew its recruits from disaffected Iraqis was called Iraqi Mijahiddin.

Here then was the nucleus of the new Islamic terror movements. Many of those involved in the later outrages can be traced back to events in Iran following Khomeini's seizure of power there. Others plotted in Iraq, or fled to Lebanon.

Ayatollah Khomeini himself had been one of those who came under the influence of the Call and the Shi'ite revival when he was living in Najaf in the 1960s after being expelled from Iran by the Shah. The old man was inspired by the teachings of the religious philosophers, and became convinced that he was the chosen one to spread revolution and religious fervor to Iran. He broadcast the word with his famous cassette sermons, recorded first in Iraq and later—after he had been expelled again during the purges—from his new expatriate home in Paris.

Khomeini was by no means the only notable figure to be greatly affected by his stay in Najaf. So too was Imam Moussa al-Sadr, another Iranian clergyman who taught theology at the Jebel Amel College in Tyre, Lebanon. He became founder in Lebanon of what he called the Movement of the Disinherited. It was from this group that the mainstream Lebanese Shi'ite paramilitary organization named Amal developed in 1975. Again founded by Imam Moussa, it appealed particularly to the impoverished coreligionists in the south of Lebanon, and he soon had a large following. One of Amal's original aims was to oppose the Palestinian forces, so thick on the ground in south Lebanon, who were behaving like an occupying army. From the beginning, the organization took a stand against PLO efforts to spread their leftist views on the grounds that such views conflicted with the Shi'ite faith. They also blamed the PLO for terrorist attacks on Israel which provoked reprisal raids, causing further suffering in the Shi'ite villages.

Moussa al-Sadr, Amal's founder, disappeared in mysterious circumstances on a visit to Libya in 1978, and it is generally believed in the Arab world that he was murdered on the orders of Colonel Gaddafi, though the Libyan leader firmly denied this. It seems more than likely that a quarrel developed between the Imam and the Colonel over the Palestinians, whose arrogant presence in Lebanon was resented by the Shi'ites, but strongly supported by Gaddafi. The Imam may be dead but his soul goes marching on, and posters bearing his picture are still to be seen everywhere in Lebanon. In the eyes of his coreligionists he has become a saint and an martyr.

It was at Moussa al-Sadr's college in Tyre that the idea of a suicide bomb was first proposed. It was an important development, for the suicide bomb was to become the trademark of the new Islamic terrorists, and then be used by other imitators. The man responsible for this innovation is believed to have been Mohammed Saad, an electrical engineering student who, after studying theology, became a leading explosives man in Lebanon. He perished when his own headquarters were later blown up in 1984, probably by the Israelis.

Amal, which came into existence through the work of Moussa al-Sadr, developed into the main body representing Lebanese Shi'ites, and was generally considered to be a respectable organization. Indeed, its leader, Nabih Berri, a quiet and thoughtful 45-year-old lawyer who although a devout believer resisted the ranting Shi'ite clergy, became a minister in the all-faction government of the Christian president Amin Gemayel after Israelis marched into Lebanon. It was the operation called by the Israelis "Peace in Galilee" which splintered Amal—whose title, incidentally, means Hope, but which is also the acronym for Lebanese resistance units. Nabih Berri was against the idea of resisting the Israeli advance at that time, and the wilder members of his group broke away in disagreement. It is interesting to observe that Berri's attitude changed with the situation and that as the Israelis finally completed their withdrawal from Lebanon in 1985 he encouraged his militiamen to speed them on the way with constant raids, and went so far as to claim credit for driving the enemy forces out of the country. Even before he involved himself so deeply in negotiations with the United States over the TWA flight held at Beirut airport there were signs that an internal struggle in Amal was under way. The supremacy of Nabih Berri was being challenged by Hassan Hashem, chairman of the movement's executive committee.

The whole history of the Shi'ite movement in Lebanon is littered with dissension and disagreement. Soon after the disappearance of the founder, Imam Moussa, rival factions began to disassociate themselves from the main body.

The first subgroup, Islamic Amal (al-Amal al-Islami), was led by Hussein Mussawi, a 40-year-old former teacher, of whom much more was to be heard later. Calling himself Abu Mirhashem, he embraced a militant Islamic ideology, and an article of the faith was to make war to the bitter end against Israel. The first act of the breakaway movement established in 1979, however, was to make war upon Amal in the Bekaa valley around the ancient city of Baalbek, and in the surrounding villages of Hermel, Bittel and Yanta. It succeeded in driving out the old Amal and in seizing their headquarters buildings and equipment. Later, with the support of the Syrians who occupied this part of Lebanon, it built there a power base and prepared to launch the campaign of violence.

From the beginning, this group whose activities spread throughout the Arab world boasted that it would specialize in suicide attacks. Mohammed Taki al-Mudarissi, one of its leaders from the Iraqi branch based in Tehran, proudly declared: "In one week I can assemble 500 loyalists ready to throw themselves into suicide operations. No border can stop me. We are coming to the end of the world . . . Only Islam can give us hope."

Islamic Amal can certainly claim to be a multinational organization with adherents in Iraq where it claimed to have made a dozen bomb attacks, as well as farther afield in the Gulf, North Africa and even in Afghanistan. Intelligence sources estimate its strength at around 1,000 active members, the majority being militia troops and minority terrorists. They believe that it is under Iranian control, and is also firmly allied with Syria.

The Call of Islam (Islamic al-Dawa) is an equally active terrorist organization, despite its mild-sounding alternative name—Lebanese Union of Moslem students—derived from its foundation in 1973/74 by the ever-active Moussa-Sadr, as an organization of Shi'ite university and high-school students in Beirut. It too broke away from a close relationship with Amal in search of bolder action and later allied itself with the more vigorous Party of God. It is headed by the notorious Sheikh Muhammed Hassan Fadlallah, who escaped from Iraqi persecution, and is strongly suspected to be the organizer of the truck-bomb attacks on the United States Marines and French troops of the multinational forces in October 1983. He is a staunch admirer of the Iranian revolution, a constant visitor to Tehran, and rarely moves without his personal guard of Kalashnikov-carrying henchmen. He explained to an American reporter: "That is for people who do not understand my concept of peace." At his mosque in the Bir Abed district of Beirut he often preached to large congregations of young men, some of them not more than 14 years old, promising a place in paradise to any of them who killed an Israeli. Sheikh Fadlallah himself has been known to give his blessing at the mosque to young men before they set out on their missions. Western experts believe that the Shi'ite clerics go in for a kind of religious brainwashing of potential suicide bombers in order to "psych them up" for their dreadful task.

The sheikh escaped unharmed when a car bomb exploded outside his Beirut home near the Bir Abed mosque in 1985 as he drove along the crowded street in his armored Land-Rover. A few minutes before a young man had parked a pick-up truck there, saying he needed to change a tire. The blast killed no less than 90 other people, and wounded 200. The Americans were blamed, and according to later reports in the *Washington Post* there was a degree of CIA involvement with the Lebanese who exploded the bomb. No American source accused the CIA of knowing in advance about the attack, but there had been cooperation with Lebanese intelligence, to explore the possibility of making preemptive strikes against anti-American terrorists. Despite a CIA statement that the agency had never "conducted any training of Lebanese security forces related to the events," suspicions remained. The Shi'ite, of course, remained convinced that the United States had launched a counter-terror campaign.

There can be no doubt that Islamic al-Dawa is one of the most extreme of the Shi'ite groups, or that it is deeply involved in terror enterprises. Its militants are recruited in the mosques of Beirut, and its organization is firmly rooted in the Lebanese capital. Shi'ite clergymen preach holy war, not only against Israel, but also against all things Western, and the United States in particular. France, too, figured prominently on the hate list. It sold arms to Iraq, including Super-Etendard jets and the Exocet missiles for use against Iran in the Gulf War.

Supporters of Islamic al-Dawa were also particularly active in southern Lebanon in harassing the Israeli army as it began to withdraw from the region early in 1985. The organization benefits from the patronage of Iran, which helps to provide money, training and weapons for its militia and terrorists groups.

One way in which the Iranians maintain their links with Shi'ite units in Lebanon is through the contingent of Iranian Revolutionary Guards permanently stationed in Baalbek and the villages around it. The Hotel Khawan there is a military training establishment. Their rear base continues to be at Zabadani in Syria, which is also the communications center for passing instructions to the terrorists groups from the Iranian foreign ministry in Tehran and from the Revolutionary Guards' headquarters there.

So far as the Iranian government is concerned, their presence in Lebanon demonstrated that despite the war with Iraq, the revolutionary regime was still capable of fighting the twin devils of imperialism and Zionism, and of giving visible support to the oppressed Shi'ites. But they were also engaged in exporting the revolutionary ideology of the new Iran by acting as a backstop for the terrorists they were there to encourage and supply. It was part of their garrison duty, apart from giving military training to Shi'ite militias and organizing the local population into an Islamic republic, to set up and even take part in terrorist attacks against a multiplicity of targets. They attacked the obvious enemy, the Israeli forces; they also fought the Lebanese army, and while they still remained in position, the multinational forces.

Another extremist group with which the Revolutionary Guards are closely connected is the Party of God (Hizbollah) created in Beirut by Sheikh Fadlallah after he returned from Najaf, and then placed under the tactical control of a very active partisan known as Abbas Mussawi who has on several occasions acted as lieutenant to the Sheikh in his enterprises. In Baalbek, Abbas Mussawi was the military boss, with Sheikh Sobhi Tufhaili as his spiritual right hand. Sheikh Ibrahim al-Amin, a 34-year-old bearded cleric trained in Iran, also emerged as a prominent figure.

Hizbollah became the most active of the Shi'ite groups there. In February 1986 a four-man crew from French television was seized after filming a Hizbollah meeting. The affiliation of this group with Islamic Jihad was confirmed when Jihad announced it was questioning the four kidnapped TV people and was holding them hostage. Other French citizens were already being held in Beirut under threat of death; this was obviously intended to put pressure on the French government on the eve of parliamentary elections.

The estimated strength of Hizbollah is 700 fanatics, but in 1985 it was claimed that the overall militia strength might have grown to 4,000. Linked with Islamic Amal, it enjoyed hospitality and facilities provided by the Iranians in central Baalbek, which became a real hornet's nest of Shi'ite terrorists and guerrillas. The main establishment was at the so-called camp of the Holy Martyrs at Janta. Another center of terrorist activity was the Baalbek barracks on a hill above the town, formerly known as the Sheikh Abdullah barracks, but then renamed, in honor of the founder of the Shi'ite faith, Imam Ali barracks.

Hizbollah is perhaps even more closely aligned ideologically with the Iranian revolutionaries than are its brother organizations; they provide it with instructors, and so do the Syrians who are also highly active in the Bekaa valley. Members of this group are largely composed of young Shi'ites from the poorest of the poor attracted into the movement by hell-raising mullahs. By surrendering themselves to the cause of religious and political revolution they receive strong spiritual support, not to mention economic security. It is certain that these young Lebanese have a sense of mission strong enough to make them volunteer for suicide operations against any target which they believe represents the enemies of Islam, and they have demonstrated their undoubted courage in action.

One other small group must also be mentioned. It is named the Imam Hussein suicide brigade in honor of Hussein the son of Ali, the founder of the Shi'ite faith. It flourishes in West Beirut, where it has carried out a number of bombing raids and other attacks. The leader is Abdullah Mussawi, who is thought to control a hundred activists. The name Mussawi continually crops up in the various branch organizations of Shi'ite terror. This fact demonstrates the power of clans within the various groups. The extended family exercises powerful influence over all aspects of Lebanese life, and it has been observed that for this reason the security of terrorist cells would be difficult to break. Family secretiveness goes hand in hand with the secrecy of the terrorists.

These, then, are the organizations which are loosely grouped together under the generic title Islamic Jihad—*jihad* being the Arabic for holy war. That description has become a sort of umbrella under which these terrorist groups are huddled. As with practically all warlike organizations in the Middle East, the main body consists of thousands of militiamen from whom are drawn terrorists with specialized training to work in assassination teams or bomb squads. There is a remarkable similarity here with what happened to the old Palestinian organizations. These represented a wide spectrum of politics and ideologies, but were nonetheless generally grouped together under the enveloping cover of the PLO. Black September, the assassination organization responsible for the massacre at the Munich Olympic games, for example, drew its recruits from Fatah, the PLO fighting unit, and also from other Palestinian groups working under the PLO umbrella.

Most of the Shi'ite factions hived off from the old original Amal movement, became ever more "root-and-branch," and involved in more and more desperate acts of resistance and terrorism. Their actions also influenced the mainstream movement Amal, which, still under the orders of Nabih Berri—who remained minister of justice in the Lebanese government—itself became more violent in its methods. Indeed, it was the Amal militia which began battling against the Arafat faction of the PLO as that organization attempted to reestablish itself in the famous Beirut refugee camps in the summer of 1985. Regular forces of Amal with the support of Shia units of the 6th Brigade of the Lebanese national army launched an all-out assault upon the Palestinian base camps at Shatila, Sabra and Bourj-al-Barajneh with the aim of destroying forever their stronghold in Lebanon. Shortly after that the Lebanon-based terrorists moved into aircraft-hijacking, and so began the drama of the TWA hostages.

Operating under the cover title Islamic Jihad (Islamic Holy War), the various squads declared their responsibility for a whole series of acts in Lebanon during 1983. Farther afield, Islamic Jihad launched a bomb attack in March 1985 on a Jewish film festival in Paris in revenge for Israeli action in south Lebanon. The following month it also bombed a suburban restaurant in Madrid much used by American Air Force people from a nearby base.

Although the main inspiration of the Shi'ite groups undoubtedly came from Iran, it would be wrong to underestimate the influence of the Syrian government of President Assad. He himself belongs to the Alaouite minority community in Syria, which is a secret religion linked to the

Shi'ite branch of Islam. The Bekaa valley, close to the Syrian border, has been under the control of President Assad's field force in Lebanon for many years, and nothing can be undertaken there without the knowledge and approval of the Syrians. There is ample evidence that President Assad has provided Shi'ite units with weapons, ammunition and explosives from his vast stores of Soviet-built equipment. His officers have helped to train them, and have arranged frequent visits by Shi'ite group leaders to Damascus for meetings with senior commanders and intelligence chiefs who give aid in operational planning. There is also a measure of coordination with the Revolutionary Guards and with the Iranians who pass into Lebanon by way of Syria.

The primary aim of Syrian policy is to ensure that Islamic terrorists concentrate on targets considered to be the enemies of Syria. Jihad and Syria certainly have plenty of common enemies—the United States, Western Europe, not to mention Arab neighbors who have incurred their wrath, such as Iraq, Jordan and Egypt. By aiding such groups as Amal and Hizbollah, President Assad hopes to gain control over them in order to tighten his grip upon Lebanon.

But the inspiration of Islamic Jihad is by no means entirely geopolitical. Behind the terror actions there is clearly the strongest of religious motivations, the desire to ensure that the will of Allah is done upon earth. The young men and women who go into action in this cause—which inspired multitudes long before their own generation—consider it a worthy one. Unlike most of the other forms of new terrorism considered in this book, the religious push of Jihad is very strong. Faith in Islam, rather than a desire to win back "national home" territory, or ambition to spread political ideology, is what brings recruits to carry out operations in the name of this organization. The tragedy is that high-minded people, blinded by their faith, become pawns on the three-dimensional political chessboard of Middle East politics.

It was the Israelis who provided the launching pad for Islamic terrorists in Lebanon by invading that troubled country in June 1982. One of the many ironies of the whole affair is that the pretext for launching the main attack was that a few days before Shlomo Argov, the Israeli ambassador to London, had been critically wounded by gunmen working for the independent Abu Nidal terrorist organization. Although that Arab group was bitterly opposed to the main body of the PLO, the Israeli government seized upon this event to order its armed forces into Lebanon with the aim of rooting out the Palestinians, who were firmly entrenched there as a state within a state. In fact, Prime Minister Menachem Begin's hard-line government had planned the operation long in advance. But the occasion for launching the big battalions was the act of terrorism committed in London.

The initial success of the assault in destroying the power of the Palestinians served to strengthen the resolve of the new Islamic movements which ever since the Iranian revolution had been preparing their forces in the fertile soil of Lebanon. The Shi'ites had always hated and resented the domineering ways of the Palestinians and their élitist presumptions; they had no love for the Israelis. When the Americans came upon the scene, as President Reagan provided U.S. Marines to try and restore peace after the Israelis surrounded Beirut, it seemed a heaven-sent opportunity for the new terrorists. For were not the Americans the villains who had given their support to the Shah of Iran? Had they not planned a huge operation to try to release the American hostages in Tehran? They were, in the utterances of Ayatollah Khomeini, "the great Satan."

In the early stages of the Israeli invasion Israel's troops were positively welcomed by the Shi'ite majority in south Lebanon on the old Middle East principle that "my enemy's enemy is my friend." They had been oppressed and bullied by the Palestinians; now the PLO was being attacked by the Israelis. But the unholy friendship could not last.

As things went from bad to worse in Lebanon despite the intervention of the U.S. forces (aided by the French, the Italians and a small British contingent), the Shi'ite organizations prepared to make their power felt. They were ready to use their terrible new weapon—the suicide bomb. The idea of using a human bomb had already been tried out in 1981, when the Iraqi embassy in Beirut was blown up by this means.

It was on April 18, 1983 that the first of the suicide bombers went into action against foreign enemies. The target was the U.S. embassy on the elegant Beirut seafront, and the truck loaded with explosives killed 45 people, including 16 Americans. Never before had this devastating form of terrorist warfare been used to such effect. This single event created an enormous impact, both in the Middle East and in the United States, whose diplomatic service was forced to recognize that its members were in grave danger throughout the Arab world.

There was nothing new about using cars, and even trucks, stuffed with explosives. The Islamic innovation was to have the explosive charge blasted by a determined person courageous enough to drive to the target and to sacrifice his own life to make the mission successful.

The next suicide bomb attack was even more devastating. On October 23, 1983 two kamikazes raided almost simultaneously the headquarters of the U.S. Marines near Beirut and the command post of the French contingent. These two explosions killed more than 300 people. In fact, terrorists in one day inflicted military casualties on the same scale as those to be expected in a battalion attack in conventional warfare. Within 10 days Islamic Jihad followed up these actions by launching a similar raid upon Israeli intelligence headquarters in Tyre, killing 61 Palestinians as well as Israelis. The political and diplomatic effects of these blasts were enormous, for it was clear that a new and horrifying dimension had been added to the terror wars.

Two days after the bombing, a statement from the new group calling itself Islamic Jihad was published in Beirut newspapers: "We are the soldiers of God and we crave death. Violence will remain our only path . . . we are ready to turn Lebanon into another Vietnam. We are not Iranians or Syrians, or Palestinians. We are Lebanese Moslems who follow the dicta of the Koran."

There was, of course, a natural desire on the part of the Western powers and Israel to strike back at the terrorists, but at what, at whom? It became apparent that the intelligence services knew practically nothing about Islamic Jihad. Until that autumn intelligence effort in the Middle East had been concentrated upon the Palestinians. Mossad, the Israeli intelligence organization, had done a thorough job penetrating their groups at high level. It was remarkably well informed, as were the Americans and the British, about the planning and thinking of the long-established terrorists. But the new group remained a total mystery. It was obviously well organized and highly secretive. How to infiltrate a fiercely religious and multinational Moslem organization was the problem confronting the intelligence services.

The first response was to send in the jets, and for American warships to shell areas where the new raiders were thought to live. They even used for the purpose the USS *New Jersey*, a refurbished battleship offshore. But you cannot destroy scattered terrorists with 16-inch shells, even when they are directed by the latest electronic devices. Israeli air attacks seemed to be no more successful; and sure as fate, the shells and the rockets hit more harmless people than terrorists. It became obvious that more information was needed before any effective counteraction could be taken.

The first serious intelligence material about Islamic Jihad began to come in as the CIA, Mossad and the French, helped by the Lebanese intelligence service, began to probe into the mysteries of the bomb attacks on the headquarters of the international force in Beirut. In this task they were also assisted by FBI agents from Washington, specially flown in to do the police work.

A clue was provided by the explosives used. In the attack on the Marines headquarters, the terrorists had used 12,000 pounds of TNT and the plastic explosive PETN. At the French post there was also proof that hexogen had been used. Such modern military explosives are difficult to obtain, even in Lebanon, without the cooperation of government or intelligence services. So their use seemed to prove the involvement of state organizations, and the leading suspects were Syria and Iran. It seemed also that a money order for $50,000, used to make preparations and also to pay local mercenaries with special skills, was paid out by Iranian diplomats.

The intelligence dossier finally named 14 individuals who had been involved in planning the operation, though this information by no means simplified the task of analyzing the organization of Islamic Jihad. They included a Lebanese fixer, a Syrian intelligence colonel, a renegade PLO officer, professional terrorists skilled at bomb making and a fundamentalist mullah. The Israelis were convinced that a key figure was Nablan Shayhk, a Palestinian who had once been a security officer in Beirut.

In Beirut the local press seized upon the name of Hussein Mussawi, the Shi'ite former teacher already mentioned as a leader of Islamic Amal. It was his cousin Haydar Mussawi who had been involved in providing the pick-up trucks used in the suicide bombing. These vehicles had been carefully chosen, and bore the markings of a Lebanese commercial airline which frequently made deliveries to the Marines' base. Hussein Mussawi himself promptly denied responsibility, but he did so in an oblique fashion, declaring:

"I salute this good act and I consider it a good deed and a legitimate right, and I bow to the spirit of the martyrs who carried out this operation."

The other notable mentioned was the fiery Islamic clergyman Sheikh Mohammed Fadlallah, from Party of God, who told Reuter: "Our aim is to expel the aggressive forces of the United States and other so-called multinational forces including the Zionists."

Hardest information about Syrian involvement with the Jihad movement came from the fact that Lieutenant-Colonel Diyab, a Damascus intelligence officer, was connected with the plotters. His name was in police records, for he had served under diplomatic cover in Paris at a time when the Syrians were involved in terrorist activities there.

A good deal of the information which came to light about the workings of the new terrorists in the Middle East was obtained from communications intercepts. At the time the U.S. Sixth Fleet, with its impressive display of electronics, was lying offshore, and the area is also within range of the British listening posts on the island of Cyprus. Terrorists with state backing used modern communications which are vulnerable to intercepts.

Why then, it might be asked, were not warnings given to the American diplomats and to the commanders of the multinational forces in Lebanon? The answer is that such warnings were given, but at that stage no resources were available for the reports to be checked out by intelligence men onshore to discover the precise nature of the threat, so that proper precautions might be taken. In any case, the commanders were overwhelmed by vague reports about perils to come. It was far from clear which ones were serious and which were simple bits of gossip. None the less, Caspar Weinberger, U.S. defense secretary, was confident enough to state that those responsible for the October bombing were "basically Iranians, with the sponsorship, knowledge and authority of the Syrian government."

Although comprehensive intelligence was still sadly lacking in the autumn of 1983, it was clear that a fresh kind of terrorist movement was putting down its roots in Lebanon. That country had become the theatre of an overlapping series of different and complicated wars. There had been the conventional war between Israel and Syria; there were the civil wars between Lebanese factions, in varying combinations—Christian Maronites, Sunni Moslems, Shi'ite

Moslems and Druses, each seeking different allies among greater powers as their fortunes varied. Each of the factions had its own militia of well-equipped regular forces to fight pitched battles, and also its smaller squads ever ready to use terrorist attacks in support of the larger militia conflicts. These terror bands, and those of the Palestinian interlopers, all had a multiplicity of targets—each other, the Israelis and the four-nation peacekeeping force of Americans, French, Italians, and British. The suicide bombings made it apparent that a new multinational terrorist organization built on an alliance of interests, Shi'ite, Syrian and Iranian, had now joined in as well.

This fresh force—operating under the blanket description Islamic Jihad—although based in Lebanon had other aims and interests in the Middle East. While the militia army of Amal, the Shi'ite organization which gave birth to Jihad, built forces ready to establish local power by harrying first the Israelis and then the Palestinians out of Lebanon, the Jihad movement under Iranian influence turned to exporting revolution, and terror, to the Gulf and to Saudi Arabia.

The first target of this new "Shi'ite international" was in Kuwait, the small though important oil state at the head of the Gulf, on the very frontiers of warring Iran and Iraq. It was a tempting place to strike, for Iran reproached the Kuwaitis for supporting Iraq and for allowing war material to pass through their ports to supply President Saddam's armies.

On December 12, 1983 a truck loaded with high explosive including hexogen, exactly like the suicide bomb used in the Beirut attack, crashed through the gates of the US embassy in Kuwait and detonated ten feet from the main building. But the Kuwait attack was even more ambitious. Apart from the embassy bomb, seven others had been placed in the city ready to be detonated almost simultaneously by non-suicide terrorists. The targets included the headquarters and rest house of the American corporation Raytheon Company (then installing Hawk missiles) and the French embassy. But it was not just foreign targets which were under attack. The terrorists also bombed local state installations—the ministry of electricity and water, the passport office and a petrochemical complex at Shuaiba.

This time Islamic Jihad had in its sights an Arab state whose rulers it hated. Furthermore, it was discovered later that together with the bomb-making explosives and detonators, they had smuggled in by sea quantities of modern weapons, including grenade launchers and machine guns which had been stored in safe houses. It looked as though the terrorists were planning to follow up a successful bombing campaign with a plot to assassinate government figures, and perhaps even to attempt a coup d'état.

Intelligence investigations revealed that the plot had been hatched in the Bekaa valley in Lebanon at about the same time that the Beirut bomb attack was being prepared in October. The Iranians had given it their blessing, and the Tehran connection was further proved by careful police work. In the debris of the US embassy were discovered the gruesome remains of the suicide bomber's hand. His fingerprints made it possible to identify the man as Raad Meftel Ajeel. He was a 25-year-old driver for a local company who had arrived three months earlier, traveling on an Iranian passport. This evidence made it possible to discover more about the score of other men involved in the operation. Eighteen of them were Iraqi-born Shi'ites, all of whom had connections with The Call, the religious revival movement that started in Najaf and now has its headquarters in Iran. Two others were Lebanese Shi'ites linked to Hussein Mussawi, already mentioned as the ever-active leader of Islamic Amal. Finally, there was a Lebanese Christian named Elias Saab, apparently a mercenary recruited for his skill at bomb making.

What forcibly struck the Kuwaiti and American in-vestigators was the professionalism of the terrorist organiza-tion. The team was divided into seven cells. There were "cut-outs" to divide these cells into watertight compartments. Final planning arrangements had been made at separate safe houses to reduce the chances of discovery or betrayal. The bombing killed five people, wounded 87 others, and caused a good deal of damage to some of the targets, though because of faulty wiring the bombs did not all explode as planned. The attack served to demonstrate that Islamic Jihad was ready to move outside Lebanon and to spread the terrorist war eastward to the vulnerable Gulf states. Several of them (Bahrain in particular) had been nervous ever since the Iranian revolution. Not only do they have a substantial Shi'ite minority living within their borders, but also Iran has long-standing historic claims to overlordship, some of which were pressed even by the Shah.

That was why the advance of Islamic terror eastward

caused such alarm on the frontiers of Arabia, where even the proud and powerful Saudis began to fear they were next on the hit list.

The Israelis picked up information that an even more terrible form of terrorism was being planned with the preparation of what was called a suicide vest. It consists of a kind of sleeveless garment with five kilos of explosive sewn into it, worn under a jacket or Arab *djellabah*. The wearer simply walks up to his target and pulls a toggle to release a grenade-type pin which detonates simultaneously the explosive, the wearer and the target. So far it is a secret weapon which, mercifully, has not been used.

This did nothing to reduce the general unease about suicide bombing. President Reagan himself made the extravagant claim that there were 1,000 terrorists, many of them Iranian, gathered in Lebanon in readiness for more such missions. The fear of suicide attacks caused special barricades to be built at the White House and at government buildings in Washington. U.S. warships in the Mediterranean were alerted to the possibility of kamikaze attacks by terrorist light aircraft. Unfortunately, the defenses at American diplomatic missions in danger areas were not tightened sufficiently to prevent new attacks, though it did turn out that there were not nearly as many Islamic human bombs available as had been predicted. Even in the world of fanatical Islam there are backsliders, not entirely persuaded of the certainty of the trip to paradise.

Even so, there had been five suicide bomb attacks in less than a year, and certainly the Kuwait example had shown that this form of hitting the enemy was more psychologically effective than older and less dramatic forms of detonation. Moreover, in Kuwait the only bomb to detonate on target was the human one piloted by Ajeel.

The personal history of Raad Ajeel illuminates the fashion in which the many arms of the Islamic terrorist monster are joined. Together with his brother Saad, he had been swept along by the theology and politics of The Call (Al Dawa) in his native Iraq, and they had both taken part in attacks on police stations. Saad was caught and executed. Raad managed to escape to Iran, and was there taken under the wing of the self-styled Supreme Council of the Islamic Revolution in Iran, the sworn enemies of President Saddam of Iraq. This body was under the leadership of Ayatollah Mohammed Baqr Hakim, one of three sons of a leading Shi'ite theologian in the holy city of Najaf, the place in Iraq where the great religious revival had begun in the 1960s.

The Supreme Council is dedicated to supporting Iran and to the overthrow of President Saddam of Iraq. In this capacity it acts as a parent organization for at least two Iraqi terrorist organizations—Al Dawa and the Mujaheddin, which was led by Aziz, another of the Hakim brothers. It is strongly suspected that the third Hakim brother, who lived in Kuwait, helped to set up the human-bomb operation of Ajeel, who had been recruited and trained in Iran by Baqr Hakim. To complete the pattern, it can be recorded that the Supreme Council of the Iraqi Islamic Revolution has links with Islamic Amal in Lebanon, led by Hussein Mussawi. And Mussawi was a follower of Sheikh Fadlallah, founder of the Party of God, who had incorporated into it the Lebanese followers of The Call.

In May 1984 a determined effort to bring together and coordinate all these elements ready for a new campaign was made at a high-level meeting in Tehran. Ayatollah Muhammed Khatami, the Iranian minister of Islamic guidance, gathered in his office a number of other ministers, together with military commanders and departmental heads, and Ayatollah Baqr Hakim, head of the Islamic Revolution in Iraq. The purpose of this gathering—reported later by Iranian exiles opposed to the present regime—was to discuss the recruitment and training of suicide squads to carry out further operations in "enemy" countries. Significantly, those countries in order of importance were: Saudi Arabia, the United Arab Emirates, Jordan and France (because of her support for Iraq in the war against Iran), and "any other countries that might oppose the Islamic revolution." Needless to say, the United States remained the number one Satan.

Detailed plans, 200 pages long, were presented for the creation of what was to be called an independent brigade for irregular warfare in enemy territories. They involved the recruitment of some 1,500 men, including instructors from the Iranian armed forces. The requirement was for men under 30, preferably bachelors, all committed to martyrdom. According to a London spokesman at the office of Dr. Shapur Bakhtiar, the exiled former prime minister of Iran, the terrorist plans were approved by Ayatollah Khomeini.

The man who seems to have made the running at the

Tehran meeting was introduced in this fashion: "Your eminences are fully acquainted with his face, but for the sake of prudence, let us refer to him as brother Mirhashem." The war name Abu Mirhashem is that used by none other than Hussein Mussawi, the ex-teacher from Lebanon who is Iranian by birth and whose name constantly comes up in connection with Islamic terror, despite his denials.

At the May meeting, it was reported, Mussawi outlined his ideas for forming the new unit which for official purposes would be a secret branch of the Iranian Revolutionary Guards, but would in fact act independently. Initially it would be formed around a few groups of up to 20 people currently serving in Lebanon, and known to the outside world as suicide groups. He asked for the secondment to his unit of army instructors with special skills. In making this request, he revealed that his groups had hitherto been assisted by five Moslems from "occupied Palestine" who were making available knowledge acquired during their many years of service with the Israelis. This may simply have been a boast to impress his distinguished hosts, or it is possible that Islamic Jihad had recruited some of the Arabs—notably the Druse—who do indeed serve in the Israeli defense forces.

Mussawi asked for a secure base, and suggested that he should get facilities for training some volunteers as pilots of light aircraft and in boat handling. Nor did he neglect intelligence work, suggesting that some members of the special unit might be posted abroad under diplomatic cover in Iranian diplomatic missions.

According to his estimate, it would take at least a year to prepare the new force for action. He therefore regretted that there might be a lull in activities until it was ready.

The fact that Shi'ite terrorist groups felt confident enough to ask for such an ambitious program of aid from the Iranian government showed how self-assured they had become. There was no doubt that their suicide bombing and other acts in Lebanon had impressed both the Iranians and other Middle East neighbors. For with some justification they could claim to have helped drive out the Americans and the rest of the international force from Lebanon. They had inflicted a kind of defeat upon the all-conquering Israeli army and had destroyed its morale. In that part of the world terrorism could be seen to be producing results.

The Islamic Jihad group also impressed the Syrians. After a visit to Damascus by the president of Iran, the Syrian government was able to reach agreement to cooperate with militant Shi'ite leaders. In return for help, both financial and military, as well as in the field of military intelligence, the Syrians got from them an undertaking that they coordinate in advance their actions with Syrian intelligence. Two senior officers from Damascus, Adnan Ram Hamdani, head of liaison with Iran, and Ghazi Kanan, Syrian intelligence boss in Lebanon, came to an arrangement with, among others, Hussein Mussawi of Islamic Amal, Sheikh Fadlallah and other chiefs. This was an arrangement of advantage to both parties. Syria remains the "big brother" controller of north Lebanon, especially the Bekaa valley where the Shi'ites are based, and nothing can be done there in opposition to Syrian interests.

While busy improving its organization on the ground, Islamic Jihad did not neglect the oldest tactic known to mankind, the taking of hostages. In 1984 it moved into a field of activity formerly much favored by the Palestinians—taking hostages in the sky. In the summer an Iranian and two Lebanese hijacked an Air France Boeing flying from Frankfurt, and eventually forced it to land in Tehran. The French refused to give in to their demands for the release of five Iranians jailed in France for attempted assassination of a former Iranian prime minister, despite threats that one French person an hour would be murdered aboard the aircraft.

Eventually the hijackers surrendered to the Iranian authorities after blowing up the flight deck. It was obvious that the terrorists had local support, for after the plane landed at Tehran, they emerged with much bigger and better weapons, obviously supplied locally. Their spokesman boasted that they had been trained for three years at Qom, the Iranian holy city.

The next hijacking carried out by the Shi'ite international in mid-December was a much more brutal affair. During the six days that they held the passengers of a Kuwaiti airliner, the terrorists murdered in cold blood two American Agency for International Development officials, wounded two Kuwaitis and beat up and tortured others. They had seized the plane after take-off from Dubai en route to Pakistan and ordered it to fly to Tehran. The hijack took place a year after the Kuwait bomb outrages, and the terrorists demanded the release of their 17 comrades arrested and sentenced to death or prison for their part in the bombing. For six days the aircraft stayed on the ground while the Iranian authorities did little except allow the broadcasting of some of the horrors being enacted inside. Freed passengers reported later that the hijackers had been provided with fresh weapons, hand-cuffs and ropes during the long stay. In fact, there was deep suspicion about official Iranian complicity in the affair, even though it seemed to bear the trademark "made in Lebanon." The eventual "storming" of the aircraft by Iranian security men disguised as ground crew did little to reassure the Americans. As President Reagan put it: "Even if they weren't in collusion, the Iranians could have done better."

There could be no doubt that Islamic Jihad had become firmly committed to the hostage game, and its leaders must have made a deliberate decision to revive this tactic. It came as something of a surprise, because the tightening of airport security had made air piracy a much more chancy operation since the days when the Popular Front for the Liberation of Palestine with the help of European terrorists had caused such alarm by seizing aircraft. Before the dramas of late 1984, it had been assumed that improved security and successful hostage-rescue operations had defeated this form of terrorist warfare. Islamic Jihad suddenly demonstrated the falsity of this assumption. By exploiting security weaknesses which always develop in the long periods of calm before a terrorist storm, they had revived hijacking. What is more, they had learned the lessons of previous terrorist defeats. The teams which grabbed the two airliners, first the French and then the Kuwaiti one, knew what reactions might be expected and were prepared for every move. In addition they understood the value of propaganda, and had deliberately allowed the broadcasting of the screams and shouts of hostages inside the aircraft at Tehran airport. As in more conventional forms of warfare, it is sometimes techniques of defense which are ahead of the game; and sometimes those of attack.

The horrible murder of two American officials aboard the Kuwaiti aircraft just before Christmas shocked public opinion in America. Two days after the murders, the American Delta force flew a squad to Masirah island, the nearest friendly base off the coast of the Sultanate of Oman. It was clear that such a unit could do nothing so long as the airliner remained at Tehran airport, but the élite U.S. antiterrorist army unit was on standby to go in for a rescue operation should the aircraft be flown to one of the Gulf states where action might become possible. Eventually the Iranians—who had earlier been giving help and support to the hijackers—ended the affair by getting their own security people to enter the aircraft disguised as a medical team to disarm the fanatics.

Yet again, as had happened after the suicide bombs, the cry went up for action against terrorism. Until then, efforts had concentrated on intelligence-gathering in the Middle East in attempts to discover who the new terrorists were and to locate their bases. Now the demand was for action, and George Shultz, the American secretary of state, spoke of more active defense. He had always taken an aggressive line on the response to terror, and he began talking about the need to strike in advance against terrorists, using American power to get in the first blow, even though full and accurate information about complicity was not available.

"They don't seem to need additional excuses to hit us. They seem anxious to do what damage they can. I haven't seen any evidence of restraint on their part."

That is precisely the advantage that the hijackers and suicide bombers enjoy in their campaigns against Western democracies. While liberal consciences in our part of the world are consumed with anxiety about how far we may legitimately go in combating the forces of naked violence, the terrorists themselves positively rejoice in their excesses, and justify every one of their brutal acts.

Nothing effective was done after the clear warnings of further Islamic terror provided by the air piracy campaign of the summer and winter of 1984. The conspirators in Iran and in Lebanon were able, unhindered, to prepare even more desperate action. But before they launched the next air-hostage operation Islamic Jihad struck at others on their enemy list.

2.

Human Bombs

The Shi'ite international extended its field of action in May 1985 to Saudi Arabia. Islamic Jihad gave Riyadh, the capital, its first taste of terrorism by planting bombs there. The explosions coincided with the arrival in Iran of Prince Saud al-Faisal, the foreign minister, making the first official Saudi visit to Tehran since the fall of the Shah.

Islamic Jihad's spokesman frankly explained that the purpose was to "shake up the retrogressive Saudi monarch." He also delivered a warning that Saudi Arabia would be further punished for supporting Iraq, and for providing millions of dollars to finance its Gulf War against Iran. The Riyadh bombing caused alarm in the Saudi hierarchy, and at least one of the royal princes called in security experts from Britain to improve his own personal defenses.

In the summer of 1985 a series of fresh attacks were also made in Kuwait, the small though influential Arab oil state at the top end of the gulf, whose capital had already suffered at the hands of suicide bombers. Its population is one-third Shi'ite. The government, like those of all the Gulf states, supports Iraq in the never-ending conflict with Iran. That in itself is reason enough for Kuwait to incur the wrath of the Shi'ites. But the specific reason given for terror raids was a demand for the release of 17 men convicted of carrying out earlier bombings at Al Kuwait, the capital. A number of them received death sentences which have never been carried out.

27

The same demand was the ostensible motive for an attempt in May 1985 to murder the ruler of Kuwait, Sheikh Jaber al-Ahmed. A suicide car bomber who drove into his motorcade almost succeeded, and did in fact kill a number of his bodyguards.

When Shi'ite groups made further bomb attacks a few weeks later this confirmed that Islamic Jihad intended to step up its campaign to rescue the imprisoned comrades. It was also a clear indication that the new terrorists had in their sights the small oil states, all of which are under the rule of Sunni families. Among the victims of these attacks was Colonel Khalil Gaith, a senior Kuwaiti police officer. The authorities arrested dozens of local Shi'ites, more than 200,000 of whom live there. Many are of Lebanese, Iranian and Iraqi nationality.

The gravity of the terrorist threat to the Gulf states as a whole was further demonstrated when the British antiterrorist squad arrested and deported eight Arabs in London who were plotting to overthrow the government of Bahrain. They were equipped with forged papers and large sums of money. Bahrain is the oldest established of the Gulf oil states, with a population largely Shi'ite, and, moreover, Iran has historic claims to control over it.

These events prompted the Gulf Cooperation Council, a regional grouping which coordinates the policies, especially defense, of six states (including Saudi Arabia) to begin considering measures to combat terrorism. Their greatest fear was that the kind of chaos prevailing in Lebanon might spread to their hitherto peaceful and prosperous area. To keep out the infection they made arrangements for the careful monitoring of foreigners, in particular the large number of immigrants needed in a sparsely populated region of great wealth. Among the imported workers are Shi'ites from Iran, Palestinian exiles, Lebanese and Egyptians, Indians and Pakistanis. During the years of the oil boom the Gulf was a magnet for thousands of impoverished people from the Third World who saw it as the only place where they could succeed and make money. But the labor market declined with the recession and the falling price of oil. The Gulf Council began thinking also about the best way of expelling Arab immigrants, especially Shi'ites whom they suspected of being ready to join in plots to overthrow established governments.

Under deepest suspicion in this part of the world are Shi'ite expatriates from Iraq. Persecuted in their own country, thousands seeking refuge in exile have been recruited by the Iraqi Al Dawa movement operated by the Supreme Council of the Iraqi Revolution, which as we have already shown is closely allied to the Shi'ite revolutionaries in Iran. Whole battalions of them were mobilized into the Iranian army for its human-wave onslaughts on the Iraqi army. But others still were taken to Iran for training in subversion and terrorism.

At Manzarieh, north of Tehran, and at Saleh-Abad, near the holy city of Qom, they are instructed together with recruits of the international terror force from Pakistan, Turkey and North Africa, as well as from the other Arab states. These are the training schools for suicide squads, where practical bomb making is taught side by side with psychological and religious preparation for death missions worldwide. It seems from the list of missions carried out in 1984-5 that those teams operated by the Iraqi branch of Al Dawa specialized in operations in the Gulf region, and began planning for the eventual assault upon Saudi Arabia, which in the eastern province has a strong minority Shi'ite population. They too often make their claims under the blanket organization name Islamic Jihad. An example of this was the claim in May 1985 regarding the murder in Kuwait of an Iraqi diplomat and his son. But the Shi'ite international does not confine its activities to Lebanon and the Gulf. The ayatollahs and the sheikhs who control it from their grand offices in Tehran have also launched their men on numerous missions in Western Europe. Intelligence officers under diplomatic cover in Iranian embassies in the West give assistance with such enterprises.

As part of the campaign to punish those connected with the Shah's regime in Iran, attacks were carried out in Paris early in 1984. Three exiles were murdered, including General Ali Oveissi, former military governor of Tehran, and his brother. In their use of French territory for murderous attempts they did not stick just to attacking compatriots. In April 1985 Islamic Jihad caused an uproar in Paris by placing a bomb which wounded 18 in a cinema during a festival of Jewish films. It was intended as an act of revenge for Israel's 'iron fist' policy in Lebanon.

The U.S. embassy in Rome was the target which had been given to a group of seven Lebanese arrested there in the autumn of 1984. Their plot was discovered when Swiss security officers at Zurich airport searched a young Lebanese and found that he was carrying detonators and five pounds of high explosive concealed in a body belt. At Zurich railway station they also picked up another five-pound pack, and from that the trail led to Rome, where the rest of the group were arrested. "It could have been a massacre," reported one officer. For the men—all in their mid-thirties, and Islamic students—were planning to mount a suicide car bomb attack on the diplomatic building in Via Veneto. In their apartments police discovered plans of the embassy, together with detailed notes about the movements of Marine guards. It began to look as though the controllers of Islamic Jihad had plans to bomb other American missions in Europe, and extra precautions were taken in both Paris and Madrid. Their ultimate ambition is to carry their terrorist war to America itself, and that is why concrete defenses to hold off suicide car bombs have been erected, not only around U.S. missions abroad, but at the White House itself.

Although Islamic Jihad had not yet succeeded in making suicide attacks in Europe, there were numerous bombing incidents in the West attributed to their organization. In June 1985 a bomb exploded at Frankfurt airport in West Germany, killing a man and two small children. Although nobody claimed responsibility, the West German Federal Criminal Bureau was certain that it was not the act of one of their home-grown terrorists, and it did coincide with the hijack of the TWA flight to Beirut.

In Madrid a bomb thrown into offices used by TWA and by British Airways killed one man and injured 25. Then offices of the Jordanian airline were machine-gunned. Police discovered that a woman and two Arabs were responsible. These attacks coincided with the trial in Spain of two Lebanese sentenced to prison for the attempted murder of Mohammed Idris, a Libyan diplomat, in revenge for the disappearance in Libya of Imam Moussa. Both men, Mohammed Abbas Rahal and Mustafa Ali Khalil, claimed that they were soldiers of Amal, simply obeying orders, and declared: "We are slaves of God." But in Beirut, The Organization of the Oppressed—clearly a Shi'ite body—said it had placed the Madrid bombs as an answer to American threats. "Let Reagan know that our hands will reach the whole world . . . We thank all the alliances which helped us to carry out the bombing."

In the summer of 1985 there were other Shi'ite bombs in European cities—one at Rome airport which exploded in the baggage hall, and one in London which was detected on the doorstep of the Iraqi embassy. According to the antiterror squad, it was "a very professional device, just like it says in the manuals." There could be no doubt that there was a real danger of terrorist attacks from the Middle East overlapping into the cities of Western Europe. But it was in Lebanon that the main thrust of the assault continued.

When the Israeli prime minister, Menachem Begin, egged on by General Ariel Sharon, ordered his army to march into Lebanon in June 1982 his aim was to destroy the military organization implanted there by the PLO. So obsessed were he and his generals with destroying the Palestinian guerrillas, and building the power of their allies the Maronite Christians, that they failed to consider the Shi'ite factor. The government paid no heed to intelligence warnings about the growing power of the Shi'ite majority. Nor did it seem to understand that southern Lebanon was the seat of the Iranian revolution. Yet, even Nabih Berri, the leader of Amal (who was by no means a firebrand), was already calling for future action to "dig the graves of the Israeli army." He claimed that the southerners had in the past defeated the Crusaders "and will be able to defeat the Israelis and free Lebanon." Nearly three years later, as the last tanks drove back into Israel, leaving the Amal militia in control, the Christian allies defeated and Shi'ite forces in command, and with Syria triumphant, it looked as though Nabih Berri's prophecy had come to pass. It was not surprising that gloomy critics of the war in Israel should have quoted from the Old Testament book of Habakkuk 2:17: "For the violence of Lebanon shall cover thee."

As soon as the Israelis had announced their intention of pulling out, Shi'ite forces intensified their guerrilla and terrorist attacks upon the demoralized soldiers. In reply, the Israelis imposed what they called an "iron fist" policy, striking back at the village bases of the Shi'ite marauders. But this only made matters worse, and when they finally pulled back into their own territory the Israelis thought it prudent to dig something resembling an ancient earthwork, 15 feet wide and 12 feet deep, along the 55-mile border, to ward off suicide car bombers from the homeland itself.

The original suicide truck bombs in Beirut had produced such a devastating effect that the Shi'ites were determined to exploit their new weapon to the full. One such attack in February 1985 drew particular attention because it came at a time when the iron-fist policy was in full swing. A 19-year-old electrical engineering student from Islamic Jihad named Hassan Qassir drove a car packed with explosive into an Israeli convoy, killing 10 soldiers and himself.

Islamic Jihad attacks of this kind were considered so successful that other organizations began to copy them by recruiting and training volunteers for suicide missions of their own. Some were Sunni Moslems, such as the Nasserites—the continuing supporters of the long-dead Colonel Nasser of Egypt. But the group which made most impact was the National Socialist Syrian Party, an interesting survival from other times, and an unexpected arrival in the suicide attack business. It claimed its first victims in March 1985, when a car exploded in an Israeli convoy near Metullah on the border between Israel and Lebanon in an area which had been considered safe. The new terrorist group concentrated upon attacks in the buffer zone which Israel had created north of the international border after its retreat, leaving behind only Israeli special units and a ramshackle locally recruited force called the SLA, or South Lebanese Army.

The new terror threat came from what was originally known as the Partie Populaire Syrienne, established in Lebanon in 1932 under the leadership of a man named Antoine Saadeh. The party was fascist, for he was an admirer of Mussolini, as indeed were a number of Arab leaders, including such Christian Maronites as the father of President Gemayel. Its aim was to establish Greater Syria, which would incorporate not only Syria and Lebanon but also Palestine, Iraq, Jordan and even the island of Cyprus. In the hope of achieving this monumentally ambitious program, the party first concentrated on trying to liberate Lebanon and Syria from French rule and domination. Its methods were sabotage and acts of terrorism. Indeed, in some respects the PPS (as it was known) is a founder-member of the Middle East terrorist circle, and many others have copied its techniques.

What is surprising is that such an antique fascist party should have come back to life to copy so successfully the suicide bomb methods of Islamic Jihad. The clue to its revival is provided by the fact that it now operates as a Syrian surrogate terror group controlled by the Damascus state intelligence service, supervised by President Assad himself. This arrangement reveals the depth of cynicism in the politics of the Levant, for until comparatively recently the

Syrian regime was doing all in its power to suppress the PPS. Yet it eventually decided that here was a useful tool for terrorism at arm's length.

In its checkered history the party has suffered many setbacks. Antoine Saadeh, the founder, was himself executed by the Syrians in 1949. Members were constantly persecuted, and it was branded as an extreme right-wing organization. However, in the 1970s it took on a new lease on life in collaboration with the Palestinians in Lebanon, working closely with George Habash's Popular Front for the Liberation of Palestine. Provided with arms and money by both Syria and Libya, it again became operational after the Yom Kippur war of 1973 from the bases it shared with other terrorist groups in the Bekaa valley.

Membership in the party is by no means exclusively Shi'ite. In its ranks are to be found Druse, Alawais, Palestinians, Sunnis and a large number of Greek Orthodox Christians. Like most Lebanese groups, it is divided into several factions, with the largest one under the leadership of Abdallah Saadeh, from the same clan as the founder, and Inam Rad. Paradoxically for an organization with a right-wing fascist history, one faction led by George Abdel Masih is closely linked with Lebanese leftists who seem to have forgotten the true meaning of national socialism.

When announcing a terrorist attack the party used the more up-to-date name National Resistance Front, and that was the organization which in April 1985 proudly announced that Sana Mahaidali had become the first woman suicide car bomber to perish in action. To draw further attention to her act the Front produced a video recording made by this nice-looking girl before she set out on her mission. This was an entirely new and macabre technique for creating posthumous terrorist publicity.

Mahaidali, dressed in a European-style two-piece suit and wearing a red beret, said that she had joined the organization after her village in the south had been attacked by the Israelis. She calmly announced, "I am very relaxed as I go to do this operation which I have chosen because I am carrying out my duty to my people. I am from the group that decided on self-sacrifice and martyrdom for the sake of liberation of land and people, because I have seen the tragedy of our people from the humiliation of occupation and oppression, the killing of children, women and old men."

Before going out to make the video and meet her fate, Sana

told her parents that she was off to buy lipstick. Then she drove away in a white Peugeot stuffed with TNT, took it alongside an Israeli army jeep near the village of Jessina, and detonated the charge which killed two soldiers as well as herself. It was the sixth such attack by her organization.

So alarmed were the Israelis by this onslaught that they went to some trouble to announce that they had earlier captured a Shi'ite would-be-suicide bomber named Mohammad Bourro. According to their version of his inter-rogation, he denied being a fanatic and said that he had been forced to agree to undertake a mission to get his father out of trouble with Amal. This may have been true, but from the outside the announcement looked like a bit of Israeli disin-formation.

The PPS-National Resistance Front struck again with two suicide bombs in the buffer zone on the same July day, killing 17 people at SLA checkpoints. One was driven by Ibtissam Harb, a Druse woman who was a former psychology student at the Lebanese university. She, too, was in a white 504 and duly appeared posthumously on a video recording to say "I hope to kill as many Jews and their agents as possible. I hope my mission will be successful, and a lesson to every enemy and traitor."

Ibtissam was a smart-looking, dark-haired young woman jauntily wearing her military shirt and the red beret of the PPS. She had made up discreetly with lipstick and eyeshadow. Behind her in the video shots was the party badge and, significantly, a picture of President Assad of Syria.

The boy suicide driver who went into action on the same day was a Syrian-born Sunni with a thin moustache named Khaled Azrak. He too had prerecorded his last words for television posterity. "I believe Israel's hand in this country should be chopped off" was the message of this timid-looking young party member, clad in combat jacket and wearing the red beret which was becoming the familiar headgear of these rather secular and innocent-looking suicide killers.

The next car bomber to kill himself and wound several Israeli soldiers at Arnoun in the buffer zone, Ali Ghazi Taleb, also used the same expression on his video. He warned "all collaborators and traitors and even Israel. We will chop off their hands." The 22-year-old Taleb also had a message for his mother: that she was not to grieve, for he had died a martyr and therefore he was not really dead.

By the summer suicide attacks were being made at the rate of one a week. At first the attacks were attributed to the Shi'ite suicide squads whose actions had made such an impact earlier. Then it emerged that this form of terrorist action by doomed men and women of tender age was less clearly inspired by religious faith and was a politically inspired imitation. It was clear that the people who sacrificed their lives in such attacks were being cleverly exploited by the Syrians and party leaders, among whom was mentioned the name of a Damascus politician, Isslam al-Mayhari. The video appearances were organized to wring maximum publicity for terrorist exploits and to give the impression that Lebanon was seething with the patriotic death wish to destroy Israelis and those who sympathized with them.

From Beirut it was learned that the average cost of such an operation is about $5,000. The party provided a car fitted out with explosives, and trained and prepared the driver. Then, according to one source, the organizers leave it to the person so equipped to choose his own time and place. Ali Taleb, whose mission took him in a Mercedes to Arnoun by the Litani river, simply waited in the square for an Israeli patrol to come along, asking local people what time it was expected.

The new suicide attacks from an unexpected source, the revived National Socialist party, took the Israelis by surprise. President Assad of Syria, by creating the new group, reinforced his hold over Lebanon, partly at the expense of the Shi'ites, and also created another front on which Israel was compelled to fight. Once again the Israelis turned to the old antiterrorist tactics which had served them so well against the Palestinians in the past. Good intelligence work pinpointed the bases of the Syrian National Socialist party suicide bombers. One of the main bases was in the town of Chtaura, on the road from Beirut to Damascus. Early one August morning, two Israeli jets swooped in low from Mount Lebanon to bomb and rocket the villa used as headquarters by the suicide bombers, which was completely destroyed.

In planning the retreat from Lebanon, Israel had attached great importance to preserving a security zone outside its northern border, similar to the one which had existed before the 1982 invasion. In face of harassing attacks against the main body of the army a local makeshift force was organized in the zone to defend Israel from cross-border attacks by Shi'ites, by then considered to be the main enemy.

Also, in the so-called iron fist campaign, the army rounded

up several hundred Shi'ite men of fighting age from the villages of southern Lebanon and transported them to Israel, to be held as hostages for the good behavior of their fellow religionists in Lebanon. The idea was that they would be useful bargaining counter in eventual negotiations with Amal to persuade that group to forbid terror raids across the border into Israel. This was a decision the Israeli government was to regret. Determined attempts by the Shi'ite international to get their people back from captivity led to the seizure of a TWA airliner which provoked a major international incident.

3.

Beirut Buccaneers

Ten minutes after TWA Flight 847 took off from Athens on June 14, 1985 and headed for Rome, two well-dressed young men moved forward to the flight deck. One of them turned by the door and faced the passengers with a 9 mm machine pistol. The other burst through to the flight deck, thrust a hand grenade in the face of Captain John Testrake and ordered him to fly to Beirut.

It was the beginning of the most remarkable and controversial act of air piracy since the high old days of Palestinian terrorism in the 1970s. Moreover, this tense terrorist scenario, the capture and torment of scores of American citizens, involved President Reagan and the U.S. administration in the most nerve-racking dilemma since the affair of the hostages at the embassy in Tehran.

Islamic Jihad spent months preparing the operation, and carefully planned it to make a giant impact on the world at large. The model was the multiple act of air piracy carried out in 1970 by George Habash's Popular Front for the Liberation of Palestine, the almost simultaneous seizure of five aircraft operated by Western airline companies. On that occasion every one of the governments concerned gave in to terrorist demands. But since that time, 15 years earlier, things had become a great deal more difficult for the air pirates. IATA (International Air Transport Association) figures speak for themselves. Whereas in 1970 IATA recorded

91 air hijacks, only 17 took place in 1984. The most significant drop in numbers came after 1974, when international agreements came into force requiring the screening of passengers and their baggage. Even so, there were gaps in the defenses waiting to be exploited. One was at Athens, and another in Beirut.

Ever since the meeting of Islamic Jihad leaders in Tehran in the summer of 1984 Shi'ite special squads had studied earlier hijacks, learning the lessons of their successes and failures, and had examined ways and means of launching their own campaign. Their people had already carried out two air piracy raids to Tehran in the summer and then in the winter of 1974. By the month of June the following year they were ready to try the big one.

International plotting was under way in the Middle East. Most of it was conducted at undercover meetings which took place behind the scenes at official gatherings of foreign ministers and during state visits. When President Ali Hamani of Iran went to Syria in September 1984, arrangements were made on the side to ensure the cooperation of Iranian and Syrian intelligence with leaders of the extremist Shi'ite organizations. In return for help with money, training and the provision of false documents the Shi'ites agreed to inform Syrian intelligence in advance about their operational plans. Senior Syrian intelligence officers were present, and so were Hussain Mussawi of Islamic Amal, Abbas Mussawi and Sheikh Sobhi Tufaili of Hizbollah and Sheikh Fadlallah. So too was Abdullah Mussawi, head of the so-called Imam Hussein suicide brigade—and the hijackers of the TWA flight eventually announced themselves as the Imam Hussein brigade.

Intelligence reports later spoke of the delivery to the Shi'ites of 35 passports, expertly forged in Cyprus by the Palestinian group owing allegiance to Abu Iyad. This followed a further meeting of state intelligence officers while the foreign ministers of Syria, Iran and Libya gathered in Tehran, officially to discuss a pact to oppose the American-Israeli alliance in the Middle East. Arrangements were made to facilitate the movement of Iranians across the Syrian border into Lebanon. Syria promised to hand over to Hizbollah 50 Soviet-made Sagger antitank missiles, also Grad missiles and launchers.

The equipment was to come from Syria, but it was paid for by Colonel Gaddafi of Libya. This was announced at an April meeting in Tripoli when the colonel inaugurated the "Arab Revolutionary Command" to liberate Arab lands. He told the conference, "What is important is the launching of an individual suicide action," and there was much talk of revolutionary violence being prepared against Israel and its ally, America.

Such was the background to preparations being made by Islamic Jihad for their big strike. Orginally they intended to capture more than one American airliner. The plot to take over another aircraft, flying out of West Berlin, was foiled by one of the rare (though not unprecedented) interventions of an eastern bloc country against terrorists. East German authorities detected two people traveling with passports from a Middle East country and carrying explosives in their baggage. They had been tipped off that the would-be hijackers were passing through Schönefeld airport in East Berlin on their way westward. The timing coincided with the Athens hijack. Even the East Germans are not keen on explosives being carried aboard their aircraft for smuggling into the West.

It is important to remember that terror operations frequently do fail before they begin. TV viewers and newspaper readers whose attention is only attracted when some spectacular affair is being reported tend to overestimate the cunning and the success rate of terrorists of all kinds. But in fact their organizations suffer from all the failures, mishaps and bits of bad luck which affect everyone else. The plan to take the TWA flight was itself thrown into disarray by the failure of the third man in the hijack team to get a seat on board the target aircraft. George Shultz, the U.S. secretary of state, went on record in the summer of 1985 with a statement that no less than 60 planned terrorist attacks around the world in the previous nine months had been "exposed, stopped or otherwise dealt with."

Before the TWA hijack the scene was cluttered, rather than cleared, by two similar air piracy operations. A man named Nazih, who led the team which seized the first plane at Beirut airport (a Boeing 707 of Royal Jordanian Airlines), said that he was acting for the Shi'ite National Resistance movement. They were clearly connected with Amal, for armed and uniformed Amal men helped them to blow up the aircraft on the ground when they returned to Beirut, after a 30-hour perambulation around the Mediterranean.

It was intended as an act of war against Jordan. The point

of that was to punish Jordan for supporting the Palestinians, then under attack in their Beirut camps by the Shi'ite militia. To complicate matters further, this affair prompted a Palestinian supporter to seize in revenge a Middle East Airlines plane in Cyprus; which goes to show how one hijack can lead to another in this volatile part of the world. But these were simply sideshows before the main event, demonstrating again the perils of Beirut airport in the hands of warring factions of private armies.

On board the TWA Boeing as it wheeled over the Bay of Salamis, the 145 passengers at first did not understand what was happening. They were the kind of people who might have been selected by a scriptwriter to figure in the cast of a doomed plane in a disaster movie—120 Americans, a Greek pop singer, some Australians and, inevitably, three Roman Catholic priests and 21 of their flock on a holiday tour and a group from Algonquin, Illinois.

Captain Testrake signaled the hijack on his special radio frequency, and the antiterror computer network promptly passed on the news to Washington, where President Reagan was informed at 2 A.M., as the crisis management team began assembling at the State Department.

Passengers and aircrew soon felt the bullying anger of the hijackers as they were forced to sit in uncomfortable postures and to surrender their passports under constant threats. Anyone who disobeyed was pistol-whipped by the excited Arabs, so constantly on the move that many people thought there were four of them rather than two. At about noon local time the Boeing made contact with the Beirut control tower, asking permission to land. The conversation was broadcast around the world as John Testrake, in that cool airline captain drawl, explained the desperate state of affairs on board. Fuel was low, and a hysterical gunman removed the pin of his hand grenade, threatening to blow up everything if the plane did not land. John Testrake was the only person around to behave with calm dignity. The control tower was swarming with armed members of Lebanese private armies, shouting and screaming.

The Boeing did land, but remained at Beirut international only long enough to refuel. Seventeen women and two children were allowed to escape from the aircraft by way of the emergency chutes before Captain Testrake was ordered to take off again and make for Algiers.

At first President Chadli of Algeria refused to allow the

flight to land at Boumedienne airport, 20 miles from the capital. He was in an awkward position, for his country had formerly been branded as a haven for hijackers, and he was anxious to demonstrate that things had changed. It was the Americans who wanted him to sanction the landing there in the hope that more hostages could be gotten off the aircraft. President Reagan persuaded him by telex to accept the hijacked plane. During the five hours spent on the ground, negotiators (joined in the control tower by the U.S. ambassador, Michael Newlin) were able to secure the release of 22 passengers, mostly women and children.

That evening at 7:15 GMT Flight 847, still under the orders of the Shi'ite duo, Ali Younis and Ahmed Ghorbieh, was airborne en route for Beirut again. Now with 113 remaining passengers, 104 of them American, it arrived over the blacked-out runways of Beirut international before midnight (GMT). When landing permission was refused by the erratic control tower the hijackers went berserk.

"I'll give you two minutes", one of them screamed over the radio, "then I will let one American loose off the plane."

The runway lights went on and the Boeing, down to its last reserves of fuel, landed safely. But immediately a quarrel broke out between the control tower and hijackers Younis and Ghorbieh, who wanted Shi'ite leaders brought to the plane. They had already discovered from their collection of passenger passports that there were U.S. Navy men on board, and had selected one of them, a diver named Robert Stetham, as a scapegoat. This brave young man had already been badly beaten, and was almost unconscious. Now he was dragged from his seat and the terrorists shouted that unless they got their way they would kill him.

"You don't believe us," one of them screamed. "We'll take this Marine, he was one of those who shelled Beirut."

Captain Testrake intervened to warn the control tower that they intended to kill a passenger. Then as a shot rang out, he reported again in his quiet-toned voice, "He's just killed a passenger." The body was dumped upon the tarmac a few minutes later.

If there had been any doubts about the brutal determination of the terrorists, it was now obvious that they would go to any lengths. Their further threats to kill all Americans on board one by one had to be taken literally, as Younis and Ghorbia pressed the demands they had first made in Algiers. They wanted the release of all Shi'ites captured in Lebanon and then taken to Israel. The demands (made in partly devout, partly obscene, language) included the cutting off of oil-sales to the West, Arab money to be removed from Western banks, and release of Shi'ites imprisoned in Kuwait.

By raising the question of men held prisoner by the Israelis at Atlit camp near Haifa, the hijackers added another international complication to the affair. Even before the seizure of the TWA plane the Israelis had already announced their intention of freeing the Shi'ite prisoners piecemeal when they believed the time was ripe. It had been argued that by removing the prisoners to Israel as they withdrew from Lebanon the Israelis were using them as hostages, and were anyway in breach of the Geneva Convention. Many things which happen in the Middle East are.

But that did nothing to ease the dilemma in which President Reagan found himself. For four years he had threatened to strike back at terrorism, taking a strong "no surrender" line, and had promised "swift retribution." He had to avoid falling into the same trap of inaction and compromise which had cost Jimmy Carter the presidency at the time of the Tehran hostage crisis. The president was reluctant publicly to put pressure upon Israel to hand over the prisoners, and in any case there was no guarantee that the Jerusalem government—which itself always opposed the idea of giving in to terrorists—would agree to this kind of action. Only a few weeks before they had done a deal with Syria by which three Israeli prisoners of war were returned in exchange for the release of 1,150 Arabs held for terrorism, which brought strong criticism at home from hard-liners.

No doubt the President would have liked to call in Delta, the U.S. army's special unit, formed and trained for hostage-release operations. From its headquarters at Fort Bragg, commandos, anxious to prove that they could be as dashingly successful as the Israelis at Entebbe and the West Germans at Mogadishu, were already planning how to storm the aircraft. A unit had flown to the Mediterranean from Polk Air Force Base in North Carolina on day one and was now in the region, probably on board the carrier USS *Enterprise* in the western Mediterranean. There were also reports that the rival FBI Hostage Rescue Team was on the move, though nothing more was heard of it.

"We're doing all we can," said the President. Warships of the Sixth Fleet led by USS *Nimitz*, the mighty carrier flagship, were already on station off the Lebanese coast.

There were contingency plans for air strikes against known Shi'ite bases, arsenals and safe houses in the Bekaa valley, including Hizbollah's barracks on the hill above Baalbek, overlooking the Temple of Jupiter. The fleet was being reinforced with extra ships and an 1,800-Marine amphibious unit. Squadrons of F-16 fighters were redeployed at bases in Turkey.

Despite the bold words of the Shi'ites on shore, they were alarmed by the proximity of this force, and its presence was certainly a factor in the panicky decision of the hijackers to get the Boeing airborne after their murderous sortie, which was a deliberate challenge. To get away from the fleet, they set course once again for Algiers.

As the Boeing headed westward through the night of Saturday/Sunday, the tactical debate continued in Washington. Bernard Kalb, the state department spokesman, warily declared: "The U.S.A. is working with all appropriate governments to secure the release of the hostages on TWA 847," adding, "It is not our policy to give in to terrorist demands." His boss, George Shultz, was known to favor strong action. He had publicly spoken of the need to put an end to the barbarism that threatened the foundations of civilized life. "It will not be a clean or pleasant fight," he had stated, recognizing the ugly truth that military action might involve the loss of civilian life if it came to a crunch.

On the other hand, Caspar Weinberger, the defense secretary, supported by his chiefs of staff, was chary of the idea of using special forces in an awkward situation which might provoke even worse retaliation. They all remembered only too well the misfortunes and losses sustained by the U.S. Marines in the earlier Lebanon intervention. And the military still bore the scars of the disastrous attempt to free the hostages at the embassy in Tehran. Furthermore, they feared that even a successful mission might result in the Shi'ites carrying out terrorist attacks in the United States itself. If there was to be a counterterrorist raid, it would need careful planning and assurance of a high probability of success.

The most favored military alternative to a rescue attempt was pinpointed air strikes at known terrorist establishments, the standard Israeli response to terror. But would that have done any good? It would certainly have placed the TWA passengers already in the hands of homicidal maniacs in even greater danger. And supposing aircraft were shot down over

Lebanon by Soviet missiles in position there, and their surviving aircrew added to the total number of hostages? Similar doubts and objections were expressed to every one of the more macho military responses.

The airliner with its wary flight crew and passengers arrived at Algiers early on Saturday morning. Obviously the hijackers knew their drill—keep the initiative, make a gesture by releasing a few passengers, then increase the pressure, as they did, by threatening one-at-a-time murders and the blowing up of the plane. Over the years hostage negotiators have developed their tactics to a fine art. But so too have the hijackers, who have learned not to let the initiative slip to the opposition in return for food and promises. These Shi'ites had made a study of such things, and because they knew the drill, they did not want to stay long in one place, giving a chance for rescue forces to plan and strike.

However, in this case, during the second stay in Algiers the two hijackers received a bonus presented by the Greek government which gave them their next victory. So anxious was the Greek government of Andreas Papandreou to secure the release of compatriots on board the TWA flight—especially the pop singer Demis Roussos—that they made concessions at once. After the departure from Athens of Flight 847, airport security had discovered and arrested Ali Atweh, the third-man hijacker who had failed to get a seat on the plane and almost ruined the plot. Now the Greeks not only agreed to free him, but had him flown to Algiers so that he might join and reinforce the terrorists holding the aircraft! This abject and speedy surrender served only to build the morale of the terrorists and to encourage them to make further demands.

In return the hijackers did hand over the Greek passengers, together with stewardesses and some others. But they held on to Demis Roussos, realizing that a pop singer would be bound to attract further publicity for their cause. There was no doubt, though, that reinforced by the return of Ali Atweh, and with fewer passengers now aboard, they had even tighter control over the plane. The hijackers demonstrated their training and expertise by releasing women, children and old people. Not only do such people cause them most trouble (because they often need special care) but also, if they are hurt, it is especially bad for the image of the hijackers. A terror expert commented at this point in the TWA hijack: "Now they're down to a useful bunch of hostages: big enough, but not too big to manage."

With hindsight, it can be seen that the Saturday spent on the ground at Algiers airport offered the best chance for a rescue raid by American special forces. The Washington task force under Robert Oakley, director of the Office of Counterterrorism and Emergency Planning, was fully operational and receiving constantly updated information about the state of affairs aboard the aircraft. Mrs. Thatcher had placed a Special Air Service (SAS) team in the British sovereign bases in Cyprus. They had no orders to intervene, but their expertise in antiterrorist warfare was available to help. From Cyprus the base electronic listening posts had been able to monitor everything said in Beirut.

To mount a rescue operation, an attack force needs at least a measure of cooperation from the host country on whose airfield the plane is held. The only examples of successes on hostile territory are the Israeli operation at Entebbe and the French rescue of hostages in Kolwesi. But in both cases the terrain was in ill-organized and ill-defended black African countries. Algeria, too, is a special case, a country no longer sympathetic to hijackers and terrorists, with a government open to persuasion for permission to storm the aircraft. The North African airport near Algiers certainly offered the best chance available for a Delta Force attack. Had they chosen to go in at Beirut they would have needed the help of a large covering force to hold off the well-armed militias.

No attempt was made, and early on Sunday morning, June 16, the three hijackers ordered take-off, and back they went to Beirut. It was at this point that Nabih Berri, the lawyer boss of Amal, the most respectable part of the Shi'ite organizations in Lebanon, made his entrance upon the scene. Berri made contact with the British and French ambassadors in Beirut with the suggestion that he might use his good offices as mediator. What he was doing, in fact, was to practice the traditional Lebanese skill of inserting himself as a middleman. Those who know Beirut well recognize that it is impossible to carry through any kind of transaction there, be it selling a cup of coffee or a new airline, without the arrival of some third-party agent skilled at bargaining. It is a traditional local pastime.

For Nabih Berri here was a fine opportunity, whether or not he had been a party to the original plan for a hijack, to demonstrate the strength of his position as a Shi'ite leader and to make a political profit for Amal through *marchandage*. If he could arrange a settlement without bloodshed, he might become the boss of Lebanon. This was a glittering prize for a bourgeois boy from the village of Tibnin, who unlike other Lebanese chiefs was not a feudal lord or spiritual leader but an upstart self-made master of the Shi'ite majority. His advantage was that to American eyes he looked right; smartly dressed in a Western suit, unarmed and disarming—so different from the scruffy beards, jeans and Kalashnikov men of the Shi'ite militia he more or less controlled.

The key moment came when before dawn on Monday, June 17, Nabih Berri got his militia to remove the bulk of the American hostages, 30 of them, and take them to three safe houses in the area they controlled around Bourj el-Barajneh. Though still in danger, these people were no longer under the sole control of the armed maniacs who had beaten passengers and murdered the Navy diver.

Furthermore, the terrorists had lost the initiative. Although they still held the Boeing aircraft and its crew, they no longer controlled the aircraft as an ideal 'prison'. For that is why planes are so sought after as terrorist prizes. They are easy to defend, difficult to assault, concentrate the attention of all, and are highly mobile. Their only disadvantage from the terrorist viewpoint is that modern electronic surveillance makes it easy for antiterrorist forces, even at long range, to monitor what is being said and done within the aircraft. Once Nabih Berri had succeeded in getting the hostage passengers ashore, eavesdropping became impossible.

The new anxiety was to know how far the Amal leader was in control of his own militia, and whether or not he could bargain successfully with Islamic Jihad, the extremists from his own side. A sinister turn of events was that passengers with Jewish-sounding names had been segregated, together with men who had U.S. services identity documents. They remained in the hands of the fanatics, and were held apart from the others. It was a reminder of what had happened during the Palestinian hijack to Entebbe, when they took Jewish passengers and held them separately, obviously with evil intent. Locked up in their three safe houses, the other hostages lived in fear of being handed back to the original homicidal hijackers. In the words of one of them, Peter Hill, "We eat, we sleep, we smoke, we pray."

Nabih Berri's strong card was that the hostages held by his men were now split up and relatively immune from any attempt at a rescue operation. They themselves, through Allyn Conwell, the Houston oil-man who had become the spokesman, were positively beseeching the United States not to attempt a rescue, and even Captain Testrake, interviewed through the window on his flight deck, declared: "If there is an attack we are dead men."

Mrs. Palmer, whose husband Jim was a hostage, put it well: "If I were sitting in my sitting room in Little Rock and watching this on television, I would say 'Reagan, send in the Marines and get them out.' But here in the hotel room in Paris, I don't want to get my husband killed. I am patriotic so long as I am sitting safe and calm in my living room, but I don't want to sacrifice my husband for the United States of America."

The Shi'ite leader still threatened that unless he got satisfaction he could hand his prisoners back to the Hizbollah gunmen. President Reagan and his men therefore faced an embarrassing predicament: tempting action with 'swift and effective retribution' was out. The only alternative was negotiation and diplomatic maneuvering, despite those bold statements—"America will never make concessions to terrorists." The *Wall Street Journal* could not resist the taunting headline, "Jimmy Reagan."

Diplomacy was two-pronged. On the one hand, the Americans had to try to persuade the tetchy Israelis to find a dignifed way of handing back their 500-odd Shi'ite captives, together with some 200 Palestinians, and on the other to bring pressure to bear upon Nabih Berri without exposing him to the wrath of Shi'ite religious bigots more unscrupulous than he. The Israelis were still smarting at State Department criticism of their earlier decision to hand over 1,150 Arabs (many of them convicted terrorists) to get back their own three POWs in Syrian hands at a very high rate of exchange.

In dealing with the Lebanese, the White House was fortunate to have at hand Robert (Bud) McFarlane, national security adviser, an ex-Marine colonel who during his earlier stint in the Middle East had had dealings with Nabih Berri. The two men had met while McFarlane was coordinating the American response to the suicide bomb attack on the Marines' barracks.

Bud McFarlane, who ran the White House situation room, was able to talk to Berri over the telephone, and this helped a great deal. Nabih Berri had his own troubles, which came to a head on Saturday, June 22, when his Amal militia, aided by the Shi'ite 6th Brigade of the national army, had to be called out to hold back the wilder elements of Hizbollah demonstrating at the airport. They felt that their hijack was slipping away from them, and that Berri was taking over their victory.

Berri had already been in trouble with the religious terrorists over Amal's attempt to throw out the Palestinians from their old base camps in Beirut. Both Iran and Hizbollah had denounced him for striking at the Palestinian enemies of Israel, and Colonel Gaddafi had described him as "worse than Sharon," the notorious Israeli general. In fact he wanted to prevent Yassir Arafat from rebuilding his forces in Lebanon in order to make guerrilla war on Israel and thereby provoke reprisal raids which would fall upon the Shi'ites of south Lebanon.

Four days of contacts between Nabih Berri and the Americans brought a solution of the crisis no closer. Finally, under the influence of George Shultz and Bud McFarlane—who had learned about Middle East politics the hard way, through contact with people on the ground—President Reagan was persuaded that only through dealing with President Assad, the real power in Lebanon, could something be arranged. The Syrian president, ally of the Soviet Union, was an old enemy of the United States, but at least he knew about *realpolitik*, and not a religious zealot. By taking a successful hand in the hostage affair, he could only increase his prestige and power. The reason he decided to put pressure upon the Lebanese Shi'ites for release of the hostages was to demonstrate that he was the master in Lebanon. By delivering a 12-hour ultimatum he forced Hizbollah to surrender the five captives held separately from the others. President Assad firmly told Sheikh Tufhaili and Abbas Mussawi, respectively the spiritual and military leaders of Hizbollah and Baalbek, that unless they did so he would sever all relations with them and cut off supplies and communications. Suddenly here was a head of a terrorist-sponsor state taking firm measures against the new terrorists.

On Sunday, June 30, all 39 remaining American hostages were driven up through the mountains to Damascus, from where they were flown to Frankfurt in West Germany.

One of the curiosities of the strange TWA hijack was the way in which the stars of the early days, the Islamic Jihad hijackers, Delta special forces and even President Reagan, faded, while those who at first had seemed only bit-part players—Nabih Berri and President Assad—became the lead players in the grand finale.

Three hooded young men—said to be Ali Younis and Ahmed Ghorbieh, who had seized Flight 847, and their colleague who missed the plane—were allowed to make a brief appearance at Beirut airport at what was called their own press conference: no questions, by order. Before they were hustled away by armed Amal militia they launched into a long anti-American tirade. Their words did nothing to answer the perplexing question, what had they and their masters really hoped to achieve? Certainly they demanded the release of Shi'ite prisoners in Israel, but that was only one demand among many. They kept adding to the list as new grievances crossed their minds—the release, for example, of other coreligionists, such as the two convicted in Madrid, another held in Paris and those in prison in Kuwait.

As always when trying to understand events in the Middle East, it is necessary in the search for deeper motives to listen to the words said and to crack the codes of their unfamiliar language.

When the terrorists broadcast from the flight deck of the Boeing, they expressed themselves thus:

> In the name of Allah, the all compassionate, the merciful. Where are you, Arabs? Jerusalem is calling you, you that claim yourselves Moslems . . . To the people who surrendered to Israel, to Mubarek (of Egypt), Arafat, Hussein, Saddam (of Iraq), to the usurpers of thrones, Jerusalem can only be liberated by the hands of the believers . . . To the people of Palestine we say, it is only through Islam that you can liberate your land.

That is the kind of politico-mystical language which must be penetrated to get an insight into the minds and aims of the Shi'ite terrorists. The enemies are listed. They are those denounced for cooperating with the United States, which tries to arrange a compromise peace settlement in Western diplomatic form between Israel and the Arabs. To the Moslem fundamentalists this is incomprehensible, and outside their terms of reference. Jerusalem is not a geopolitical capital, but the site of one of the holiest places in Islam. Their feeling for it would have been understood better by devout Christians among the Crusader hordes in the Middle Ages, who saw Jerusalem as the holiest place of Christendom disgracefully in the hands of the infidel. The Moslems are the faithful now; the Israelis and the Americans are the infidels to be driven out and humiliated. So too are their "supporters," including "Godless Iraq," Egypt, Jordan and the usurpers of thrones in Saudi Arabia and the Gulf. There is Allah's hit list.

It was generally taken for granted that the TWA hijackers had won a victory for terrorism. But what had they achieved in real terms? Israel did begin repatriating the Shi'ite prisoners, but it would have done that anyway, even if the hijack had never taken place. The difference was that they returned home as heroes to reinforce Amal, not simply as discharged prisoners considered unimportant to their captors. The Shi'ites, with a permanent chip on their shoulder, had demonstrated that they were capable of getting back their own people as effectively as the Palestinians, with the help of Syria, had done only a few weeks before in bargaining three Israeli POWs for the release of 1,150 of their own. On that occasion neither the Palestinians nor the Syrians had bothered about their fellow Arab Shi'ites.

In America many declared that the Shi'ites had drawn attention to their cause, though few seemed capable of explaining what that cause was, except the desire to be top dog in Lebanon and to spread Islamic revolution to that country and elsewhere. It is the difference between those two aims which divides the Shi'ite movement in Lebanon. Those who carried out the hijack were zealots for the faith inspired by Iran and the fundamentalist clergy and the desire to spread their revolution to the shores of the Mediterranean by establishing the Islamic Republic of Lebanon. Nabih Berri and the Amal supporters who took over the hijack and negotiated have the more local aim of bringing the Shi'ite majority in Lebanon to its rightful place at the top of the hierarchy of diverse religious groupings in that country, above Sunnis, Christians and the Druse.

Certainly in the end Nabih Berri gained prestige in Lebanon, but such prestige in the factional city hall-style politics of Beirut is pretty ephemeral. President Assad was able to demonstrate his influence over the country at the expense of the other warring sects there, and to prove to the United States that without him there is no possibility of making a lasting arrangement between the Arabs and the Israelis, which is optimistically known as the "peace process." But all that he managed to wring out of the United States in return for his help was a statement that it supported the integrity, stability and security of Lebanon, which was its policy anyway.

The terrorists of Islamic Jihad were none the less satisfied that this demonstrated American "submission to our will." America remains the 'Great Satan.' They knew quite well that the best way to win glory and prestige in the Middle East was to challenge the United States, the greatest power on earth, and to humiliate that nation in Arab eyes. Because they were convinced that a victory had been won the new terrorists were encouraged to strike again. Indeed, when the hijack affair was all over, the Islamic groups were still holding captive seven American and five French and British citizens seized by armed men as they went about their business in Lebanon.

"We will not rest until justice is done," declared President Reagan, expressing determination to go after the hijackers and punish them. But after all the brave talk during the crisis about Western powers uniting to fight terrorism, little was done. The call to arms was forgotten—until the next big terrorist attack. There was hardly any response to the American lead in boycotting Beirut international airport.

Lawrence Eagleburger, formerly of the State department, summed up the lessons of the TWA hijack and all that happened because of it when he declared: "I don't think anybody has discovered an antiterrorism policy that works . . . we are all facing a new kind of warfare, and we don't know how to deal with it."

Part Two

The QUARTERMASTERS

4.

The Flaky
Barbarian

I find he's not only a barbarian, but he's flaky
—President Reagan

Among the many governments in the Middle East that use terrorism as an executive arm of diplomacy that of the Libya stands out because of the *braggadocio* style of Colonel Muammar al-Gaddafi. From the moment that he seized power from old King Idris in September 1969 and sent him into exile, Gaddafi deliberately committed his country and its burgeoning oil wealth to terrorism as the correct, indeed, divinely ordained, way to defeat Israel.

Ambitious and eager to succeed his hero, Colonel Gamal Abdel Nasser of Egypt, as the leading revolutionary in the Arab world, he was equally determined to strike at Israel. The catch was that as ruler of a state which consisted largely of sand, with a population of only around three million, he lacked the men, the equipment and infrastructure to make any real military contribution to the war against Israel. And that conflict was the main focus of political interest in the world of Islam. In any case even the powerful armed forces of Egypt, Syria and Jordan had been roundly defeated in the field by the Israelis in 1967. For that very reason the despairing Palestinians themselves had turned to subversive warfare as the only means left to them.

Though short of men the new Libya had plenty of money—

petrodollars from the newly developed oilfields—and the dictator began spending it in the Soviet Union to buy a surfeit of modern weapons, far more than his small army and air force could use effectively. Even when he had built up the strength of the army to 58,000 in 1986 and lavishly equipped it with armor and artillery, and despite the fact that the air force had more than 500 combat aircraft and the navy was equipped with six submarines and two score patrol craft, Libya still did not count in terms of a real Arab-Israeli war.

Gaddafi's prime reason for setting up as the sponsor of any and every terrorist movement with Israel and friends of Israel as its enemy was that he realized how impotent his country was to make conventional war. Fatah, the Palestinian guerrilla and terrorist organization built by Yassir Arafat, had set the example which the Libyan chose to follow. Subversive warfare was the trick and Muammar Gaddafi fought it with a two-pronged series of campaigns directed first against Libyans who opposed him and then against Israel, Europe and America.

The plotting revolutionary army officer at the age of 27 had come to power with a ready-made list of foes. Israel headed it, but others figured prominently—Italy because it had once colonized Libya; Britain and France because they ran, and subsidized, the country after 1945, and the United States because it had an air base, shared with Britain, at Wheelus Field near Tripoli, the capital. The Anglo-Saxons were branded from the start, not only as friends of Israel, but also as imperialists. Furthermore they were capitalists; their companies ran the Libyan oilfields. For all these reasons of hatred he targeted them all.

As this curiosity among political leaders evolved his own political theory, which was a strange mixture of Islamic faith, ill-digested Marxism and clan loyalty, he proudly declared, "I have solved the problem of democracy." At home he looked after the interests of his people, spending lavishly on welfare, housing and industrialization projects. "The Guide," as he liked to be called, aspired to create a system of government by which political power was in the hands of Revolutionary Committees, but control of those bodies often fell into the hands of his own relations and clansmen in the Gdaf, a minority tribe only 600 strong. He quarreled with his revolutionary officer comrades who had brought him to power. Several went off into exile and denounced him. So did middle-class emigres deprived of their property and businesses.

Colonel Gaddafi became paranoic about their plots against him, both imaginary and real. That was one of the arrows which pointed him into the paths of terrorism. Anyone not with him was against him, and he and his young revolutionaries organized hit squads to go abroad to seek out and to kill those "enemies of the state" who stubbornly refused to return home. At first the Libyans, despite the swashbuckling of their leader, turned out to be not very good at murder. That led the colonel to hire trained and proficient gunmen from elsewhere in the Arab world.

There was no shortage of such people in the 1970s among the proliferating and quarreling segments of the Palestine liberation movement. The militant oil baron of Tripoli made use of the mercenary Carlos and his international band; he employed Abu Nidal, the Palestinian rebel whose group was able to strike down its own enemies, including a score of moderate Palestinians owing allegiance to Yassir Arafat, in countries as far apart as Portugal and India, as well as those of Libya.

They were ready and willing to kill Gaddafi's enemies in return for largesse enabling them to set up their camps in Libyan territory at his expense. By 1986 the regime was maintaining no less than 34 instruction facilities for terrorists in Libya. Abu Nidal's men were installed near the oasis of Sebha. Petrodollars were readily available, especially after the oil price crisis following the Yom Kippur war, and Libya was ready to disburse large sums and promise even larger ones to any group anywhere in the world ready for action against Israelis, capitalists and imperialists. Colonel Gaddafi bought huge quantities of modern weapons from a Soviet Union more anxious to earn hard currency even than it was to stir up trouble for the West. In 1976 he signed a contract with the Kremlin to buy $12 billion worth of military equipment including 2,800 tanks, and the Soviets were glad to get the dollars, no matter what their Arab customer planned to do with the weapons.

Nor were Arabs and Russians the only people to cash in on the terror boom. The renegade CIA agent and arch-villain of the American intelligence community Edwin Wilson helped to supervise the training of Libyan so-called special forces and acted as Libya's unofficial quartermaster. In the process he amassed a fortune in excess of $15 million and bought a 2,000-acre property in Virginia before he was lured to the Dominican Republic and taken back to the United States where he is now serving a total of 52 years in prison for assorted crimes. Together with Frank Terpil, another former intelligence man, he sold to Colonel Gaddafi quantities of modern explosives and detonators. Included in the shipments were 21 tons of American-made C-4, the most powerful plastic explosive in the world. They also arranged to supply 100,000 Texas-made electronic delayed action timers on the pretext that they were to be used for clearing a wartime minefield for oil companies working in the Libyan desert. Wilson's Libyan go-between was Abdullah Hajazzi of Libyan military intelligence, who later became liaison officer with Abu Nidal.

Omar Maheshi, one of Gaddafi's original revolutionary officers who became a minister before defecting from the regime to Cairo, reported dealings with Frank Terpil. He had recruited Terpil to train terrorists in return for a cash payment of $1 million and $20,000 a month. The American then persuaded active Green Berets on leave to help with the task.

Edwin Wilson went further and became involved in the Gaddafi campaign against Libyan dissidents abroad. In 1976 he was responsible for hiring an assassin who tried and failed to kill Omar Mehaishi in Cairo. One of his former Green Beret connections, Eugene Tafoya, shot and wounded another Libyan exile, Faisal Zagalai, who was a sociology student at the Colorado State University. When they arrested him police found in his possession a hit list of 100 Libyans living in North America.

Flattered by the attention of foreign experts and notorious terrorist leaders come to his court at revolutionary headquarters in Tripoli, Muammar Gaddafi became more expert in the theories and tactics of subversive warfare. They helped him establish state security and intelligence. They gave assistance in training and operating Libyan hit squads who were sent roaming in Europe. Libyan embassies were transformed into people's bureaus abroad, which as young revolutionaries replaced old style diplomats, became centers for terrorist activity worldwide. Libya perverted the convention of the diplomatic bag, by which civilized embassies have a right to import supplies and documents without customs examination, by using the privilege for the regular supply of weapons and explosives intended for use by assorted terrorist groups. The bureaus abroad were able to supply authentic passports and identity documents for a host of violent troublemakers.

An actual case history of a Libyan hit man caught and

arrested in Europe for killing two people demonstrates the technique. He told his interrogators that he had been noticed for efficiency and initiative while serving in the army as corporal on the Chad expedition. The talent spotters told him that he had been selected for duty with the Operations Team of the Revolutionary Committees. This special force has many duties as an armed militia with terrorist cells, and as a force of "parallel police" to sniff out sedition within the country.

The corporal was posted to a training unit near Tripoli where instructors turned out batches of apprentice hit men, 40 at a time. While he was there three separate courses were under way. Recruits learned to handle all types of small arms, some with silencers, explosives and many of the devices of terror. After six months he graduated as a fully trained operative and was dispatched on a mission. They gave him a genuine doctored Tunisian passport and sent him to Europe to await orders.

After several weeks during which he obeyed instructions to the letter and, using public phones, regularly telephoned the case officer in Tripoli, he was given the name of a man to kill and left to choose when and how to do it. He had arrived in the country clean but weapons and equipment presented no problem. All he had to do was go to the Libyan people's bureau, speak the correct code word and be left to choose from its extensive "diplomatic" armory of weapons and explosives.

He selected an Israeli-made Uzi automatic and killed his man. Things only went wrong because an accomplice provided with a motorbike to speed him away from the scene panicked and left him behind. The helper got away, made for the nearest international airport and was flown home to Tripoli, courtesy of Libyan Arab Airlines. The corporal was arrested. That is how it works, and nobody knows just how many Libyan hit men like the corporal are currently at large in our part of the world simply awaiting the word to strike.

Using such teams the Libyan state mounted a sustained campaign against its own expatriates living in Britain, Europe and the United States. There have been killings of such people in London, Birmingham, Manchester, Rome, Athens, Bonn, Stockholm and Vienna, as well as in North America. In 1981 Hosni Farhat attempted to murder a Libyan named Farag Ghesuda together with his English wife and two young children simply because he refused to leave

Britain and go back to Libya. The two men, who had served together in the Libyan navy, knew each other. Hosni Farhat visited the Ghesuda home and gave to the children a packet of peanuts coated with thallium, a lethal poison. Fortunately for the children they played "one for you one for me" with the nuts and most of the coating rubbed off. Even so they were both seriously ill and needed emergency treatment. Their pet Pekingese dog which picked some nuts did in fact die. The poisoner Farhat was sentenced to life imprisonment by a British court.

In another case Ali al-Giahour, a flamboyant Libyan businessman remanded on charges of conspiracy to cause explosions in London during March 1984, was found murdered in his apartment. He had been arrested after a series of five bomb attacks on places where Libyan exiles gathered in London and in Manchester. According to Libyan exiles, Ali al-Giahour had been forced by Gaddafi agents to prove his loyalty by taking part in the bomb plots. When he was arrested they feared that he would reveal details of their organization to the police and therefore killed him, making him kneel before shooting him in the head at close range. By his body was a note in Arabic.

> This is the punishment for the one who is employed to do a job and does not succeed in doing it. Signed Al Fatih and the committees everywhere.

Al Fatih means "the conqeror," a title used by Colonel Gaddafi, and the committees are the people's ones which are supposed to govern the country.

Al-Giahour's murderer, who was never caught, was obviously a professional. The pistol with silencer and six bullets and the notebook and pen used to write the message were all dumped in a bath in an attempt to destroy fingerprint evidence.

Other assaults on people described by the Libyan leader as "stray dogs" have been less successful. In November 1984 Tripoli radio announced the execution of Abdul-Hamid Bakoush, a former prime minister in the King Idris regime, exiled in Egypt. He was accused of selling his conscience to the enemies of the Arab nation and was in fact leader of the Libyan Liberation Organization, an anti-Gaddafi movement enjoying the support of the Egyptian government. The hit team reported their success and produced pictures of a bloodstained body. In fact they themselves had fallen victim to a plot hatched by the Egyptian secret service. The day following the Tripoli announcement Abdul-Hamid Bakoush appeared alive and well at a Cairo press conference and joined the Egyptian interior minister, Ahmed Roshdi, in denouncing Colonel Gaddafi.

The story they told was that two British businessmen, Anthony William Gill and Godfrey William Shiner, had been hired by the Libyan ambassador in Malta, together with two Maltese, Romeo Chakambari and Edgar Cahia, to kill the exiled politician. Gill later said that he had been offered £50,000 to organize the murder. But from the moment they flew to Egypt all four were under surveillance by the Egyptian secret service, which had been tipped off about the plot. When the plotters set about hiring Cairo criminals to do the deed, Egyptian agents fixed it so that the contract killers were covert Cairo security men. Using real blood from a hospital stock and careful makeup, they faked realistic Polaroid photographs of Bakoush bound and gagged, then lying in a pool of blood with a bullet hole in his head.

The evidence was taken to Malta by an Egyptian agent, together with a letter confirming that the assassination had been carried out. It was claimed by the Egyptians that these were handed to Colonel Gaddafi himself during his meeting in Crete with President Francois Mitterrand of France and the Greek prime minister, George Papandreou. A triumphant broadcast from Tripoli was quickly followed, to the embarrassment and chagrin of Colonel Gaddafi, by the Egyptian account of what had really happened.

Even this chastening experience did not discourage the Libyans from going ahead with their campaign against the exiled "stray dogs." In a long speech in March 1985 Colonel Gaddafi declared: "We have the right to take a legitimate and sacred action—an entire people liquidating its opponents at home and abroad and in broad daylight." He announced the recruitment of a new force of 150 specially trained men called Mutarabesun (Ever Ready). Its task was to seek out and destroy any Libyan considered an enemy of the regime.

Colonel Gaddafi's justification was that he considered the exiles to be the real terrorists. Indeed, he accused European governments of sheltering them. He even considered it legitimate for his men to open fire on opposition Libyan demonstrators in London who—to his way of thinking—were being protected by the London police. He even had the gall to claim that it was the police who were responsible for the death of a policewoman.

Action against dissidents was only one part of Libyan state sponsorship of terror. Colonel Gaddafi encouraged dissident Palestinian war bands to attack Americans and Europeans, usually in embassies abroad, but sometimes in their home countries. The general aim of the plans for anti-American action using the services of guerrilla bands backed up by Arab state intelligence officers was to improve his standing and image in the Arab world as a brave leader capable of striking down the friends of Israel. Muammar Gaddafi attempted to justify his actions by using every propaganda trick in the book to try to prove that he was the innocent victim of Reaganite imperialism. He was encouraged by signs of European anxiety about bold action by the Americans.

Colonel Gaddafi's true feelings about the terrorism he had done so much to encourage were summed up in one paragraph from a speech made at Sibha, central Libya in September 1985 when he said:

> We have the right to take deterrent measures against all capitulationist Arab regimes . . . We are always wronged. Therefore we have the right to export terrorism to them because they have done everything to us. . . If we really want to face up to our responsibilities then Libya has no alternative but to be a base for liberation. If Libya does not become a base for liberation, then we will be escaping from our responsibilities . . .

The first clear signal that Libya intended to set up as the sponsor of violence worldwide came with the Munich Olympic Games massacre in September 1972. When five Palestinian gunmen killed in the shootout at Furstenfeldbruck airfield were given martyrs' funerals in the Libyan capital, the colonel marched at the head of the procession. He also handed out $5 million reward to Yassir Arafat's Fatah organization, which had carried out the Munich operation under the cover name Black September. And when the three surviving members of the gang were released by the West Germans in November 1972 in exchange for a Lufthansa airliner seized in a subsequent hijacking planned for the purpose, they were welcomed as heroes in Tripoli.

Rashid al-Kikhya, the then Libyan foreign minister, spelled out his leader's attitude in an interview with *Stern* magazine: "We say openly; Yes, in Libya, volunteers from 18 Arab countries are preparing for the fight against Israel. The stagnation in the Arab world has been ended by the Libyan revolution. Now we are in a position to be able to radicalize the war. And naturally we Libyans will support in this phase every Palestinian commando operation. I stress: every operation."

Colonel Gaddafi lived up to his word. He gave encouragement, money, arms and shelter to the most notorious terrorists. No act, however cruel, caused him to withdraw his support. His only criticism was that they were talking too much and not killing enough. He was involved in the Black September attempt to seize the Saudi Arabian embassy in Khartoum which led to the murder of Cleo Noel, U.S. ambassador to Sudan, George Moore, another American diplomat, and the Belgian chargé d'affaires, Guy Eid, who was killed because the hit men believed he was a Jew.

Gaddafi helped and encouraged Carlos, the international terrorist, in planning the kidnap raid on OPEC headquarters in Vienna. The later confessions of Hans Joachim Klein, one of Carlos' men, left no doubt about his part in this affair and its aftermath. The Libyan leader allowed hijackers of a number of aircraft to land in his country, to make their deals and then cover their tracks.

He rejoiced at the slaughter carried out by three Japanese Red Army killers on behalf of the Popular Front for the Liberation of Palestine at Lod airport, Tel Aviv. Using grenades and assault rifles, they killed 26 people and wounded 76. Two of the Japanese died in the shooting and the survivor, the mad Kozo Okamoto, said at his trial in Israel that the people he killed "become stars in the sky." Gaddafi told the Palestinians that their action should be of the type carried out by the Japanese.

Two Egyptian submarines on secondment to the Libyan navy were ordered by him to torpedo the British liner *Queen Elizabeth II* as it sailed towards Israel carrying 500 American and British Jews to Haifa for celebrations to mark the 25th anniversary of the founding of Israel. The submarine commanders, somewhat surprised by these orders, signaled their own navy headquarters at Alexandria and asked for further instructions. President Sadat ordered them to return to base. The Egyptians themselves made the facts public and so incurred the hatred of Colonel Gaddafi.

In July 1984 the colonel sent the Libyan roll-on, roll-off ferry Ghat through the Suez canal to lay mines in the Red Sea. These Russian-made devices damaged 18 ships. During an international mine-sweeping operation in which the U.S. Navy took part, one of them was recovered by the British warship HMS *Gavington*. The fact that it contained only a quarter of the normal weight of explosive indicated that the plan was to damage ships rather than to sink them. The real purpose of the cruise of the Ghat was to frighten away ships from the Suez Canal in order to damage the Egyptian economy, as punishment for what Libya saw as Egypt's betrayal of the Arab cause by making peace with Israel.

Such wild behavior led Colonel Gaddafi into bitter quarrels, not only with other Arab leaders, but also with the Palestinian organizations. He clashed with Yassir Arafat when the PLO leader, having used terrorism to bring his cause to world attention, began employing diplomacy to further that cause. By the spring of 1983, Gaddafi was openly supporting Palestinian factions opposed to Yassir Arafat and urging them on to ever more desperate acts.

When even his promises of money and weapons failed to win him control over the main Fatah group, he set up his own organization, the National Arab Youth for the Liberation of Palestine, commanded by Ahmed al-Ghafour, the PLO representative in Libya who had defected to join the Libyans. But Al-Ghafour's enterprises were so horrific that they appalled the PLO which condemned him to death as a traitor and he was shot dead by a Fatah "elimination squad."

Despite snubs and failures, Colonel Gaddafi never faltered in his belief in the efficacy of terrorism. He aided dissident groups and "liberation movements" in many parts of the world. The list of countries where he has intervened is truly astonishing. Oman, North Yemen, Sudan, Morocco, Tunisia, Lebanon, Egypt and Chad are among the Arab states in which Libyan help has gone to antigovernment forces. And, before his rapprochement with King Hassan of Morocco in 1984, he supported the Polisario nationalists in their Sahara desert war against the royal regime.

Nor were his efforts confined to Arab countries. He backed antigovernment groups in the Azores, Madeira, the Canary Islands, Eritrea and the Philippines. Libyan agents became increasingly active in Latin America, particularly Nicaragua and El Salvador, and in West Africa, where both Ghana and Liberia complained about his activities. Numerous threats were also made to sponsor urban terror groups in European countries when their governments refused to do as Colonel Gaddafi told them.

In February 1985, for example, the official Libyan newspaper, "Green March" threatened that the Red Army

Faction would be financed and armed by Libya to renew its terror campaign if the Federal government failed to hand over eight Libyan dissidents living in West Germany. Similar threats of support for the Italian Red Brigades were uttered when Italy refused to take action against exiled "anti-Libyan terrorists." Although such threats are not always carried out, it is known that various European separatist movements received supplies from Libya.

The best documented example of his support for a European nationalist movement, in this case the IRA, is provided by the *Claudia* affair. The *Claudia*, a coaster operated by the Giromar Cypriot company, was itself owned by Gunther Leinhauser, a convicted West German arms smuggler. The ship was detained by the Irish Republic navy on March 28, 1973 as the crew tried to unload five tons of arms from Libya, including 250 Soviet-made automatic rifles, pistols, ammunition, grenades, mines and explosives. The *Claudia* had been shadowed all during the voyage by the Royal Navy, which passed it on to the Irish navy as it approached the Republic territorial waters. Among those on board was Joe Cahill, a former commander of the Provisional IRA in Belfast. According to Leinhauser he had been given a shopping list of Gaddfi-furnished arms by the IRA, and had arranged the deal with Cahill in Tripoli.

Libyan support for the IRA slackened after this affair, not only because of the scandal, but also because the Ulster Defense Association, (UDA) an illegal counterterrorist Protestant group, sent a delegation to Libya asking for Gaddafi's support in their fight against the republicans. This incident served to display the Arab leader's amazing ignorance about the complications of Irish politics. He was apparently under the impression that the whole of Ireland was a kind of colony occupied by British troops against whom both the IRA and the UDA were engaged in a liberation struggle. He considered them simply as rival bands fighting the same cause, rather like the rival Palestinian groups. Gaddafi had no idea about the difference between Catholics and Protestants, or the chasm separating Republicans and Loyalists. That did not prevent him from threatening to intervene again whenever he was at odds with the British government.

The Provisional IRA fostered the idea that Libya was its ally. In December 1976 the "Voice of the Arab Homeland," broadcasting from Tripoli, gave what it claimed were extracts from a letter smuggled out the the Maze prison by IRA prisoners: "We, here in our internment camp, greet the 1st September revolution and its leader Colonel Muammar Gaddafi. The voice of this leader reaches us despite the solitary confinement cells and the prison guards. We also greet the Palestinian Arab revolution and our companions in the Zionist interment camps. Long live the Arab-Irish struggle."

Gaddafi resurrected his threat to help the IRA in the wake of the killing of policewoman Yvonne Fletcher by Libyan "diplomats" firing a Sterling submachine gun at Libyan dissidents demonstrating outside their people's bureau in St. James's Square, London in April 1984. As a result the British government broke off diplomatic relations with Libya and expelled more than 60 officials and supporters.

Five days after the policewoman's murder the "Voice of the Arab Homeland" said:

> The people's committees will form an alliance with the secret IRA in view of the fact that it champions the cause of liberating Ireland and liberating the Irish nation from the tyranny of British colonialism. The people's committees will open branches for the secret IRA in all Libyan towns, and if Britain tries to use any means to pressurise and oppress Libyan Arabs, the revolutionary committees will enable the IRA to do whatever it wishes in Britain and retaliate twice as strongly.

The leader himself followed up by declaring: "We do not consider the IRA a terrorist army; they have a just cause, the independence of their country . . . this is a just cause and we are not ashamed of supporting it with all the means we have . . ."

After the U.S. raid on Libya from British airfields Colonel Gaddafi again renewed his threats to increase support for the IRA. When Prime Minister Thatcher was explaining her reasons for supporting President Reagan she listed Libyan terror plots against foreign countries and mentioned the discovery in January 1986 of a major arms cache at Sligo and Roscommon in the Republic of Ireland which she described as the largest ever found there. Among the stores discovered were rifles and ammunition from Libya. The government of the Irish Republic protested vigorously at Libyan backing for the IRA which it, too, considers to be an illegal organization. That also must have surprised the Libyan leader who hardly seemed aware that the Irish Republic was an independent state.

Long before that Americans had been the targets of Gaddafi-inspired terror and threats to strike back in revenge. Following the first air action over the Gulf of Sirte, in October 1981, Maxwell Rabb, the U.S. ambassador to Italy, was flown home at once when it became known that he was a target of a Libyan assassin. Rabb was visiting Milan at the time and the danger was considered so pressing that he was hustled to the plane without even having time to get a change of clothing. Soon after that the French authorities learned of a plot to murder Christian Chapman, the U.S. chargé d'affaires in Paris. He and his chauffeur had a narrow escape. Other hit squads had been set up to attack U.S. embassies in Athens and Ankara as well.

Two months later there was a fresh scare in Washington when it was reported that a five-man Libyan hit team, which included an East German, had entered the United States with orders to kill President Reagan. According to federal officials the hit team considered plans to shoot down Air Force One with ground to air missiles; to blow up his limousine with a rocket propelled grenade; or to make a suicide attack on the president with automatic weapons. Although a massive manhunt for the would-be killers was launched, no trace of them was discovered. Indeed, doubts were expressed about whether they really existed. But no chances were taken.

Unable to execute his melodramatic plans the Libyan leader chose instead to aid groups in the Caribbean and in Central America opposed to the United States. The extent of this support was revealed in documents captured as a result of the 1983 American invasion of Grenada following the murder by extremists of the "New Jewel" movement of the Marxist prime minister, Maurice Bishop.

The documents proved that Libyan agents had moved in to set up ties with the "People's Revolutionary government." Their opportunity arose as relations between Grenada and Britain and America deteriorated. In February 1983 a Libyan people's bureau was established in the capital, St. George's. Headed by Abdullah Attir, a hard-line Gaddafi man, it had a staff of six Libyans in addition to locally employed people, with an office much bigger than was needed for normal diplomatic representation.

Colonel Gaddafi planned to use Grenada as a stepping-stone in a campaign to spread his influence through the area. One batch of papers outlined his plans for funneling military and economic aid worth some $60 million a year to the

Sandinista regime in Nicaragua. But Libyan promises are notoriously long on words and short on performance, and it is not known if the money was ever handed over.

Gaddafi had ambitious plans for the Caribbean. Selected students were being sent to three camps in Libya for courses on military tactics and to learn Arabic. They were earmarked as the vanguard of the West Indian campaign. It emerged also that the next target for subversion was to be St. Lucia. When governments of friendly Caribbean countries were informed of these plots by the Americans, Sir Paul Scoon, governor-general of Grenada, broke off diplomatic relations with Libya and sent the people's bureau packing, along with diplomats and advisors from the Soviet Union, Cuba, North Korea, East Germany and Bulgaria.

Colonel Gaddafi switched his attention to the American mainland during the 1984 campaign for the Democratic party's presidential nomination. The Reverend Louis Farrakhan, leader of a black Moslem movement, the Nation of Islam, came to national prominence as he offered support to the black candidate, the Reverend Jesse Jackson. Because of his openly anti-semitic views the Rev. Farrakhan turned out to be a great liability. He praised Hitler as a very great man and spoke of Judaism as a "gutter religion." The black fanatic first made contact with Colonel Gaddafi at a government sponsored conference in Tripoli in April of 1984, attended by a number of black nationalist organizations, one of the delegates being a colleague named Akbar Muhammad. A Gaddafi speech was transmitted live from Tripoli to a Chicago rally to mark the International Savior's Day Convention of the Nation of Islam attended by 12,000 American blacks. Even by Gaddafi's standards the 40-minute performance was remarkable. He told the cheering delegates that the United States must be destroyed, and suggested that as a first step blacks in the American armed forces should mutiny and form a separate army.

He promised to provide arms and fight with them "to destroy white America. We will fight shoulder to shoulder. The final victory will be soon." Although this might be dismissed as yet another flight of Libyan fancy there was some danger that such ranting might inspire some among the discontented black followers of the rabble-rousing Rev. Farrakhan to follow the Libyan lead.

It must not be forgotten that while the "Colonelissimo," as Gaddafi likes to sign himself, masterminds so many international plots he is constantly worried that others, even close associates, may be plotting against him. In the fall of 1985 he began to suspect Colonel Hassan Ishkal, governor of the military region of Sirte, his cousin and his deputy. The Ishkal affair demonstrated just how ruthless the leader could be even with friends and relations.

The fact was that Hassan Ishkal had become too ambitious and successful after saving the day by leading the counterattack when an anti-Gaddafi suicide squad attacked revolutionary headquarters in May 1984. He took over security, made money and bought property in Italy and in Egypt, and married an Egyptian woman. Furthermore, he had the temerity to speak of the "dirty war in Chad," saying that the army was fed up with it.

On the return from a November trip to Moscow with Gaddafi he was summoned to revolutionary headquarters from a dinner party to attend a cabinet meeting on the crisis caused by the massing of Egyptian forces on the border. His wife, Jamaalat, got a telephone call the next day to say that her husband had died after a road accident between Tripoli and Sirte where he was going because of the crisis. The other version is that he was shot in the head with revolver bullets inside the barracks and that his staff officers were arrested.

Immediately afterwards Major Abdul Salaam Jalloud, a long-term and disciplined crony of Gaddafi's was back in favor with the other three "historic" leaders—Aboubakr Youness, chief of the general staff, Mustepha Kharroubi, inspector general, and Khouildi Hamidi.

The ranks needed to close up because exiled dissidents were beginning to hit back against their tormentors. The most active anti-Gaddafi movement is the National Front for the Salvation of Libya (NFSL). It is a well-organized group enjoying the support of the Saddam Hussein regime in Iraq as well as that of Egypt. In January 1985 the NFSL had held its second national congress in "a friendly Arab country," attended also by representatives of the Libyan National Movement, the Libyan Liberation Organization, the Preparatory Committee for the Libyan National Charter and the National Union of Libyan Women.

A congress communiqué issued by the secretary-general and former diplomat, Dr. Mohammed Yusuf al-Magariaf, called upon "all Arabs and Moslem states and all peace-loving countries of the world to lend material and moral support to the Libyan national struggle against Gaddafi, in order that the Libyan people can restore peace, freedom and democracy in Libya . . . "

In May 1984 a 15-man unit of the front's military wing, the Salvation Corps, attacked revolutionary headquarters in Tripoli. It was a forlorn hope. The fortress is guarded by T-55 tanks dug in on either side of the main gates; its battlements carry multibarreled antiaircraft guns. It is protected by electronic guard devices and closed circuit television. The garrison consists of handpicked bodyguards. The Salvation Corps attackers were all killed, though in a five-hour gun battle they inflicted casualties on the guards. Among those who died leading his men in battle was Ahmed Ibrahim Ehwass, founder of the Corps. The assault so alarmed Colonel Gaddafi that he launched a campaign of repression within the country and a new hunt for exiles abroad.

This provoked a wave of counterterror by Gaddafi's opponents. A group calling itself al-Borkan, the Volcano, shot the regime's ambassador to Italy, Ammar al-Taggazya, in January 1984 and killed another Gaddafi man in Athens later in the year. Volcano is in fact the terrorist arm of the NFSL. Although they deny this, NFSL was ready to justify acts carried out by Volcano. After the shooting of another Libyan diplomat in Rome their newsletter commented: "The Libyan diplomat gunned down in Rome had spent three years in Italy and had achieved a reputation for harassing Libyan students in that country. The reaction to him was an understandable one—as was last year's shooting of the Libyan ambassador . . . It can only be said that the regime itself breeds this kind of response."

Those who live by the sword of terror are always in danger of perishing by it. But such thoughts did not deter Colonel Gaddafi as in the wake of the Israeli invasion of Lebanon he moved in to exploit the chaos of that country for his own ends. When the Palestinian Fatah fighters, beleaguered in Beirut, ignored his unhelpful advice to them to commit mass suicide rather than evacuate the place under Israeli guns, Gaddafi began his most ambitious project. He allied himself with President Assad of Syria, controller of the PLO rump, and with the Iranian revolutionaries of Ayatollah Khomeini. So the triple alliance of terror came into being with Gaddafi as its quartermaster. And it was that development which convinced President Reagan that the Libyan was the most dangerous man in the world. This alarming combination was intent upon striking at Americans and Europeans as a means of getting at the old enemy, Israel.

5.

America
Strikes
Back

Take That, Gaddafi--New York Post headline

When intelligence evidence accumulated at the beginning of 1986 that the Libyans and the Syrians were engaged in the systematic expansion of terrorism in Europe specifically aimed at American targets, President Reagan finally lost patience with Colonel Muammar Gaddafi. In April 66 U.S. aircraft bombed terror targets in Tripoli and Benghazi.

The sequence of events leading to this formidable counterattack began the previous autumn off the coast of Egypt with the piratical seizure of the cruise liner *Achille Lauro*. This PLO operation had little to do with the Libyans and was aimed at Israel and not specifically at the United States, but the murder of Leon Klinghoffer, an elderly Jewish New Yorker on board, at once involved the U.S. Its forces in the Mediterranean were alerted. Naval aircraft intercepted the Egyptair flight taking the pirates back home to Tunisia and forced it to land at Sigonella, an American base in Sicily. President Reagan wanted them taken to the United States for trial on charges of murdering an American citizen. But on instructions from Rome the Italian carabinieri seized the terrorists. Their leader, Abu Abbas, was released on the grounds that there was insufficient evidence to hold him. Yet, when the pirates were eventually brought before a Roman court in the summer of 1986 he was, in his absence, convicted of masterminding the plot. Italian caution and fear of becoming further involved in the war without end prevented decisive action. Italian governments had a long tradition of attempting to avoid trouble with terrorists by making little deals with them. General Ambrogio Viviani, former head of military intelligence, revealed in the magazine *Panorama* that Italy had agreed to return known terrorists to Libya so as to get immunity from attack and to protect Italian commercial interests in that country. Robert Oakley, head of the State Department's counterterrorism office, accused both Italy and France of making deals with terrorists, saying: "they acknowledge in private they've had such arrangements blow up in their faces, figuratively and literally."

It had long been the custom both in Italy and in France to keep trouble away from their own territory by prevaricating. They quietly expelled Middle East terrorists arrested on their national territory instead of taking stronger measures. The French Foreign Ministry had once connived at the quiet expulsion back to the Middle East of the Palestinian Abu Daoud then being shadowed by their own security people because he was wanted both by the West Germans and by the Israelis for terror acts. The diplomats wanted to stay friends with the Arabs. In the *Achille Lauro* affair another factor was involved—Italian national pride. The government feared that if it handed over to the Americans prisoners forced down on Italian territory by the Americans it would be accused of toadying to Washington.

The latest example of Italy's caution and its refusal to surrender the prisoners only added to President Reagan's frustration at being unable to strike back at the elusive and many-headed enemy. It began a great crisis of misunderstanding between Europe and the United States, which became critical at the time of air strike against Libya.

Again in November when American officers flew with the Egyptian "Thunderbolt" commando unit sent to Luga airport in Malta to assault hijackers of an Egyptair Boeing, the counteraction was only half a success, even though the forces of terror suffered a setback.

Two days after Christmas, hit squads from the Middle East coordinated simultaneous machine-gun and bomb attacks upon seasonal travelers as they lined up at the El Al desks in Fiumicino airport, Rome and in Vienna airport. This time 19 people, five Americans among them, lost their lives and more than 100 were wounded. The sole survivor of the killer band at Rome had on him a paper threatening the West with "rivers of blood."

The only consolation was that yet again this was a bungled attack by ill-trained Arabs. The hit men had intended to seize hostages and use them to force the authorities to provide an aircraft so as to begin a fresh saga of air piracy. In this they failed because armed guards at the airport fought back, killing or wounding all them. From later intelligence reports it seems likely that the two attacks were originally intended to coincide with raids upon other airports in Paris and in Madrid, but that these plans were foiled in advance. The seven killers had arrived in the European capitals, four in Rome, three in Vienna, staying in cheap hotels before they drew their weapons from "friendly" embassies. In Rome they exploded a canvas bag near the airline desk before opening fire indiscriminately with Kalashnikov assault rifles. When Austrian police counterattacked at Vienna, the killers stole a car to make their escape and were caught in a firefight some distance away.

As the interrogation of these men proceeded it became clear that they had been recruited by the Abu Nidal faction run by Sabri al-Banna, the renegade PLO leader. At first there was some confusion about which group was responsible because a Vienna survivor said that he belonged to the PLO. The truth was that in his understanding he did, for the Abu Nidal faction calls itself the true PLO—as opposed to the one run by Yassir Arafat with which it quarreled. Mohammed Sarham, the terrorist wounded in Rome, told an Italian investigator that he had trained in Lebanon after being chosen with 35 other volunteers, before being sent to Europe. He stated that he was a supporter of Abu Musa, the boss of yet another offshoot of the mainstream PLO. So many are the divisions and subdivisions of the Palestine movement that even the adherents become confused. Such evidence confirms the belief that the Arab terrorists operating in Europe in early 1986 were jointly operated by several terrorist bands under the control of Libyan and Syrian intelligence officers.

Those hit men responsible for the Rome and Vienna attacks had been equipped with genuine Tunisian and Moroccan passports, a fact which implicated Colonel Gaddafi. Libya has an endless supply of genuine North African passports seized from Arab workers who enter the country illegally in search of work and who can be picked up at will by the local police. Because entry is illegal there is no embarrassing

Libyan visa in the document. All the terrorists need to do is to change the photograph and merge with the thousands of Arabs who make their way to Europe in search of employment.

Two of the wounded terrorists, one in Rome and one in Vienna, admitted also that they had been trained in Lebanon by the Syrians. So there could be little doubt that in this final terrorist enterprise of the year 1985, both Libya and Syria, the major sponsors of subversive war in the Middle East were involved up to the hilt. As if to confirm the Libyan involvement a spokesman in Tripoli praised the attacks as "heroic operations by Palestinian martyrs."

In Washington the identity of the culprits seemed proven. "It is clear that responsibility lies squarely with the terrorist known as Abu Nidal and his organization," said the President. In the words of the State Department, "We believe Gaddafi has given Abu Nidal and his group a considerable amount of financing and assistance." But the Palestinian faction boss, elusive as ever, was not just the hireling of Gaddafi. Admiral Fulvio Martini of Italian intelligence was not the only intelligence source to assert that he also worked for Syria and Iran.

Again there were warnings that a military option had to be considered as a riposte to such attacks and as the new year began the Reagan administration reviewed its options for an armed confrontation with Colonel Gaddafi. The weapon ready at hand was the Sixth Fleet already deployed in the Mediterranean and within striking range of Libya. President Reagan cleared the decks for action by freezing Libyan assets in U.S. banks and by ordering the 1,000 Americans still working in Libya to leave the country.

Muammar Gaddafi was at this period by no means inactive. At his invitation a secret gathering of Palestinian terror organizations and other Arab radical groups assembled in Tripoli between February 2 and 4, 1986. It was attended by 200 representatives of more than 20 Palestinian, Lebanese, Iraqi and Kurdish organizations. The meeting was described as a session of the national leadership of Arab revolutionary forces. It was masked by an overlapping gathering of representatives from most of the malcontents of the Third World.

The conference provided a valuable insight into the devious ways of the Libyan leader in acting to support and to control subversive campaigns. His skill is that he can manipulate a whole range of different organizations and persuade them to carry out acts of violence throughout the world in return for promises of cash and weapons. When such operations appear successful to Colonel Gaddafi, he claims the credit. When they go wrong he washes his hands of them, and for good measure, often throws out an equivocal condemnation of violence into the bargain.

In the course of closed sessions at the February gathering it was decided "to escalate the armed struggle" and make plans for attacks against Israeli and Western, mainly American, targets. There was also an agreement to set up "revolutionary suicide forces" trained to carry out these special operations. Use of the word *suicide* in this context is to be interpreted as a polite nod towards the successes of the real suicide squads of the Shi'ite revolution rather than as an indication that genuine suicide forces were to be set up. The meeting marked an important step in Gaddafi's plan to build his prestige as an Arab leader by appearing as the chief sponsor of the revolutionary campaign against the United States and the Western world.

Among those present were George Habash, head of the Popular Front for the Liberation of Palestine (PFLP; the fringe group responsible for the spectacular hijacks of the 60s and 70s), together with Ahmed Jibril, head of PFLP-General Command and his deputy, Talal Naji. There was no sign of Abu Nidal, who cautiously avoids big gatherings where he might be in danger, but he did send along Mustafa Murad, operational commander of the Abu Nidal faction, and head of its Syrian branch. The faction had reason to be grateful to Gaddafi who made an annual contribution to their funds of $5 million and had offered a similar sum as a bonus for its recent murderous attacks at Vienna and Rome airports.

Abu Musa, boss of the dissident anti-Arafat Palestinians, and Abu Khaled, the organization's secretary, were present together with Abdal Ghanem, head of the radical wing of the Palestine Liberation Front (PLF). This group works under the auspices of Syrian intelligence. To this jamboree of trouble-seeking Arabs there also came representatives of the Iraqi underground and opposition, and prominent leaders of the Syrian Baath Party who promised to give help to the assembled leaders.

It was at the end of the conference that the Israeli air force intercepted a Libyan executive aircraft over the Mediterranean and forced it to land in Israel, in an attempt to capture key terrorist leaders. They picked the wrong aircraft. The only passengers were Syrian political leaders. This failure cheered the Libyan leader and in turn encouraged him to intensify his new campaign.

Reassured by the support of his allies, Muammar Gaddafi, who had boasted of his desire to make never-ending war, committed himself to a foolish gesture. On March 24, he ordered his missile batteries to fire two SAM 5s at U.S. naval aircraft from the Sixth Fleet flying in international airspace over the Gulf of Sirte. The aircraft were on patrol over waters considered to be international by all nations except Libya but inside what the Colonel had dramatically called the "line of death." More missiles were fired without result after the initial salvo and the fleet at last had a perfect opportunity to strike back at the tormenting Libyans. The Libyans had been trapped into making a false move creating an opening for President Reagan to flex his naval muscle.

In Operation Prairie Fire warships and aircraft hit four Libyan patrol boats with Harpoon anti-ship missiles, sinking two, and made two attacks using Harm weapons against missile sites onshore.

In the war of words which followed—and Gaddafi is undoubtedly at his best when fighting with such weapons—the scene was set for further clashes between conventional military power and terrorist dirty tricks. "We humiliated America and its forces," screamed Gaddafi who falsely claimed to have shot down three U.S. aircraft. While he raged with threats to turn the Mediterranean into a "sea of blood," the President in New Orleans declared:

> We are aware of intensive Libyan preparations that were already under way for terrorist operations against Americans. Mr. Gaddafi must know that we will hold him fully accountable for any such actions.

As the naval battle group which had concentrated for operations in the Gulf of Sirte began dispersing, the terrorists went into action again. This time their target was a TWA Boeing 727. It was making the same ferry run, bearing 103 incoming passengers from the United States, via Rome to Athens and Cairo on which the ill-fated Boeing hijacked by the Shi'ites a year earlier had been flying. As Flight 840 headed over Corinth towards Athens at 11,000 feet there was a flash of light and a loud bang in the passenger compartment. Captain Richard Peterson on the flight deck thought that a window had blown out. But when a passenger named Janet Chaffee looked back she could see blue sky were seat 10F had been.

A bomb had blasted a six-foot hole in the side of the aircraft and through that gap four Americans, a baby among them, were sucked out to their death. Down below a Greek shepherd who looked into the sky thought that it was "raining bodies." The aircraft managed to land safely, though had the bomb exploded 10 minutes earlier while it was at cruising altitude the chances are that it would have been totally destroyed.

FBI investigators who arrived in Athens concentrated their attention on seat 10F and concluded that the explosive device had been placed there, probably in the life jacket under it. Suspicion therefore focused on a Lebanese woman boutique owner named May Elias Mansur, who had sat there on the plane's earlier flight from Cairo to Rome. Fellow passengers reported that she had kept the table down throughout the flight, and it would have been simple for her to place and prime a small charge smuggled aboard without being noticed. The Egyptians claimed that she had been searched in Cairo where she arrived late at the airport and was taken to the aircraft by car.

This mysterious lady had transitted through Athens and returned to Beirut aboard Middle East Airlines. She promptly made a public appearance in Lebanon fiercely denying that she had planted the bomb. She did, however, admit to earlier activities on behalf of the Syrian Social Nationalist Party, which has carried out terrorist attacks in Lebanon. It would have been totally out of character for such a group to carry out this kind of operation.

An organization calling itself Arab Revolutionary Cells made a telephone call in Beirut saying that its unit was responsible for the bombing. As is customary in the terrorist world, the actual unit had been named in honor of a "martyr"—Ezzedin Kassem, a man hanged in 1936 for leading an uprising against the British in the time of the Palestine Mandate. Arab Revolutionary Cells is one of the titles used by the Abu Nidal faction and it was not long before this notorious body was being blamed for the attack. The only drawback to this theory was that the faction usually went in for assassination rather than bombing. It now seems that Abu Nidal was at the time under pressure from his paymasters both in Libya and in Syria to do something quickly. In face of strengthened airport security, which made hijacking more difficult, and the fact that hijackers in recent acts of piracy had taken losses as antiterror forces counterattacked them, tactics were changed. In their attempts to find a weak spot, the terrorists turned to the more brutal method of blowing up airliners in flight. Tetro nitrate explosives now available are especially difficult to detect. Use of compact sheet or pliable plastic such as RDX explosives requiring only miniature nylon detonators makes it possible to smuggle them aboard without their registering on the line scanners used by airport security. For this purpose women are more effective than men.

There is a natural tendancy among public figures in Western countries to think like news editors. They therefore assumed that because the TWA bombing closely followed the naval action against Libya, it had been planned in revenge for it. The claims of terror groups were quick to exploit such assumptions. Such a view ignores the complexity of organizing a terror attack and the amount of time it needs. The chances are that this incident, and, indeed, the bombing of the Berlin nightclub which followed it, were the result of the February get-together in Tripoli rather than a consequence of American naval action. Shimon Peres, the Israeli prime minister, declared, "I think they planned it even before this [meaning the raid]." He believed that Abu Nidal was responsible, but that on this occasion he had been working under Syrian auspices in conjunction with Abu Musa, leader of the PLO faction controlled by Damascus.

By the spring of 1986 it was clear that plans were afoot for a series of terror attacks. CIA reports spoke of no fewer than 35 overseas American targets, including a number of their own station chiefs, being under terrorist surveillance. It was reported that Tripoli was signaling agents in Geneva and Paris to ready themselves to carry out "the plan." The fact that this intelligence had substance was borne out by the fact that the French forestalled an attempt to attack people lining up for visas outside the U.S. consulate in Paris and promptly expelled two Libyan diplomats involved in the plot.

Only three days after the TWA incident a bomb placed close to the bar blasted La Belle night club in a suburb of West Berlin. It was 1:50 A.M. and the place was crowded with American servicemen from the 6,000-strong Berlin garrison. The explosion brought down the ceiling, started a fire and turned the club into a bloody shambles which reminded

Germans present of wartime horrors. Sergeant Kenneth Terrance Ford, a young infantry NCO from Detroit, died in the blast and so did a Turkish woman. More than 200 others were injured. Those who escaped will not easily forget the sight of blood-spattered soldiers and women in torn leisure clothes making their way back to McNair barracks. The bombers had given no warning and obviously intended to kill as many Americans as possible.

Although there was early talk of possible involvement of West German Red Army Faction extremists, the attack bore the hallmarks of an Arab raid. On this occasion there was more substantial evidence to back the conviction that the Libyan/Syrian-controlled war bands were responsible and that Libyan diplomats from the people's bureau in communist East Berlin had transmitted the orders and helped with infrastructure. West German police discovered that a Libyan diplomat who had been a member of his country's embassy in Bonn before going to East Berlin was implicated. His name was Abdullah al-Amin. U.S. intelligence had hard evidence of its own.

So determined was President Reagan to convince the American people of Libya's determination to kill Americans abroad that he overrode objections by security advisers and revealed the contents of coded signals between Tripoli and the people's bureau in East Berlin, which had been intercepted by the National Security Agency (NSA). The President made detailed disclosures, saying that on March 25, the day after the Libyan missile batteries opened fire on the Sixth Fleet, Tripoli had ordered the East Berlin bureau to mount an attack on Americans in Germany. On April 4 the Berlin Libyans reported that the operation would take place the following day. After the La Belle bomb they reported the "great success of the mission" and said that the attackers had gone underground and could not be traced.

"Our evidence is direct; it is precise; it is irrefutable," said the president on television.

He went on to disclose some details of the attack planned at the U.S. consulate in Paris, which with French help had been forestalled. And Larry Speakes, the White House spokesman, added that there was reliable evidence that Gaddafi and his lieutenents were planning attacks on U.S. citizens and installations in Europe, the Middle East and Latin America. Libyans preparing for raids in Africa had conducted surveillance on American facilities in 10 countries.

It was without precedent that an American president should disclose in public the results of code breaking of foreign countries' diplomatic signals. The National Security Agency, most secretive in the American intelligence community, was opposed to such revelations on grounds of security. Not only would Arab terrorists and their state sponsors become more cautious and possibly abandon electronic in favor of courier communication, but should they change their codes, it might take months or even years before cryptographers could crack the new ones. In the meantime the United States might be deprived of vital intelligence information at a critical time.

Despite the production of this evidence, the Europeans in general remained unconvinced. Many on the continent, indeed, did not want to be convinced, for they were already trembling at the prospect of American counteraction against Libya and its possible consequences. Among the Atlantic statesmen, only Mrs. Thatcher stood ready to back the president. There was no doubt in her mind that information about the origins of the Berlin bombing was sure. Indeed, Whitehall sources were able to add that the British government had its own information on the subject and was not simply relying on American sources. Their intelligence related to past Libyan involvement in terror and also to Libyan participation in planned future operations. It was assumed that the British source was the communications monitoring center in the Cyprus sovereign bases run by GCHQ, Cheltenham, which is the British equivalent of NSA and works in cooperation with it.

Ever since the Libyan people's bureau in London had been closed down after the so-called diplomats there shot dead a London policewoman from the windows of their office, Mrs. Thatcher's agencies had kept a close eye on Gaddafi's activities. They knew that Libya was supplying weapons to the Irish Republican Army and had information that an arms cache discovered by the Irish Republic in Sligo and Roscommon in January included rifles and ammunition from Tripoli.

It took President Reagan just three days to decide that the time had come to strike back at Colonel Gaddafi. As operational plans were completed he was assured of the support of the Conservative government in London. His special envoy, General Vernon Walters, explained in detail to Mrs. Thatcher what was planned and even produced the target list, for

British cooperation was crucial. It had been decided to make a low-level night attack on Libya and although carrier-based A-6 planes could manage the job there were not enough of them aboard the fleet carriers. Land-based F-111s provided a better military solution, and those based in England at the East Anglian airfields had been earmarked for the task. A force of Tristar tanker aircraft needed for in-flight refueling would also be operating from English airfields.

The prime minister agreed to the plan, provided that she could approve the target list, and sanctioned use of airfields on condition that everything would be done to ensure that the air strikes were surgical. She wanted an assurance that a special effort should be made to limit civilian casualties and damage to nonmilitary targets. It was agreed that if aircraft captains had any doubts about certainty of hitting the target they would abort their attacks.

Mrs. Thatcher explained later:

> The President assured me that the operation would be limited to clearly defined targets related to terrorism, and that the risk of collateral damage would be minimized.
>
> He made it clear that use of F-111 aircraft from bases in the United Kingdom was essential, because by virtue of their special characteristics they would provide the safest means of achieving particular objectives with the lowest possible risk both of civilian casualties in Libya and of casualties among the United States service personnel.

It was a tense weekend as 28 tankers flew into British airfields. The air combat group of 66 planes being assembled was to be the biggest to fly off from Britain since World War II. At fields named RAF Mildenhall and RAF Upper Heyford, American crews prepared for the mission over Africa while Air Force spokesmen remained tight-lipped and spoke only of NATO exercises.

President Reagan had little trouble in getting broad support for military action on Capitol Hill. Meanwhile, General Walters, continuing his mission in Bonn, Paris, Rome and Madrid, was having a harder task to convince European Community leaders. None of them would even agree to allow the U.S. bombers to fly through their air space, let alone to refuel at NATO bases. All manner of arguments were put forward to justify refusal to cooperate, but they all boiled down to the fact that public opinion in their countries would instinctively condemn an American air raid against

Libya. Certainly fear of Arab terrorist reprisals of a kind with which they were already familiar, played a part. So too did the desire not to offend the Arab powers, especially from those countries like France and Italy which depend industrially on oil from the Middle East. Meeting in The Hague only hours before the raid, foreign ministers of the 12 European Community nations put out an urgent appeal for "restraint on all sides."

European hesitation and alarm greatly increased the difficulties of those planning the air strike. The only route to Libya available was the long way around from Britain down to Gibraltar and through the Mediterranean towards the shore of Tripoli 2,800 miles away. An air fleet of tankers had to go along to refuel the bombers in flight.

At 17:13 GMT 28 flying fuel tanks, KC-10s and KC-135s took off from the English fields. Just half an hour later F-111 bombers, 24 of them, were airborne while the carriers *America* and *Coral Sea* still busied themselves preparing to launch the naval air strike five hours later. The fleet was to send A-6 bombers to attack Benghazi and to provide overall fighter cover with F-14s. In addition they flew command and control aircraft and others equipped with radar-busting missiles.

The lights of Tripoli still blazed out in the early hours of the morning when the first fighter bombers, 18 of them, hurtled across the North African shoreline dead on time at over 500 miles an hour just 200 feet above the dunes. Two groups of six fighter bombers hit the Sidi Bilal naval base and its terrorist training installations and the Bab al Azizia, the Revolutionary Command headquarters of Colonel Gaddafi. The third group of six zoomed away round the city to blast the Tripoli military airfield, the base of Soviet-built Ilyushin transports used by terror groups and Libyan MiG-23 fighters.

The bombing technique was to climb to 500 feet so that electronic aiming devices could locate the target. Then the weapons officers held it in the cross hairs of the infrared scope at the range calculated by lasers. As it appeared he lobbed the bombs away onto the laser-illuminated path to the target. The rules of engagement ordered crews to make a double lock aim, using both scope and radar, and they had been instructed, if in doubt, to refrain from bombing. Indeed five of the 18 F-111s did abort, including two of those assigned to Gaddafi's headquarters. The raid lasted just 11 minutes.

In military terms the attack by naval aircraft on Benghazi

was as successful as that upon Tripoli. The Sixth Fleet managed to slip the surveillance of Soviet warships which always trail its movements. Certainly there was no sign that the Soviets had given any warning to their friend Gaddafi and no attempts were made by the Red Fleet to interfere with the operation. The first wave of low-flying attackers launched a missile strike with Shrike and Harm weapons on Libyan antiaircraft defenses after deliberately attracting and then electronically confusing their radars. Vice Admiral Frank Kelso, the fleet commander, reported, "They came at us with a wide spectrum of surface-to-air missiles, and there were antiaircraft guns of all kinds." Despite that, no naval aircraft were lost. The attack upon the Benina military airfield, where cluster bombs were used, was particularly effective in knocking out Libyan military aircraft, especially MiG fighters. The Jamahiriya barracks was also hit, though there was damage to civilian buildings.

In the Tripoli action, although Libyan defenses were taken by surprise, it was not long before antiaircraft batteries opened up. The most effective were not the surface-to-air missiles which had been confused by electronic warfare action but the old-fashioned ZSU-23 "quads," multi-barreled guns mounted around Fortress Gaddafi at Bab al-Azizia. It was there the Americans lost an F-111 to ground fire. Captain Fernando Ribas-Dominci fought to get his stricken bomber out to sea before ejecting, but the plane exploded in flames as it crossed the coast and crashed into the sea killing both the pilot and his weapons officer, Captain Paul Lorence.

It seems likely that bombs from this aircraft were the ones which fell so far off target in the fashionable residential area of Tripoli near the French embassy. The theory was put forward that Captain Ribas-Dominci tried to release his 2,000 pound bombs, but that one of them hung on and was only dislodged as he made a sharp turn seawards. This may have been the weapon which caused casualties and damage.

The tragic accidental bombing of civilians was to have a great impact on world opinion. Libyan officials helpfully escorted TV cameramen to film damage to obviously civilian buildings, and also to the bedsides and gravesides of victims. Mainland America has never suffered aerial bombardment and Americans are therefore perhaps less sensitive to the ghastly results on the ground of air attack. The British still remember the devastation caused by Hitler's bombers and in Europe within living memory few major cities have escaped the attentions of air raiders. It was inevitable, therefore, that in that part of the world sympathy went out to the bombed than the bombers, and that the first result of the air strike was to make people forget that its purpose had been to strike back at Colonel Gaddafi and his foreign legions of terrorists. Within hours of the raid the public reaction was one of indignant anti-Americanism.

Once again arguments raged on the subject of what the West can do about international terrorism. The conclusion drawn by the opponents of heavyweight counteraction by the West's armed forces was that small bands of desperate men cannot be defeated by air strikes. The Shi'ites had not been put out of action by shelling from the sea. It seemed that such countermeasures simple stirred up the hornet's nest. As the *Economist* succinctly put it: "Most Europeans but very few Americans conclude that America was wrong to use its bombers against Libya. Aerial bombardment rarely serves a political end."

The first stage of political recrimination in Europe centered on two aspects of the air strike. There was the feeling of horror that an air raid had killed so many apparently harmless people, including the allegedly adopted daughter of Colonel Gaddafi. Apart from that there was genuine fear that the raid would provoke a devastating series of terrorist assaults. Reaction to this threat varied between a vague fear that something nasty might happen and downright hysteria.

In the immediate backwash of these events which aroused great controversy in Europe and in the Middle East, a number of violent events took place. Fears seemed to be confirmed by news from Beirut that Peter Kilburn, librarian at the American University, and two British hostages held there had been murdered in revenge. U.S. diplomats were attacked in places like Khartoum. A terrorist bomb exploded in Regent Street in the heart of London and Arab terrorists were blamed.

Some of the violence, like the murder of foreign hostages in Lebanon, was spontaneous. Other actions, although they were represented as reprisals for the bombing of Tripoli, had in fact already been organized before the American raid. Indeed that strike was planned to discourage the men of violence from continuing their bloodthirsty campaigns. The most notable of such events was the failed attempt to smuggle a bomb aboard an El Al flight for Tel Aviv at London airport.

The carry-on bag containing 10 pounds of high explosive, timers and detonators was discovered at the final Heathrow checkpoint before passengers boarded the aircraft. The disquieting feature of this was that it had already passed unnoticed through the usual airport controls. Ann Murphy, a young Irish chambermaid several months pregnant, had been given the bag by her lover, Nezar Hindawi, a 31-year-old good-looking Jordanian who promised to join her later in Israel. Although he escaped, police picked him up quickly after he had taken refuge with relations at a London hotel. It soon became clear that the Irish girl had no idea that she was carrying a package of death which, had it exploded when the airliner was in flight, possibly over London, would have killed 400 passengers and crew—including herself. She was released and returned home to Ireland with no charges made against her.

The bomb itself was a highly professional affair. Investigators came to the conclusion that, because a similar model had been discovered in Rome and was known to have been provided by a Syrian-backed group of Palestinians, the London embassy of Syria was involved. Commander George Churchill-Coleman, chief of C 13, the Scotland Yard antiterrorist branch, wanted to questions three Syrian diplomats, but the ambassador, Dr. Loutof al-Haydar, refused to waive diplomatic immunity, though he agreed to questioning in the presence of other diplomats. As a result of that refusal the British government expelled the three a week later because of their alleged involvement in terrorist activity in Britain and Europe. Their departure was followed by that of Georges Shiha, another attaché, thought to be the Syrian intelligence station chief in London. The Damascus connection was established, not only with the attempted El Al bombing, but also with the earlier bomb attack on the Berlin nightclub. A Jordanian suspect in Germany told police that he had collected a carton of explosives from the Syrian embassy in East Berlin and had smuggled them through the Berlin wall.

Disquieting though the aftermath events were, the more important question was, what had been achieved by the attack on the ground in Libya? Although a number of bombs missed their targets and killed Libyan civilians, others did inflict significant damage in Tripoli and in Benghazi. One notable success was the destruction of Colonel Gaddafi's command post at Revolutionary headquarters in the Bab-al-Azizia barracks. At command headquarters it was not only the famous tent of the ringmaster of international terrorism which sagged to the ground.

The nerve center for the control of Colonel Gaddafi's foreign adventures and the international terrorist network was in heavily guarded barracks. From his office there and surrounded with batteries of telephones and electronic communications equipment, the Colonel sent out orders to his hit squads in the field. Until the damage could be repaired, loss of this control center made it much more difficult for him to sustain the long-planned terror campaign. Temporarily the control center was moved to the large building in Tripoli which houses the Pan Arab-African Trading Corporation. That is used as cover for the headquarters of the Libyan intelligence service.

It is known to Western intelligence that the procedure for hit-men moles working for Libyan-directed terror in Europe was to lie low with instructions to keep in touch with their case officer at the Gaddafi control center in Tripoli. In such operations radio communication with Libyan missions abroad was all-important. Other terror nests taken out by the air strike included a well-known villa, not far from the French embassy. It was used to accommodate Middle East terror leaders who gathered in Tripoli for the forward planning conference in February.

Perhaps the most significant effect of the military action was psychological. It surprised and alarmed the Libyan people and shook their confidence in their leader. As for Colonel Gaddafi himself, alarmed and shaken, mourning the death of his adopted daughter and deeply upset by injuries to his sons, he survived the raids to fight again. But in a mood of fear and depression he hastily left the capital and hid in Sebha. Not even the prospect, normally so irresistable to such a showman, of appearing on television at mass gatherings at funerals to denounce the wicked Americans could lure him back. Such video appearances as he did make revealed a depressed and uncertain leader with the stuffing knocked out of him. Observers began talking about the "richochet effect" of the raid.

There was wild and unexplained shooting in Tripoli the day after the raid. Salvation Front exiles who from Britain constantly telephone friends and relations back home reported a mood of black depression. They even dared to hope that Gaddafi had fled the country and that the end of his regime was in sight. In this they were overoptimistic.

Yet there were signs that the leader was losing his touch. Despite the regime's efforts to suppress news of trouble there was some evidence of growing internal dissension and discontent as falling oil prices undermined the economy. Within five years Libyan oil revenue had slumped by 75% to around $5 billion. An austerity program led to food riots when a long-awaited banana boat finally docked. The army was called in to control disorders in Benghazi. Ministers were given extra protection and bodyguards. The demonstrations seen on Western TV screens with enthusiatic chanted support for Gaddafi had to be carefully stage-managed with loyalist troops in civilian clothes marshaled by their officers.

Gaddafi's failure to appear in the stricken streets suggested to Western intelligence that he might be afraid for his life. It was known that army officers were uneasy about his leadership, especially after the murder of Colonel Hassan Ishkal.

While the Libyans licked their wounds and made a few halfhearted threats it slowly became apparent the dire consequences of the great American raid, predicted by many Europeans, had not come to pass. The Soviets made no great attempt to help their Libyan customers. There was no immediate and terrible terrorist onslaught. Even the foreboding forecasts that the entire world of Islam would rally round Gaddafi to make the West suffer proved false. They could not even agree among themselves to come together for an Arab summit and plans for it were abandoned.

Certainly the official noises being made in Middle East countries were sympathetic to the victim of the mighty Sixth Fleet. Even so, the Arab nations are realistic in their appreciation of where real power lies. They are controlled by absolute rulers, men who live by power and who understand it, even when it is exercised against them. They were not slow to notice that the Russian ally of Libya offered nothing more than verbal encouragement when it came to the crunch.

The fact is, also, that Gaddafi is hated by Arab governments as a posturing troublemaker. He is isolated from all but a few, the most notable being Syria, a country which needs his financial subsidy. Saudi Arabia and the Gulf states are wary of him because of his constant threats to bring republican revolution to the kingdoms and sheikhdoms.

In the eyes of the Arab masses he may be a bit of a hero. But he is a hero 30 years too late, for he is cast in the Nasser mold of out-of-date Arab nationalist socialism. Colonel Gaddafi is not in tune with either of the two main forces in the Arab world, the Shi'ite revival and orthodox Islamic fundamentalism.

In these circumstances even the most timid of Western

statesmen began to realize that as nothing too terrible was about to happen they might well profit from the American initiative by taking measures against world terrorists in general and against the Libyans in particular. The most lasting effect of the raid on Tripoli proved to be the fresh impulse it gave Western efforts to step up the battle against international terrorism.

When the European Community ministers gathered on the eve of the raid, restraint had been their watchword. In April the EEC response to plans for sanctions to be taken against Libya was woefully inadequate. France and Italy did expel a number of Libyans and cut down people's bureaus by a few diplomats, but none of their missions were closed down. Only Britain, which had shut down the people's bureau in London two years earlier, sent packing a great number of Libyan suspects.

By the time the seven major democracies gathered again at the Tokyo summit they had, with American encouragement, summoned the courage to do something more positive. Even when a few rockets were launched by Japanese anarchists as the meeting opened—"They missed," said Ronald Reagan cheerfully—Mrs. Thatcher expressed the general mood by telling journalists, "The rockets are worrying you more than us, dear."

The seven heads of state declared, "We . . . strongly reaffirm our condemnation of international terrorism in all its forms, of its accomplices and those, including governments, who sponsor or support it. We abhor the increase in the level of such terrorism since our last meeting, and in particular its blatant and cynical use as an instrument of government policy. Terrorism has no justification. It spreads only by use of contemptible means, ignoring the values of human life, freedom and dignity. It must be fought relentlessly and without compromise."

Summit statements, of course, are always good on fine words. But on this occasion they were backed by a number of practical measures such as an agreement to refuse to sell arms to countries sponsoring terror. Strict limits were to be placed on the size of the diplomatic missions of rogue nations and if necessary their diplomats' movements could be restricted. Persons, diplomats included, expelled by one of the allied countries should not be allowed to enter any of the seven major industrial nations. There were provisions also for improving extradition procedures, always a delicate business as the long wrangle between Britain and the United States over IRA suspects living in North America showed. Agreement was also reached on stricter immigration controls on citizens of places mixed up with terrorists. Finally, there was to be closer cooperation between police and security organizations.

The seven recognized the need to intensify the exchange of information about threats so as to combat terrorism within the framework of international law. They pledged themselves to fight against the scourge of terrorism. Although experience shows that such words are not always a guarantee of subsequent firm action, especially in cooperation, there was no doubt that this was the strongest affirmation of a general will to stand up to their terrorists and their allies.

George Shultz, the secretary of state, was sufficiently moved to speak of "a long and very good day for democracy, for freedom, for the fight against terrorism and for the cohesion of the West." The message for Colonel Gaddafi in his words, was: "You've had it, pal. You are isolated. You are recognized as a terrorist."

Libya had been specifically named despite original worries on this score from the French and the Japanese. Mrs. Thatcher, basking in presidential approval for her stand over the airfields and described by George Shultz as "a terrific leader," had overridden their objections and then succeeded in toughening up the six specific measures outlined in the final draft.

The Tokyo summit went some ways to reassure the Americans that Europe was not entirely populated by persons too scared to fight back against the terrorists. But even in Britain and certainly in parts of Europe public opinion went on being more exercised about President Reagan's use of force than about the continual use of force by the terrorists. Deep disenchantment with Western Europe remained detectable in Washington. "We need to know precisely where our allies are," said Robert Dole, the Senate majority leader. Not only had most countries refused to help and support the air operation against Libya, but even after Tokyo some of them still seemed reluctant to face up to the undoubted and continuing threat of state-sponsored terror.

6.

The Fox
Of Damascus

Syria is a far more dangerous and more effective state sponsor of terrorism than Libya. This fact was obscured so long as Western, and especially American, attention concentrated upon the North African lair. Within days of the Tripoli raid it became apparent in London that Syrian diplomats were implicated in the failed attempt to place a bomb aboard an Israeli airliner at Heathrow. Even as President Reagan issued a qualified warning in May 1986 that Syria too might expect retribution as a harbor of terror, evidence emerged that the Syrians as well as the Libyans had a hand in the Berlin night club bombing. Within a month another explosive device identical to the London one was discovered at El Al's check-in desk at Madrid airport. The Arab who had paid a Spanish petty criminal to take it on board belonged to a Syrian-controlled gang.

These incidents demonstrated that for once the shrewd and soft-spoken President Hafez Assad, a head of state usually so careful to conceal his tracks in the jungle of terrorism, had been found out. Despite the indignant denials, he was every bit as much involved in promoting campaigns of death as was his more publicity-conscious ally Colonel Gaddafi. His capable intelligence service headed by an air force brigadier occupies itself with little else than planning covert operations on many fronts at home and abroad. But Hafez al-Assad had usually displayed fox-like cunning in

89

manipulating a selection of Arab terrorist organizations while keeping himself at a distance, the better to raise his hands in innocence when accused of complicity with them.

As a close neighbor of Israel, his country had been at war ever since 1948. From the Golan Heights on the southern frontier the Syrians could look down upon Galilee and in 1973 their tank columns had battered through the Israeli defenses and had almost reached the lake itself before being thrown back. The central conflict of the Middle East was right there on the doorstep and it was inevitable that Syria should become active in both the big wars and the small subversive wars which developed out of them. It was, moreover, a nation which saw itself as the heartland of the Arab nationalist renaissance of the twentieth century and therefore the natural defender of Palestine.

The difference between Libya and Syria as sponsors of terrorism was that Hafez Assad was a much subtler, more devious and skillful head of state than Gaddafi, and a man who knew when to be aggressive and when to appear more reasonable. Colonel Gaddafi used the terror weapon like a shouting maniac with a bludgeon; President Hafez used it in silence like a rapier for selective purposes, as he did to undermine the Hussein-Arafat peace attempt in 1985. As a fighter-pilot general who seized power by coup d'etat in 1970, (the 20th such coup since the country became independent after the Second World War), and who had held on to it longer than any other president in the troubled country, in troubled times, he had mastered statecraft and patience. As a member of the oppressed minority Alawite branch of Islam ruling a nation populated by a sea of Sunni orthodox Moslems, he knew the advantages of compromise and maneuvers.

His country had for years been on the American blacklist of countries engaged in state-supported terrorism. Yet twice within a year, and no doubt for tactical reasons of his own, he had done the United States some service by withdrawing his support of the Palestinian war bands at critical moments. When American airmen from the Sixth Fleet were shot down while attacking Lebanon in the time of the international peacekeeping force, the Syrians handed them over after a visit to Damascus by the Reverend Jesse Jackson. The temptation must have been to hold them as hostages, but the Syrian head of state scored points by deciding otherwise.

President Assad had certainly helped to resolve the crisis brought on by the hijacking of the TWA flight to Beirut in

1985. Using his power and influence in Beirut he intervened to help save the hostage passengers and crew. They were taken to Damascus to be flown out westward to safety. It should not be forgotten that his army and his intelligence men controlled a good part of Lebanon, including the Bekaa Valley, which was one great training camp for the assorted practioners of subversive warfare.

Again in 1985, the Syrians wisely forestalled trouble for themselves by refusing to allow Abu Abbas to dock the *Achille Lauro* with its pirate crew in the Syrian port of Tartus. When their plans to seize the ship in an Israeli port went wrong the terrorists headed their prize towards Syrian waters. It looked for several tense hours as though they would find safe haven there. Had they done so the crisis would have become much more complicated and President Reagan would have been faced with the decision whether or not to deploy the fleet in a rescue attempt in the port of a heavily-armed regional power. He was spared that awkward problem by Assad's firm refusal to aid this particular crowd of Palestinian terrorists. Later there were suggestions that Hafez Assad was prepared to be helpful in trying to obtain the release of five American hostages held in Beirut by various guerrilla groups. That was perhaps because he was hoping to feed his people with a few hundred thousand tons of American cut-rate wheat which he could not afford to buy on the open market.

At least he displayed more realism and flexibility than, for example, Colonel Gaddafi in his assessment of the risks involved in running terror groups and the dangers of overstepping the mark. With an ever-watchful Israeli intelligence and military machine just down the road, he had to be.

Right from the beginning, when the state of Israel was first established in the late 1940s it had been Syrian policy to exploit the Palestinian cause for the greater glory of the Greater Syria, which Damascus had always sought to create. The rival was Egypt; the enemy was neighboring Iraq, especially after the overthrow of the monarchy there when a rival branch of the Syrian ruling party, Baath (Renaissance), came to power. The two parts of this very Arab socialist party could never come to terms and frequently quarreled over abstruse points of political doctrine, as indeed did the Syrian party itself.

Egypt, especially under the long rule of Colonel Gamal Abdel Nasser, was the big power in the region. With Soviet help after his famous quarrel with John Foster Dulles and

President Eisenhower, when they refused to finance his cherished Aswan Dam project, Nasser took the lead, both as the champion of Arab decolonialization and as the protector and exploiter of the Palestinians. Both Syria and Egypt unsuccessfully made war on Israel in 1967 and in 1973, ostensibly in the Palestinian cause. But both countries had taken good care to keep the refugees who fled from the old Palestine when the Jews took over there, in camps close to the borders of the new Israel. The refugees were not allowed to disperse through the Arab world. They were forced to stay in misery, close at hand as a warning sign.

From 1948 onward Syria was fully engaged in recruiting guerrilla groups, raising funds for them and providing them with weapons. The regular army of the Palestinians organized in brigades was run from Syria and used by President Assad. When he decided in 1976 to intervene in Lebanon at the start of the civil war the first troops he sent in were those of the Palestine Liberation army, under the tight command of Syrian officers.

Damascus became the headquarters of the proliferating terrorist groups. "We support the PLO . . . without disparaging the fight of the other organizations," said Dr. Abdallah Sa'adah, chairman of the ruling Nationalist party. The Palestinians were an irregular force in being. It was the children of their camps, brought up in squalor with a burning hatred of the Israelis and their friends the Americans and the Europeans, who grew up to become terror leaders in the fin de siècle period.

When Fatah was established as the guerrilla force of the PLO with its boss Yassir Arafat in overall charge, both Egypt and Syria did their best to keep it on a tight rein. It needed freedom of movement for trans-border attacks into Israel which neither Egypt nor Syria would tolerate across their borders with the Zionist state for fear of reprisals against themselves. To escape their control the PLO took itself to Jordan. When King Hussein launched his Bedouin army and forced the PLO out of Jordan, they reestablished themselves with Syrian help in Lebanon. It was the unfortunate consequence of that move and of the subsequent Israeli invasion which landed both poor Lebanon, and the Western world, in its present pickle.

Syria bears heavy responsibility for building up the multifarious irregular forces now deployed in the secret war. The ancient capital city of Damascus was, and still is, alive with their headquarter offices. One segment of the PLO led by Abu Musa, also of the Popular Front for the Liberation of Palestine, and indeed almost all the Palestinian groups appearing in the list at the end of this book are housed there. Every Palestinian radical movement and most of the Iranian-inspired Shi'ite squads have base facilities in the Bekaa valley of Lebanon, where the Syrian army rules.

Their clandestine units, particularly those of Abu Nidal and of Abu Musa, are regularly used to conduct strong-arm diplomacy. When in 1985 King Hussein of Jordan got together with Yassir Arafat to begin a peace process in the Middle East, the Syrian government signified its disapproval by letting loose its dogs of terror to assassinate a number of Jordanian diplomats and Arafatist moderates. Such campaigns have become a normal feature of diplomatic exchanges in the Arab world and they kill more Arabs than foreigners.

The better to manage terrorism as a weapon in the tactical interest of state, the Syrians also set up their own organization and named it Sa'iqa, which translates as Thunderbolt. That is a totally Syrian-government-run terrorist group under the firm control of state intelligence services. Many of those serving in its ranks are Palestinian volunteers but before they are admitted they are all carefully screened and vetted to ensure their loyalty to Syria and to guard against recruits being the agents of other groups. Regular soldiers from the Syrian army are regularly drafted in to ensure total loyalty. Every operation they carry out must be approved at the highest level in the government.

The most notorious son of this monstrous regiment is Captain Ahmed Jibril, Syrian Army, retired—but not from terrorism. On behalf of President Assad he runs the Popular Front for the Liberation of Palestine—General Command. A shrewd and quarrelsome man, he has in his time fallen out with many terrorist leaders usually on tactical grounds. He always favored operation on the ground against Israel rather than publicity-seeking international ones. His greatest coup was to organize the bartering of three Jewish soldiers captured by his group to get the release from prison in Israel of 1,154 Arab prisoners, including convicted terrorists. Significantly, it was because of a dispute with Ahmed Jibril while Syria was cracking down on Palestinian activity in Lebanon that Abu Abbas, the *Achille Lauro* pirate, went his own way to become boss of a subgroup despite the fact that originally he had been one of Jibril's recruits. Ahmed Jibril was also a favorite of Colonel Gaddafi, who liked him for his hard-line determination to hit hard at the Israelis. As far back as 1970 Jibril first visited the Colonel, then newly installed in power. Since that time he has received hundreds of thousands of dollars' worth of Libyan aid while still remaining the faithful servant of President Assad. Jibril was among the notable masters of terror who attended the Gaddafi campaign planning conference in Tripoli in February 1986. After it he warned people "not to travel on American or Israeli planes from now on."

Like many of the Syrian-controlled terror masters Jibril has on several occasions visited the Soviet Union and was trained there in guerrilla and subversive warfare. The Israelis report that he is a man in close touch with Soviet KGB agents in the Middle East. Certainly he has been supplied with Soviet weapons and equipment brought in from Bulgaria. This is not surprising, for relations between the USSR and Syria are close and friendly. There is a treaty of friendship and alliance between the two countries. This was an important deterrent factor when Washington was considering military action. It is well known that the Kremlin bosses are sticklers for protocol and much more likely to react in favor of a country to which they have formal treaty obligations. President Assad had better reason than Gaddafi to believe that in time of trouble the Russians might come to his aid. They had already demonstrated loyalty to the Middle East protegé by flying in tanks and ammunition to replace losses in the Yom Kippur war, and again by quickly replacing MiG fighters shot down by the Israelis in air battles during the invasion of Lebanon.

Such actions gave a measure of confidence to the Syrians as they faced counter-action because of their terror war involvements. They helped demonstrate big brother support for the main aim of Syrian foreign policy which is to achieve strategic parity with Israel.

For subversive war offensive capability President Assad made frequent use of the mercenaries of terror. The Abu Nidal faction was even more deeply involved there than in Libya where it had training facilities. Air Force General al-Khoury, the Damascus intelligence boss, and his network helped with planning operations. There was a base at Hamara in the Bekaa valley. Despite the close alliance, Abu Nidal's office in Damascus was officially but discreetly closed down shortly after the Christmas 1985 attacks mounted by the faction at Rome and Vienna. When questioned about it officials speciously explained that it had been a political and propaganda office, rather than a terrorist center. That is the way the Syrians work. They are always ready to cover their tracks and make their surrogates lie low to facilitate denials about their activities. When Sir Geoffrey Howe, the foreign secretary, admonished Farouk al-Sharaa, the Syrian foreign minister on a visit to London for his country's links with Abu Nidal, he felt able to express ignorance on the subject. Even better concealed was the part which Syria played in encouraging assorted militia attacks upon the four-nation international army which served in Lebanon as a peacekeeping force.

The smaller Palestinian groups and factions, of which the Abu Nidal organization is the most notable, assumed increased importance because of the breakup of the mainline Palestine Liberation Organization of Yassir Arafat. The Israeli invasion of Lebanon of 1982 eventually succeeded in bottling up their main forces in Beirut. Syria had shown itself unable to prevent this despite the proximity of its armed forces. In the end Yassir Arafat was compelled to agree to evacuate his people by sea and to disperse them throughout the Arab world, making his own headquarters in distant Tunis. This by no means suited all his former supporters, several thousand of whom were taken out by road through the mountains to Damascus. There, and to the satisfaction of President Assad, they were securely under his command. It was at this stage that a mass defection took place of former supporters and many old friends of Arafat who set up in Damascus under their new leader Abu Musa. There they simply became the tools of the Syrian government, unable to take independent action, either military or diplomatic.

To complicate things even further, a new Palestinian dissident movement was set up in 1986 with headquarters in Baghdad. Led by Abu Zaim, whose real name is Atalla-Atalla, with the backing of the Iraqi government, it was established to rival the Abu Musa rump in Damascus and the Arafat originals in Tunis. It also provided President Saddam of Iraq, whose hands are by no means unstained with terrorist blood, with a Palestinian tool. This development demonstrated how eager are the Middle East powers to vaunt their close connection with the Palestinian cause.

It came at a time when Syria found itself in bad trouble

because of terrorist attacks on home ground. Even states which sponsor terror attacks abroad can themselves fall victim to the same tactics. In the early part of the year a number of bomb attacks, some 20 in all, were made in Syria. Responsibility was claimed by two groups, one calling itself "17 November," though nobody could remember what that date commemorated, and by the Syrian Liberation Organization which, whoever ran it, was clearly against the government.

In March a refrigerated truck stuffed with explosives blew up in Damascus, killing, according to some reports, 60 people. News of it was suppressed for several weeks. Then al-Sharaa, the same foreign minister who had expressed surprise in London at accusations of Syrian terror activities, made a statement claiming that the truck bomb was the work of the Iraqis. A Lebanese agent had confessed to driving the vehicle to explode near the Officers' Club on orders from Baghdad.

No doubt many arrests were made, for the regime is a harsh one and the Muhabarat, the security police, frequently round up thousands of suspects who then just disappear. It is by no means unusual to see public hangings in Martyrs' Square in the city center and for them to be left there as a warning to others. But nothing more was said.

The following month seven bombs went off simultaneously in five towns, causing many casualties, and there were several more attacks mostly on bus stations. Even the secretive Syrian government had to confirm these happenings for by then stringent antiterrorist measures were being enforced on the streets and in bus stations. A wide range of Assad opponents had motives for such attacks but at first officials claimed, though without conviction, that Israel was responsible.

Blame was eventually placed upon ancient enemies of the Syrian regime—the Moslem Brotherhood, a politically motivated group of Sunni orthodox fundamentalists. It was naturally assumed, the Middle East being what it is, that the people ultimately responsible for helping the Brothers were neighbors in Iraq.

This was not the first time that the Alawite regime had been in trouble with Sunni extremists. While its forces were engaged in Lebanon, Sunnis in the Syrian town of Hama revolted in February 1982. The president ordered in the army, led by the Special Forces then commanded by his brother Rifaat, which brutally suppressed the rebellion, killing at least 20,000 people. Not content with that Assad dispatched six hit squads to Europe to strike back by murdering leaders of the Moslem Brotherhood in London and in Stuttgart whom he held responsible for stirring up the Hama rebellion. That is the kind of force which Arab leaders use to fight back at terrorists who affect their own interests.

The 1986 outburst of bombing did not seem to amount to a serious threat to Assad's position. That could only come from within the governing clique of men anxious about the prospect of a brutal fight for the succession which would follow his departure. There had been general alarm two years earlier when the President suffered a heart attack and again when after a quarrel, his brother, Rifaat, commander of the Special Forces, took himself off in a huff to live in Parisian exile.

Disquiet in Damascus led to a clash between Syrian intelligence chiefs. General Ali Duba, a senior Alawite military intelligence officer, strongly criticized Brigadier Mohammed al-Khoul of air force intelligence for failing to crack the Moslem brotherhood's covert network. The brigadier is the same officer who had such close dealings with Abu Nidal and who is intimately concerned in coordinating state terrorist operations abroad.

Western intelligence sources learned that in this clash of generals, responsibility was being placed upon al-Khoul for the failure of the recent terror campaign in the West, the one which had been planned in Tripoli, Libya. The clumsy attempt to place an explosive device aboard the El Al flight in London, the Berlin nightclub bomb, and a failed attempt in Turkey to hit an American officers' club were put down as disasters for the Syrian intelligence service.

As a result of those setbacks both the Syrians and the Libyans began reassessing their tactics. They came to the conclusion that it had been a mistake to act in haste against European targets using badly trained young bunglers. The conclusion was that more time and planning was needed to ensure success and that greater use should be made of mature intelligence operators rather than leaving things to enthusiastic young guerrillas. This was not entirely bad news for Western counterterrorist officers who reckoned that they were better informed about Arab intelligence professionals than about boys from the camps and would therefore have greater opportunities to penetrate networks and discover plans in advance.

Syria is in many ways the most enigmatic of the states involved in terrorism. In conventional military terms it is the most powerful of the Arab states with an army more than a quarter of a million strong which is equipped with modern Soviet-built equipment of high quality. It has more tanks than Israel, though only 1,000 out of the total of 4,200 are the latest model T-72s. The air force too is strong, and so are the antiaircraft defenses though Israeli superiority in electronic warfare has always enabled them to down Syrian aircraft without sustaining too many losses themselves. The unknown factor is the effectiveness of the thousands of Soviet Red Army instructors who help to control the SAM missiles and MiG fighters.

Military strength goes with economic weakness. Unlike Libya, President Assad's country does not enjoy oil riches, and the state-dominated economy is burdened with debt through overspending on military hardware and on subsidizing terrorists. In the summer of 1986 the country was in bad financial trouble with virtually no currency reserves at all. There was a shortage of grain and no money to buy it. The Syrians at one stage had only enough money to purchase grain a week at a time. They depend for cash upon Saudi Arabia which hands out up to $700 million to Assad. This is partly sentimental money for the Arab cause and partly protection money to keep trouble at a distance. Because the Saudis are conscious of American reproaches that they are thus subsidising terror at second hand, they have cut down the size of their gifts and imposed conditions. The Saudis are critical anyway of Syria's alliance with and support for Iran in its war with Iraq, a fellow Arab state which also benefits from Saudi largesse.

For some years Muammar Gaddafi provided both oil and cash subsidies to keep Damascus in business. Indeed the generous subsidies explain the closeness of the relationship between the two entirely different countries and their joint patronage of the forces of terror. But as oil prices tumbled, cutting Libya's income by some 75%, even the tyrant of Tripoli began to think twice about the size of his cash flow towards Damascus. He already had to bargain with the Russians, trying to barter his crude oil which the Soviets did not really want in payment of massive debts for military equipment. The other source of oil, without which the Syrian war machine would grind to a halt, was Iran, the third pillar of the terror alliance. Khomeini's regime had been offering oil well below the market price which to President Assad was worth something like $1 billion in hard currency. But even Iran, locked in the interminable war with Iraq, could no longer afford to subsidize the government of Syria on the former generous scale. To get supplies President Assad who owed millions of dollars to Iran for oil already exported was forced to start sending military equipment and spares to that country to help with the war effort.

That is part of the price which Syria has had to pay for its lust to establish itself as the vanguard nation of the Arab cause by manipulating the terror forces of the Middle East. It also has to put its faith in continuing support from the Kremlin. Of the three pillars of state-aided terrorism in that part of the world, only Iran remains independent of the Soviet Union. Without Russian weapons, encouragement and propaganda support, neither Gaddafi's Libya nor Assad's Syria would dare to pursue their chosen path in face of American hostility.

7.

Kremlin Connivance

Are the Russians responsible for the slaughter and plotting by the terrorist international? That is the question asked whenever violence boils over. Yes, they are deeply involved; but no, they did not invent it, and they do not mastermind a giant world plot. The guiding rule of the Kremlin is public condemnation of the idea of terror and clandestine support for some selected practitioners. There is no evidence to prove that the Soviets themselves set up terrorist groups. They do not need to, for such organizations are self-generating.

Moreover, there is no shortage of states which are prepared to do for them the job of supporting and directing the forces of subversive warfare. In the Middle East the two most important helpers are Libya and Syria. In the case of Libya the Russians have even been able to use Colonel Gaddafi and to make a profit out of him. They did not simply supply him with weapons, some of which he passed on to an assortment of terror bands; they charged him the going rate for all this material and presented a bill for $15 billion. In their eyes he is a customer who until the oil market upset was willing and eager to pay in dollars for every tank and every jet received. In addition to that Gaddafi in his heyday in the 1970s was financing the USSR's other Arab client state and sponsor of terrorism, Syria. He also supplied millions of dollars to provide weapons, many of them bought from Russia, as well as ammunition for the Palestinian sects battling it out in the

Lebanese civil war. It was a cosy arrangement for the Soviets and well worth the trouble of providing military advisers to Libya.

Despite that, he can be almost as tiresome to them on his frequent visits to Moscow as he is to the Western world, for the Russians are embarrassed to be too closely and publicly identified with such an obvious terrormaster. The more so after Soviet citizens were taken hostage by Arab guerrillas in Lebanon and one of them was murdered. It was noticeable on Gaddafi's first Moscow trip after Mikhail Gorbachev came to power that things did not go so smoothly as they had before. Strains were revealed when the temperamental Libyan failed to turn up at a Kremlin reception in his honor. The feeble excuse was that his driver had been given the wrong address. The tiff was likely caused by Russia's shelving plans announced in 1983 for a treaty of friendship between Moscow and Tripoli. It must have been a relief to the Soviets that they had moved so prudently, for it allowed them to leave Libya at the mercy of air attack without loss of face for failing to go to the rescue under an aid treaty. Although the Libyan had proved a useful ally, he could not count on the Soviet Union to rescue him from troubles of his own making.

The proof of that came with the Russian reaction to the American raid on Tripoli. Although Tass, the official news agency, put up a barrage of hostile words denouncing American action as "barbarous and totally unjustified aggression" there was no sign of counteraction. The only gesture was to cancel an arranged meeting between Soviet and American foreign ministers.

If the Kremlin was aware that the attack was about to take place there was no indication that any advance warning was passed on to Tripoli. The Red Fleet in the Mediterranean made no attempt to hamper the operations of the Sixth Fleet when it sailed into the Gulf of Sirte. The Russian flagship cruiser *Drozit* pointedly sailed from Tripoli the day before the raid and did not return until the dust had settled. Nor was there any sign that the Soviet advisers and training teams in Libya were prepared to give much of a hand with the defenses when the U.S. forces went operational.

Only one helpful gesture was made and that was to fly in replenishments for missiles fired by the Libyans—with, presumably, the bill to follow. When the colonel told Soviet correspondents that their country should regard any fresh American assault as an attack on the USSR they described the remark as "unfortunate" and the Russian media did not even carry the story.

The message is that Soviet leaders believe it is all very well to flatter the vanity of Arab states by advising and helping to train their military and their guerrilla forces for actions which alarm and damage the West, but that the prospect of an armed clash with the rival superpower is too high a price to pay from the advantages gained. It seems to be recognized even in the Kremlin that Gaddafi is an alarming joker in the pack. They even began lecturing him on the dangers of terrorism and urging restraint. The interests of the Soviet Union must come first and on this occasion the Kremlin was content to make the most of the obvious propaganda line by denouncing President Reagan as a Rambo-like warmonger.

Ever since the Cuban missile crisis, the USSR has shown marked reluctance to become involved in military operations which might lead to an armed clash with the United States. This fear was demonstrated in the case of the Soviet's other Arab client state, Syria. When, during the invasion of Lebanon, Israel knocked out Syria's missile bases which were supplied and partly manned by Russians, and shattered its fighter force, Russia refused to come to the rescue in case America moved in to protect Israel. On that occasion the Kremlin was content to resupply the Syrians. But this did not alter the fact that at a critical moment protection was not made available.

The Soviet Union prefers to influence Libya and Syria by providing warlike stores and military expertise while still remaining at arm's length. This enables KGB officers to make discreet contact with sympathizers and communist recruits in those countries and to prepare them as agents of influence to move closer to the centers of political power. A survey by the International Institute for Strategic Studies published in London accused the Soviets of "assisting low-level violence against the west, particularly if this can be done without an embarrassing display of complicity."

It is natural that the Kremlin should be satisfied to observe and sometimes encourage disorder and confusion in the West; for it serves to convince the Soviets that the communist analysis of the sickness of nonsocialist countries is correct and that the crisis of capitalism is at hand. They are as delighted to examine signs of imminent Western collapse as some religious sects are happy to contemplate the "last days" and the coming millennium.

At a more banal level Soviet agents from the KGB, or from GRU military intelligence, make cautious contact with already established terror groups. It is usually a cautious relationship, for Soviet, East German and Bulgarian agents in Europe and the Middle East are not to be found in front-line positions. Their mission is first to get information, then in selected cases, to offer help with the provision of weapons, and eventually to arrange for suitable men and women to attend training courses. These are held, in either the Soviet Union itself, the East bloc or the countries of Third World supporters. The Russians act as suppliers and advisers to handpicked terrorist movements. There is no sign that they completely control or direct any group. Thus the Kremlin can get the best of all worlds by using its covert state security forces as watchdogs and as shepherd dogs, without officially having to commit itself to open involvement for insurgent movements. A further advantage is that public opinion in the Soviet bloc knows nothing of such activities, sheltered as it is from intrusive TV coverage and the activities of native investigative journalists.

International terrorism presents the Soviet Union with an opportunity and a dilemma. In assessing their policies towards it, Russian leaders are sandwiched between the desire to present their socialist society as a respectable, grown-up member of the world community and a pillar of the United Nations, and the preachings of Lenin, the founding father. The revolution could only come about, so he declared, through civil war between the proletariat and the bourgeoisie in advanced countries, combined with "a whole series of democratic and revolutionary movements, including the national liberation movement in the underdeveloped, backward and oppressed nations."

Yet, on numerous occasions, modern day Leninists have publicly condemned such activities. A great difficulty is that there are so many different kinds of terrorists, guerrillas and insurgents. The attraction of them all from a Kremlin eye view is that they are doing their best to disorganize and destabilize society in the capitalist world and that they are people, moreover, who use the language of Marx and Lenin. But doctrinally they are considered unsound by the purists of true communism. Moreover, they are "adventurists" of the worst kind, almost impossible to control, and in general unsatisfactory. Such people have been condemned from time to time as elitists, serving only the interests of the class enemy and encouraging international forces of reaction. These strictures, of course, apply in particular to what we have called doctrinal terrorists, such as the new outfits in Western Europe. Indeed, some of their activities smack of Trotskyism, and we all know what that unfortunate movement led to.

In their relations with terrorist bodies in Western Europe the Russians are even more cautious than in other parts of the world. Only on one occasion, in 1978, was a KGB man discovered actually meeting a European terrorist, an ETA Basque codenamed "Anchon." Officers of the intelligence service in our part of the world are, anyway, fully occupied with espionage, disinformation and technological industrial espionage. They also have to prepare sabotage networks to go operational in time of war. Defectors like Oleg Lyalin, have revealed that they also reconnoiter targets for Spetnaz special service units of the Red Army to attack at a time of general conflict. In this task they also benefit from the fact that after World War II, the partisan units established in Italy and France provided a useful structure for continuing clandestine communists after the war. The underground networks were preserved and Soviet agents still use them in making preparations for the next war. This activity must provide for the possibility of using terrorist groups for attacks on the military infrastructure of the Western alliance. When the pan-European terrorist groups began attacking specifically NATO installations and people in Europe, Western intelligence investigated the possibility that some of the targets, such as the European military fuel line, might have been suggested to them by the Soviets. But West German security authorities considered it more likely that secret plans of the fuel installations had been acquired by the groups themselves as a result of lax security at American bases.

There can be no doubt that the Soviets act with great caution in their on-the-ground contacts with foreign "doctrinal" groups. At various times they have used surrogate supporters. A notable example was Carlos Ramirez Sanchez, the Latin American mercenary trained in Havana and Moscow, who carried out his most notorious acts in conjunction both with Red Army faction people and with Palestinian extremists. A KGB trainee, he succeeded as leader of a Palestinian squad in Paris after the murder of Mohammed Boudia, also branded by Israeli intelligence as a KGB operative.

A logistics network supplying false documents, money and support for both European and Third World fighters was run in Paris in the 1970s by a staunch old communist named Henri Curiel, who was a relation of George Blake, the British intelligence officer and defector to Moscow. The organization, then known as *Solidarité*, was financed by a Russian bank. It provided safe houses and other forms of backup for the Carlos crowd and for other terrorists.

The testimony of Antonio Savasta, a "penitent" Italian terrorist during the trial of those charged with the murder of former premier Aldo Moro indicated Soviet and East bloc involvement with the Red Brigades. He had a tangled tale to tell about the origins of the plot in 1981 to kidnap Brigadier Dozier, an American officer serving with NATO forces in Italy. He claimed that Bulgarian agents had been in touch with the Italians to offer support in this operation, so as to keep guerrilla action going. An Italian trade union leader named Luigi Scricciolo, a self-proclaimed Bulgarian spy, claimed that help from Sofia had been offered in return for secret information extorted from the Brigadier before his Red Brigades' captors released him. There was even mention that Soviet-made weapons could be offered to the Red Brigades through the agency of the Palestinians. Of course, useful though such information is, evidence from terrorist defectors must always be treated with caution, for they often tell their interrogators what they think the authorities will like to hear.

But it is known that the Soviets have made generous use of the Bulgarian secret service to carry out missions in which they do not wish to be too closely involved. Bulgaria does serve as a convoluted interchange for the movement of gunrunners and drug smugglers as well as for terrorists moving between the Middle East and Europe. It is also a convenient crossing place between Western Europe and the East bloc. Many cases are on record of the Bulgarian authorities permitting the passage of armed terrorists with their supplies.

The government of this hard-line communist country has also been implicated in the plot which almost succeeded in murdering Pope John Paul. In the confusion of rumor, disinformation and intrigue let loose by investigation of the wounding of the pope, few facts are sure. The only hard ground is that Mehmet Ali Agca, a demented Turk, did intend to murder the pontiff in St. Peter's Square, Rome, and did wound him. For this offense he received a sentence of life imprisonment. In prison he began to recount strange tales. In particular, he claimed that he had not acted alone, and that seems to be the case. But he enlarged the story with circumstantial evidence that he had been working for and with the Bulgarian secret service through their embassy and airline officials in Rome. For months while he was questioned by an examining magistrate, the Bulgarians denied any part in the plot. Then, when Ali Agca finally appeared publicly in open court to give his eagerly awaited version of these strange events, he destroyed all belief in the truth of what he had been saying by an astonishing announcement that he was in fact Jesus Christ. Once the star witness had made such an incredible claim, it became impossible to have much faith in any of his other revelations. The pope plot therefore remains, and seems likely to remain forever, an impenetrable mystery.

In earlier Italian goings-on there was harder evidence of Soviet connection with Giangiacomo Feltrinelli, the strange Italian millionaire who helped to establish terrorism in Italy. His publishing house was the first in the West to publish Boris Pasternak's *Doctor Zhivago*. He used his profits and his personal fortune to finance terror groups in the West. A violent playboy, he was in touch with the leaders of any number of troublemaking organizations in Europe, the Middle East and Latin America. Among those he entertained in style at his Milanese property was Ulrike Meinhof, the original German terror mother.

Meinhof herself, founding member of the Baader-Meinhof gang, and her husband, Klaus Rainier Rohl, had been card-carrying members of the East German Communist party. Her husband ran a trendy left-wing magazine which was subsidized from East Germany to the tune of $250,000.

More recently a spokesman at the West German attorney-general's office in Karlsruhe declared that there was no decisive proof that the new terrorists were being subsidized by the Soviets. Nonetheless, carefully laundered money from East Germany does go into their war chest. The BKA antiterrorist unit has drawn attention to the number of journeys by terrorists which either begin, or end, in East Berlin. That segment of the former German capital is used as a staging post, both for European terrorists and for Middle Eastern ones traveling westward on missions. After serving a sentence in France, the woman terrorist Magdalena Kaupp returned for a while to West Germany, then made her way to East Berlin and from there flew to Libya to marry her lover, Carlos. In Europe the connections are there, but they are neither obvious nor easy to document.

When it comes to their relations with nationalist movements using terrorism and guerrilla warfare to gain control over their homeland, the Soviets have an easier time of it. They have a ready-made escape clause permitting them to favor "national liberation" movements, though support for such movements is highly selective. One Soviet man's liberation movement is another Soviet man's gang of bandits. Political expediency makes it reasonable to support, for example, the Palestinians, in their fight against the forces of international Zionism. The growth of the terror industry in Latin America presented too good a chance to miss of helping to stir up trouble and confusion so close to the United States. The Soviets were able to achieve their purpose fairly inconspicuously at arm's length by allowing Fidel Castro's Cubans to act as aggressive middlemen. The other important odd-job man in purveying Soviet support to resistance movements in the Western Hemisphere, and in Africa, was Kim Il-sung, the boss of North Korea. Terrorists trained in his country have been detected in a whole range of countries.

All such activities in the nonsocialist world were considered to be legitimate. The strict rule is that at home there must be neither terrorist gangs nor liberation fighters. If a resistance movement of Moslems in Soviet Azerbaijan tried to fight in the cause of liberation from Russian rule that would be a heinous plot. Hypocrisy is a common stance in assessing terrorist movements, and, it has to be admitted, in the West we are not immune to it. The Soviets get around the problem by making arbitrary realpolitik decisions on which wars of liberation are just wars, and which are unjust. But in this decision taking, they are conscious of the risk that by overencouraging liberation movements in the outside world, they may be setting a bad example to all those discontented ethnic groups within the Soviet empire. They do not want to upset things abroad too ostentatiously at the price of encouraging similar troubles within the "socialist camp."

This consideration also applies to the new-style religious terrorists such as the Islamic Jihad. Moscow recognizes the power of religion, be it Moslem or Christian, and every possible repressive measure is taken to prevent that power spreading in the world they control. When it comes to Islam, the need for caution is at its most acute. In central Asia within the borders of the Soviet Union are millions of followers of the Prophet Mohammed. It is a principle aim of Kremlin policy to prevent the spread of the Iranian religious revolution northward across the border. The religion of Moslems within the USSR is kept tightly under state control to the extent that only very small numbers of approved persons are permitted to make the Haj pilgrimage to Mecca, although it is the duty of every good Moslem to visit the holy places in Saudi Arabia once in his lifetime.

Islamic Jihad, therefore, is unlikely to get any great encouragement from the Soviet Union. The only way in which the Shi'ites benefit from its support is by way of Syria, already heavily dependent upon the Russians for military supplies. Syria is now the most important power in Lebanon, and the sponsor of terror outfits operating there, such as the suicide bombers controlled by what used to be called the Syrian National Socialist Party, a conglomerate affair which incorporates people of many factions and religious persuasions. But on the ground in the Middle East neither KGB men nor agents of the GRU are to be found anywhere near the scene of action.

The instructors and manipulators come into their own in the training camps inside the Soviet Union and in the East bloc countries, safe from the prying eyes of interfering Westerners. Most of the information about these camps comes from Israeli intelligence and is based upon the interrogation of Arab prisoners. The Israelis in making their case also rely heavily on documentation discovered in Palestinian bases in Lebanon after the Israeli conquest of a large part of that country. Naturally the information released is selective and intended to justify Israel's case against the PLO and its many offshoots.

Putting aside the question of the legitimacy of Palestinian claims to a homeland in territory now occupied by the state of Israel, it must be recognized that so far as the Soviets are concerned, the PLO has proved a useful vehicle for their purposes, despite initial misgivings. It is a rich organization, well financed by prosperous Arab countries salving their consciences after failing to help fellow Arabs in trouble. Therefore, no great subsidies are needed from Moscow. Indeed, the Palestinians can perfectly well afford to purchase their weapons and pay for them in hard currency, which is always a lure for the Soviets. The further attraction was that Arab liberation fighters could be offered training facilities in guerrilla warfare techniques within the Soviet Union, with communist indoctrination as an extra facility. This is a process which has continued for two decades. When the Palestinians returned to Lebanon and the other countries where they had their bases, they set up instruction establishments of their own which became in turn places where other guerrillas, both urban and rural, from Europe and other parts of the world, might learn their trade. Thus a generation of Western terrorists passed through the Palestinian camps before "Base Lebanon" fell to the enemy and their forces were dispersed. Since then fresh camps have been established to carry on the work in Aden, the People's Democratic Republic of Yemen, where the East Germans are particularly active, and Colonel Gaddafi's Libya. Such places remain the spawning ground of modern terrorists worldwide.

In passing, it is worth recording that specially trained gunmen from around the world provide a reservoir of mercenaries ready for use as hit men by secret services when they do not dare to be too closely involved in such enterprises. There are now so many anonymous trained Arabs, for example, that they flood the market with offers to ply their grisly trade on behalf of a wide range of interests, both state-run and criminal. Certainly the Russians have such people on their books for use when the need arises, and it would not be surprising if other countries, too, had at least considered making use of their talents.

Within the Soviet empire a whole range of place names are frequently cited as the location for the formation of guerrillas—Baku and Tashkent, Simferopol in the Crimea, Odessa on the Black Sea. An Israeli estimate is that since 1973 some 3,000 Arabs from the different Palestinian groups have been trained in terrorism, subversive activities and sabotage by the Soviet Union. Similar courses in low-intensity operations are on offer at various establishments in Czechoslovakia, Hungary, Bulgaria and East Germany. Detailed information about the nature of specialist classes available, like explosives work, assassination and small-arms instruction, has been published by the Israeli authorities. For intellectuals, for agents of influence and "sleepers" from likely countries, places are offered at establishments such as the Patrice Lumumba University in Moscow. Such activities will continue so long as Marxist-Leninist factions of the resistance movements go on preaching communism in their publications and public statements, thereby doing the Soviet Union's work for it.

Precise assessment of the Soviet role in international terrorism, nonetheless, remains a difficult task. Propagandists can easily distort the available evidence to exaggerate the importance of it, and give the impression that it is all the fault of the Russians, that somewhere in Moscow exists an all-powerful figure who orders hijack here, a kidnap there, and that action squads everywhere are awaiting such orders. It is not like that. The Kremlin exploits and prudently makes use of forces already in being.

In a thoughtful speech on the state of the art, George Shultz, the U.S. secretary of state, put the thing into perspective. After saying that in many parts of the world terrorism would have withered away without outside support, and that the Israelis had produced "irrefutable" evidence of Soviet arming and training of groups, he commented:

> Today, there is no reason to think that Soviet support for terrorist groups around the world has diminished . . . The Soviets condemn terrorism, but in practice they connive with terrorist groups.

It is a connivance which the Russians may yet have cause to regret, for they themselves are not invulnerable to terrorist attack. Until now commentators on subversive warfare have always taken it as an article of faith that in the USSR there is no terrorism. Yet there are already signs, ominous for the Russians, that this state of affairs may not last. In Afghanistan they find themselves on the other side of the fence with the Red Army under attack from "freedom fighters." They are the targets now. The response has been to train and operate Spetnaz special forces in the same essentially antiterrorist role as the Delta force and the British SAS.

The role reversal process may not confine itself to Afghanistan. The Soviet Union is in fact the only great surviving empire in which Europeans, in this case Russians, control and dominate a collection of essentially Moslem Asian states. Those states of central Asia are inhabited by a fast-growing population whose religion is Islam. They cannot forever remain unmoved by what is happening to their coreligionists in Afghanistan. Indeed Afghan units of freedom fighters/terrorists in 1986 carried the war across the Afghan border into Uzbekistan—into Soviet territory. This is just the beginning of future troubles.

The Iranian Islamic revolution which has made such horrifying use of the scimitar of terror against the West is seething just south of the Soviet Union. Can the Russians prevent the same form of Islam-inspired holy revolution from seeping across the line on the map and into their territory? That is a question to which the Kremlin will have to give a great deal of attention before the century ends.

PART THREE

TERROR
IN
EUROPE

8.

Soft Option?

From terrorist statistics alone, terrible though they were, it is difficult for outsiders now to comprehend the deep anxiety which struck German society in the 1970s. In the first decade of the armed struggle 31 people were killed, including nine police, four prosecutors and three diplomats. Nearly 100 had been injured; 25 bomb attacks were recorded and 30 terrorist bank raids took place. That was bad enough, but worse things had happened in Northern Ireland, for example, and elsewhere, without causing such dramatic consequences. In Germany, it was the choice of victims, the horror of the crimes—Hanns-Martin Schleyer had his throat cut after being shot dead—and fears about spreading contamination and disaffection among the young, which brought such panic. The country was going through its worst postwar ordeal. The baffling thing was that for the older generation there seemed no reason for it. The Federal Republic was a flourishing democracy built upon the ashes of Hitler's Reich, it was prosperous and well ordered. There was no regional or religious conflict as in Corsica, the Basque country, or in Ireland, nor did there appear to be social tension. Robin Smythe, writing in the *Observer* (London) from Bonn at the time shrewdly drew his own conclusions:

> Terrorism has struck at the foundations of German self-confidence. It suggests that there might be something in the national character which refuses to accept the whole idea of well-being.

115

A storm of terrorism shook the countries of continental Europe in the 1970s, but nowhere did it succeed in its aim to destroy Western society. For a while, in 1977, it did look as though destabilization of the Federal Republic of Germany was a possibility. The attorney-general, Siegfried Buback, was killed, together with his guards; an attempt was made to rocket the federal justice offices; numerous murders of police officers took place. This series of events culminated in the kidnapping of the prominent industrialist, Hanns-Martin Schleyer. Terrorists held him prisoner and then killed him. The discovery of his mutilated body conincided with the defeat of their combined hijack operation with the Arabs against an Air France flight taken to Mogadishu in Somalia.

These events caused general alarm. Something close to panic was detectable in the government of the Federal Republic. Political life was interrupted. A visit to Bonn by James Callaghan, the British prime minister, and his foreign secretary was postponed and terrorism became the main item on every agenda.

The deep disquiet caused by these dramatic events, soon to be duplicated in Italy, France and the Low Countries, and the strategies which each hit upon to defend themselves against the new menace had a profound effect on their reactions to the great crisis of international terrorism of 1986. By then the Europeans had learned to live with the phenomenon and each country in its own way had managed to contain the threat and to live with danger.

Simultaneously they had to cope with another offensive linked with the national assaults, and that came from the Middle East, turning the old continent, Britain included, into the killing ground and target area for Palestinians keen on bringing their war to the West. Because the European nations already had their hands full at home the tendency was to bargain a way out of trouble with the Arabs. Some terrorists, like Leila Khaled, the woman hijacker, were simply expelled. Abu Daoud, the wanted Arab terrorist, was allowed to leave France when both Israel and West Germany laid charges against him. Not wanting to make further trouble for themselves, countries simply returned troublemakers and potential troublemakers to their countries of origin.

In fact this policy did not work, but because it was an easy way out European Community members continued to operate it long after it had been rejected by the British. The temptation remained, for each country is selfishly but naturally more keen on fighting its own individual terrorist enemies than other people's. Like the Americans, the continental countries constantly irked the British by expressing sympathy for, giving aid to, and refusing to agree to extradition of, members of the IRA.

When the Arabs became part of the equation, the Middle East powers were wielding simultaneously the terror weapon and the oil weapon after 1973. That oil was desperately needed by the industrial powers and they were reluctant to risk an entire economy just to prosecute the war against terrorist irritation.

Terrorism had been a fact of life for the old democracies for nearly a quarter of a century before the great upheavals and high dramas sprang from the Middle East in the mid-1980s bringing American intervention on a superpower scale. In a way it was part of the price for, if not peace, at least absence of world war, ensured by the nuclear balance.

The explanation, if not the justification for European reluctance to march with President Reagan towards the sound of the guns in the spring of 86, was fear that superpower naval and air force action against Colonel Gaddafi might precipitate something worse. Each of the Community countries had managed to contain terrorism by other means. Granted that some had gone too far along the path of compromise and soft options, they had by and large achieved a measure of coordination against those forces which threatened them. Much of the cooperation was on an "old boy network" rather than a formal basis. A good example is the working of TREVI and the so-called Berne Club, semi-informal networks which regularly bring together police officers, intelligence people and diplomats of the nations concerned to exchange information on the terrorist threat and those responsible for it. Each individual country had set up special antiterrorist units, both defensive and offensive, in the form of such forces as the British Special Air Service Regiment and the West German GSG 9.

Great though the agony of Europe had been, the Community countries had not suffered the American trauma of the embassy seizure in Tehran, the giant bombings of embassies and U.S. Marines units in the Middle East. Those were the events which led up to the great American strike back when Libya, Syria and Iran began their provocatively anti-American campaigns. There was, however, still a tendency towards that latent feeling of old-nation superiority, partly based on envy, which is always detectable in Europe. Statesmen on the eastern side of the Atlantic, Prime Minister Thatcher excepted, tended to think that the United States, having come late upon the terrorist scene, was overreacting to the threat from Islam.

That said, it was unforgivable that the NATO countries, especially France, Italy and the new member Spain, should have refused overflying rights to American aircraft on their way to Libya. An alliance is an alliance for all that. Already the Italians had shown a lack of confidence in their superpower ally when they refused to hand over Abu Abbas and his *Achille Lauro* pirates to American justice after they had murdered a U.S. citizen. Even worse they had released him for lack of evidence, though he later became the principal accused. Of course, lawyers may argue forever about the technicalities of that case, but when the Atlantic alliance is at stake such debates become less important.

Italy has a special relationship with Libya, its former colony. Thousands of its citizens live and work there. Italian contractors did a great deal of business in the north African country and were in fact owed huge sums of money by the regime which has never been a prompt payer. Gaddafi over the years had bought his way into Italian industry and indeed still owns a substantial number of shares in Fiat motors, a fact causing great embarrassment.

Many factors lay behind the cautious decisions of the European countries, both economic and political. There was national pride about being seen to take orders from Washington. There was also alarm at upsetting the Arabs and provoking more attacks—in Europe, not in America. The Italians were even apprehensive about their island of Lampedusa, out there in the Mediterranean too close to Libya for comfort. Above all stood the fear that large-scale action might provoke the Soviet Union and end all hope of some kind of summit arrangement on world tension and nuclear-arms reduction.

In terms of strictly terrorist sub-warfare the Community considered the benefits of other ways of dealing with the threat, of a kind which had proved effective in the past against their own national groups. At the time of the Vienna and Rome airport attacks they had placed a ban on arms sales to Libya. After the Tripoli raid, and under the strengthening influence of Margaret Thatcher and Hans-Dietrich Genscher, the West German foreign minister, stronger measures against the Libyans were agreed, though Greece, controlled by the Byzantine policy scrambling of Andreas Papadandreou, dissented. The socialist prime minister at first flatly refused to go along with Community sanctions against Libyan diplomats. He justified his stand with an astounding declaration to the effect that "violence in the context of the Palestinian liberation struggle is not terrorism." George Shultz, the secretary of state, was so furious that he obtained a retraction.

Even the French, so persistently devoted to their own self-interest took a stronger line than before. They attracted American sneers for putting it about that they had only refused to help with the Tripoli raid because at heart they did not believe that the action taken was powerful enough.

Most of the 10-point plan presented by the British was in fact accepted. The main effect was to clamp down on the activities of Libyan peoples' bureaus and those employed by them, by limiting their movements, by cutting down diplomatic representation, and ensuring that a diplomat expelled from one country would be banned by all. Although such measures did not go as far as Britain wanted, notably in closing down Libyan bureaus altogether, they were a step forward from the position previously adopted. "They will be seen as an effective response by a concerned Community, and thank heaven for that," declared Sir Geoffrey Howe, the foreign secretary, with an obvious sigh of relief. He had managed to convince his colleagues that the bureaus really were being used "as terrorist command and communication outposts."

There was, however, no discussion among the foreign ministers of outright economic sanctions against Libya. This was partly because of Prime Minister Thatcher's mistrust of the effectiveness of such measures, especially with the South African case looming, and also because the Germans flatly refused to compromise their supply of oil from Libya. On the day that 21 Libyans were expelled from the U.K. (later to be followed by hundreds more), Mrs. Thatcher told Parliament: "We would have liked a lot more to have been done and we must consider how much further to go ourselves."

President Reagan, too, would have liked sterner stuff. Diplomatic pressure was put upon the 12 member states to ensure that the measures agreed were put into operation. Each had been left to apply the decision in its own way and in its own time. That did not prevent Colonel Gaddafi who was clearly worried at the change of attitude across the Mediterranean from denouncing the Community for "ominously adopting the frenzied actions led by the USA and Britain."

Hundreds of Libyans—students, diplomats, trainee pilots and businessmen—were eventually sent home from Europe. Their disappearance from the scene made the task of Western security a great deal easier. And the fact that a lull broke out in the war without end appeared to show that the measures taken were at least partly effective.

9.

Don't Argue—Destroy

Don't argue—Destroy —Campus wall slogan, West Germany

The origins of the first terrorist assault on continental Europe were very different from those of the second wave from the Middle East. The long martyrdom began with the reign of terror inspired by the Baader-Meinhof gang, born with the shoot-out rescue from prison in May 1970 of Andreas Baader in which both Ulrike Meinhof, the radical chic lady journalist, and Horst Mahler took part. The name was replaced by the title Red Army Faction, (RAF) to imply that it was a part, or faction, of an international army of revolution, an idea which originated in this context with the Japanese Red Army. Two other forces became similarly active: the 2nd June movement, named after the date of the 1967 shooting in Berlin of a student named Benno Ohnesorg, and the Revolutionary Cells. RAF was the most dangerous movement, representing as it did the rootless generation whose motto painted on campus walls was "Don't argue—destroy."

It had the most convincing ideological conception and political aims. It also had the greatest capacity for criminal potential and benefited from support among groups that did not themselves break the law, yet shared its indignation about their smug, self-satisfied parent generation. They condemned it for failing to stop Hitler, and then relaxing back to enjoy the benefits of postwar-imposed democracy. Even more galling for the young Marxists and anarchists was the undoubted fact that the working class was just as bad, and showed every sign of contentment.

In face of invincible proletarian reluctance to make a revolution, RAF leaders (introduced to the idea by the philosopher Herbert Marcuse) saw themselves as the vanguard of the workers to make war upon the bourgeoisie. The objective was destruction, politically, economically and militarily, of "the imperialist feudal system" through the armed struggle. This justified the attack, internationally, upon NATO and upon the armed forces of Germany, the allies of the United States. Nationally the main enemies were the police, the federal border guards and the security services, who represented what they called the "monopoly of power of the ruling class." American imperialism and multinational power structures figure as frequently in today's communiqués and statements as they did in the outpourings of Ulrike Meinhof and Horst Mahler in 1972, when they were carrying out the original series of 15 bomb raids in West German cities from Munich to Hamburg. They set the semantics of revolutionary language which outlived them. The sequence of the assault was from bank raids to bombing, from bombing to kidnapping and deliberate assassination. 1977 marked the climax of "revolutionary terror." By that time the hard-core RAF people, half of them women, were spread throughout the country in 25 groups of five-person units. They had become professional terrorists. They lived the clandestine life, were precise and intelligent in planning and execution and enjoyed the help of scores of supporters known as "criminals without crime."

But the time of gravest crisis passed. The security forces were beefed up to meet the threat. The BKA, the federal criminal office at Wiesbaden, increased in strength from 900 to 2500. Its resources and equipment were modernized, and a powerful data bank was created. It was expanded to act as the central information and communications center for the fight against terrorism.

GSG 9 (Grenzschutzgruppe 9), the special antihijack unit of the federal border guard, was set up within three weeks of the disastrous affair of the terrorist attack upon Israeli athletes at the Munich Olympic games in September 1972. The new force showed its mettle at Mogadishu by storming a hijacked Lufthansa jet which had been forced to fly there. Since then it has expanded to become the spearhead of counterterrorism in West Germany. Its main job is still to deal with the seizure by terrorists of planes, trains, buses and ships, but it now has a wider spectrum of tasks. After the formation of an extra group in 1984, GSG 9 consisted of four combat units, each composed of 36 men. Two of them specialize in surveillance duties and action in support of BKA, the federal police, and of the *Lander* forces of each of the federal states.

Unit 2 concentrates on the protection of maritime targets. Germany has oil rigs in the North Sea and in the Baltic, and also a fleet of tankers which are considered possible targets. Unit 3 goes in for parachuting, especially free fall, which can be used when all other means fail, to get to a building or other area held by terrorists. Recruits do normal police training first, then four months' special instruction in five-man teamwork including the tactics of "room penetration." Each year there is an international combat team competition for special units, held at the GSG 9 headquarters in St. Augustin, near Bonn. In 1985 the competition was won by South Bavarian police, with U.S. army Delta force second, and the U.S. Navy Seals third.

Responsibility for overall intelligence in the war against terrorism lies with the Federal Office for the Protection of the Constitution which also handles counterespionage in Germany. Using modern methods and electronic equipment, its officers collect and evaluate information.

Prosecution of terrorists, and all the legal side, is handled by the federal attorney-general's office in Karlsruhe. Of necessity, the buildings look like a fortress. They are protected by heavy bomb-proof doors, high walls, barbed wire, TV and electronic surveillance, and spiked revolving doors at entrance and exit.

In a street only 200 yards from this place a terrorist hideout was discovered in July 1984. It contained weapons and was obviously intended as the base for an attack. Alexander Prechtel, the lawyer spokesman of the *Generalbundesanwalts*, told the authors, "We also found a hit list and I figured on it. They know us and they hate us."

Since 1976 this organization has been responsible for the investigation and prosecution of all cases of terror, espionage and of matter affecting the security of the state. The present attorney-general is Professor Dr. Kurt Rebmann, successor to the Siegfried Buback who was murdered by the Red Army Faction.

Effective measures against terrorism depend upon a steady flow of information and help from the public at large, and at first this was not forthcoming. It was one of the alarming features of the worst stage of the RAF offensive that as it escalated people became less willing to help the security authorities. This was an indication that West Germany was so shaken by the onslaught that people began to believe it was more dangerous to help the authorities than just to lie low.

The most controversial feature of the war on terrorists was the federal government's decision to change the law in ways which reduced the right to personal freedom so carefully built into the Federal Republic's postwar constitution. The most opposed and bitterly criticized step had already been taken before the worst of the outrages took place. In response to the student demonstrations and violence of the New Left, federal Chancellor Willy Brandt issued a decree in 1972 to vet applicants, and if necessary exclude political extremists from millions of jobs in the German civil service. This resulted, as he admitted later, in "grotesque abuses."

It was one thing to make a law to punish those who took hostages and planted bombs, but liberal opinion was further shocked by plans to give the police the right to shoot to kill and to change the rules about the right of defense for arrested persons. The reason for legal reform was that the RAF had quite blatantly made use of sympathetic left-wing lawyers to aid its activities, and had incorporated some of them in its organization. For example, when their car was stopped for a routine check on the autobahn in 1977 it was discovered that two lawyers, Siegfried Haag and Roland Mayer, were carrying papers showing that new actions were being planned. In addition, they were in possession of currency which had been stolen in bank raids at Cologne and Hamburg. Indeed, Haag was leader of one group, and even after his imprisonment, he exercised remote control over its members, who were responsible for several notable assassinations.

Of course, most German lawyers behaved correctly and simply defended their clients to the best of their ability. However, several law offices specialized in not only defending imprisoned terrorists and others still in action but in aiding them by acting as couriers. Klaus Croissant, a 48-year-old advocate, had established a lawyers' cooperative in Stuttgart where several terrorist recruits, especially women, worked.

Croissant had been arrested in 1975, but he had jumped bail and fled to France. Amid a wave of left-wing protests he was eventually extradited and sentenced to two and a half years for operating an information network on behalf of the terrorists.

It was for such reasons that the law was altered to exclude a defense lawyer from a trial if he was suspected of involvement in the crime of the defendant. Other measures were successively taken to weaken chain-of-command connections between lawyers and their terrorist friends and clients.

Such moves caused an outcry, and there were accusations of fascism and that a general assault was being made on the liberty of the individual. Many protests sprang from general alarm, but a campaign was mounted by the supporters of terrorists themselves, specifically planned to undermine government authority, and to give the impression that Germany was going back to nazism. It was one of the strengths of the RAF that committees were already in being whose aim was to support the revolutionary movement. Such bodies as 'Red Help' and the 'Solidarity Committee for Political Prisoners' existed in many German cities. They sprang into action to publicize claims that isolation torture was used against Red Army prisoners who in fact enjoyed notable privileges in the prisons of West Germany. The proof of linkage between these support groups and the terror organization was that many of their members eventually went underground and joined the RAF itself. None the less, all this had a disquieting effect on public opinion, and other Europeans began to voice anti-German misgivings about the dangers of a reversion to nazism in the Federal Republic, a cry quickly taken up by Marxists and leftist abroad.

Such themes were further developed when another new law permitted police search of whole apartment blocks suspected of harboring terrorists. At the same time it became legal for the police to set up control points on the roads for large-scale checking operations against the terrorists, and even to make personal strip searches. Although the countermeasures taken at this difficult time seemed excessive, even to many moderate Germans, and there were accusations about panic measures, they proved effective in breaking the power of the main German terrorist organization. In despair at the failure of their 1977 grand offensive, the principal leaders who were already in prison, Andreas

Baader, Ulrike Meinhof, Gudrun Ensslin and Jan-Carl Raspe, committed suicide at the Stammheim high-security establishment. So successful were the police and security forces in Germany that it began to look as though the anarchists and Marxists who had caused so much trouble and suffering had been routed in their attempt to overthrow the system.

This was partly because of the vigorous response. But it also seemed unlikely that they could rally again because the emotional causes which at first inspired such movements as the Red Army Faction and similar ones elsewhere in Europe simply faded away. Now, in 1985, the great issues which fueled the university protest movement and the teach-ins of the New Left, the incubators of violence, seem remote and historic. The first actions in Berlin were directed against the Shah of Iran and Moise Kapenda Tshombe of the then Congo. The Shah is dead and gone, and who can remember the activities of Tshombe? Even the Vietnam War, about which they got so excited, came to an end. As if that was not enough to discourage them, there was another factor. Young revolutionaries consistently worried and fretted about the consumer society and the evils of materialism; they denounced Western prosperity, and felt guilty about sharing it. But then, with the oil crisis, the slump began. Excessive prosperity ceased to be such a compelling reason for deep anxiety, either in the United States or in Europe. They had to search for new causes along the old neo-Marxist lines to justify new campaigns of violence.

Despite the fact that the old motives were forgotten by the world at large, the revolutionary armed conflict went marching on, and signs appeared in the summer of 1984 of a resurgence of warlike activities by new versions of the old groups. Despite its many setbacks and the arrest of nearly 100 of its field men and women, the Red Army Faction was again operational. Also, it had become the pacesetter for new groups establishing themselves in the neighboring countries of Western Europe. Western intelligence officers now know that in June 1984 representatives of most of the long-established European terrorist movements met in Lisbon and agreed to cooperate in a disruptive campaign.

The warning sign came in June when an armed raid was made on a quarry at a place in Belgium called Ecaussines, not far from Brussels. The raiders made off with 1,800 pounds of high explosive and detonators. Over the following months traces of this material were identified at the scene of numerous bomb attacks made upon installations in Belgium, France and West Germany. It was detected in August in a car bomb which failed to explode outside the Paris office of Western European Union. A bomb composed of the same explosive planted by the RAF in December also failed to detonate at the NATO officers' school at Oberammergau.

These bombs revealed the existence of a new trans-European terrorist alliance, the "Political-Military Front." This grandly named organization consisted of the rump of the old Red Army Faction, reinforced by new recruits; a revivified French organization named Action Directe, supported by a brand-new group from Belgium—CCC, the French-language acronym for fighting communist cells. It was not until 50 separate bomb attacks and two assassinations later that the new Euro-terrorists officially announced their existence in a long and convoluted communique handed to a news agency in Paris.

The inspiration was German. Fresh leaders had taken over the shattered remains of the old groups, both the Red Army Faction and its offshoot, the 2nd June movement. They succeeded in recruiting new and younger people for training and blooding. In mid-1985 the German public prosecutor's office in Karlsruhe estimated that during the second half of the previous year 12 fresh members, women as well as men, had gone underground as potential full-time bombers and murderers. Even allowing for the seven members caught by security forces, this left the organization with a net gain in personnel of five.

Such figures help to get the scale of terrorism in Europe in its true perspective. The official estimate of the Red Army Faction's order of battle is that it consisted in 1985 of some 20 hard-core members, backed by 200 willing militants capable of taking part in urban guerrilla attacks. Behind this active force there were some 2,000 enthusiastic supporters who could be relied upon to help with infrastructure by providing safe houses and so on, or simply being ready to pass messages and to scrawl slogans on a wall.

Wanted notices offering a reward of DM 50,000 listed 22 names and pictures with the old leaders at the top of the posters and newcomers below the line. Of these hard-core people no less than 13 were women, their ages varying between 24 and 44. Some of the most notorious of them are known to have taken refuge abroad, especially in the Middle

East. For example, three women of the older generation—Susanne Albrecht, Monika Helbing, and Friederike
Krabbe—have been tracked down to their Iraqi hideout in
Baghdad. "We know their address," declared an official in the
public prosecutor's office, "and exactly where they are, but
there is no means of getting them because the Iraqi government refuses to help."

Another notorious exile was Inge Viett, a 41-year-old
former nursery-school teacher and daughter of a Hamburg
bricklayer, grown middle-aged in the service of terrorism. As
a veteran RAF and 2nd June movement member she had
often been to the Middle East, where she had an established
connection with the Popular Front for the Liberation of
Palestine, and through it with the Carlos organization. She
took refuge across the border in France, where she was
detected when a Paris traffic policeman tried to stop her for
the minor offense of riding a motorcycle without wearing a
crash helmet. When he signaled her, she shot and wounded
him.

Inge Viett was suspected of being one of the principal
organizers of the New Red Army Faction. She used her long
stay underground in France to help reactivate the French
equivalent group, Action Directe. In fact, the RAF took
advantage of the fact that 19 French terrorist leaders were in
prison to get control of Action Directe, and to tighten up the
organization and thereby transform it from a small-time
entity into something more powerful, by linking its groups
with like-minded people across the border in the Federal
Republic.

Another important element in the revival of European
terrorists is the apparent ease with which those underground
seemed able to communicate with the old imprisoned leaders
in German top-security establishments. This was largely
accomplished with the help of defense lawyers sympathetic
to the cause who had the right to visit their imprisoned
clients. Earlier legislation had failed to prevent a small
number of left-wing lawyers from using their privileged position to act as middlemen of terror. To prevent written
messages and objects being handed over, lawyers may only
talk to clients through glass screens and in special rooms.

In spite of all the precautions, the "Old Brigade" of convicted RAF terrorists in prison were able to help in coordinating arrangements for the new onslaught of the European
alliance. It was planned to coincide with a hunger strike of 30

incarcerated RAF terrorists beginning in the autumn of 1984. Originally the idea was that it would lead to the death through starvation of prominent terrorists such as the new-generation boss Christian Klar. He was serving a life-imprisonment sentence. This was a tactic which the Irish Republican Army had used with great effect to draw attention to its cause. The Euro-terrorists believed that they could do the same thing, but time showed that they did not possess the stamina and determination of the IRA men, and eventually the hunger strike was called off. The publicized demand of the imprisoned RAF people was that they must be treated as political prisoners, and that instead of being split up among a number of high-security prisons in West Germany, they should all be kept together in one place. Obviously their idea was to play a more effective role in organizing the new terrorism from behind bars.

To that extent the plot failed. Even so, the strike, lasting several weeks, was used as the signal that other operations should start. The campaign was to be in three stages. First the hunger strike, then bomb attacks upon property, and, finally, the assassination of prominent persons. Operations were carried out in sequence by Germans, French and Belgians, acting as national (and not as mixed) hit teams. Bomb attacks were made upon NATO installations in Western Europe, and multinational firms and companies connected with defense production. The ambitious aim was to force such companies to stop working for defense programs. They made a point of picking on enterprises connected with nuclear energy and computers. A murder list discovered in a West German safe house contained the names of 90 important executives taken both from newspaper clippings and from articles in technical and industrial magazines.

The new factor was not so much that national groups were cooperating as that they had agreed in advance to make NATO and the defense industry their joint target. Having earlier tried and failed to destabilize the Western democracies politically, the Euro-terrorists launched their new campaign against the military defense preparations. Their idea was to exploit the sympathy of the hard pacifist lobby on the continent, which at the time had just suffered defeat in the campaign against installation of cruise missiles. They hoped also to blame American capitalism for all economic ills, and for financing the military-industrial complex which they believed caused unemployment. It was their plan to use disillusion caused by unemployment to win allies and recruits among the young.

The strategy of the alliance of European doctrinal terror groups shows most clearly in the catalog of actions mounted in the year 1984 by the newly revived French group Action Directe. At the beginning of the year they decided that they were ready to launch "a European guerrilla attack against the Americanization of Europe." Ten bomb attacks were made, causing much damage. Among them were the Paris offices of Panhard, makers of tanks and military vehicles; the Atlantic Institute of International Affairs; the French Ministry of Industry; the Paris headquarters of the European Space Agency; Western European Union, the defense assembly of the Common Market countries (where a car loaded with 23 kilos of TNT failed to explode); Messier-Hispano-Bugatti; the offices at St. Cloud of Marcel Dassault, the French aircraft manufacturer; RPR headquarters, Paris; and, finally, in December, the offices of Elf-Aquitaine, the oil company.

The choice of these organizations—all connected with technology and the defense industry and its political control—gives an insight into the minds of the new terrorists. To their way of thinking the organization of defense against the Soviet threat is in itself wicked. It is what they call "the machinery of oppression." In their eyes, to be involved in any high-technology industry is to be enslaved to the United States.

But it would be a mistake to assume from this that the new terrorists are simply admirers and tools of the Soviet Union. Meticulous examination of their published propaganda by German security analysts shows that they are almost equally critical of the Kremlin. A senior West German police officer at BKA, the Federal Criminal Police headquarters at Wiesbaden, reported: "So far as it mentions the Soviet Union at all, the Red Army Faction is anti-Soviet in its statements." He went on to say: "We have no hard information about active support from the Soviet Union, though there is some evidence that the East bloc gives finance to leftist groups, and some of this may get through to RAF."

In all the European movements now under consideration there is constant harping on the themes of antiimperialism, mainly a form of anti-Americanism, on the dangers of nuclear war and of new technology which is designed, they believe, to enslave the people in capitalist society. These themes march hand in hand with anti-Zionism. Israel is considered by the ideologues of terror to be almost as much the work of the devil as is the United States. Like the first generation of urban guerrillas, the new wave tends to blame all Third World disasters and shortcomings upon the capitalist world of the West. But for all that, the new movements are very different from the ones which developed in the 1970s from a guilty and emotional desire to help the Third World, and which in the process became simply a European prolongation of Middle East terror. The early members of the RAF, for example, all took themselves to training camps run by the PLO in the Arab countries. Statistics from an Israeli source show that as late as 1981 no less than 2,400 people received terrorist and guerrilla training in Middle East establishments run by the various Palestinian factions. Of that total 950 were from Europe. There was much common ideological ground in shared hatred of imperialism and Zionism, and the Europeans benefited from the operational experience gained by the Arabs.

What is remarkable in the present European terror groups is their ideological coherence. This makes possible a much higher degree of international coordination than has existed before. Their other trademark is the well-organized violence of their attacks.

It was early in 1985 that the new *internationale* of terror turned to deliberate murder. Warning of what was to come had been given by the Belgian CCC, which earlier announced that it had been decided, "Human life is not absolute in itself, it has no mystic value." In a carefully prepared ambush gunmen shot dead General René Audran as he parked his car one evening outside his Paris suburban home. It was the first time that Action Directe had gone in for deliberate murder as part of its campaign, and the choice of victim was important. For the general was, to their way of thinking, a powerful symbol of all that they hated. As international affairs head of the French defense ministry he controlled French arms sales abroad. After the two superpowers, France is the world's largest supplier of arms. The industry, directly or indirectly, provides employment for a million French people.

Only a few days later, the Red Army Faction was in action against a similar personality in Germany. Just before dawn on a February morning, a young woman rang the doorbell at the Munich home of Ernst Zimmermann, a leading industrialist whose firm makes engines for the Tornado jets used by NATO forces in Europe. She asked him to sign for delivery of a letter, and as he did so a man with a sub machine gun rushed forward and he and the woman crashed into the house. They forced Zimmermann into a bedroom and killed him with a bullet in the head from a heavy Colt automatic. Frau Zimmermann, who saw them both at close quarters, was able to identify them from police wanted lists. She was convinced that the women was Barbara Meyer and that the man was Werner-Bernhard Lotze, 37, a former student from the Ruhr who was drawn into terrorism in 1978 after doing small jobs for the RAF, such as carrying blackmail letters in the Schleyer affair. Barbara Meyer, 28, from Stuttgart, was a new recruit.

An anonymous caller to a local news-agency office later announced that the killing was the work of the Red Army Faction in alliance with the "West European guerrilla movement." Police knew that Zimmermann was on the hit list. His picture, biography and newspaper clips about him had been found months before in a hideout at 344 Bergerstrasse, Frankfurt. They were convinced that he was selected because those higher on the list were too well protected, and he had refused guards.

General Audran and Herr Zimmermann were on friendly terms. They had often worked together on projects, and had met for the last time only a few days before the assassination of Herr Zimmermann.

These two assassinations provided a clear signal that the new terrorists had meant what they said when they issued a long communiqué in Paris announcing that a new terrorist network was operational. The declaration was headed, in both French and in German, "For the Unity of West European Revolutionaries," and it bore the imprint of both the RAF and Action Directe. It announced the opening of a new phase in authentic revolutionary strategy and the creation of a West European guerrilla "political-military network," as part of the worldwide clash between the proletariat and the imperialist bourgeoisie. The aim would be to break the imperialists' strategy of maintaining their economic and military domination of the world.

According to this verbose and highly partisan analysis, the imperialists were intent upon using NATO to weld together the countries of European order to "roll back" liberation movements in the states of Asia, Africa and Central America (the peripheral countries, they are rather insultingly called, as opposed to the center ones of Europe). They were also alleged to be preparing for war against the socialist countries of the Eastern bloc. "Imperialism is fighting and preparing to fight everywhere," and Europe was falling under total domination of the United States.

The authors of this extraordinary pronunciamento drew attention to the implantation of missiles in Europe, and plans for Franco-German cooperation in a joint nuclear striking force. They also claimed that NATO was mounting a great counterinsurgency campaign (described as a counterrevolution) against Third World countries. To this end, they believed that a war economy was being established which would deprive millions of their jobs, as industry was "robotized" to ensure supreme power for the bourgeoisie.

In these supposed circumstances the terrorist groups were acting on behalf of the proletariat of the West European countries and the oppressed peoples of the periphery to aggravate the "crisis of the system." Their proclaimed revolutionary strategy was to deploy for attacks upon central imperialist projects to "bring about the destruction of imperialist structures, so as to conquer the ground upon which can develop the consciousness and the power of the proletariat."

Such phrases give the flavor of the confused, "small-c" communism of the new terrorists, and help to explain the kind of action they have been taking. Although it was only the Germans and the French who subscribed to the January statement, evidence—to which we shall draw attention later—has emerged that other like-minded European groups were also involved in their plans. The Belgian CCC has already been mentioned. But in addition to that, an Italian connection was apparent, in that Italians had been identified in a shoot-out as allies of Action Directe, and banknotes stolen in a French raid surfaced in a Milan safe house. Two years before the fusion of RAF and Action Directe, the French organization had allied itself with COLP, Communists for the Liberation of the Proletariat, and connections existed too with another Italian group called Prima Linea. There were indications too that a Portuguese group named Popular Forces of April 25th, which attacked NATO and West German targets in Portugal, was linked with the consortium of terror.

Further proof that the Euro-terrorists were ready to murder as well as to bomb in order to achieve their farfetched objectives came in June of 1985, when Action Directe struck again, though failed, in its attempt to murder General

Blandin, a senior officer at the defense ministry, connected with integration of the armed forces and the defense industry. This time the hit squad opened fire while the general's car was stopped at traffic lights on his way to work. Fortunately, the driver saw in his mirror an armed man running forward. He accelerated sharply, and zigzagged away at speed under fire. The general escaped unhurt.

Action Directe later took the unusual step of putting out a communiqué acknowledging the failure. It was due to an accumulation of "technical failings:" first, a machine carbine jammed, then the communications system went wrong, and there was no back-up hit man available. Such self-criticism rarely comes from a terrorist outfit, and this one displayed a rare degree of confidence in admitting failure.

The actual unit involved was named the Antonio Lo Muscio commando in honor of a Red Brigades terrorist shot dead by the carabinieri in 1977. It is one of the characteristics of the new alliance that they name hit squads after "historic" terrorists. The one who killed Herr Zimmermann was dubbed (in honor of an Irish terrorist) Patrick O'Hara—an IRA man who died in a hunger strike—and the assassins of General Audran called themselves the Elizabeth Van Dyke, after an RAF woman killed by West German police. It is the martyr system of nomenclature, and it was first used by the Red Army Faction. Although many of the outward trappings of that organizaiton and its language were still familiar to those who remembered its origins, the new-model RAF was a much tougher and more cohesive group.

10.

Reds Under
The Republic

Victories over terrorists soon fade as new leaders appear to take the place of fallen comrades. When the GSG 9 border guard commandos stormed the hijacked Lufthansa jet at Mogadishu and freed the hostages, there was a great feeling of relief in West Germany. It began to look as though the end of the affair was in sight, and the impression was heightened when the old terror chiefs in despair at the failure of their great effort killed themselves in prison. But less than a year after the euphoria felt in West Germany at the success of operations against the Red Army Faction, that movement had come to life again. It was being directed by Christian Klar, son of a Karlsruhe headmaster, who became involved in the politics of the violent left as a student of politics and philosophy at Heidelberg university, and joined the Siegfried Haag group. After apprenticeship in helping with terrorist infrastructure, he graduated to operations and was suspected of taking part in the Schleyer kidnap. By then a good-looking young man of 30, Klar was the only one of the surviving leaders with real charisma.

The first sign that yet more trouble was in store came when, together with Peter Stoll and Adelheid Schulz, posing as a film crew, he rented a helicopter and flew over the area between Heidelberg, Frankfurt and Wiesbaden, spying out the ground for the relaunch of a new assault upon U.S. imperialism, in the shape of U.S. forces in Europe. They were also seeking new recruits to go underground and to rebuild infrastructure for the next round, and working on plans to free those still in prison.

One group, under Knut Folkerts, Christoph Wackernagel and Gert Schneider, went to the Netherlands in 1977 to set up a branch of the antiimperialist "camp" there. Dutch antifascist groups lent a helping hand. In fact the West Germans were spreading into neighboring countries.

In June 1979 they tried to kill General Alexander Haig as he drove to SHAPE (Supreme Headquarters Allied Powers in Europe) headquarters in Belgium. This was the first sign of what RAF groups called the "new orientation," to concentrate less upon West German targets and more upon the "imperialists." They wanted to attack both the military installations of NATO forces and those of the U.S. contingent in Europe, as well as senior officers in command.

A number of survivors from the first generation of Red Army Faction people had not only taken refuge in France but were active there in planning new operations in conjunction with sympathetic non-Germans. They were also in touch with international terrorists. An interesting insight into the way of life of the terrorist expatriates was provided in May 1980 when French police raided an apartment in Left Bank Paris at 4, rue Flatters. It was a kind of terrorist hideout peopled by RAF and 2nd June movement women who stored in it their weapons, false papers and 1,000 rounds of ammunition. In the original raid the officers grabbed Sieglinde Hoffmann, an old Baader-Meinhof hand, and Ingrid Barabass, who had been involved in several actions. These had included the kidnapping in Vienna of the Austrian textile millionaire Walter Palmers with demands for a four million marks ransom, though she had later been acquitted by the Austrian court. After arresting these two, French police staked out the apartment, and the following day ambushed three more German women who also made use of this international nest of terrorists. It was another blow struck at the German groups when they were extradited for trial in the Federal Republic, but there were still plenty left to launch new operations.

In August 1981 it was the turn of U.S. Air Force headquarters at Ramstein to be attacked with terrorist bombs. Such raids need a great deal of preparation. Before each new series the RAF had to gather resources to rob banks in order to provide funds, and to get weapons and explosives. The death in a car crash of Juliane Plambeck revealed she had been told to prepare for a big operation by establishing safe houses and stealing eight cars. Ms. Plambeck, of the Inge Viett group, was a former student of philology known to male colleagues as "the erotic challenge cup trophy."

In September came a determined attempt to kill General Frederick J. Kroesen, U.S. commander in Europe, in a sophisticated ambush. For the first time the RAF made use of a Soviet-made rocket launcher, which had for years been a favorite weapon in armories from Belfast to Beirut—the RPG 7. It proved that they were reorganizing and equipping themselves with heavier weapons. The general's life was saved thanks to the skill of his driver, but also because the military limousine was armored. The timing of this attack was important, for it came 48 hours after a big anti-American demonstration in Berlin against a visit there by Alexander Haig, by then U.S. secretary of state. Pamphlets bearing his picture, and the caption "only 2.7 seconds too late," were handed out by demonstrators as a reminder that the former NATO supreme commander had himself almost been assassinated. The Kroesen attempt coincided with the "militant pacifist" European campaign against President Reagan for deploying U.S. nuclear weapons in NATO bases. It was a high-intensity effort in Germany, and the RAF was trying to build up support for its activities among the fringe radicals, so zealously campaigning against nuclear weapons, especially Western ones. It is likely that they hoped to win recruits in such a milieu.

In such well-planned enterprises German antiterrorist experts suspected the leadership of one of the old first-wave executives of the movement, Inge Viett. She had learned her trade in action with the 2nd June movement, of which she became the boss. While waiting trial on charges connected with the murder of a judge, she broke out of the Moabit prison in West Berlin in 1976, but two years later she returned there in an armed raid to free a fellow terrorist. After that she crossed the border into France and began establishing the first firm links with Action Directe, the Gallic equivalent of the RAF. There can be little doubt that this woman has played an important part, both in reactivating the RAF and also in creating the alliance of European new terrorists. After the arrest of her only real rival to the title, Christian Klar, and his women associates Brigitte Monhaupt and Adelheid Schulz, she became, at the age of 41, the most significant of the terror bosses in the mid 1980s.

Klar's arrest in October 1982 following attacks on U.S.

military establishments marked a notable success for the
security forces. It came about when people out looking for
mushrooms in the woods around Gravenbuch, not far from
Frankfurt, noticed some odd goings-on and signs of digging,
which they reported to the police.

The BKA federal investigation center was alerted, and they
called upon the services of GSG 9, the antiterrorist squad.
That year, command of the unit had passed to Colonel Uwe
Dee, a rangy and lean officer, known to his friends as "Easy"
Dee. He is a descendant of a Scottish Protestant family that
emigrated to Prussia in the eighteenth century.

Colonel Dee told the authors about the difficulties of the
operation he commanded. A five-man team was placed in the
woods and dug themselves into heavily camouflaged
positions. Their discomfort in the autumn chill was great. "At
first, we worked on 12 hour turns," said the colonel, "but as it
got colder and began snowing, I cut the duty spell down to 8
then 4 hours. There seemed to be a lot of people around in the
forest, and passers-by kept approaching the men as they lay
hidden around the terrorist cache, asking what they were
doing there. I began to think that this activity must have
given our presence away to the terrorists." There was even
discussion after five days of vigil about whether it was
worthwhile to continue. Eventually GSG 9 decided to give it
just one more day.

"Then, on the sixth day, two people appeared, crawling
through the undergrowth to their hide. They had heads
down, and never saw us until they were jumped."

The two were top women on the wanted list, Brigitte
Monhaupt and Adelheid Schultz (who was later sentenced to
life imprisonment). Two years earlier Adelheid Schultz had a
narrow escape when the car she was driving crashed, killing
her friend Juliane Plambeck. What cheered the security men
was the discovery that the hide was a terrorist depot, in the
words of a federal police officer, "a veritable RAF logistics
base." The hideout was full of documents, for it is a fault of
RAF administration that it seems to be as bureaucratic as do
many other German organizations. There were boxes full of
explosives and firearms, and also forged military passes,
registration papers for stolen cars and reports from spies
watching both U.S. military bases and the movements of
German politicians. The notes were written in code, but
police cryptologists succeeded in cracking it. Detailed maps
of other such caches let to the discovery of no less than 14 un-

derground depots of arms, explosives and documents, and also enabled police to set an ambush for Christian Klar.

Only five days later, he was lured to another supply dump in pinewoods near Hamburg. Police seized him as, dressed in a blue jogging suit, he began digging up a money-box containing about $4,500 worth of stolen Deutschmarks. He was pale, and, depressed over the arrest of his long-term girlfriend, Adelheid Schultz, he surrendered without resistance. He might even have been thinking about using the money to flee the country. Although the federal prosecutor, Kurt Rebmann, described this and the other recent arrests as a "catastrophic blow" to the RAF, both he and other leaders of the campaign against terror were well aware that others still survived in the underground to carry on the struggle.

Inge Viett had taken refuge in France, and lived in Paris from 1980 to 1982. After a short stay in Germany at this critical moment in the fortunes of the RAF, she crossed the border and spent another year at Vincennes, in the suburbs of the French capital. French police, by that time working in closer collaboration with their colleagues in the Federal Republic, were keeping watch over German activity, most of it directed by the women who were taking over the German movement. There was also clear evidence of their getting together with French radicals. In fact the way was already open for the collaboration of European groups which was the central feature of terrorism in the mid-1980s.

In West Germany itself another new breed of revolutionaries was becoming active. They called themselves Revolutionary Cells (*Revolutionäre Zellen*), often known as Red Cells. This was a movement which began in 1973 with just one cell, but which even by 1976 had spread all over Germany. Revolutionary Cells considered themselves to be a part of the armed left, urban guerrillas, and they were equally intent on disrupting the social order. Antiimperialist and anti-Zionist, like the Red Army Faction, they concentrated on organizations they considered were connected with defense industries—genetic and biological research, computers and electronics. The cells also tried to exploit social and industrial disputes in order to win public sympathy and support.

In 1985 they carried out 200 attacks, not all of which succeeded. It was estimated by German security services in 1985 that there are five active groups, each with between three and five members. Mystery still surrounds their organization, though it is believed that to some extent membership overlaps with that of the more hard-nosed terror groups. What seems probable is that the Revolutionary Cells provide a training ground for some of those who later graduate through violent exploits to become full-fledged agents of terror.

The cells are very adaptable, and their structure is extremely difficult to penetrate, because most of the members are inconspicuous, in that they live normally and have regular jobs. They dress correctly, and are sometimes known as "day-off terrorists," or part-time terrorists. Ties between the different cells remain fairly loose, so that individual cells have great liberty of action.

Even when security men managed to arrest some cell members they resolutely refused under interrogation to reveal anything about their cell structure. But in 1984, BKA had a lucky break when a Red Cell man named Feiling blew himself up with his own bomb. Both his legs were amputated. He agreed to talk about the organization of which he was a member. Despite that, and the fact that surveillance was carried out on arrested suspects who were later released, it was still almost impossible to name names. "We are faced with a blank sheet," said Kriminalrat (Superintendent) Werner Loew, head of TE 2, the BKA control intelligence unit of the antiterrorist division, known by its German acronym TE. He runs a team of 23 out of an antiterrorist staff of 300 at headquarters, a well-protected bureaucracy building on a wooded hill above the old spa town of Wiesbaden.

"There may be an ideological brain somewhere for they have been putting out various publications. The only major declaration of position came in one of these, entitled 'Revolutionary Anger.' But whether there are 'leaders' in the classic sense, or not, we just do not know. Certainly we have no names."

Side by side with the Revolutionary Cells there developed what is literally a sister movement known as Red Zora—in fact, an autonomous women's terrorist movement. Working in fully compartmented cells, they attack property and buildings rather than people, and tend to specialize in targets where they claim that work to the disadvantage of women is carried on. For example, in April 1985, they made an unsuccessful explosives attack on the Heidelberg Institute then under construction, on the grounds that it was planned to do research into human genetics there.

Members of Red Zora give the impression that they are against operations which cause death and human suffering. Nonetheless, they shot dead Herr Heinz Karry, the 61-year-old Hesse minister of the interior, as he lay asleep on May 11, 1981. Afterwards they issued a communiqué declaring that they had not intended to hurt him. Herr Karry made many enemies with his plans to extend Frankfurt airport, to build a plant for processing nuclear waste and to build new road networks.

Red Zora cells are differently structured from Revolutionary Cells, and the organization is very personal. They attack bodies concerned with issues attracting public attention, such as the controversy in West Germany about whether or not speed limits should be imposed upon drivers on the autobahn.

A similar tendency to choose newsworthy targets for bomb attacks could be seen in Revolutionary Cells actions when they attacked a miners' trade union headquarters and the offices of a coal merchant in the Ruhr. This, they said, was in revenge for the export of coal to Britain during the prolonged miner's strike of 1984. During that industrial conflict there had already been explosive and incendiary bomb assaults in Hamburg and the Ruhr to express revolutionary support for British miners. The West German coal industry was accused of using the misfortunes of British miners to unload its surplus stocks of coal. In fact, the cells were turning their attention to industrial troubles in order to try to attract the working class to their revolutionary cause. They began specializing in the bombing of industrial concerns, while the RAF stuck to its offensive against military installations. The campaign of the new revolutionaries took a nasty turn with the use of bombs made from lengths of pipe placed in a bookstore. Condemning what he described as a "new form of terrorism," Wighard Hardtl, an interior ministry spokesman, said, "Innocent bystanders are the target now."

Despite that, West German terrorists were winning a measure of encouragement. In singularly ill-timed letters, the Greens, the German left-inclined ecological party, thought fit to send "cordial greetings" to Christian Klar and his imprisoned comrades. Ministers described such messages as "monstrous," but the Greens lamely defended their action by claiming that they had meant to invite the terrorists to renounce their violent methods. The Greens have consistently taken a sympathetic attitude towards the terrorists. During the prison hunger strike their members in parliament criticized conditions in prisons where RAF leaders were incarcerated, and forced a vote ensuring that hunger strikers would only be force-fed if they were too weak to signify their own intentions.

To confuse the German terrorist scene further, there have come into existence what antiterrorist specialists call "resonant cells," so called because although they put out slogans and declarations in the same style as Revolutionary Cells, it is not certain that they are authentic terrorists. They give the impression that they have the same aims and structure, but they don't seem quite authentic. This sets a puzzle for security officers, who can never be quite certain whether such cells will in fact develop actions which they claim they are preparing.

Together with both the Revolutionary Cells and the RAF itself, the resonant cells showed signs in mid-1985 of renewed concentration in an attempt to exploit social conditions in order to woo the workers whose support they so strongly desire. Werner Loew at BKA pinpointed the trend:

> They have turned to the workers and the proletariat as a subject. For example, they are trying to exploit the problems of unemployment at enterprises like Volkswagen. If that happens, and attacks begin on the leaders of industry in general, we have told them that we cannot provide protection for everybody. We shall publish information and make it available to industrial organizations and to the local police. Prevention is the best defense and we shall encourage industry to be aware of the danger and to take their own precautions.

Documents discovered in a raid on an RAF safe house in Frankfurt demonstrated the scope of their plans for disruption. It came about because an old lady reported that she had seen a terrorist—whom she recognized from wanted notices—entering the apartment. Police investigated, and when they approached they came under fire. The odd thing was that the people grabbed were not those that the old lady thought she had spotted, but for all that she knew a terrorist when she saw one. Inside the building police found and examined 4,000 pages of papers. There were piles of clippings and papers and magazines, including technical defense journals. Among them was a hit list consisting of hundreds of names (including that of Ernst Zimmermann, who was murdered later) and bomb targets, such as the NATO officers' school at Oberammergau, the scene of an attack in December 1984.

What kind of people are the new terrorists? That is the question constantly asked, and even for experienced security experts in Europe it is not one easy to answer. Not even the copious biographical records of arrested or wanted wrongdoers kept by BKA, the German federal police headquarters, and by the public prosecutor's office in Karlsruhe can provide a complete picture.

What does emerge is that they live in small groups, dominated by women members, where much time is given over to endless discussions intended to "politicize" incoming recruits. They are to be found now in all parts of Germany, usually in the big cities. In a way the groups are headless, which makes it difficult to identify leaders. The underground living groups are usually 20 or so strong, and apparently spend a good deal of talk time discussing targets and how to attack them, and what their doctrinal value is.

New terrorists may be less fanatical but seem to be sharper and more skillful. The fresh wave of RAF people are less highly educated than most of the original Baader-Meinhof crowd: it is no longer true that they are predominantly middle-class students. As the number of sociology students declines, the proportion of non-university people increases. Among the practitioners of trades now represented are carpenters, an electrical engineer, an electrical worker, a wood-carver, school help, a hospital worker, a laborer, an office boy and—perhaps least likely of all—two salesclerks. They are, of course, mostly young people in their early twenties, though some of the survivors from an earlier age of violence are now into their forties. It would be a mistake to suppose that they are always efficient in action. Bombs fail to explode, and sometimes detonate too soon, blowing up those who are constructing them.

Tactics used have been passed on to the new RAF and its European equivalent movements from the pioneers who launched urban guerrilla warfare, still clutching their copies of the famous mini-manual written by Carlos Marighella. They may be influenced, on the copycat principle, by outside terror actions practiced in the Middle East, and they may be tempted by the Shi'ite big-bang terror. But they are realist enough to try only what they know they can do. Never since the Mogadishu act of air piracy which failed have they tried hijacking and kidnapping. Such operations need complicated logistics, special arms, many supporters, hideouts and so on. They are difficult to organize for groups like the RAF, groups that unlike their Islamic counterparts, are under constant pressure.

True to the traditions of terrorist warfare, the new Europeans only try a spectacular attack when they believe that they can use the advantage of surprise. When Western heads of state and prime ministers met in Bonn for an economic summit in the early summer of 1985 they presented a broad and tempting target. But great precautions were taken to protect President Reagan and his friends, so the terrorists did not attempt any action in Bonn. To mark the occasion they caused an explosion in a French factory in Cologne which supplies electronics to the German army; they planted 55 lbs. of explosives which failed to explode at a military procurement office in Koblenz; and an unfortunate U.S. army sergeant was injured when his car blew up in West Berlin. Such occasions reveal something of the scope of routine action available to the terrorist alliance in between major events.

The cautious assessment of the BKA is summed up by Werner Loew in Wiesbaden:

> Ever since the Zimmermann affair we have been prepared for the worst. It is clear that the RAF is prepared to mount military-style attacks and to kill people. But it is not easy to forecast what is going to happen. The RAF are cautious, susceptible to pressure and they like to make careful preparation before attacking a particular target.

In 1982 there were 600 bombings and firebombings, mostly directed at private-enterprise establishments. Banks were attacked as symbols of capitalism, and warehouses as the temples of consumerism.

But the hard-core RAF was becoming more brutal as it went for the nerve centers of the state and of the NATO alliance. In August 1985 a joint message from RAF and their French ally Action Directe proudly announced that they were responsible for blasting a car bomb at Rhein-Main, the U.S. base near Frankfurt, killing two and injuring 16. It was the seventh such claim of the year, but the first one claimed as a joint field operation. For the first time, too, they named the attackers in honor of an American, calling the attack team the "George Jackson Commando" after a Black Panther killed in 1971.

This time an even more ominous circumstance came to light. The joint terror groups forwarded to the Reuters office in Frankfurt with their 'communiqué' the military ID card of

Edward Pimental, an American serviceman whose body had been found in the woods. He had been shot dead after leaving a disco with a man and a woman only a few hours before the bomb blast. The fact that for the first time RAF/AD had killed a man to get his pass, so that they could enter a U.S. base, marked the beginning of an even uglier phase in their campaign. BKA warned that it was not an isolated incident, and that more similar attacks "of a different quality" might be expected.

Even before that, Ministry of the Interior figures for the first half of 1985 had recorded 160 attacks, of which 111 were firebombs and 39 explosive.

11.

Target
Nato

The public boast that the big bomb attack was the combined work of the Red Army Faction and of Action Directe is a clear indication of the importance which the German terrorists attach to the idea of the antiimperialist front. They see that front as their achievement and as proof that there really is an international red revolutionary army in action, no matter that the notion was originally borrowed from eccentric Japanese mystics who first created the Japanese Red Army in 1969. The concept of a "front" in Western Europe was originally put forward by Renato Curcio, the "historic" leader of Italian Red Brigades, who dreamed of the formation in Europe of national revolutionary armed forces fighting a great war against the massed bourgeoisie.

It is one of the characteristics of terrorist bands (which they also share with guerrilla forces) that they see themselves as much grander institutions than they really are. The ambition of every guerrilla leader, be he urban or rural, is to place himself at the head of a formidable military force. Everyone of them carries in his pack, if not a field marshal's baton, at least a field marshal's military ambition. For this reason the Irish nationalist formation calls itself the Irish Republican Army, and its boss styles himself "Chief of Staff," though in fact there is no general staff, and the "Brigades" he controls are just handfuls of terrorists. In the same way the Palestine

Liberation Organization was never more satisfied with itself than when it set up in Lebanon a "regular" army, and equipped it with uniforms, tanks and heavy artillery. It is in this way that irregular forces become a parody of the regular armies which oppose them.

Another curiosity of this form of warfare is that as the terrorists and guerrillas build their institutional ego with fine titles and bigger and better guns, so the regular armies resort to guerrilla and counterterrorist tactics to fight more effectively against them. Units like the British Special Air Service and the American Delta force seek their inspiration by deformalizing themselves as army units. Badges of rank become less conspicuous; tactics more flexible. They operate in units which resemble the cell system adopted by the terrorists. *Ruses de guerre* transform themselves into dirty tricks.

The truth about European urban guerrillas, for all their communiqués announcing bomb and bullet victories and their pronunciamentos of political doctrine, is that they have not succeeded yet in building a true front with international cooperation. Dangerous and disquieting though the joint German-French terrorist campaign may become, it is at present a rather homemade effort to draw public attention, a collaboration among a comparatively small number of individuals and underground groups. In the opinion of Reinhard Rupprecht, *Ministerialdirigent* at the Bonn ministry of the interior and a leading expert in terrorist strategy, what they lack at the moment is a genuine big international cause to exploit in order to build their strength, and to draw in a mass of recruits from their sympathizers. The old Baader-Meinhof and similar European movements drew their support from general hostility to the war in Vietnam and disquiet about the Shah of Iran. The best hope of moral reinforcement for their successors in 1985 was offered by growing indignation over apartheid in South Africa, as violence spread through that country. Here at last was a full-scale international drama whose terms of reference fitted in neatly with the Marxist interpretation of history favored by the European terrorist groups. America, the European Community and the Third World countries all condemn the South African government for its policies of oppression against the blacks. Here then is the raw material of genuine political outcry in the liberal states, ready to be processed by the new terrorists to justify their war upon society in the

West, whose governments they can accuse of a hypocritical attitude towards South Africa, their capitalist ally. To draw attention to the danger of perfectly proper and reasonable expressions of public opinion being subverted by terrorists is in no way to condone the kind of fierce racism practiced in South Africa, or to condemn people who abhor it.

A key factor was that by mid-1985 anti-South African demonstrations, both in the United States and in Europe, were beginning to attract the big battalions of young idealists, and their camp followers of entertainment stars, who in turn attract less desirable elements. Activists were at work retooling the protest industry on many an American campus. In West Germany, where such demonstrators can easily turn nasty, an anti-apartheid march in Frankfurt degenerated into public disorder, when a crowd of 2,000 began smashing the windows of banks to indicate their anger at German investment in South Africa.

Shareholders had already campaigned to pressure companies in which they had holdings to withdraw from South African business. Herr Rupprecht at the Bonn Interior Ministry pointed out that the West German newspapers, radio and TV stations were publishing lists of German companies with business interests in South Africa. That is precisely the kind of information which finds its way into the dossiers of the terrorist alliance. It is a short step from there for those same terrorist organizations to include company premises on the hit list for their bombings. Of course, those who so bitterly condemn the wickedness of South Africa might think that such institutions deserved to be attacked. The conventional liberal attitude is to declare: "Of course we do not approve of violence, but after all it is understandable that these young people are frustrated when governments refuse to listen to them. We sympathize with their indignation." If the Red Army Faction is willing to bomb a coal merchant for selling his product to Britain during a miner's strike there, why should it not bomb a company selling equipment to South Africa, which to their way of thinking might aid the oppression of blacks?

Another alarming possibility for the future is that the European alliance may develop links with the Shi'ite holy-war terrorism of the Middle East. In the 1960s and 1970s strong bonds developed between the Palestinian groups and the Europeans active at that time. They came to know each other on terrorist-training courses in the camps of Lebanon and other Arab countries, and indeed began working together. Inge Viett, the German lady so active, was a graduate of Lebanon and Aden. With many other West Germans she fought side by side in the terror war with her friend Carlos and the PFPL. It was almost, as one French antiterrorist expert has put it, like army experience, where officers on exchange courses develop friendships which last a lifetime as they keep meeting unexpectedly in changing circumstances. So far there has been little sign of similar relationships developing among the new wave of terrorists with the Shi'ites, though there is no doubt that international terrorists do have a tendency to come together. The poor relations are always attracted to the richer, better-equipped ones, who have all the benefits of state resources and secure training and organizing facilities provided for them. It must not be forgotten that George Habash, the present leader of PFLP, is still active in Lebanon, where he has his strong con- nections with the new men of Islamic Jihad.

For the time being the new Europeans have to make do with their own resources, paid for with money from raids and hold-ups, and on weapons bought illegally or stolen. The RAF proved most adept at self-supply. They were better organized, and with their dedicated, predominantly female leadership—women are often more persistent than men—they had little difficulty in imposing their will upon French urban guerrillas, who in the early stages were never very effective.

Terrorism of the Baader-Meinhof pattern was slow to develop in France. The reason was that until the mid-1960s the French were much more inward-looking, through the circumstances of painful decolonialization in North Africa. French affairs were dominated by the long-drawn-out and complicated war in Algeria. Both the war of independence and General de Gaulle's brutal solution to it brought waves of terrorism to metropolitan France, but it was of a different kind and quality. First, the Algerian National Liberation Front began its campaign of bombing and assassination. Then counterterrorists of the Secret Army, the OAS—an un- holy alliance of French settlers and rebellious right-wing army officers—set upon Algerians and anyone suspected of supporting them. It was a time of *coups d'état*, high drama and alarms, which left little space for activity by Marxist- anarchist groups of the kind already forming in Germany and Italy.

When the mass student protests of the 1960s hit France they did so with a bang rather than a whimper. Beginning on the campuses of the United States, and then in West Berlin, they spread throughout Europe. When the students of France began going critical in the spring of 1968, it was not long before they converted protest into revolution, and turned the boulevards of Paris into a battlefield of barricades. University buildings were "occupied," to use the jargon of the time, and the new generation fought it out with riot squads under clouds of tear gas. The conflict almost brought down the regime of the great General de Gaulle, who at one critical stage helicoptered away to stay with the French army in West Germany.

It was not until all those troubles had subsided that France began to get the taste of a different kind of action by the new-style terror movements. Like London, Paris became by extension a killing-ground of the Arab-Israeli conflict. The French capital also began suffering from the assault by nationalist territorial terrorist groups, Breton and Corsican.

The first sign that doctrinal terrorism might manifest itself in France, as it had done in neighboring Germany and Italy, came with the emergence in 1977 of a group named NAPAP (*Noyaux armés pour l'Autonomie populaire*), led by a young man called Frederic Orbiach. Its declared aim was "to overthrow a rotten society and build a new one," and according to the French police it began to do this by murdering Zentano Araya, Bolivian ambassador to Paris, because he was implicated in the killing of the revolutionary hero Ché Guevara. The group also murdered a night watchman at the Renault car factory, claiming that he was responsible for the death of a Maoist worker during a demonstration there.

More was to be heard later of Orbiach. His armed bands were merged in a new movement known as Action Directe which had its baptism of *firing* in September 1979, when its members sprayed the French Ministry of Labour with a burst of machine-gun fire. Such tactics were the specialty of AD's first round of activity. In March 1980 a man and woman opened fire with machine pistols on the façade of the Ministry of Co-operation, and there were other similar attacks. Such tactics were the speciality of AD's first round of activity.

Action Directe seems to have sprung to life under local leaders more or less spontaneously, and its cells spread in rather the same way as those of the Revolutionary Cells in West Germany. By the time that it made its first public appearance, it was thought to consist of a hard core of 40 members, around whom floated a few hundred supporters. Inevitably their money came from hold-ups, euphemistically called "proletarian expropriation." They produced a journal called *L'Internationale*, which was a kind of new magazine about terrorist activities worldwide, printed in Meaux and distributed through an anarchist bookshop in Paris.

The man who assumed control was Jean-Marc Rouillan, a 32-year-old from Toulouse in southwest France, with a passion for the clandestine life, and for action in what he called his antiimperialist war. Even as an adolescent be began his career working (under the code name "Sebas") with an anarchist anti-Franco group, the Movement for the Liberation of Iberia. In 1973 he was with Puig Antich, the Spanish guerrilla leader, when they came under fire from Civil Guards in Barcelona. Rouillan managed to escape, but Antich was taken and condemned to death. Back home in France, Jean-Marc Rouillan took part in the actions of GARI (*Groups d'action revolutionnaire internationaliste*), whose aim was to pressure Europe into action against the fascist regime in Spain. GARI mounted a violent campaign in vain attempts to save Antich from death by garrotting.

In December 1974 Rouillan was arrested in Paris, using a false identity and with weapons concealed in his car. During the two and a half years which he spent in prison he moved towards revolutionary communism. At the time that he was released in 1977, NAPAP was still in action, though it was showing more interest in Italy than in Spain, where the Franco regime was being dismantled. Action Directe, of which Rouillan became boss, was born of remnants of GARI and of NAPAP, both of which had strong connections with the Italians who were forming the Red Brigades. It was Rouillan who brought them together for his antiimperialist war. In the process he met and became attached to a woman supporter, Nathalie Menigon, a slim Parisian girl from a working-class family who had worked in a bank. The terrorist group which they jointly controlled launched its first symbolic operations by machine-gunning the façades of public buildings.

In one of these attacks on the Ministry of Overseas Cooperation Nathalie Menigon, then 28, proved herself cool under fire. After she had emptied a 30-round clip from her machine carbine, and while police guards fought back, she calmly reloaded and went on firing.

An even more formidable figure in the newly active group

was Régis Schleicher, also 28, and known (because of his German-sounding name) as "Klaus." Police reports described him as "an intellectual killer" given to quoting bits from Nietzsche. Son of a Christian trade-union leader, he had never worked, and devoted all his effort to the clandestine life and politics. Schleicher greatly admired the Italian groups, which through him brought their influence to bear on the French terrorists.

At this stage all that AD could claim to have achieved was a score of minor attacks which had made little enough impact. That is why the French police were not inclined to take the emergence of this local terror group too seriously. Police intelligence networks provided detailed knowledge about the organization and its members, and they had no difficulty in penetrating the cells of young enthusiasts involved at that time. To discover more about the workings of French terrorists, French police made use of a Lebanese informer named Gabriel Chahine, who passed for a supporter of Action Directe. Eventually they manipulated him to lure into a police trap both Rouillan and his mistress, Nathalie Menigon. The bait for this ambush was Carlos, the Latin-American star of the international terrorist milieu. Chahine was coached to tell his terrorist friends that Carlos was planning to blow up the Aswan Dam in Egypt, and that he wanted to consult with Rouillan and ask his help.

To the young French terrorist this was an irresistible offer, proving that he was now recognized by one of the world's most famous terrorists. He gladly accepted a rendezvous at a Paris apartment in the rue Pergolese. He arrived with his girlfriend to be greeted, not by the famous man himself, but by a posse of armed police. Nathalie Menigon was with him, and opened fire with a handgun, but was overpowered. As an impotent act of revenge Rouillan's gang machine-gunned the outside of the Ecole de Guerre in Paris two days later. Before long a gunman shot and killed the unfortunate Gabriel Chahine who had betrayed the leader.

Rouillan did not stay for long in prison. Before he could even be brought to trial elections had taken place in France, and the socialist politician Francois Mitterrand became president of the republic. Among his election promises was one that he would put an end to Corsican separatist terrorism. He would do this the nice way, through making political concessions to reasonable people. As a gesture of goodwill he abolished the state security court which had dealt with political subversion, and he reduced the amount of time police might hold a prisoner without charging him from six to three days. In 1981 the new president declared a general amnesty for terrorists under arrest, which was really meant as a gesture of goodwill towards the Corsican separatists. But it applied also to the two leaders and 25 other members of Action Directe then in detention. In the words of Captain Barril, an antiterrorist officer in the Gendarmerie, "It was a time of general demobilization in our teams."

For a time there was a sort of truce, at least so far as the separatists were concerned, but soon they decided that after all there was little chance that they would get everything they wanted, and resumed their campaigns. Meanwhile, the stage in France was left free for outside international terrorists like Carlos and Abu Nidal, who were dubbed the "superstars of violence," to continue their own vendettas on French territory.

In the period of relative calm the newly freed Rouillan and Nathalie Menigon went underground again and began the task of reorganizing their movement and preparing new actions. They published at this time wordy tracts entitled *Towards a Communist Project* and *On American Imperialism* which gave clues about their intentions. Already AD had strong connections with COLP, and in Belgium, the traditional center for the illegal arms trade. It is now known that they were also getting help there from the nascent CCC, the so-called Belgian fighting communist cells (*cellules communistes combattantes*), which later became the auxiliaries of the Franco-German front. Quietly and methodically, they began preparing for fresh action. Their speciality during this period was bank robbery. Between 1982 and 1984 they carried out 40 or so hold-ups. These raids not only helped to fill their war chest; they also served as fieldcraft exercises for new terrorists serving their apprenticeship. They did not hesitate to fire on the police when disturbed, but did not use murder as a deliberate tactic. The favorite weapon was a Colt .45; they chose, as another trademark, to use stolen Renault 20 cars. Quite a number of their recruits came from Parisian squats. Two squat leaders, the brothers Halfen—Claude and Nicholas—later captured by the police were the sons of a militant communist.

Action Directe started again in earnest in summer of 1982 with a number of anti-American attacks, timed to coincide with President Reagan's visit to Versailles for a summit conference. Even then it was clear that the French terrorists were firmly under the influence of the German RAF missionaries in France whose doctrinal aim was to hit American imperialists and Zionists. Midsummer terrorist raids by a variety of international groups that year, culminating in attacks on Jewish targets in Paris, including a synagogue and a well-known Jewish restaurant, produced the most serious consequences. President Mitterrand himself attended a memorial service for the victims. Although Action Directe denied responsibility for attacking the restaurant, and even condemned it, Mitterrand's patience with the terrorists in general was exhausted.

On August 18, 1982 Action Directe was declared a banned organization. As an act of defiance the terrorists marked the occasion by making a bomb attack at the offices of Minute, a right-wing weekly magazine. Rouillan fled to Italy, and then made his way to Belgium.

President Mitterrand spoke of the need to reorganize in face of the threat, and affirmed "the will to defeat terrorism wherever it appears, and to track it to the very roots." He appointed Joseph Franceschi secretary of state in charge of public security. A special group of gendarmes to ensure protection for the president, the GSPR, came into being, and there was also a high-level consultative body, UCLAT (*Unité de coordination de la lutte anti-terroriste*). As frequently turns out with such reorganization, there were more acronyms than actions.

Chef d'Escadron Prouteau of the Gendarmerie Nationale was put in command of a special unit at the presidential Elysée palace, charged with antiterrorist coordination, intelligence and action. As a captain, Christian Prouteau had for several years commanded GIGN, the gendarmerie intervention unit, formed and specially trained for hostage-release and antiterrorist duties, after the Munich Olympic games massacre alerted the governments of Western Europe to the scale of the new menace.

In style and composition GIGN was similar to the British SAS and the West German GSG 9, though despite several successes it had never been called upon for an operation requiring great panache of the kind carried out by those units. It was undoubtedly a useful move to create the unit and give it the advantage of presidential prestige, but it was nonetheless a sign of disarray. President Mitterrand had chosen the gendarmes because he did not trust his police and intelligence services, many of which were hostile to any form of socialist government. The French have always been at a disadvantage in the fight against terrorism because of the multiplicity of rival, even warring, police forces in the republic.

There has always been animosity between the national police and the Gendarmerie Nationale, which belongs to the Ministry of Defense and is proud to proclaim itself the oldest regiment in the French army, with a long and honorable tradition of service in both military and police work. The force is less political than the police. Furthermore, the police are divided into a number of different units, all involved in antiterrorist work. The police Judiciaire, the criminal investigation branch, have a hand in it, together with the 6th Section, an offshoot which specializes in arms-traffic investigation. In addition, there are two special forces, the RG, *Renseignements generaux*, with specifically political responsibilities, and the DST, *Direction de la surveillance du territoire*, responsible for anti-espionage and subversive activities. Even on top of all those, France has special air and frontier police units. To make matters more complicated still, various forces have over the years set up their own intervention squads, rather like American SWAT teams. All these varied sections and units are controlled by the Ministry of the Interior, ever watchful for interference in its affairs by Ministry of Defense gendarmes.

Defense also has charge of the DGSE, *Direction generale de securitie exterieure*—French secret intelligence service—and of military security, DPSD, *Direction de la protection et de la securité de la defense*. In such a jungle of envious and backbiting state organs it is not surprising that the French effort against terrorists, both local and international, has not been entirely successful. A report by French senators commenting on inter-service conflict maintained: "It is significant to note that when the DST needs information, either on foreign terrorism, or about support given to terrorists outside our frontiers, it is more willing to seek it from certain foreign services than from colleagues in the DGSE."

In his book *Missions très spéciales*, the gossipy Captain Barril described security conferences of different groups at the Elysée palace as being "like a liar poker session." Although the Captain is a man with many axes to grind, he did serve as number two in the special antiterrorist force of gendarmes, and must be taken seriously when he declares: "Terrorists in France are so much at ease that even our own French ones do not bother to flee the country."

He should know, for he was called upon to make contact with Jean-Marc Rouillan after the terrorist leader had been interviewed in October 1982 by the newspaper *Le Matin de Paris*, declaring, "When I learned from the press that I was wanted, it was agreed that I should surrender, but we soon learned that the state would not agree to a surrender. Police surrounded the office of the *juge d'instruction* to prevent me entering freely . . . In these circumstances I thought it better to wait."

Barril met the journalist Jacques Bacelon, and asked to be put in touch with Rouillan, then went to see his lawyer. Arrangements were made for a meeting, but first Rouillan demanded, and got, a letter signed by Christian Prouteau on Elysée notepaper as a guarantee of his safety. Subsequently the letters were leaked to *Le Canard enchaîné*, the Parisian satirical weekly; a general outcry followed.

It had been an error of judgment to free the AD leaders in the first place; now it became obvious that the error had been compounded by using Captain Barril from the presidential unit to try to negotiate a sort of gentleman's agreement with terrorists. This is an absurd concept, for such people will not and cannot accept the rules of democratic society. They are prisoners of their overwhelming desire to achieve power, and to display their ability to destabilize the liberal state. Terrorist philosophy may be summed up as "I kill, therefore I exist." Once he negotiates, the terrorist is nothing.

President Mitterrand learned the lesson the hard way. Other terrorist problems also weighed upon him. They were largely the result of the historic commitment of France to belief in the principle of the right of asylum (dating from the French Revolution of 1789) to those who are politically persecuted in their own countries. The trouble is that in recent years foreign terrorists from neighboring countries have taken advantage of this worthy concept to hide in France—not from political persecution, but from retribution for their terrorist deeds. Thousands of Italians from the Red Brigades and similar movements, thousands more Basque activists of the ETA (Basque Homeland and Liberty) separatist group, settled in France and continued their violent political activities there. It was not until 1984 that the

French government finally acceded to constant reproachful requests from the Spanish government and agreed to extradite three wanted Basque terrorist leaders.

The same reluctance to harm the proud image of France as a *pays d'asile* affected the Italian dilemma. President Mitterrand affirmed that he would not willingly allow extradition of suspected terrorists, "if they were willing to renounce violent acts in return for asylum." No fewer than 120 applications for extradition had been made by the Italian government. So far as Italy was concerned, the trouble was that although numbers of those who fled did indeed renounce their former ways, many expatriate terrorists simply used French sanctuary to carry on their transborder activities. Giovanni Spadolini, Italian defense minister, reproached France for "sheltering a terrorist multinational."

Furthermore, Italians from Prima Linea and COLP merged and cooperated with French urban guerrillas of Action Directe and taught them the tricks of the trade, learned through experience. In the early days of native terrorism, France had been fortunate in that Action Directe leaders were by no means top-class, and organization was poor. But under the influence of experienced outsiders they got better at it, and imposed a coherent organization in the big cities.

They set up a vertical structure with a military front responsible for all urban guerrilla actions; a logistic front provided weapons, false papers, money and safe houses, and even what is was called a prison front, on the German model, to ensure continued relations with captured comrades, usually by way of friendly lawyers. Of course, it must never be forgotten when considering terrorist organizations that their structure sounds much more impressive than is justified by the relatively small number of people involved. They always think big. One of the theoreticians of the French outfit is Eric Moreau, son of a police inspector, who has harangued courts with abstract political lectures derived from the Italian theoretician of the *autonomes*, Professor Antonio Negri, arrested in Italy charged with organizing a terrorist network and released from custody after being elected to parliament as a fringe candidate. He was among those who took refuge in France.

While AD was in its regrouping phase in 1983 it had its setbacks. Police intervened in one of their bank raids and shot dead an Italian collaborator called Ciro Rizatto, a COLP man. A further indication of Italian involvement was the arrest in Paris of Vicenzo Spano. The bloodiest incident was the killing of two police officers in central Paris. The terrorists had been trailed by a three-man plainclothes police patrol after Régis Schleicher emerged from a safe house under surveillance, in company with Mohand Hamami, an Algerian, and Nicholas Halfen (known as 'Nic the Cap'). Two Italians from Prima Linea, Gloria Argano and Franco Fiorina, were also with them. Challenged by the police, they opened fire before making their escape.

When he was arrested some time later, Schleicher became "leader" of Direct Action prisoners and symbol of the movement. Mohand Hamami, the Algerian Maoist in this oddly assorted band, had been arrested in 1980 charged with three hold-ups and acquitted, though at his trial he justified the acts committed.

Among other imprisoned AD leaders was Frédéric Orbiach, who in 1980 had bombed the Paris office of West German railways as an act of solidarity with RAF and "to reforge memories of the combat of the German proletariat, lost in the Nazi period, and through the imposition of the American model." He no longer supports Action Directe, having decided to concentrate on the "anti-Zionist struggle" while reading Palestinian literature in prison. Despite that, in April 1983 his friends raided the museum of the Legion of Honor in an effort to demand his release.

With so many of the original members out of play, it was the Germans and the Italians who forced Action Directe and its new people into a harder mold and prepared it for the joint campaign which began in the summer of 1984. By that time Jean-Marc Rouillan and Nathalie Menigon had taken refuge in the Brussels suburb of Ixelle, though they were occasionally able to cross the border into northern France. They had several narrow escapes; on one occasion they seized a Belgian police officer sent to arrest them.

The wave of 10 bomb attacks in France in 1984—all upon buildings connected with NATO, the United States, or the defense industry—provided full confirmation that Action Directe had a tough-line terrorist organization with the same targets in its sights as had the Red Army Faction. It was clear that harsher leaders were by then in charge.

On August 23 at nine in the morning a Renault 20 stuffed with 24 kilos of high explosive, and stolen in Belgium a year before, was parked in front of the Western European Union building in Paris. By great good fortune the bomb failed to detonate. If it had gone off the death toll would have been high. Paris police who at first ignored telephone warnings simply collected the car and drove it to the police pound, where it stayed for four days without being examined. This was despite the fact that Nathalie Menigon—who apparently has no taste for mass murder—telephoned the police and AFP, the French news agency, several times to warn of the danger.

That was the beginning in France of the European guerrilla assault against what they called the Americanization of Europe. AD had changed into a new and fearsome organization. The French, in alliance with the West Germans, escalated their campaign from bombing to include assassination when early in 1985 they killed General Audran outside his own home. Their determination to try again was exemplified in the summer when they made an attempt on the life of another senior French defense ministry officer, General Blandin.

The road by which a comparatively mild Western European anarchist group has passed into full-scale and brutal terrorism can clearly be traced. It passes through Belgium, the small buffer state with many frontiers, between France and Germany. Herr Rebmann, the West German attorney-general, has drawn attention to the existence in northern France, the area between Paris and the Belgian border, of a support organization known as "Active Rebels." He is convinced that they were recruited by RAF and Revolutionary Cells as clandestine agents to work in liaison between the Germans, the French and the newly emerged Belgian fighting communist cells. Most of them are not directly involved in terrorism, and those arrested have only been charged with receiving. But they provide essential services on the roads linking France, Germany and Belgium.

12.

Triple C

Brussels is not just the capital of Belgium; it has also become the first city of the European Community and seat of the international bureaucracy of government. Furthermore, within a few miles of the city and close to the airport are located the administration offices of the North Atlantic Treaty Organization, and the military ones of the Supreme Headquarters, Allied Powers in Europe (SHAPE). In these establishments the United States and its friends and allies in the West plan and coordinate their military measures to discourage the real red army, the armed forces of the Soviet Union, from ever daring to launch an assault upon the old continent.

It is hardly necessary to say more than that to explain why Brussels in particular, and Belgium in general, are targets of high attraction for the raggle-taggle red armies of European terror. As we have shown, the international gangs of the 1980s are geared to hatred of militarism, and what they are pleased to call the Americanization of Europe. It ought not therefore to have come as an amazing surprise when in 1984 that country's peace and quiet was suddenly disturbed by a series of bomb explosions and terrorist outrages. But it did.

It was known that the reactivated Action Directe in France made frequent use of the friendly open frontiers of Belgium. Both Rouillan and Nathalie Menigon had often hopped across them, using the neighbor country as a kind of fall-back base. When Belgian police, alerted from Paris, waited to arrest the "infernal couple," an officer was seized at gunpoint and his car hijacked to make their escape. But apparently they were then able to live undisturbed in the Brussels suburb of Ixelle, though a few of their suspected anarchist supporters did go underground. Until then, the Belgian extreme left, though active in pamphleteering, had kept clear of violence.

Indeed, Belgium had been relatvely terror-free, apart from the attentions of outside groups. The most notable attack was in 1979, when an attempt was made on the life of General Haig, NATO supreme commander. Even after that the authorities thought it prudent not to seem overzealous, hoping that if they made no vigorous response the country might escape the worst of terrorist attacks being suffered by neighboring countries. As a result of this attitude Belgium became the refuge base for a number of organizations such as GARI, the international anarchist movement and then of ETA, the Basque group whose emissaries often traveled to Brussels to buy weapons on the black market. German RAF people and Irish terrorists from the IRA, not to mention various Arab groups, operated from time to time within the country.

Nevertheless the Belgian authorities seemed to have no idea that a new native group was springing up from within. The first indication was the now-famous armed raid upon Scouffleny quarry at Ecaussines in June 1984. The marauders got away with a great quantity of explosives and detonators, shared out for use later in the European terrorist campaign. Some of the explosive was F15, a plastic mix of high power.

The new Belgian terror group that had come into action called itself CCC, the fighting communist cells. Its first communiqué, bearing a symbolic five-pointed red star which was the same as that shared by the Italian Red Brigades and by Action Directe, announced that it was beginning "the armed struggle against the imperialist bourgeoisie." The rhetoric of *Ligne Rouge*, its publication printed on a clandestine antiimperialist press, resembled in style those of AD. It featured communiqués and terrorist bulletin board under the heading "News from the Front." But there was also a strong local element of political news which showed a clear and up-to-date grasp of political events in Belgium.

In a statement its leaders explained, "Revolutionary

guerrilla actions are never directed against the people, but always against the enemies of the people," which of course meant that they felt confident to decide who *were* the enemies of the people.

Despite the bold words, it seemed at first as though the CCC had been set up as a logistic structure with the task of providing arms and explosives for more active co-groups. They were known to be getting liaison help from a strange anarchist body known by the peculiar, catch-all title Bakounin-Gdansk (Bakunin the nineteenth-century terrorist, and Gdansk, the home of the Polish Solidarity movement) whose main platform was to oppose Western defense policies. Before long that judgment had to be revised as tougher spirits took control and Belgians went into action on their own account.

In October attacks were made on the office in Belgium of companies working in the defense industry, and over the following few months CCC was responsible for 14 eye-catching incidents. The list of raids showed the increasing ambitions of an organization which gave every sign of being well-structured and directed. The first six were bomb attacks against the offices of multi-national companies and Belgian political parties. Then on December 11, 1984 came more spectacular action against NATO fuel lines passing from the ports into Germany to supply allied armies in case of Soviet assault. The scope of the bombing operations was shown by the fact that within an hour six bombs had been positioned in a district 30 miles by 60.

Some of the pumping stations chosen for the attacks were marked by signposts to indicate that they were used for both military and civilian purposes. But it was noteworthy that CCC blew up only the exclusively military pipeline installations—no doubt in order to justify its claim to be a fighting army, though its actions also demonstrated the quality of intelligence information available to its leaders. Before attacks ever took place, German security men raiding an apartment used by the RAF in Frankfurt found plans of the NATO pipeline which they thought might have been obtained from an American base with bad security. It was a discovery which showed the terror groups to be capable of joint staff work and reconnaissance. In the words of Jean Gol, Belgian minister of justice, "We are not dealing with amateurs."

Until the beginning of 1985 CCC attacks had not put people at risk. However, when they parked a stolen car packed with explosive, and detonated it outside a U.S. Army administrative building, two American soldiers barely escaped injury. To mark this climax to the first stage of their antiimperialist campaign, a special communiqué was issued.

> This morning's action is the most complex and the most offensive which we have so far mounted. The obvious importance of the objective determined our decision to launch our first attack which might have wounded or killed Yankee soldiers and their accomplices.

In simultaneously announcing the start of a new campaign, it declared, "Human life is not an obstacle in itself. There is nothing sacred about it."

These events at last goaded the Belgian authorities into counteraction as they launched "Operation Mammoth," a series of police raids involving thousands of officers. The former policy of deliberately refusing to arrest terrorists so long as they did not attack targets within the country was abandoned overnight. The only trouble was that now the authorities could not find any terrorists to arrest. In an attempt to reassure the public the police presence on the streets was suddenly trebled, as the police force spent almost half its annual budget in one month. The government also began drafting a prevention of terrorism act similar to the British one.

A special antiterrorist squad, the 30-strong *Groupe de répression de terrorism*, was reactivated. It had been set up as a gesture towards reassuring public opinion after an earlier terrorist incident, but since then had not shown much sign of activity.

Like the French, the Belgians divide responsibility for action against terrorists between police and gendarmes. At the time in the early 1970s when all European governments were setting up special forces in the backwash of the Munich affair the Brussels government designated a special gendarme unit for hostage-release operations. The very existence of this unit, code-named "Diane," was kept secret, and its commanders, Captain Lemignouse and Lieutenant Lievin, were forbidden to speak publicly about their force. It was modeled on the German GSG 9 to operate in action groups of five men each, and it had been trained to the highest European standards. Unlike most similar units, the Belgian one also has its own intelligence group trained for electronic surveillance work. Its members dress in plainclothes and have at their disposal a mobile laboratory.

"Diane" gets its recruits from a special gendarmerie unit, the Légion Mobile, which is responsible for the security of the Belgian government, and also for the international organizations which have their headquarters in Brussels. It has 1,000 men.

Operation Mammoth, despite the wide scope of its raids in Belgian left-wing circles, was a failure. Little new information emerged from the interrogation of more than 150 people pulled in for questioning and then released. The only positive result was to demonstrate that their number-one suspect as CCC leader was a man named Pierre Carette.

Carette was born in the mining district of Charleroi in 1952. He became known as an "antiimperialist printer" while studying at the Beaux Arts in Brussels, where he helped to produce various left-wing publications. He drew himself to the attention of the police through being among troublemakers who invariably resorted to violence during otherwise peaceable street marches and demonstrations. It was noticed that his pamphlets praised Belgian miners in their 1983 strike, and in Brussels he was active in setting up a support group for West German RAF prisoners.

In 1982 he had a road accident while driving in France on the Autoroute du Nord with Nathalie Menigon in his car. In the damaged vehicle police found 15,000 Direct Action pamphlets, most of them printed by him. In the same year he was distributing a revolutionary review called *Subversion* to local radio stations. Careful examination of such literature provided fascinating hints about Carette's connection with terrorist outrages. For example, *Subversion* drew attention to an attack on the Litton Corporation in Toronto. One of the first CCC actions was an attack on the corporation's Brussels office. Did this mean that the idea of selecting it as a target had come from Carette?

The Belgian police, fumbling for clues, were left speculating about such minimal indications as pressure increased for them to do something. That is why they issued such a jubilant victory bulletin just before Christmas 1985 announcing that they had at last succeeded in arresting four suspects, including Pierre Carette. He was picked up with the other armed men at an address at Namur, 30 miles from Brussels, in the aptly named rue de L'inquietude. By that time CCC had carried out with impunity 27 bomb attacks upon international companies, banks and NATO installations.

The marked increase in terrorist incidents in Western Europe, and especially the fact that the perpetrators singled out NATO installations, provided a warning that more was to come. Belgium was not the only new country to be affected, and other groups made their appearance on the scene apart from the Franco-German Belgian alliance. Not a single European country has escaped the attentions of terrorists owing allegiance to one alliance or another. There have been outrages in Portugal, Greece, Austria and the Netherlands, where a demonstrating group wrecked a train, and even in neutral Switzerland, where the so-called "autonomes" have blasted off their devices in Zurich and in Berne, the capital.

In January 1985 an organization calling itself FP-25 (*Forças Populares 25 de Abril*) mortared NATO warships in the harbor at Lisbon. Only a week later an extremist group in Greece bomb-blasted a café near a U.S. air base outside Athens, injuring 70 American servicemen and 8 others. The confused state of affairs in the Greek capital makes it difficult to discover for certain who did it.

NATO itself took a surprisingly relaxed view of the dangers of the attacks in the territories of member states, which were dismissed as simply imitative ones brought on by publicity. West Germany, hardened by long experience of terror campaigns, was less sanguine about the state of affairs in Portugal. In January FP-25 blew up 15 cars belonging to Germans at their training base in the town of Beja, and there were attacks on other military installations as well as upon NATO headquarters in Lisbon. The actual lobbing of mortar bombs towards the warships was a feeble affair, but the FP-25 communiqué taking responsibility echoed the language and declared aims of the other European movements. It wanted "to combat imperialism and capitalism, and to get Portugal out of the orbit of NATO and the super-powers."

The Portuguese movement set up shop in 1980 with a fireworks display of 110 small bombs and a ritual announcement on paper bearing the ritual red star and automatic rifle: "A revolutionary army has been formed to overthrow the capitalist dictatorship and those of the old fascist regime now returning to power." For its title it seized upon the date of the outbreak of the "revolution of the carnations" of April 25 1974 when the Portuguese armed forces overthrew the old-established right-wing dictatorship.

In five years of activity the group has bombed a variety of targets, many of them commercial, and its members have mortared the U.S. embassy. It claims to have murdered 10 people. When in response to these outrages the security police arrested 73 suspected members and supporters of FP-25, they caused a sensation by also pulling in Lieutenant-Colonel Otelo Saraiva de Carvalho, one of the best-known leaders of the successful 1974 revolution, who was at that time something of a national hero. With his arrest, preparations for the trial became an important political issue in Portugal. Although he denied it, the prosecution alleged that his left-wing Popular United Front not only shared the ideals of FP-25 but also had links with the terrorist organization.

The trial, which had been due to begin in the summer of 1985 in a high-security court in Lisbon, specially built at a cost of half a million dollars, was postponed. A key witness for the prosecution was José Rosa Barradas, who was himself a repentant terrorist. However, Barradas was shot seven times, and died of his wounds some weeks later. FP-25 promptly announced that they were responsible. There was a notable reluctance among jurors to take their place in court, and fear of reprisals persuaded some to pay a $1,000 fine rather than take the risk.

The most confusing terrorist hotbed in Europe is in Athens, which claims to be the birthplace of Western civilization. In the strong words of Constantine Mitsotakis, leader of the conservative opposition party New Democracy, the country has been transformed "into a hospitable den for international terrorism where the law of the jungle reigns supreme." In a party statement he declared: "In the past two years bomb attacks and murders have been aimed at celebrities, political persons and newspapers." Naturally, he blamed the socialist regime of Andreas Papandreou, the prime minister. There is no shortage of highly placed Western security and intelligence people who would agree with him on this point.

Athens in fact has become a sort of transit camp for terrorists of all kinds. The intelligence estimate is that no fewer than 10 Arab and Islamic groups have their representatives installed in Athens. Some of their activities are described in another part of this book and it is generally believed that the Greek government has an arrangement with some of them that so long as they do no harm to specifically Greek targets, they will not be interfered with. The new European terrorists have also made use of this crossroads of Europe and the Middle East for their own purposes, and there are also local Greek terrorist bands which sometimes work in cooperation with them. The most notable of these is an extreme-left organization known as "November 17"—another of those date-names, this one in honor of a student killed in a demonstration. It first declared itself after the murder of Richard Welch, the Athens station chief of the CIA, and has also killed an American naval officer, two police officers and a prominent Greek newspaper publisher. Its statements are full of hatred for that well-known target "American imperialism," and declarations that it advocates what is called a violent shortcut to true socialism. Whether or not this home-produced urban guerrilla group is strongly connected to the red armies of Western Europe is a matter of debate. However, when a 13-lb. device was planted near the West German embassy this action was claimed by people describing themselves as "friends of the Red Army Faction," and that may provide a clue.

Because they are few in number but expert in living the clandestine existence, the new terrorists easily exploit the frontiers of Europe to meet up on the "old-boy network of violence." They come together for a while, then move on to form new cells and make fresh brutal mischief. Among the most skilled of the frontier-jumpers are the multifarious groups of Italian terrorists, some of which have been active for more than two decades.

13.

Death,
Italian Style

Ezio Tarantelli, a 43-year-old economist and adviser to the Catholic trade unions, had just finished giving his weekly lecture at Rome university on a March morning in 1985. He was getting into his car when two young men pushed forward and shot him down with a rapid burst from a machine carbine.

It was the beginning of another phase in the 16-year-long war against Italian society conducted by the Red Brigades, who promptly claimed responsibility for the murder. For more than a year they had been lying low, and the new outrage came as a shock just at a time when all seemed well. After the bad years which almost succeeded in disrupting public social life in the cities, prominent citizens were seen out again without bodyguards, and the newspapers reported a slump in the sale of armored private cars. It really did seem as though the so-called "columns" of Red Brigades in each of the main cities of Italy had been broken by vigorous police action. Their network was fragmented, and many of their members lived in exile abroad. Red Brigades had always worked on this system of local columns supposed to be under the general control of the "Strategic Committee" which directed—at any rate in principle—their politics, and their terrorist moves.

The signal for the start of what the Italians call the third wave of terror came in the form of a red-covered dossier composed by terrorists from the "foreign column." The date

169

was March 1984, and the document was the 19th "Strategic Resolution" of the Red Brigades. According to Piervittorio Buffa, of the Rome weekly *Espresso*, its was "written in Paris, printed in Madrid, posted in Switzerland." Like their comrades elsewhere in Europe, the Italians are much given to the production of doctrinal papers, and only those skilled in decoding the language can understand the message contained. This one, for example, was filled with phrases such as "the perspective for class organization is positive." It went on to declare that possibilities were opening for the workers' vanguard in the antagonist movement (themselves, that is to say) by the political struggle of the working class against Prime Minister Bettino Craxi. The issue chosen was the famous Italian sliding scale (*scala mobile*), which ensures that wages automatically rise with the cost-of-living index. Professor Tarantelli was the academic economist who had argued convincingly that the time had come to control inflation by cutting the famous sliding scale and by establishing wage increases in advance. The socialist prime minister had forced parliamentary legislation in this matter despite opposition from the powerful Italian Communist party which was demanding a referendum on the question.

It appeared from the captured Red Brigades policy document that a quarrel had broken out within its executive group. One faction was keen to intensify the "armed struggle" in the context of a long war. The other, arguing that the defenses were too strong for such military action to succeed, favored political intervention by infiltrating the masses with the aim of stirring them into insurrection against the state. In this fierce quarrel the action group won the day. They chose Ezio Tarantelli as their first victim, hoping that by branding his economic theories as anti-working class they might succeed in their endless quest to win favor with the workers. At about the time that similar terrorist movements in France and West Germany were murdering senior men in the defense industry the Red Brigades chose an economist as their target; it was the launch of new terrorism—Italian-style.

Judge Ferdinando Imposimato, Rome's foremost analyst of terrorist groups and their motives and a man who has talked with terrorists and with penitent terrorists, made a close study of the 70-page document. He concluded that, as frequently happens with national groups under pressure, a phase of silence, during which regrouping took place, would soon be followed by a sudden explosion. The aim of this new burst of activity was clearly political, to exploit social tensions over pay scales and to cause trouble among the parliamentary parties.

As an experienced terror watcher he had already noted other signs. Captured documents revealed a schism in the leadership followed by a decision to resume armed action. After that came an obvious fund-raising expedition to hold up an armored van, in the course of which a prominent woman RB member, Cecilia Massaro, was arrested. His conclusion was that tougher times were coming.

Judge Imposimento calculated that there were then some 40 active guerrillas, and certainly not more than 100, but they had been using their temporary quarters in Paris to recruit new professional terrorists. Some of them began filtering back across the borders. Front Line (Prima Linea), which had once rivaled the Red Brigades, showed little sign of life, except that 13 of its activists were known to be commuting between Rome, Milan and France, while others had transferred their allegiance to the RB columns. Prima Linea operates like a secret society, whose members are part-time terrorists. They have regular jobs, and for this reason get along better with working-class organizations. That is also the aim of another of the many Italian terrorist groups called Continuous Struggle (*Lotta Continua*), which also favored mass violence through demonstrations, strikes and pickets. The Autonomists, who are also active in Italy, are even more difficult to pinpoint as a terrorist movement, since they are highly individualist anarcho-socialists. Their watchword was "neither with the state nor with the Red Brigades."

Craxi, the socialist premier, was well aware of trouble spreading from northern Europe by way of Red Brigades fugitives who had settled themselves in France and elsewhere. His suspicions about links between them and Direct Action and the West German Red Army Faction were reinforced by the discovery early in the year of another RB paper. It made the first mention of an "external column" whose role was to protect the clandestines abroad and also to recruit new militants for active service. Paris was one of the main centers of Italian preparation for new attacks, as was demonstrated by the arrest there of Giorgio Frau who kept a list of a thousand names of supporters.

Yet again the French government was criticized for its failure to prevent foreign terrorists using its national territory as a base for reorganization. Attention has already been drawn to the French desire not to infringe its ancient principle of offering a haven to political refugees, and no doubt quite a number of the hundreds of Italians living in France were genuinely in fear of being unjustly arrested merely on suspicion that they had terrorist connections. But by no means was that true of all of them. A number of dangerous Italians had already been picked up in Paris. Two years earlier French police had killed an Italian terrorist called Ciro Rizatto, taking part with French comrades in a bank hold-up. Further links with Italian activists were confirmed by the arrest in February 1984 of Vicenzo Spano, operating with Direct Action.

After the new campaign of political murder in France and Germany in early 1985 Giovanni Spadolini, the Italian defense minister, complained about France's "harboring" multinational terrorism capable of striking throughout Europe." Signor Craxi himself weighed in to express his fears about the development of Red Brigade connections with the new breed of Euro-terrorists, and drew attention to the fact that 120 demands of extradition of Italian terrorists from France had been made. The wanted list of Italian suspects from leftist groups totaled 295, of whom 204 were living outside Italy, with the largest number, 143, in France.

As President Mitterrand of France came under stronger pressure to act against his own native terrorists by himself becoming unpleasantly active he became more sympathetic to demands for extradition. Against this, he insisted that most of the Italian political refugees in this country had in fact severed their links with the urban guerrillas. This, too, was the view of Oreste Scalzone, who had received a 36-year sentence in Italy before taking refuge in France. He declared that many of the Italians were people who had of their own free will dropped out of the game. Among those in Paris was a teacher of political science from Padua university, Antonio Negri, theoretician of the extra-parliamentary left, and sometimes described as the ideologue of the autonomists. He had certainly argued in favor of industrial sabotage, declaring "Proletarian opposition must consolidate itself in practical destruction, in subversion." In this fashion he justified terrorism as part of an incipient civil war in which he considered Red Brigades to be engaged as the armed vanguard in the clash with the imperialist state of the multinationals.

A Roman court sentenced him in his absence to 30 years

imprisonment for running an armed band and for involvement in kidnap, robbery and manslaughter. Following
earlier detention, he was released after being elected a
member of the Italian parliament. He then escaped to
France, and still denies any involvement in terrorism.

Ever since the initial violent outbreak of terrorism in 1969,
bombing and assassination have been part of the everyday
drama of Italian life. The first acts ended a rare state of affairs
in Italian history, when for two decades there had been hardly any violence, though just below the surface a deep cultural
and social malaise was to be detected which gave rise to
subsequent unpleasant events. It all began in the
universities, which were crammed with students, many of
whom became "perpetual students" without any hope of ever
making their way in the professions, and who were yet too
grand to seek any other kind of employment. They were the
cannon-fodder of revolutionary warfare as the festering
universities became centers of mass protest, at first
organized by *Movimento Studentesco*, a quaint radical body
combining Maoism and Catholic Christianity. Such
organizations foundered as their members moved off to join
extreme leftist "extra-parliamentary " parties, and together
with some of their professors drifted into terrorism. There
were workers' demonstrations, too, as the old unions lost control over the factories under inflationary pressures and with
the growth of the black economy.

It was a social situation which thoroughly alarmed the
respectable and conservative classes of Italy, Unlike other
Europeans in a similar situation, their first reaction was to
defend themselves by going back to the old ways, and turning
to fascism. Not only did more people vote from the extreme
right at election times but they lent support to the fascist
squads which sprang up with the aim of simultaneously
restoring order and fighting the left. Such bodies as New
Order (*Ordine Nuovo*) and Mussolini Action Squads (*Squadre
di Azione Mussolini*), were certainly not notable for the
quality of their leadership, but they seemed to have plenty of
money, and were linked to the more conventional right-wing
political parties such as *Movimento Sociale Italiano*.

Moreover, they enjoyed the support of a number of police
officers and security men. Their so-called strategy of tension
was intended to create a state of chaos which would force the
army to take over and impose martial law as a preliminary to
overthrowing parliamentary democracy. It was a fascist

bomb placed at the Piazza Fontana in Milan in December 1969, killing 16 people and wounding 90, which inaugurated the time of terror in Italy, even though it was in response to the student demonstrations of the hot autumn of that year. Since that time a number of bloody acts have been right-wing inspired. In 1974 their terrorists killed seven demonstrators at Brescia; they derailed the Italica express in the same year, and 12 people died. Six years later the right-wing Armed Revolutionary Nuclei, NAR (not to be confused with the left-wing Armed *Proletarian* Nuclei, NAP), blew up the restaurant at Bologna station during the holiday season, slaughtering 84. The typical right-wing terrorist attack caused mass slaughter, whereas Red brigade actions pinpointed specific targets for individual killing.

The difficulties of bringing to justice such terrorists were well illustrated by the fact that five years later two senior officers of Italian military intelligence were sentenced to long terms of imprisonment for belonging to an illegal organization within the service. It was alleged that both of them, General Pietro Musumeci and Colonel Giuseppe Belmonte, had falsely attempted to implicate a West German guerrilla group for the Bologna explosion.

Right-wing groups made a speciality of rail terror, and their gangs were suspected of being responsible for the most frightening attack so far upon a train. Just before Christmas 1984 a bomb was exploded in a coach of the Naples-Milan express in a tunnel. It killed 15 and wounded 100, but casualties in the constricted space might easily have been much higher. The task of investigators was not helped by the fact that no less than 23 organizations of the left, as well as of the right, and even including one claiming to be from Islamic Jihad, said that they had done it.

Fascist organizations never managed to achieve a coup d'état like the successful one launched by the Colonels in Greece. For a brief moment Prince Valerio Borghese, a recycled war hero, did manage to "occupy" the Ministry of the Interior in 1970. There was constant talk of scandals in the Italian secret service, and the former head of it who later became a member of parliament was arrested at one point for treason. The strategy of tension failed.

However, it did serve to encourage the groups on the left who were equally intent upon making trouble. Suspecting that the state itself was in league with the fascists, they felt that this justified their attempts to overthrow the republic, as their fathers and uncles in the wartime resistance had helped to destroy Mussolini. Both the moralistic, prosperous students and the penniless workers recruited to work in the factories were dedicated to the idea of overthrowing the system and fighting fascism.

Among the first generation of Italian terrorist leaders were a number of extravagant figures. The first left-wingers in action belonged to the *Gruppidi Azione Partigiana*, founded by the remorseful millionaire publisher Giangiacomo Feltrinelli, who eventually blew himself up during a training exercise with a bomb he was planting under an electric pylon at Segrate, near Milan. He drew his original inspiration from the Tupamaros in Uruguay, as well as from Castro and Mao. His money and undoubted organizing ability made possible the first wave of left-wing terror in Italy.

Renato Curcio, "historic" leader of the Red Brigades who became the best known of Italian urban guerrillas, was the bearded, operatically good-looking revolutionary leader. The illegimate son of Renato Zampa, brother of film director Luigi Zampa, he had a strict Roman Catholic upbringing before going to university at Trento in northern Italy, where sociology is the special subject. His first venture into violent politics was as a supporter of left-wing Catholic causes, but he was converted by the atmosphere of revolution at the university. One of his professors drew attention to the fact that both Curcio and many of his supporters came from very old-fashioned Catholic families and added, "They are basically religious people who come to politics and violence with all the conviction of zealots." Other early RB members like Alberto Franceschini and Roberto Ognibene, both from Reggio Emilia in the north, were the product of the powerful joint influences in Italy of the church and the Communist party. There is a parallel between the left-wing religious zeal of these young Italians and that of the Shi'ite Moslems.

Renato Curcio's career as a terrorist began with the seizing of "enemies of the people," such as Ettore Amerio, personnel director of Fiat and a fascist trade-union leader. After mock trials before "peoples' courts" in the name of proletarian justice the prisoners were released. There followed a number of symbolic attacks in which cars were set on fire. Although the group was formed in Milan in 1970, it was not until four years later that the Red Brigades committed their first murder.

Renato Curcio had met and married at the university a

quiet, religious girl named Margarita Cagol who was also drawn into the movement. Soon she was at work with her husband trying to persuade factory workers (many of whom were staunch communists, reluctant to take counsel from young students) to occupy their premises. At that time the ancient crime of kidnapping flourished in Italy. Some 300 cases a year were being reported. In 1975, after the Red Brigades had turned to this form of terror, Curcio and his wife seized a member of the Gancia wine family and imprisoned him in a lonely Piedmontese farmhouse. They were discovered there, and surrounded by the carabinieri. During a gun battle Margarita was shot dead, though her husband escaped and survived in the clandestine world for another year before being wounded and captured.

By that time harder men and women, schooled in tactics in the Middle East and East Europe and armed with the latest weapons, were taking over the Italian terror groups, which proliferated in remarkable numbers. There were at least 150 of them. Some were political parties, with a military wing; others were simply called autonomists, who held sway in a factory, or port, or in a university faculty. By the late 1970s official figures listed some 2,000 acts of terror each year, with up to 40 murders a year included. State politicians all fell victim to terrorist bombs and bullets. In the boom years between 1974 and 1979 Red Brigades won ascendancy over the come-and-go groups which imitated them. Regular attacks were made before the Brigades felt ready for their big strike at "the heart of the state."

When the great climax of terrorism came in Italy—as it does to all states so afflicted—with the kidnap and murder of the Christian democrat elder statesman Aldo Moro, it did not turn out to be the triumph which the Red Brigades had hoped for. Terrible though it was, and dramatic the decisions which had to be taken by the Italian government, the republic emerged unscathed. In retrospect it can be seen that this tragic affair simply demonstrated the futility of the terrorist philosophy and proved that even a country so riven with dissension as Italy was unlikely to be overthrown by them. The kidnap had been carefully timed politically to take place on the day that Prime Minister Andreotti resolved a long cabinet crisis with the help of Aldo Moro, and just as he was about to present his program with the support of the Communist party. The timing of other murders and kidnaps to coincide with elections or important parliamentory debates—on, for example, legalizing divorce—also revealed the political aims of the plotters.

On a March morning in 1979 a well-practiced squad of Red Brigades ambushed Aldo Moro's car in Rome, killed his five bodyguards and abducted the old man. They held him for 54 days, during which time they conducted a parody of a trial, and forced him to denounce former colleagues. It was, as a State Department official said at the time: "The strongest attempt we in the Western world have seen by terrorists to destabilize a democracy." At first the terrorists made no demands in exchange for his release, and only later insisted that arrested comrades had to be freed in return for his life. They were making a political gesture; they wanted to strike at the heart of the state.

The government made no response. Eventually in May the Red Brigades shot Aldo Moro dead with a Skorpion machine pistol and dumped his body in the trunk of a Renault car. Symbolically, it was left halfway between the party headquarters of the Communists and those of the Christian Democrats, both of which parties had been opposed to making concessions to the terrorists. Indeed, the first political consequence of the Moro affair was that these unlikely bedfellows formed an unexpected alliance to condemn the methods of extremists they both despised.

In reality the grand gesture so carefully planned backfired upon the Red Brigades themselves. Even among their supporters there was shock at the brutal murder of an old and distinguished man, while the militants felt bitter disappointment at the failure of their attempt. The Red Brigades, though they did not disappear, degenerated into a demoralized sect. From this point onward they were under heavy pressure, as in the backlash the Italian parliament passed tougher antiterrorist laws and gave new powers to the police and the paramilitary carabinieri. The Reale law authorized them to hold suspects longer and permitted them to open fire on suspected terrorists.

That same summer a portly 57-year-old carabinieri general named Carlo Alberto dalla Chiesa, with long experience of fighting both terrorists and *mafiosi*, was appointed to coordinate operations. He had a large but secret budget, and was able to use the resources of other law-enforcement agencies in the country. Using traditional police methods, he relied heavily on informers, managed to infiltrate the terror gangs and employed underworld criminal contacts to provide information. The general personally led his own carefully chosen team in action, and was soon able to break the so-called columns into which the Brigades were divided. His men also rounded up numbers of supporters and apologists. General dalla Chiesa became in the process something of a national hero. Having struck formidable blows at the terrorists, he was sent to Sicily in an attempt to master the Mafia. In 1982 he was murdered in Palermo, together with his wife, by that brutal organization of criminals.

By the mid-1980s it seemed that despite the fact that new terrorists of both left and right remained in existence to launch fresh attacks their chances of success in destabilizing the Italian republic were not great. Even with the help of their "external column," the Red Brigades found it difficult to recreate the high old days of terrorism in the face of more determined and efficient reaction from the state. Another blow was struck at the network with the arrest in Ostia, near Rome, of Barbara Balzarini, implicated in the murder of Aldo Moro. By then aged 36, she was the last of the old Red Brigades leaders still operational, and a strategic Committee member. She had directed the Milan column for years, and helped to organize one of the rare sorties of the Red Brigades against non-Italians, the kidnapping of Brigadier Dozier of the U.S. Army from his apartment in Verona. This American officer, who was serving with NATO forces in Italy, was later rescued. For a while the Dozier affair raised fears that the Red Brigades were copying the tactics of similar terrorist organizations in France and Germany by directing their thrust against Americans. Barbara Balzarini was herself involved with COLP, the group which helped to reactivate Direct Action in Paris. Copies of the declaration of alliance between the French and German groups circulated in left-wing circles in Italian factories and universities. There still exists a possibility that in alliance with the newly activated groups in Western Europe, Red Brigades will turn to the military-industrial complex targets which so fascinated other pan-European urban guerrillas.

14.

The Old
Incorrigibles

From the world of Islamic religious and pan-European political terror it is a long march to Ireland and Spain, the Western strongholds of the oldest-established of the nationalist homeland guerrillas, the Irish Republican Army and the Basques of ETA. So long have their micro-armies been in the field that it is not easy to think of them in terms of "new" terrorists. Yet despite years of long service and bad conduct, they are still forces in being, and have shown themselves capable of great tenacity of purpose. So continuous is the cause which inspires them that from generation to generation young men and women are always found who are ready to take to the gun and the bomb to assert their nationality. The Basques and Irish in this sense have a great deal in common. They are descendants of ancient races with a strong sense of history and determination to secure independence for their national states. Each is proud of its own national language and resentful of the fact that most Basques speak Spanish, while the Irish majority is more at home in English. In the Basque country, as in Ireland, the power and influence of the Roman Catholic church is great. Indeed, the clergy helped to keep alive the Basque language—which is a powerful force in nationalism—partly in order to shield their people from corrupting ideas more freely available in more cosmopolitan languages.

179

In both cases it becomes apparent that there can be no end to their terrorism without a political solution; but equally there can be no political solution until terrorism ends. Democratic Spanish governments have made concessions and suggested compromises to meet the more reasonable demands; nothing would please the British government more than to end the Irish wars by similar means, if this could be done without creating new grievances among the Loyalist Protestant majority in Northern Ireland. It must not be forgotten that the Loyalists too have their terrorist groups, engaged in sectarian murdering and ready to fight bigger battles. The sad truth is that, whenever things begin to look hopeful in either region, hard new men take control over the old movements, demand ever more and once again reactivate the old blood feuds. The old movements revive; the new terrorists who step forward are capable of constant innovation.

There is evidence of "togetherness" between Irish and Basque terror groups. Some of their activists meet at training establishments in Libya and South Yemen. On occasion the IRA, have provided explosives for ETA, as when they acted as suppliers of material used to blow up the then Spanish prime minister, Luis Carrero Blanco. Years later the Royal Ulster Constabulary had information that the Basques were trying to persuade their Irish comrades to copy their tactic of assassinating prominent persons, rather than making easy kills of off-duty soldiers and policemen. Cooperation between IRA and ETA began in 1972, when Basque activists visited Ireland to update themselves on Provo tactics. Contacts continued, and little deals were arranged, including the exchange of M-16 rifles from Ireland in return for explosives from the Basque country. In 1980 a captured Basque revealed that at least 15 of his people had attended an Irish weapons and explosives training course. The Republican terrorists also have some friends in Europe, especially in France, and they have occasionally ventured there to make attacks upon British diplomats and soldiers of the British Army of the Rhine. But it would be wrong to overestimate foreign influence on the Provisional Irish Republican Army (PIRA), which is an intensely insular organization, ill at ease with foreigners.

The IRA and—after it declared a truce and went out of business—its successor movement, the breakaway PIRA, have been fighting against the British for the last 60 years in their own individual fashion. They are convinced that they alone represent the legitimate republic, and this strongly held view makes the 'usurpers' in Dublin, the government of the Irish republic, every bit as much of an enemy as the British government in London. From such a cast-iron position the IRA leaders take upon themselves the right to justify any violent means to further their cause, believing it legitimate and justifying any action, however brutal. They feel as little compunction about knee-capping an erring supporter as they do about placing a bomb in a Brighton conference hotel with the aim of blowing up the entire British cabinet.

In the campaigns in Ireland and in England they fight as terrorists, by planting bombs, kidnapping and shooting down people in the street. They have never gone in for new-fangled tactics such as hijacking or suicide bombing. They also fight as guerrillas by raiding British army units and Irish police establishments in Ireland. Indeed, on one famous occasion in 1979 their men appeared in the terrorist and guerrilla roles almost simultaneously on the very same day. In Sligo, on the west coast of Ireland, they detonated a boat bomb which killed Earl Mountbatten, a famous wartime leader, and the queen's uncle. Near the east coast, at Warrenpoint, they ambushed with great skill troops of the 2nd Parachute Regiment, and by killing 18 men inflicted upon them casualties as numerous as the regiment suffered subsequently in action against the Argentinians at the battle of Goose Green in the Falkland Islands.

In England they act purely as terrorists, placing bombs in department stores, in the street and in public houses, and by murdering prominent people like Airey Neave, MP (who was in fact killed by the Irish National Liberation Army [INLA], a breakaway faction of the IRA). Occasionally they pretend to be assaulting military targets, as when they bombed soldiers from the Brigade of Guards returning to barracks by bus and blew up a military band playing in a park and horse soldiers from the Household Cavalry on a ceremonial parade. But such claims fool nobody: all these attacks were clearly terrorist ones.

The bomb has been an Irish speciality ever since the famous day 100 years ago when their Fenian forebears planted an infernal machine at Scotland Yard and blew up the lavatory used by their enemies of the embryo Special Branch. In the post-1969 hostilities an IRA leader named Daithi O'Connell (who later became one of the movement's leading political thinkers) is credited with being the originator of the car bomb.

For the British the words IRA and bomb have become synonymous, bringing to mind a long catalogue of famous explosions. The most recent of these were the Harrods bomb and the 1984 one at Brighton. Specialists in British army and police squads responsible for dealing with their devices have great professional respect for the diabolical skill and cunning of some of the bomb makers. They are the aristocracy of terrorists across the water, and the estimate in 1985 was that the IRA largely depended on the services of only four or five master explosives artificers. Such men, who learned their trade as electricians and as repairmen for pin-ball machines, have over the years learned to build in sophisticated timing, and long-term delayed-action devices, radio controls, blast accentuators and cruel multi-booby traps. Their skills are matched only by the expertise and cool bravery of bomb-disposal officers and NCOs in the British services.

The old IRA which emerged after the failure of the first attempt in 1916 to establish an Irish republic over the whole island fought a brief campaign against what was regarded as the betrayal of partition. It opposed the 1922 division of Ireland into the Free State in the south and British Protestant Ulster of the six countries in the north. The fight continued with the campaigns against the fledgeling Free State in the 1920s and 1930s. It was then that that grandiose and old-fashioned force established its "brigades," controlled by an Army Council, and named its leaders "Chief of Staff" and "Quartermaster-General" in a touching attempt to give the impression that it was a real and legitimate army. After the Second World War—which swallowed up the smaller war on the island—it was some time before the Irish fighters were able to go operational again in a spasmodic guerrilla campaign on the border dividing the two Irelands between 1956 and 1962.

But the terror and guerrilla war began in earnest six years later, inaugurated by the civil rights marches of the Catholic minority in Northern Ireland in protest against their undoubted suffering at the hands of the overweening Ulster Loyalists, and their exclusion from political activity. The Loyalists saw this as an attempt at subversion of the state, and the police force they controlled struck back so harshly that the British army had to be called in to protect the Catholics. There were 3,000 at first, but within three years, as the bombing and shooting began in earnest, the force had grown to 21,000 and the soldiers were seen not as protectors but as enemies and targets. Not all the shooting came from the terrorists. In a badly handled affair during a protest march at Londonderry in 1972 on what came to be known as Bloody Sunday, the Parachute Regiment opened fire, killing 13 men.

The British army, little though it liked internal security duties, had long and hard experience of such work from imperial time, and during the twilight of empire. Under tight political control, and forbidden to open fire except in extreme danger, the army began perfecting its low-intensity warfare techniques and was able to make life difficult for PIRA and its supporters. After many setbacks the Irish fighters were compelled to reorganize themselves and rejigger their organization following the pattern set both by wartime resistance movements and by the guerrilla tactics being developed in many countries.

Their volunteers, surrounded by boastful and talkative hangers-on—for in Ireland drink is the curse of the fighting classes—were easy for informers to penetrate. IRA men in pubs and clubs, singing the old songs, would hold up various numbers of fingers to denote the number of the Belfast battalion in which they served. Soldiers (especially those of the SAS, the Special Air Service, who were experts in counterguerrilla operations) mounted covert operations. As a result the "bhoys" took some hard knocks and lost many of their leaders. The Special Powers Act made possible the detention of suspects. The security forces were getting a great deal of information from interrogation, sometimes employing methods which were psychologically painful, to help break the "Army."

It was under such pressure that the new leaders began reshaping PIRA, and transforming it into a more secretive and deadly organization. As if to prove the need for it, the 'Staff Report' containing proposals for more secrecy and tighter discipline fell into British hands. It included such comments as:

We are burdened with an inefficient infrastructure of commands, brigades, battalions and companies. This old system with which the Brits are familiar has to be changed. We recommend reorganisation and remotivation, the building of a new Irish Republican Army . . . we must gear ourselves towards the Long Term Struggle based on putting unknown men and new recruits into a new structure. This new structure shall be the cell system.

By the 1980s the Provisionals had dissolved the old and hallowed units, except for ceremonial purposes, and established clandestine cells usually consisting of four people with cut-outs to prevent them knowing what was happening in other cells. An important feature of the new underground movement was training in how to resist interrogation. IRA men already in prison, especially in H-blocks of the Maze prison (so called because of their architectural shape), at once approach new arrivals to debrief them about how they were caught and who arrested them. This information is smuggled out to IRA intelligence officers still operational to put others on their guard. Cells began to specialize in, for example, sniping, bombing, intelligence. Others concentrated on bank raids to provide finance for the organization without compromising units engaged in other business.

The provision of money has always been a pressing problem for Irish terrorists, and the current estimate is that they need at least two or three million pounds a year for routine expenses, and for the purchase of weapons. On the whole the IRA is self-financing and gets a good deal of money, like the rest of us, from banks. The only difference is that whereas we go cap in hand, they go gun in hand. An important external source of cash is contributions from Irish-Americans. Fund-raising efforts in New York and other cities with large Irish minorities tap sentimental supporters in the United States, who often do not realize that their money is going to finance murderous raids. It helps to keep the terrorists in business. The activities of collecting organizations are well known, though their leaders always claim that money goes only to support charities and relief work for "political" prisoners. British diplomats spend a good deal of time and effort trying to convince Americans intent on campaigning against international terrorism that one useful step would be to dry up the supply of dollars to the IRA. The only other proven source of money from abroad is that which has been supplied by Colonel Gaddafi of Libya, ever anxious to lend a helping hand in such enterprises.

On at least one occasion, when he dispatched a cargo aboard the *Claudia*, he had also provided weapons and explosives. That cargo was intercepted. More recently another gun-running ship was seized upon the high seas. On that occasion it was allowed to enter territorial waters, after being kept under surveillance by various intelligence services, before being stopped by a warship of the Irish

Republic. Although the Provisionals occasionally use more sophisticated weapons, such as the Russian-made RPG 7 rocket-launcher probably procured from Middle East sources, they are by no means lavishly equipped with hardware.

The American Armalite and the Soviet Kalashnikov are their favorite weapons, together with a variety of handguns purchased on the arms market. Explosives are normally stolen commercial products or homemade stuff—known locally as 'Coop mixture'—made from ingredients available in local stores. The terrorists have displayed some ingenuity in making bombs from modified oxygen cylinders and using them and similar materials to fabricate do-it-yourself, multiple-barrelled mortars used to bombard army and police posts. The IRA's parsimony with weapons is demonstrated by the fact that after they have used them in an attack they deposit them in hideaways, to be recovered by others and returned to stores. Sometimes two or three stages are involved in such operations to prevent loss of weapons or the arrest of guilty men. Men chosen for an operation collect their weapons or bombs just before they go into action so as to minimize the risk of being caught red-handed. The most professional always take care to go at once to a safe house, where they can not only change clothes and have a good wash but also scour their nails to remove traces of explosive. They are well aware of the dangers presented by the forensic skills of the Royal Ulster Constabulary and its Special Branch.

The reorganization proposals of the IRA, which were so successfully implemented on the military side, also set political guidelines, making it clear that Sinn Fein—ostensibly the acceptable face of the Republican movement—"should come under Army organizers at all levels."

Sinn Fein [it translates as 'Ourselves Alone'] should be radicalised under Army direction, and should agitate around social and economic issues which attack the welfare of the people. SF should be directed to infiltrate other organisations to win support for, and sympathy to, the Movement. SF should be re-educated and have a big role to play in publicity and propaganda departments.

The new role of Sinn Fein, officially described as the political wing of the Republican movement, became apparent in this sense at the time of the great hunger strike to the death among convicted IRA men held in the Maze prison. The hunger strike was an old and favored tactic for drawing sympathy and attention. When a prisoner went the whole way he became a powerful symbol as a martyr. The 1981 strike was launched in an attempt to secure special status as political prisoners for IRA men, resentful of the British government's insistence that they were in fact convicted criminals. Prime Minister Thatcher refused to give way despite a great deal of international criticism and pressure, and it became inevitable that some would die. In fact, before the hunger strike finally did end after seven months of anguish, no less than 10 prisoners had starved themselves to death, of whom the best known was Bobby Sands. The undoubted courage and conviction of those stalwart enough to sacrifice their lives made a big impression on public opinion. In the United States sympathy for the IRA increased, as did contributions to funds for Ireland. But what was of greater importance to the leaders of the reorganized IRA and Sinn Fein was the way that Irish sympathy for the martyrs might be exploited politically.

There can be no doubt that it was a powerful factor in the success of Sinn Fein in the election of 1983. Gerry Adams, president of Sinn Fein, and former chief of staff of the IRA, was himself elected as member to the Westminster parliament for West Belfast. He declined to take his seat, but the mere fact of his election placed the British government in an awkward situation. He was known to be a powerful leader of the IRA terrorist organization, and he was the man who had drafted the paper to reorganize the Provisionals which had turned them into a formidable force. Yet there he was, a member of parliament and an elected representative of Ulster, to prove that his strategy of using both the bullet and the ballot box—so bitterly opposed by IRA hard-liners—had worked by rekindling overt electoral support for Sinn Fein IRA.

In style and in physical appearance—bearded, and with steel-rimmed spectacles—Gerry Adams more closely resembles the typical intellectual radical leader of the 1980s than the more traditional Irish working-class colleagues within the Republican movement. Aged 36, and born in West Belfast, a Republican fief, he had a modest education, worked only as a barman, and was a young recruit to the cause. As he made his way up the ladder he was twice interned, though never convicted of terrorist offenses. It is nevertheless generally accepted that he devised the "economic bombing" campaign during which 21 devices were planted in Belfast city center in one afternoon—the notorious "Bloody Friday."

It is a characteristic of the leaders of the new-model IRA, as it was of the older form, that the leaders are local boys of humble origins. Unlike the ideological movements in Europe, they cannot boast a high proportion of intellectuals, university people and academic theorists. Martin McGuiness, another important figure who may or may not be the present chief of staff—for the Provisionals always keep tight-lipped on such subjects—was a butcher's assistant. When he appeared in a controversial, and at first banned, BBC television feature, he was careful to present himself as a modest family man, domesticated and surrounded by children. But even in that film he did appear at an IRA funeral surrounded by admirers as they watched masked Provisionals in black and distinctly fascist-style paramilitary gear firing the traditional hand-gun volley over their defunct colleague.

Most of the other leaders, members of the 13-strong Army Council and of the seven-man executive which controls the campaigns of terror, are simple men, many of them from the back streets of northern Irish cities. Ivor Malachy Bell, a veteran gunman and hard-liner, was originally a mechanic. Only two of the older leaders, a teacher and a solicitor, had any social pretensions, and Danny Morrison, who handled publicity, was put down as a thinking man.

In his political role Gerry Adams set about cultivating left-wing politicians in London, such as Ken Livingstone, the eccentric leader of the Greater London Council, and even leaders of the Opposition Labour party. Before the 1983 elections he was hoping that they might defeat Margaret Thatcher and once in government show themselves more sympathetic to the idea of withdrawing from Northern Ireland. He was disappointed on both counts, partly because of the public-opinion backlash in Britain caused by the pre-Christmas bomb at Harrods in London. This attack was an obvious blunder, and blame for it was placed upon Kevin McKenna, one of the bosses at the time.

Once Mrs. Thatcher's Conservative government had been reelected with a great majority the Army Council despaired of a political solution and again went military. In Ireland itself they contented themselves with a war of attrition, murdering off-duty policemen and members of the Ulster Defence Regiment, a part-time volunteer force, a kind of Northern Irish national guard. Such regular attacks were punctuated by the occasional big bang against a more obvious target. In 1984-5 things were noticeably more relaxed in Ulster; people started going out again at night, and shopping thrived. The government had spent untold millions in improving housing in Belfast, especially in the Catholic areas, and the place began to look better. The British army presence had been reduced to some 9,000 troops of whom some were simply on normal garrison duties, as they might be anywhere else in the United Kingdom. Most security duties, except in hot spots on the border with the Republic and elsewhere, were in the hands of the reformed, restructured and reinforced Royal Ulster Constabulary.

This, of course, did not suit the purpose of the new Provisionals, whose estimated frontline strength was around 50. To back up the top terrorists there were some 300 others, both men and women, trained to shoot as well as to act as auxiliaries. At least another 200 were ready for intelligence work, the provision of safe houses, and weapon collection and disposal. And, of course, it must not be forgotten that in the Republican areas thousands more might be relied on for sympathy and noisy passive support. All the same, the Provos' resources were limited, they were plagued by jealousy and infighting from the bosses downward, as well as by doctrinal quarrels with INLA, the smaller Irish National Liberation army, which had broken away from the Provos years before. Fear and suspicion in the ranks was also caused by the many successes of the security forces, acting on evidence provided by repentant terrorists—or supergrasses, as they are known in police language. They are hated and feared, though occasionally the subject of that famous good-humored Irish wit, as in the ominous Belfast wall-painted slogan: "Remember the supergrasses!" Under which someone had written: "I hope to God they don't remember me."

The most difficult place for the "active service units" to operate is in England, where even from the substantial minority of Irish people living there they receive little support. It is more difficult to smuggle in explosives and weapons. Yet one such unit did succeed in planting a bomb with a long delayed-action timing device in the bathroom of a suite at the Grand Hotel, booked for the Conservative Party conference in the autumn of 1984. When it exploded Margaret Thatcher and many members of her cabinet were staying at the hotel. By great good fortune they survived this most powerful of all IRA attacks, a deliberate attempt to vent its political frustration by destroying at a blow the entire British government. Of the ministers, only Norman Tebbit was badly injured, though five other Tories lost their lives and many were hurt.

Part Four
MISSING LINKS

15.

Forlorn
Causes

There is one great difference in the task confronting European terrorists, whether their inspiration is nationalistic or ideological, and that of Arab groups. The Europeans aim to destabilize well-established states and governments. Palestinians and their international allies have no need to do that, for the whole Middle East region in which they operate is destabilized already. In Lebanon, the cockpit of the terror wars, they can only magnify the existing chaos whatever they do.

Terrorists are united by their belief that only by fighting unorthodox campaigns of murder can they achieve their aims. Some of the strands drawing them together for reasons of self-interest have already been traced in this book. But there is one more organization which provides, so to speak, the missing link between Europe and Asia Minor. It bears the undistinguished acronym title FARL, derived from its French name—*Fractions armées révolutionnaires libanaises* (Lebanese Armed Revolutionary Groups).

Appropriately, FARL came to life in Lebanon, the crossroads between Europe and the Arab world, in 1980. Marxist-Leninist in ideology, most of its small force are Lebanese Christians from two small northern villages, Qubayat and Andaqat. To judge from its record of attacks, it believes in international terrorism as a force, and the sole aim is to strike at American and Jewish and Israeli targets in

199

Europe. In religion and politics it has connections with the Popular Front for the Liberation of Palestine through the leader George Habash, who is both a Christian and a marxist. It seems likely that on occasion FARL carries out missions on his behalf. Certainly the fact that most of its attacks have been in Italy and France convinces intelligence sources that the Lebanese group works in conjunction also with the Italian Red Brigades and with Direct Action in France. The use of such a title as "Lebanese armed revolutionary faction" gives a clue to its aspirations to be considered as a part, however small, of the European red army conglomerate. It also shared their revolutionary hatred of Americans, imperialism and Zionism. Like-minded violent groups seem always willing to encourage each other.

FARL first attracted attention in 1981 when one of its gunmen tried to shoot Christian Addison Chapman, then U.S. chargé d'affaires in Paris, as he left home on the way to the embassy. With great presence of mind the diplomat dived under his car and escaped unhurt as the hit man fired six rounds at him. At first there was little inclination to believe the claim from a hitherto unknown organization, and blame was placed upon better-known groups.

The existence of FARL was soon confirmed when its men used exactly the same methods in January of the same year, and succeeded in murdering Lieutenant-Colonel Charles Ray, the American assistant military attaché, with a single shot in the head, as he left home in Passy. A letter written in Arabic and delivered in Beirut justified the killing by accusing the United States of leading a "fascist, Zionist, reactionary alliance" against the Lebanese people.

Within a few weeks, the same organization turned its attentions to Israelis abroad. From a fast-moving car, they fired bursts at the building where an Israeli defense ministry delegation was working. In 1982, a female assassin shot dead with three bullets Yacov Bar-Simantov, an Israeli embassy second secretary. When his 17-year-old son, Avi, gave chase, she ordered him in French: "Stop, or I'll shoot." That incident was followed by two more attacks in Paris in the same year; a parcel bomb delivered to the American commercial attaché killed two police officers, and a bomb in the car of an Israeli diplomat injured a number of others.

The group claimed no more outrages until February 1984, when in Rome one of its gunmen murdered Leamon Hunt, an American diplomat who was director-general of the multinational peacekeeping force in Sinai. This attack was followed by a failed attempt on the life of the U.S. ambassador in Strasbourg.

Until the summer of that year very little information had come to light about the composition of the mysterious FARL, such a small and obscure though dangerous organization. New facts came to light with the arrest in Trieste of Abdalla Muhammad al-Mansuri, a 19-year-old Arab traveling aboard the Orient Express through Yugoslavia to France. He carried a false Moroccan passport and seven and a half kilos of explosives. Under interrogation, he revealed the names and addresses of collaborators, and international investigators were able to piece together some picture of FARL activities.

Then an extraordinary thing happened. In October 1984 a tall bearded man who said he was an Algerian electronics engineer on vacation walked into a police station in Lyons and asked for protection because, he said, Mossad agents were about to kill him. But the men tailing him were French counterintelligence agents and under cross-examination his pretense of being an Algerian crumbled away.

He agreed that his real name was Georges Ibrahim Abdallah and then boasted that he was FARL's leader. He had the effrontery to argue that he should be released because he had withdrawn all his operatives from France and had no intention of carrying out any more attacks on French soil.

The French government, as usual unwilling to have terrorists as long-term prisoners, and anxious to secure the release of a number of French hostages being held in Lebanon, partly went along with this argument and charged him merely with possession of forged papers and membership in an "association of criminals."

However, before he came to trial, two of his six brothers—FARL is a family organization—took out extra insurance by kidnapping Gilles Peyrolles, director of the French Cultural Institute in Tripoli, Lebanon, and started to bargain for an exchange. The French agreed, but when the deal was about to be concluded, intelligence agents raided an apartment in Paris which had been rented by Abdallah. There they found a cache of explosives and arms. And among the weapons was the pistol which had killed both Charles Ray and Yacov Bar-Simantov.

The French government then came under intense pressure from the United States and Israel, making it impossible for the French to go through with the exchange. But they waited until FARL released Peyrolles before reneging. In July 1986 Abdallah was sentenced to four years' imprisonment. Under the circumstances it was a very light sentence and, given the two years he had already spent in prison, he would have been eligible for conditional release in October 1986. But FARL, furious at what they considered double-dealing by the French, refused to wait for his release, and in September 1986 launched a devastating bombing campaign in the heart of Paris designed to force the immediate release of their leader.

The aims of this curious organization remain obscure. The belief grew in Paris during the bombing campaign—which coincided with attacks by Shia gunmen on the French contingent of the UN peace-keeping force in Lebanon—that it was being used by the Syrians for their own political ends, in this case the removal of French influence from Lebanon.

The multifarious organs of terror include a number of such arcane groups, whose motivation and aims remain impenetrable and who seem, eventually, to exist for terrorism itself. At the same time there are groups whose ambitions are well understood but which are totally unattainable. The most glaring case history in this category is provided by the Armenian terrorists.

Their aim is encapsulated in the title of their most redoubtable organization, the Armenian Secret Army for the Liberation of Armenia, ASALA, established 1975. It seeks to liberate and reestablish the homeland. More of the story is revealed by the names of rival movements—Justice Commandos of the Armenian Genocide, Avengers of the Armenian Genocide and the Armenian Revolutionary Army. They all share the same forlorn hope that one day Armenia will live again, and that vengeance will be theirs for the injustices inflicted upon their forebears in the final years of the Turkish empire. It is indisputable that in 1915 the ruthless Turkish regime of Enver Pasha deported 1,750,000 Armenians to Syria and Mesopotamia. At least one-third of them perished or were massacred. There can be no doubt about the horrors of that time.

Revenge for historical wrongs and deep desire for a homeland are indeed powerful forces, and they are the ones which inspire modern Armenian terrorists. Unfortunately for the young and ardent nationalists, their country is now divided by the line between the Soviet Union and the West. Less than 50,000 Armenians live in Turkey, while some two million are incorporated in Soviet Armenia, the smaller geographical area of what was once Armenian territory. It is difficult to imagine circumstances in which all Armenians, including the exiles and expatriates now scattered through 30 foreign countries, can ever be reunited in their own independent state.

It is most likely such despairing thoughts which have converted the nationalist enthusiasts of ASALA into one of the world's most effective and alarming terrorist organizations. The main difference between ASALA and the Justice Commandos is that ASALA is more left wing, and hopes to establish the new Armenia with the help of the Soviet Union. JCAG would like to control such a state without Soviet intervention.

Operating internationally, ASALA has already launched scores of attacks on Turkish targets in a score of different countries, and specializes in the murder of Turkish diplomats. When in 1983, an especially active year for them, they assassinated Dursun Aksoy of the Turkish embassy in Brussels, he was the 28th such victim. The very next day a bomb exploded at a Turkish airline desk in Orly airport, Paris. Had it not been spotted in time by a member of the public, another would have gone off at Holborn in London soon after. An indication of Armenian feeling was given by Zaven Bedros, arrested in London that year with a cache of arms while planning a raid on the Turkish embassy, when he said: "Killing is a cheap thing. It is done for our people and our country to get recognition of our rights, because it is better for a people without a country to die." The Armenians have also launched operations to punish third-party countries which imprison their people captured after terrorist raids.

Both ASALA, which is the most powerful group, and its rivals have carried out bomb attacks in North America. Justice Commandos assassinated the Turkish consul-general at traffic lights on Wilshire Boulevard. The FBI was especially alert to the danger of Armenians attempting to use the Los Angeles Olympic Games as an arena for their activities, but careful investigation and surveillance of exile groups succeeded in warding off the threat. However, the most tempting target for ASALA is Turkey itself. In 1983 they managed to penetrate strong defenses to launch an attack on people in a crowded bazaar in Istanbul. It was the first successful assault since Ankara airport was machine-gunned the previous year.

Turkey is, of course, always alert to such obvious dangers and has made things difficult for Armenian terrorists. In this respect there is an obvious comparison between the Armenians and the Palestinians. Both groups were thwarted in attempts to raid in the countries which are their principal enemies, Turkey and Israel, so they turned instead to international operations. It was not surprising that groups brought together by similar aims, like-minded political positions, and the presence in the Middle East of many Armenian exiles, should begin to cooperate.

The Palestinians offered training facilities, weapons and money to assist their Armenian comrades. All the familiar weapons of terror bearing the label "made in USSR" were soon available to ASALA. Its leaders, men like Hagop Hagopian, joined the select group of "old boys" of the Middle East military schools, where they were in contact with "terrorists international." A large Armenian community, a quarter of a million strong, lives in Lebanon, and in 1981 arrangements were made by the PLO to train 200 Armenians there and to help their cause by providing operational intelligence. Hagop Hagopian, an energetic hard-line boss of ASALA, moved to Libya after his men were forced to evacuate Lebanon with the retreating Palestinians.

In their different ways, both FARL and the Armenians became a kind of bridge between Europe and the Middle East, where the Palestine Liberation Organization, despite its many setbacks, is a continuing force in world terrorism.

Part Five

THE PALESTINIANS

16.
Arafat Strikes Again

The seizure by armed Arabs of the Italian liner *Archille Lauro* and the murder of an elderly Jewish-American passenger in the autumn of 1985 marked a return to the terrorist battlefield of the mainstream PLO forces. It was the first attempt to carry out a big eye-catching raid by Yassir Arafat and his Palestine Liberation Organization since its troups were pushed out of the Lebanese bases by the Israeli invasion. While rival forces regrouped and fragmented as thwarted warlords quarreled after that disaster, the story of the Palestinians was one of the armed squabble rather than the armed struggle.

Never were the fortunes of Yassir Arafat so low as in those dangerous days when his PLO fighters were forced to march out of the Beirut stronghold to be taken away by sea and dispersed throughout the Arab world. Thousands of others took the road to Damascus, and this faction, led by many of the chairman's old friends, including the military commanders Abu Musa and Khaled al-Amlah, rebelled against him and set up their own organization under the strict control of President Assad of Syria. Even worse, they began plotting against the Arafatists whose headquarters were transferred to Tunis 1,400 miles away from Lebanon—and from Palestine.

They were gloomy days for the mainstream PLO. Some of its members went to Jordan, some to South Yemen, and others to Tunisia. Just to marshal the dispersed forces, the chairman had to spend most of his working life in airliners. The only consolation was that he had managed to keep control over the PLO war chest, a budget comparable in size to that of some Third World countries. This fact enabled him also to maintain the network of PLO representatives around the world who enjoyed quasi-diplomatic status. The Liberation Organization has always been a many-sided thing, with its own regular army, its terrorist groups, and political, industrial and diplomatic services.

It was during the time in Tunisian exile, while outside attention concentrated upon the dramatic activities of Islamic Jihad, that Yassir Arafat began restructuring Force 17, the loyal bodyguard whose services were so essential when even his best friends were plotting against him. The plan was that eventually this unit could be used offensively when a suitable moment came to demonstrate that the PLO remained a fighting force.

For the time being Yassir Arafat had other things on his mind. Although at the beginning of 1985 he announced that the armed struggle was his main tactic, he had been heavily engaged in diplomacy for several months. The trap for him was that in order to justify his leadership he had to be seen to be capable of military action, even while he was trying to figure principally as a peacemaker. Yassir Arafat has to play both ways in order to get some sort of consensus in the divided Arab world. Israeli leaders share the same difficulty; only those who have demonstrated their ability to make war dare to take the risk of trying to make peace. That is why Yitzhak Rabin declared: "Israel wants peace as soon as possible, but reserves the right to fight terror with terror." The same words might equally have been used by the PLO leader himself.

In February Yassir Arafat reached an agreement in Amman with his old opponent, King Hussein of Jordan, to present a new negotiating position. The essence of it was the principle of "land for peace," the land being a miniature Palestine on the Israeli-occupied West Bank, confederated with the Kingdom of Jordan in return for Arab recognition of the state of Israel. Later, President Hosni Mubarak of Egypt gave his blessing, Saudi Arabia and Algeria were favorably disposed, and the Americans and the British became involved too.

A hostile response was immediately forthcoming from the hard-line Arab states, such as Syria and Libya, which automatically opposed any concession to Israel. The Damascus rump of the PLO, in the person of Khalid al-Fahoum—who had once been speaker of the Palestine National Council—promptly announced the creation of the Palestine National Salvation Front (PNSF). Incorporated in it, to "block the deviant path" of Chairman Arafat, were the Fatah rebels and all the old extremist groups so active in the world of terror. The PFLP, the Popular Front for the Liberation of Palestine, joined, and so did the PLF, the Palestine Liberation Front. Their stated objective was to foil the Amman agreement by escalating the armed struggle in cooperation with the Shi'ite terror organizations, especially Amal.

This was a clear indication of the schism which had developed between the old and the new branches of the Palestine movement. In the beginning there was the PLO, a political and military superstructure designed to give legitimacy to a dozen subgroups engaged in both political and guerilla/terrorist activities to regain the Palestinian homeland. The strands, both personal and organizational, which bound them together were tangled and complex. But the leaders, comparatively few in number, all knew each other well and understood each other, despite constant quarrels and differences of opinion on tactics and strategy. They often confused the outside world by insisting on the use of war names—Abu this, and Abu that. It was common in disputes among the big Abus (that simply means "Fathers") for factions to splinter off from the main groups and to form their own personal armies to fight in their own fashion. The new formations usually kept the old name but attached a qualifying phrase to it, such as, for example, "General Command" to follow the initials PFLP. After the great schism some of them remained loyal to the Arafatists, while others aligned themselves with the Syrian-backed alliance, which now calls itself the National *Salvation* Front, and some reinsured by backing both sides.

Faced with the Syrian-backed assembly of hardliners, ready and able to discredit their former leader by taking the kind of action which would disrupt any hope of a peaceful arrangement, Yassir Arafat felt it necessary to prove once again that he too could fight the Israelis. To strike at enemy Israel is an essential test of manhood for any Palestinian leader, even when negotiations are in hand. But it is never an easy task for terrorists to operate inside Israel, and this no doubt influenced Yassir Arafat's choice of Israeli targets outside when he activated Force 17 as a kind of terrorist navy. Deprived of operational centers in Lebanon, his men changed tactics and decided to try seaborne operations against the coast of Israel.

By that time the main body of PLO fighters were garrisoned in places as distant from Palestine as South Yemen and North Africa. The Arafatists installed themselves on the island of Kamaran, not far from Aden, which became their main training area. A number of foreign volunteers were reported to be under instruction. The island also has an airstrip, and specially selected Palestinians had flying lessons there.

Two separate units were in training for terrorist duties, Force 17, based in Tunis, and the so-called Western Sector. In command of the latter was Abu Jihad, whose real name is Khalil al-Wazir, a founding member and commander of Fatah who was trained in China. He acquired a fearsome reputation as leader of the PLO terror group, Black September. His first post-Lebanon task was to prepare attacks against Israel from Jordan, but finding it difficult to penetrate the land borders of Israel—especially as little help was forthcoming from the Jordanians—he began making plans for seaborne assaults upon the Mediterranean coastline. For the first one, in the spring of 1985, Abu Jihad trained and prepared his men in Algeria.

After careful briefing the 28 men of the force selected went aboard the small freighter *Atavirus* in Algiers. The plan was for them to split into three groups off the coast of Israel, each with its own rubber assault boat, equipped with outboard motor. Their attacks were timed for the 37th anniversary of the foundation of modern Israel. One target was the Ministry of Defense in Tel Aviv.

Off Israel on April 21, the *Atavirus* was detected and challenged by an Israel patrol boat, whose captain asked the ship to identify itself. The heavily armed squads answered his request with a barrage of rocket-propelled grenades and bursts of automatic rifle fire. The Palestinians did not stand a chance in the face of counterfire from the warship, which was armed with 20-mm and 76-mm cannon. Their vessel sank within seconds with the loss of 20 men, shot or drowned. The eight survivors were taken prisoner.

Abu Jihad took the blame for failure of the mission. In the sharp recrimination which followed the postmortem, allegations were made that his Western Sector units had been infiltrated by spies and could no longer be trusted. Yassir Arafat considered that the failed operation had been too ambitious, and that his loyal Force 17 must take the lead in future operations. Mustafa al-Natour (known as Abu Tayeb), who was its commander, explained that the organization had developed from the 10-man bodyguard formed originally to protect Chairman Arafat against assassination. Although the unit was established in 1970, it made no public impact, for its task was internal security, to ward off attacks on the "boss," mostly from his compatriots.

Abu Tayeb had long been preparing his dramatically named unit for more spectacular service. During the last days in Lebanon it has already expanded into a commando-style force of 1,000 men. Then it recruited at least another 500, including non-Arabs to help with operations outside the Middle East. Training was improved, and instructors were called in to provide courses in sabotage, bomb making and intelligence work. The unit established cells in Europe as well as in the Middle East, ready to take the offensive against enemies of the Arafatist organization. Their first targets were the Arab foes such as Fatah rebels, and their backers in Syria and Libya. Two suspected members of the force were arrested in Madrid while plotting to bomb the Syrian embassy. Force 17 was already being developed as an élite offensive unit.

Its first claim for a notable action came in May 1985 after a bomb had exploded in Jerusalem, and a number of others had been found and made safe. This event coincided with the arrival there of George Shultz for talks with the Israeli government. Even in this matter Yassir Arafat was in public dispute with the Palestinian defector Abu Musa, who claimed that *his* outfit had planted the bombs.

Despite the failure of the initial seaborne mission, the PLO persisted with its attempts to land commandos in Israel, and in the summer Force 17 was ready to make its first attempt. By that time the Israelis were anticipating further naval attempts on their seaports and had reinforced naval patrols. When late in August the motor yacht *Casselredit* appeared off Sidon in southern Lebanon, it was speedily intercepted. The eight guerrillas on board, including Force 17's deputy commander, Faisal Abu Shar, surrendered, together with an American and an Australian manning the yacht who had been hired to ferry the Palestinians from Algeria. It emerged that the fighters had been training there for a year. They had hoped to evade Israeli warships by keeping close to the Lebanese coast, and thought that a yacht might not attract attention. According to the Palestinians, they were heading for Sidon on a mission to protect Arafatist notables who were under attack. The Israeli version was that they intended to raid Israel.

Within a few days of that event, gunboats came alongside the *Ganda*, another motor yacht, outward bound from Cyprus. It too carried a Force 17 squad which was arrested together with the British owner of the vessel and his Greek partner. At this point the Israeli government declared that it considered it had a right to take action against any vessel on the high seas on suspicion of warlike activities, whether or not it was bound for Israel. Yitzhak Rabin declared that his country claimed the right to take naval action, "against terrorism not only along our shores, but wherever and whenever it is needed in the Mediterranean." The declaration upset the Cyprus government, which feared further trouble in the area. Its alarm was soon justified.

On the Jewish Day of Atonement 1985 two Arab gunmen and a very blond Briton murdered three Israelis on a yacht in the marina at Larnaca, Cyprus. The timing of this alarming terror raid was doubly emotive. It took place on the holiest day in the Jewish calendar, and also on the anniversary of the launching of the joint Syrian and Egyptian assault on Israel which began the Yom Kippur war. There was no doubt in Jerusalem that the PLO had intended to mark the occasion with a particularly nasty event. Yassir Arafat, the old original founding Abu, suddenly launched upon the world a brand-new action group. This reinforced the Israelis' conviction that at heart he was still the archterrorist and they made great play of it in their propaganda.

The unit held responsible for the Larnaca affair was Force 17. Its three-man squad boarded an Israeli yacht at Larnaca in Cyprus, shot an Israeli woman and took hostage her husband and another man. At first they demanded the release of captured Force 17 men, which included their deputy leader. Finally, after abandoning these demands, they murdered the two men, in Russian execution style by blowing off the back of their heads at close range with heavy-calibre handguns. PLO headquarters in Tunis promptly claimed that the three Israelis were in fact agents, and that they had been "executed" for spying on ship movements in the Cypriot port. Their claim was firmly denied in Jerusalem.

Israel soon hit back with an air strike at long range which destroyed PLO headquarters at Hammam Plage outside Tunis, killing 50 people. When Shimon Peres, the Israeli prime minister, was defending his country's action in attacking Palestinian installations in neutral Tunisia, he declared that he had sure intelligence that it was Force 17 which carried out the Larnaca raid. He further claimed that eight men of the force captured earlier had given positive identification of the three gunmen responsible for the murders in Cyprus as individuals and as members of their unit. Among those held by the Israelis was Faisal Abu Shar, deputy commander of Force 17, taken when his boat expedition was intercepted off Sidon, Lebanon, a month earlier. One of the Larnaca three was recognized as a Briton named Ian Davison from northeast England who had joined the PLO three years earlier.

His parents, decent folk from the coastal town of South Shields, who went to visit him in Cyprus, said he had telephoned them earlier from Tunis. They were at great pains to insist that he wanted them to say he was not a mercenary but a man who genuinely believed in the Palestinian cause. Fair-haired and with a moustache, he wore combat gear and seemed hugely pleased with his exploit. In London, *The Times* newspaper reported that he had been seen in Lebanon among the PLO fighters being evacuated in the summer of 1983. Cyprus police, who believed that he was in fact leader of the trio, discovered that he had flown to the island on a valid British passport, arriving only a few hours before the attack. Ian Davison is a fascinating example of a new type of recruit. A bit of an adventurer, restless and unemployed at home, he set out to hitchhike round the world, "with £10 in his pocket," according to his mother. In the Middle East he fell in with Palestinians, liked them and was no doubt convinced by their emotional arguments that they were fighting to get back their homeland in what is now Israel.

Davison is by no means the only European who has thrown in his lot with the Arab fighters. It is unlikely that such people are attracted by money, which amounts to only $250 a month, though some no doubt enjoy the excitement and glamor of guerrilla forces. Red Army Faction girls from Germany had enlisted with the PLO foreign legion, and at least one was killed in an Israeli artillery barrage. In 1984 an attractive 24-year-old nurse from the south of France named Francoise Kesteman, who fought for the Palestinians, met her death while on a raid against the Israelis. She had been moved by seeing at first hand the horror of an air attack on the refugee camp where she worked, made by French-built Mirages of the Israeli air force. That was the emotional reason which persuaded her to become a fighter. In a letter home she wrote, "I am happy now to be fully engaged in the Palestinian revolution."

Despite all the military/terrorist efforts made by Yassir Arafat's PLO in the summer and autumn of 1985, the chairman had very little to show for them. The peace talks were not making progress, and he had failed to impress the Arab consensus as a warlord. Yet he was still determined to make some impact on world opinion, and to show that he could pull off a terrorist coup to rival that of the Shi'ites who earlier in the year had captured the TWA airliner.

The PLO was still thinking in maritime terms, but for the big effort the chosen team came, not from Force 17, but from the only faction loyal to Yassir Arafat in a small and divided branch organization known as the Palestine Liberation Front. It is one of the advantages enjoyed by Arafat that he can pick and choose a terrorist group for a specific operation from the wide range of Palestinian factions. By so doing, he can disassociate himself after the event, and wash his hands of responsibility for violence when he slips back into a peace-making role.

The group selected for the piratical seizure of the Italian cruise liner *Achille Lauro* was the PLF breakaway section led by Abu Abbas—also known by his war name Abu Khaled—a man loyal to, and financially dependent upon, Chairman Arafat. Muhammad Zaidan Abbas, to use his full name, at the age of 37 had a lifetime of terrorist experience behind him. He looks the part of a guerrilla leader, wound-scarred, tall and muscular with dark eyes, tousled black hair and drooping Mexican moustache. A heavy smoker of Gitanes cigarettes and possessing a sharp temper, he usually moves with armed bodyguards and himself carries a Czech-made 9-mm automatic. It is not surprising that he has been able to claw and fight his way up through the ranks to top leadership in the Palestinian movement.

Born in Galilee at the time when Israel was becoming a nation, he was taken by his parents to neighboring Syria, and spent his childhood in the Harmoulk refugee camp near Damascus. It was while studying for a university degree in Arabic literature in the Syrian capital that he developed a taste for Marxist student politics. That led him into the PLO forces, where he was talent-spotted by Captain Ahmed Jibril, boss of a Palestinian faction named PFLP-GC (Popular Front for the Liberation of Palestine-General Command). Within that organization he made his mark both as a speaker and as a fighter and in 1973 at the age of 25 he was selected for training in the Soviet Union as a battalion commander.

Abu Abbas had fought in backstreet battles both in Jordan and in Lebanon, usually against fellow Arabs. He established himself as an up-and-coming leader, and no doubt benefiting from his command course in Russia, he emerged as spokesman for his group and developed his talents for planning terrorist operations to be carried out by others. In 1976 his people hijacked a KLM airliner to Tel Aviv in an attempt to get the release of captured comrades. The attempt failed.

The Israelis hold him responsible for organizing a 1979 PLF raid on a block of apartments in the northern town of Nahariya during which a local family was wiped out. Two of the raiders who survived were sentenced to life imprisonment, and it was significant that the name of one was top of the list of 50 prisoners whose release was demanded by the pirates who seized the *Achille Lauro*. The most melodramatic of Abu Abbas's operations were those launched in 1980, when he dispatched two of his men in powered hang gliders to bomb the oil refinery at Haifa. One of the flights landed in south Lebanon; the other dropped hand grenades before crash landing in Israel. At first sight these operations seemed futile, but Israeli security took them seriously, for they had information that 15 pilots were being trained in Syria by a competent woman instructor. In the same year Abbas's men again made fresh bombing attempts, this time using two hot-air balloons.

By that time Abu Abbas had acquired the reputation of being a publicity seeker. He set up as spokesman for the group, ever anxious to impress visiting pressmen in Beirut. He had already quarrelled with Ahmed Jibril, his original sponsor, and boss of the General Command. The occasion of the dispute was the behavior of Jibril's Syrian friends, who had begun to crack down on Palestinian activities in Lebanon. One section hived off to form a PLF branch under the direction of Talaat Yaqub, and Abu Abbas became his second-in-command in battles against former comrades. Then in 1982 the ambitious young guerrilla leader led his own breakaway to set up a personal group of 100 fighters known as PLF-Abu Abbas and threw in his lot definitively when he was short of friends. As a reward the PLO appointed him to the inner cabinet and arranged for him to get military aid, a training camp for himself and an Iraqi diplomatic passport.

This was the man who in the summer of 1985 set about organizing a terrorist venture tailored to attract worldwide attention, and intended to establish him as a big figure in international terrorism. The planning began with a visit to the Italian port of Genoa by Masar Kadia, one of Abbas's trusties bearing a false passport describing him as a Greek shipowner. His task was to make a reconnaissance and to book passage on the *Achille Lauro*, a 23,629-ton Italian luxury liner making cruises to Egypt and the Holy Land. Tickets for the four terrorists under the names recorded in their false passports cost five million lire (about $3,000). When the liner sailed on October 1, Majed al Molky, Hallah al Hassan, Ali Abdullah and Abdel Ibrahim were installed in cabin 82.

On that same day a squadron of Israeli jets flew westward across the Mediterranean to blast the headquarters of the PLO in Tunis in revenge for the murder of three Israelis on the yacht in Larnaca harbor. This raid was to have an effect upon the Palestinian operation just beginning in the port of Genoa, a few hundred sea miles north. The terrorists needed to keep in touch with their base, and were alarmed to hear about destruction of the Tunis headquarters which was their communications center. Abu Abbas and his controllers were cut off from their men in the field and busy at home with damage-control assessments. The operation started badly.

There had already been trouble at the Genoa end because Issa Mohammed Abbas, a relation and henchman of Abu Abbas, who had been sent to Italy to control the operation, has been arrested by the police five days before the liner sailed. In the false bottom of his car gas tank they discovered four Kalashnikovs, eight grenades and some detonators. He had been sent as quartermaster as well as group leader. In his absence the four 20-year-olds were left to make their own decisions.

The original plan, according to later statements by Abu Abbas, was not for the gunmen to take over the ship. Their orders were to stay under cover until it reached the Israeli port of Ashdod and to remain on board while the passengers went ashore on their tour. Then by night they were to leave the ship and fight their way to port oil-storage tanks and an ammunition depot, which were to be blown up.

"Their mission was not to hijack the Italian ship or to threaten the lives of the passengers," said Abu Abbas, talking to the Middle East News Agency in Belgrade. "Their destination was the Israeli port of Ashdod for the purpose of carrying out a suicide mission inside occupied territory."

According to his version of events, things went wrong because the gunmen were discovered, and this forced them to act prematurely and seize the ship. It is obvious that these inexperienced young men did indeed panic, and that may have been because they were spotted, or anyway thought that they had been detected. Aboard ship they were thoroughly out of their element, anxious about the happenings in Tunis, and alarmed that no fresh orders had reached them since they sailed from Genoa.

Whatever the reason, the fact was that after many of the passengers had gone ashore at Alexandria and the liner was sailing in international waters for Port Said on Monday, October 7, the four armed men suddenly erupted into the dining room, firing machine guns and pistols. Threatening Captain Gerardo de Rosa on his own bridge, they seized control of the *Achille Lauro* and ordered the master to sail northward towards the Syrian coast. There were still 427 passengers on board, many of them Americans, and 80 crew. They were all hostages.

The alarm bells started to ring in Washington, as well as in Rome, where Prime Minister Craxi began squaring up to the intractable horrors and frustrations of a hostage situation. On Tuesday the terrorists, thwarted in their aim of docking at a Syrian port, made their demand for the release of 50 Palestinians held by the Israelis, and threatened to kill passengers one by one, beginning with the Americans and Britons. When they did murder Leon Klinghoffer in his wheelchair, the fact that he was Jewish, and a spirited 69-year-old gentleman from New York who bravely refused to be intimidated by armed men, merely served to emphasize the horror of what was happening aboard ship.

Action was being taken. The Italians dispatched paratroops to the British bases in the island of Cyprus off the Levant coast; President Reagan put armed forces on standby and sent specially trained SEAL frogman commando units of the U.S. Navy and Delta army teams to a base in Sicily. Attempts were made to begin negotiations with the pirates on board, though there was little that could be done in the way of hostage bargaining.

As is usual in the early stages of a terrorist crisis, news was sketchy and rumors were wild. The only hard information came by way of American electronic spy planes which were monitoring events on board, but that was kept secret. Then suddenly the *Achille Lauro* was reported to be heading back to Port Said, and the four Palestinians announced themselves ready to leave the ship free. A deal had been arranged by President Mubarak of Egypt with the PLO. The man who helped to fix it was none other than Abu Abbas, the PLF leader who on behalf of the PLO had planned the operation in the first place, and who was now there in Egypt instructing his men to abandon the ship they had held captive for 51 anxious hours. It was indeed a cynical exercise of the kind for which the PLO has quite a reputation. The Palestinians simply decided that nothing more could be achieved by the seajack and that the time had come to cut their losses by calling the whole thing off. An added attraction was that it gave them their chance to make sententious declarations that terrorism had nothing to do with them. Arafat, the PLO chairman, had certainly been deeply involved from the beginning. That did not prevent him from denying any responsibility, even though he told his own people: "The operation was most important because it made the world tremble before the Palestinian warrior. I prophesied that if we were not listened to a volcano would erupt, and indeed, it has erupted."

What irked the Americans in particular was that the gunmen who had seized the ship and murdered Leon Klinghoffer seemed certain to escape punishment for their crimes. Once ashore in Egypt, they were whisked off to Cairo by the local authorities to the understandable indignation of the U.S. Ambassador, Nicholas Veliotes, who was heard shouting over the telephone to his colleagues in Cairo: "You tell the foreign ministry that we demand they prosecute those sons of bitches." His undiplomatic language well expressed the strong feelings of Americans and their friends and allies when it became obvious that the four self-satisfied pirates were to be flown back to PLO headquarters in Tunis, and no doubt congratulated for their deed.

The mood in the White House was gloomy too as reports came in that the Palestinians had left Egypt, and the military state of alert in the Mediterranean was wound down. But in Egypt, American intelligence men were still at work, and came up with fresh information that President Mubarak had lied when he said that the four had already left. Preparations were being made to fly them back to Tunis from Al Maza airbase near Cairo aboard a Boeing 737 of Egyptair. As soon as this became known the plan was hatched to intercept the flight, and orders went out from the situation room in Washington to alert the Sixth Fleet, and to send back to Sicily the Navy's special unit, Team Six of the SEALS, which had already started pulling back to Gibraltar.

The decision to go ahead was not an easy one to make, for the Americans were only too well aware of the diplomatic repercussions there would be in the Middle East, and especially of the danger of undermining the normally friendly President Mubarak of Egypt. But after tense discussions the U.S. president finally approved the plan. A fleet of F-14 fighters was scrambled aboard the USS *Saratoga*. Controlled by a Hawkeye fleet radar aircraft and an electronic warfare Prowler, they set up an air-traffic checkpoint south of Crete as the Egyptian airliner flew westward. By night they successfully picked up the airliner, and zooming around it with lights flashing, ordered its captain to divert to Sigonella airbase in Sicily.

The one flaw in an otherwise highly successful operation was that because of the need to keep things secret, Washington had failed to inform the Italian government until the aerial parade was about to enter Italian airspace. When they landed the aircraft became the center of an unseemly altercation between hastily alerted Italian carabinieri and the newly arrived navy commandos of SEAL Team Six. For a few moments it seemed that there might be an actual exchange of fire between the two units, each of which claimed the right to take custody of the Palestinian prisoners and their escorting mastermind Abu Abbas. To avoid further trouble the Americans were compelled to give way. That was how it came about that the four pirates were charged by an Italian court and escaped being whisked off to face American justice.

The other unfortunate consequence was that Abu Abbas himself was released by the Roman authorities, and was allowed to make good his escape by way of Yugoslavia, back into the terrorist world of the Middle East despite all the efforts of the U.S. authorities to extradite him. Even so, it was a famous victory which brought jubilation in the United States. "Thank God, we've finally won one," exclaimed Senator Daniel Moynihan (D., N.Y.).

On June 18, 1986 proceedings began in the Italian trial of the *Achille Lauro* terrorists. Three of the hijackers, including Abu Abbas, had to be tried in absentia. All of those three were given sentences of life imprisonment, the court finding them responsible for the organization and engineering of the hijacking. Obviously, the likelihood of their ever serving their sentences is very slim.

Four of their Palestinian henchmen, however, were detained by the Italian government. Of these four, three were indicted (the fourth being a minor, his case was tried separately) and sentenced to prison terms ranging from 15 to 30 years.

The Italian *Achille Lauro* trials charged 15 men and convicted 11 of them. American public opinion found these sentences extremely soft, in view of the nature of the crimes. No matter what the diplomatic consequences on the tangled affairs of the Middle East, there can be no doubt that the United States will go on hunting the terrorist chief Abu Abbas to serve his time in prison. Still ringing in Abbas' ears must be the words of President Reagan: "You can run, but you can't hide."

17.

The Armed Squabble

The one tactic upon which the mainline PLO and all its many offshoots and quibbling factions are in agreement is the desirability of raiding within the territory of the state of Israel. That is a form of guerrilla warfare by no means easy to conduct. Israel considers itself in a continual state of alert, and great attention is paid to internal security. Mossad, the Israeli secret service, has on many occasions managed to penetrate the terrorist organizations, and remains remarkably well informed about their leaders and their plans.

An additional safeguard so far as Israel is concerned is the attitude of the Arab neighbor states, Syria and Jordan. Neither of these countries, sympathetic though they are to the Palestinian cause, is willing to give a free hand to units operating into Israel from their territory. Large-scale attacks draw reprisals, and the Arab neighbors are rarely willing to draw such countermeasures upon themselves just to please the Palestinian brothers.

Nevertheless, some PLO terrorist activities were tolerated by Jordan's King Hussein until July 1986. Abu Jihad established himself in Amman where he cautiously conducted operations from the PLO's main office. Weapons and explosives were smuggled into the Israeli-occupied West Bank where they were distributed to Arafat's supporters.

221

Nothing was done to invite reprisals from the Israelis. But King Hussein put a stop to even his low level activity when he quarreled with Arafat following the collapse of the joint Jordanian-PLO peace initiative. Hussein, feeling that he had been betrayed, made his peace with Syria and ordered the closing of Arafat's 25 offices in Amman. Abu Jihad was given 48 hours to get out of Jordan.

However, despite his failure at sea warfare, Abu Jihad had already brought to fruition a remarkably simple and effective form of "do it yourself" terrorism within Israel. His agents had worked like termites in the villages of the West Bank, distributing weapons and encouraging the young men to make opportunistic attacks on solitary Israelis.

Men and women from the armed forces are often to be seen waiting for lifts by lonely roadsides in Israel, where hitching is a normal way of getting about the country. They became one of the principal targets of the "do it yourself" killers, as did foreign tourists. In addition, bombs were planted in buses and grenades thrown in crowded streets. This campaign continues and causes much alarm. In the six months to September 1985 12 separate such incidents were reported, costing the lives of 15 Israelis. The overall effect was dramatic, as the steady drip of shootings, stabbings and explosions sapped Israeli morale.

Ze'ev Schiff, a leading Israeli military commentator, wrote:

> The events in Judea, Samaria and Gaza are sustained by the reality in the area itself. In the same way that the underground organizations of the Jewish people in order to rebel during the British mandate, so the Arab residents do not need to be spurred by the Palestinians in exile in the Arab states in order to act against the Israeli regime.

In face of the sporadic terrorist attacks on the West Bank and elsewhere Shimon Peres's government reinforced security by deploying regular troops, and took repressive action against the Arab population, making many arrests and deporting people branded as troublemakers. It is not without irony that in the process the Israelis used emergency legislation originally formulated to enable British authorities during the Mandate to cope with Jewish terrorists. There were also ugly scenes in some places as Israeli extremist groups took the law into their own hands and attacked and sometimes murdered Arabs. In one month local Palestinians reported four of their people killed and 14 wounded.

The mainstream PLO is not the only force trying to spread terrorism within Israel. Mention has already been made of Captain Ahmed Jibril, who having started life as a Syrian army officer became the director of the Damascus-controlled breakaway group entitled PFLP-GC, the Popular Front for the Liberation of Palestine, General Command. Ahmed Jibril always favored sending his men on raids into Israeli-controlled territory. His view was that the armed struggle could only be effective on the soil of Palestine. A typical Jibril operation was carried out in the northern town of Qiryat Shemona in April 1974 when a three-man squad seized an apartment building and murdered 18 people before being itself killed by the Israeli army. Ahmed Jibril said the raid had been planned to bring into existence a "new school of struggle based on the highest degree of revolutionary violence," and he claimed it was a success because they had succeeded, even if only for a short time, in occupying a small part of Palestine. Despite the preference of General Command for such operations, the Israelis hold it responsible for a number of mid-air bombings of passenger planes never claimed by anybody else, especially the destruction, with the loss of 47 lives, of a Swissair flight from Zurich to Tel Aviv.

Ahmed Jibril has a long record of quarreling with rival terrorist leaders, whom he accused of a lack of martial zeal. He took his General Command out of the original PFLP run by Dr. George Habash and Dr. Wadi Haddad to demonstrate his disapproval of the showy international operations which were its specialty. Wadi Haddad created the international alliance which carried out the first campaigns of terror in Europe and the Middle East in the early 1970s. He was responsible for such dramatic acts as the multiple hijacking to Dawson's Field in Jordan. That affair in turn led to the "Black September" expulsion of the Palestinians from Jordan, and to the massacre of 26 people by the Japanese Red Army at Lod airport in Israel. Ahmed Jibril thoroughly disliked international operations of that kind.

Curiously enough, Ahmed Jibril's greatest success was a nonviolent one, achieved through negotiation. It came about in this way. During skirmishes in Lebanon his group captured three Israeli soldiers. Jibril knew the importance which Israel attaches to getting back prisoners held by the Arabs, and exploited this fact in shrewd bargaining through Austrian mediators over an 18-month period. Eventually, in return for the three, he secured the release of no less than

1,154 Arabs, of whom 879 were convicted terrorists held in Israeli top-security establishments. The exchange of 394 mainly Palestinian prisoners took place in Geneva after the arrival there from Damascus of the three Israeli soldiers. The remaining Arab prisoners chose to return to their homes in the occupied territories.

When it became known that many released Palestinians had been found guilty of terrorist crimes, and that among them were foreigners like Kozo Okamoto, the only survivor of the Japanese Red Army group responsible for the slaughter at Lod airport, there was general indignation in Israel. Convicted killers were allowed to return to their home towns and villages, where they could be seen in public by relatives of people who had been their victims. One great fear expressed was that the deal might tempt Palestinian groups to kidnap Israelis simply to get bargaining counters for the release of more of their men. The government was forced to declare that if this happened, then the Palestinians in the big exchange deal would be rearrested.

This led to a debate in Israel about the wisdom and morality of releasing such people. It became fiercer in that it coincided with the trial of 18 people from a Jewish group which actually called itself Terror Against Terror, for assaults upon Arabs. Ariel Sharon, an extremist general still known by his war name "Arik" and also a minister, declared in a revealing turn of phrase that it was inconceivable that "terrible killers can be released while members of the Jewish *underground* remain behind bars." Yitzhak Shamir, the right-wing deputy prime minister, argued that because of the release of the Palestinians all Jews imprisoned for terrorism should be pardoned.

The acrimony did not save the Israeli terrorists on trial at the time from being sentenced. Three men, Menachem Livmi, Uzi Sharabaf, and Shaul Nirv, received life sentences for murdering three Palestinian students and wounding others during an attack upon the Islamic college in Hebron in 1983. Twelve others were sent to prison for terms ranging between four months and seven years. Their crimes included the car-bomb attacks which maimed two prominent Arab mayors of West Bank towns, and an attempt in 1984 to boobytrap Arab buses in Jerusalem. They had also plotted to blow up the Dome of the Rock in Jerusalem, one of the holiest places of Islam. Supporters of these people (who can only be described as terrorists) appeared outside the court with banners proclaiming: "The Gentiles get freedom and the Jews suffering." Nonetheless, the rule of law was upheld.

Ahmed Jibril considered the exchange deal a great success, both because it struck a blow at Israeli self-confidence and also because it strengthened his hand in challenging Yassir Arafat for leadership of the PLO. His principal backer, President Assad of Syria, who had given his support during negotiations, was equally satisfied.

The history of the Palestinian terrorist movements is a long saga of quarrels and disputes among the temperamental and violent warlords who direct them. The group which spawned so many others as a result of internecine struggles was the Popular Front for the Liberation of Palestine, originally under the joint management of two doctors, George Habash and Wadi Haddad. Habash was the "progressive" philosopher and his fellow doctor the revolutionary man of action. As Haddad's operations became increasingly outrageous—even being condemned by the Soviet Union and China—a chasm opened before the former friends. After a bitter and public row in 1972, Habash renounced all international terrorist activities on behalf of the Front.

Dr. Haddad stormed out to form a splinter Special Operations Group, and took his terrorists off to the Iraqi capital, Baghdad. It was from there that he organized the kidnap of OPEC oil ministers in Vienna, and the hijacking which eventually ended in Entebbe. Members of the European doctrinal terrorist groups were in contact with this group, and so to a lesser extent were IRA men and Basque separatists. Some foreigners actually took their place in Haddad hit teams. The first to achieve notoriety was Patrick Arguello, a Nicaraguan, shot dead in a gun battle during an attempt to hijack an El Al Boeing over the Thames estuary. The famous woman terrorist Leila Khaled was arrested on this occasion. Carlos, the international practitioner, was one of his men, and he also used German terrorists in a number of operations. Wadi Haddad, more than any other Palestinian leader, made terrorism international.

After Haddad's death in East Berlin on April 1, 1979, of natural causes, the special operations group fragmented. Salim Abu Salem, who was Haddad's lieutenant and the action man of the old organization, inherited leadership of the breakaway group (renamed Special Command of PFLP). Consisting of some 50 gunmen, it followed Haddad's warlike example. Salim took the war name Abu Mohammad, and continued the European connection with the new terrorists there, and also gave his patronage to ASALA, the Armenian Terrorist group. The speciality of Salim Abu Salem's organization has been wanton attacks upon Jews and Jewish institutions in Europe and elsewhere. In October 1980 his men bombed a synagogue in rue Copernic, Paris, killing four. Two months later 16 people lost their lives when Special Command exploded a bomb at the Jewish-owned Norfolk hotel in Nairobi, Kenya. The following year two more fell victim to his bombers, who blasted off a car bomb near the Portuguese synagogue in Antwerp.

Since that time PFLP Special Command has been less obviously conspicuous, partly because it lost the backing of Iraq. Its place as the most vicious of the Palestinian terror factions has been taken by the Abu Nidal organization.

18.

The
Terror
Lords

Some élite antiterrorist squads are more elite than others. That was the stark lesson of the brave, though bloody, attempt by Egyptian commandos of the "Thunderbolt" squad to rescue Egyptair Flight 648, which in November 1985 had been seized by armed Arabs after taking off on the Athens-Cairo run. Before the Boeing landed at Luqa airport on the island of Malta, passports had been examined and the passengers were sorted into national groups.

Once again in a hijack, the Americans, Europeans and Israelis aboard were selected as scapegoats and with lunatic zeal the neurotic gunmen began shooting them one by one to reinforce their demand for refueling of the aircraft. Mercifully their unbalanced state of mind, and their lack of small-arms ability, ensured that some of the victims were wounded and not killed.

Clearly the circumstances of this affair were special. The murderous intent of the terrorists was so obvious that neither the Maltese authorities, nor the Egyptian commander in position there, had very much choice left in deciding how to act. There was nothing to show that the air pirates were sane enough for negotiations and bargaining to take place, and they had already shot five hostages. Robert Kupperman, the prominent expert in terrorism at the Georgetown University Center for Strategic and International Studies, wisely summed up the case: "One could argue that more effort at

227

negotiating might have softened the terrorists, but when they start shooting people and tossing them out, does it really look that way?" Indeed, the only way to discourage terrorists from murdering selected passengers is to make it clear that as soon as the killing starts negotiation becomes impossible.

President Mubarak was anxious to show after the humiliations of the *Achille Lauro* business that he was capable of coping with terrorists. The Egyptian special unit dispatched to Malta was well trained and ready for action. The troops were accompanied by several senior American army officers, and their commander, Major-General Muhammad Kamal Attia, was keen to show how good his men were. It was their tactics which came in for hostile criticism later, because so many people died as they stormed the aircraft, killing two of the three hijackers after blasting a hole in the baggage compartment. Of the 98 people originally on board the Boeing, 57 died in the assault. A disaster of this kind was bound to happen eventually. After the highly successful rescue operations at Entebbe and at Mogadishu in 1977, the impression got about that daring was enough to win against air pirates. In fact a unit must be very lucky as well as very good indeed to succeed in a situation which is militarily almost impossible. Few experts would ever rate the odds in favor of complete success at anything better than 60-40 in favor.

The ugly truth must be faced that as Mediterranean hijackers become ever more desperate, the danger for air passengers in this area is bound continually to increase. It cannot be assumed that the rescuers—be they Egyptian, British or American—will always win. This reality has already been faced by the Israelis, and must now be accepted by the international community. It does not mean that attempts should not be made to rescue seized airliners. Risks have to be taken to prevent the terrorists from winning.

In the minds of key witnesses aboard the aircraft there was certainly no doubt about the correctness of the Egyptian decision to make the assault. Captain Hani Galal reported that each time the hijackers shot another passenger, "They joked and danced about. I became convinced as it went on that the plane would be stormed, because it was the only solution." As the Egyptian troops moved in he proved his conviction by doing what many flight captains in similar situations must have longed to do. He grabbed the emergency hatchet and smote down the armed bully who had just tried to shoot him.

It was easy for Secretary of State George Shultz in Washington to say: "The way to get after these people is to get after them with both barrels." But Tony Lyons, an Australian businessman from London who lived through the whole nightmare from the time when a nervous, sweating and well-dressed Arab sitting next to him drew a handgun to scize the aircraft, said afterwards that he welcomed the Egyptian counterattack despite the danger. Mr. Lyons had been selected as the next passenger to be shot.

Blame for the slaughter at Luqa airport rests upon the terrorists who took the airliner there rather than on those who came to the rescue. Who were they?

President Mubarak of Egypt unhesitatingly accused the old Arab enemy next door, Colonel Gaddafi of Libya, of ultimate responsibility. Americans hinted that they had similar suspicions, but President Reagan's entourage felt that the case was circumstantial, and that the final element of "smoking gun" evidence could not be obtained. The basis for suspected collusion of the Libyan leader—who needless to say issued his customary denials—was that the terrorist group which announced that its men had hijacked the plane was the one led by Sabri al-Banna. Better known by his war name Abu Nidal, this PLO rebel and renegade, with a lifetime of terrorist activity, was known to have rebased his "Abu Nidal" faction in Libya. After himself putting about the disinformation story that he had died of a heart attack in November 1984, the leader moved there from Damascus in Syria. Indeed, he was photographed in consultation with Colonel Gaddafi.

Of all the bands of hit men traveling the world in search of prey, none are more persistent, vengeful and outrageous than those controlled by the Abu Nidal organization. Formed in 1973, the faction was estimated 12 years later to have 200 trained men available.

The Abu Nidal outfit resembles a mercenary body ready and willing to act in diverse interests, even though it pretends to be devoted to correcting the errors of Yassir Arafat and his PLO Fatah fighters. The group even styles itself "Fatah—The Revolutionary Council." Before that the name used was Black June, chosen to mark Abu Nidal's disapproval of the original Syrian 1976 intervention in Lebanon at that time on the side of the Christians. The title was hastily abandoned because it became necessary for the leader, Sabri al-Banna, to move to Damascus and sell his services to those same Syrians.

Sabri was the son of a prosperous Palestinian Arab family. His father, Haj Khalil al-Banna, exported fruit to Europe. The family lived in style, with houses in France, Turkey and Egypt. One of his brothers was quoted as saying: "We had horses at stables in Ashkelon and orange groves all over the land." He now lives in Nablus as an influential businessman on the occupied West Bank. When Israel came into being in 1948 the family left their big house in Jaffa and finally took refuge on the West Bank, which at the time was part of Jordan. Sabri al-Banna studied engineering in Cairo and then took a job in Saudi Arabia, where he mixed with fellow exiles working in the oil fields. He joined Fatah, and took the war name Abu Nidal. A close friendship developed with Yassir Arafat, and soon he was looked upon as a rising star among the group's leaders.

In 1969 he was appointed representative of Fatah in Baghdad, an influential post which brought him into contact with Iraq's ruling Baath Party, supporters of a tough line against Israel. When after the failure of the Arab powers to defeat Israel in the 1973 war Yassir Arafat showed signs of wanting to come to terms with the Israelis, Abu Nidal denounced him a traitor. He then declared that he himself was true leader of the armed struggle. Supported by Iraq, which had taken a leading role among the rejectionists condemning any kind of accommodation with Israel, Abu Nidal began gathering round himself a band of well-trained men for terrorist operations.

The nucleus came from the National Arab Youth for the Liberation of Palestine (NAYLP), originally led by another renegade from Fatah named Ahmed al-Ghafour (Abu Mahmoud). His career illustrates the kind of in-fighting common in terrorist movements. As the PLO man in Libya, he, like Abu Nidal, accused Chairman Arafat of selling out to the enemy. This was a point of view shared by Colonel Gaddafi, who persuaded Abu Mahmoud to take over the leadership of the NAYLP. With Libyan backing Abu Mahmoud embarked on a series of outrages so shocking that they threatened the political credibility of the PLO, even though it was not responsible for them.

One of his gangs threw thermite bombs into a Pan-American plane at Rome airport in December 1973, burning to death 32 passengers. The group claimed responsibility for planting a bomb which blew a TWA flight out of the sky over the Aegean the following September with the loss of 88 people.

For these crimes, and the damage they did to the Palestinian cause, PLO headquarters sentenced Abu Mahmoud to death. Despite that he flew back to Beirut, confident that Colonel Gaddafi's backing and his position as head of such a formidable gang would protect him. The so-called Fatah elimination squad shot him dead. His NAYLP was broken, but the remnants made their way to Baghdad to join Abu Nidal, who inherited the bloodstained mantle of Mahmoud.

Abu Nidal too was in trouble with PLO leaders who claimed that he had misappropriated the organization's funds in taking over their assets in Iraq. Furthermore, he was plotting to assassinate Yassir Arafat, and other leaders incurring his hatred. It was for this reason that Fatah sentenced him to death, and dispatched a seven-man squad to do the deed. The eliminators were themselves arrested by the Iraqi authorities. Abu Nidal survived, but from that time on he made perpetual war upon the official PLO, sending out his teams to murder any of its representatives branded by him as a moderate.

Among the victims was Said Hammami, PLO man in London, shot and killed in his Mayfair office in 1978 after holding tentative discussions with Israeli radicals, which marked him as a traitor. Abu Nidal gunmen also murdered PLO representatives in Kuwait, and in Paris that same year. Abu Daoud, another Palestinian leader, was badly wounded in Warsaw in 1981, and the Brussels representative was killed. A further victim was Issam Sartawi, heart surgeon and former member of the Palestinian "war cabinet," who sick of conflict had explored contacts between the PLO and the Israeli peace movement.

Sartawi loathed everything that Abu Nidal stood for, and dared to speak out against his terror actions, declaring, "Abu Nidal ought to be put on trial." He knew the risks, and took every precaution. But even so Abu Nidal's men, after many failed attempts, caught up with him at the Montechoro Hotel at Albufeira in Portugal while he was attending a conference of the Socialist International.

Abu Nidal gloated over the murder in a communiqué: "It is our pleasure to communicate . . . our success in implementing the death sentence towards a criminal and traitor. The bullets that killed Issam Ali Sartawi are the bullets of Palestine . . ."

In counterpoint to the murders of compatriots, the group was also carrying out attacks on behalf of its Iraqi protectors, usually against the hated Syrian neighbors. At the time this arrangement suited Abu Nidal, who had named his squads Black June. There were two attempts upon the Life of Abdul Halim Khaddam, the Syrian foreign minister, and in 1976 Abu Nidal's men blew up the Semiramis Hotel in Damascus. Three of the terrorists involved were caught and publicly hanged in the Syrian capital. Despite such events, the organization was able to win favor with the Syrians, and although the main protector was still Iraq, it was able for a while to serve two mutually hostile masters.

Abu Nidal's act of terrorism from which most lasting consequences flowed was the shooting in June 1982 of Shlomo Argov, Israeli ambassador to London, as he left the Dorchester Hotel in Park Lane. This respected diplomat was badly wounded in the head and never completely recovered. The wider significance was that Israel seized upon the affair as a pretext for the invasion of Lebanon which had such far-reaching effects.

The shooting was the work of three men: Ghassan Said, who actually fired the Polish WZ-63 machine pistol; Marwen al-Banna, the armorer, who was a kinsman of Abu Nidal; and Nawaf Rosan, a colonel in the Iraqi intelligence service seconded to the group. All three pretended they were students. Said, the gunman, was wounded in the throat by an armed police officer who pursued him, and eventually received a 35-year sentence. The other two got 30 years each. They were told by Mr. Justice Mars-Jones: "We will not tolerate gangs of terrorists operating in this country or their campaign of violence being conducted on the streets of this capital city . . . there can be no mercy from the court."

No mercy was to be expected either from Abu Nidal, who issued a threatening and arrogant statement warning the British government that it would pay a high price for imprisoning his men. "The time will come when the Zionist judges of Britain will learn what justice is and how to practice it."

In revenge for the imprisonment of the hit team, the organization did strike back by killing British officials abroad. In 1984 Kenneth Whitty, cultural attaché at the embassy in Athens, was murdered, and so was Percy Norris, deputy high commissioner in Bombay. Both were shot at close range in their cars. Telephone calls announcing these crimes were made in the name of the Revolutionary Organization of Socialist Moslems, the new style being used by Abu Nidal. The justification given was "to stop their aggressive interventions and their detention and torture of fighters." Neither of the murdered men had anything to do with Middle East politics.

The same organization was probably responsible for the kidnapping in 1985 of a British freelance journalist in Beirut, Alec Collett. The private war of attrition against Britain continued in the same year with a grenade attack upon an Athens hotel full of vacationers from the U.K., and demands kept coming for the release from prison of the three killers.

By that time Abu Nidal's headquarters had been transferred from Baghdad to the capital of his former enemy President Assad in Damascus, and the main campaign was against Jordanian diplomats. A first secretary in Ankara, Ziyad al-Sati, was shot in the head and killed. Threats were made by the organization that it was planning to "execute" King Hussein himself.

Unlike many Palestinian leaders, Abu Nidal had always been a secretive man, so it came as no surprise when reports circulated in November 1984 that he had died of a heart attack at the age of 46. They originated with a member of his family. Then a friend who visited him said he was paralyzed and close to death. It was known that he had suffered from heart trouble, and according to the PLO he once traveled anonymously to London for surgery in a private hospital.

An anonymous telephone call later denied the story about Abu Nidal's death. His brother said that he had received a message both from the Red Cross and from another member of the family saying that he was still alive. Later still a man who claimed that he was Nidal gave an interview to a French journalist, and after that he appeared several times for interviews with foreign journalists.

Such tricks seem to have been intended to conceal the fact that his organization had once again changed its allegiance. The Abu Nidal faction had come to an arrangement to work in Libya in the interests of Colonel Gaddafi. There was an unconfirmed report that the Libyan leader had paid him several million dollars for services to be rendered. Nidal's deputy, Mustafa Muradi (Abu Nizar), and the spokesman, Abdurrahman Issa, who were superintending operations, put out a cryptic statement:

"Abu Nidal is not just a person but a symbol and a fighting organization which will fight to the end against imperialism and Zionism."

At first it was read as an obituary. In fact it was a warning that the organization, with its long record of plotting and assassination, was preparing more ambitious acts of terrorism. Until December 1985 Abu Nidal had never been involved in air piracy. What tempted his organization into this form of terrorism was the hijacking of the TWA flight earlier that year by Shi'ites of Islamic Jihad. The resurgence of air piracy was by then having its effect on many groups envious of what they considered to be a success. Terrorism thrives on imitation.

The Egyptian counterattack on the aircraft prevented the three hijackers from ever making their plans. Had those demands been made it is probable that they would have included release of the Abu Nidal kinsman and his two comrades serving a long sentence in Britain. There can be no doubt that Mrs. Thatcher figures on the organization's enemy list, partly because of the men in prison and partly because the prime minister invited two moderate Palestinian leaders to London as part of a Jordanian-Palestinian delegation in 1985. An Abu Nidal spokesman declared: "We warn these two against participating in this treason which is a criminal act against the people's cause. We announce to our Palestinian people, to the Arab nation and to the press, that we have decided to shed the blood of these two in case they do not heed this warning and the will of our people in continuing the armed struggle."

During their brief visit in October 1985 the two leaders in question, Mohammed Milhem and Bishop Khoury, were heavily guarded, but the anger of the terrorist group against Britain was manifest.

Abu Nidal confirmed that Prime Minister Thatcher was on his death list in an interview with the Abu Dhabi newspaper *Al Wahda* on January 8, 1986 in which he said: "Margaret Thatcher is high on the list of people to assassinate because of her pro-Zionist leanings . . . We are working with anti-Thatcher forces such as the IRA. She got away with it in the Brighton attack, but I can assure you she will not escape next time. I don't want to say any more about this bitch."

The interview consisted largely of a diatribe against his enemies—Zionists, imperialists and the Americans. "I can tell you one thing, whenever we have a chance to do even the slightest damage to the Americans, we shall not hesitate to do it; between them and us it is war without mercy. We want them to fuck off from our territory. Whether they want to elect as President a ballet dancer, a cowboy or an actor, that is their business, but when American aircraft bomb our houses, that is terrorism and we shall strike back."

Asked whether President Reagan was on the hit list he replied that he certainly was. "If we get him we shall make sure he gets the place in history that he deserves."

He acknowledged his responsibility for the coordinate attacks on the El Al desks at Rome and Vienna airports on December 27, 1985, in which 16 people were killed: "Yes, I organized the attacks at Rome and Vienna. Such actions are completely legitimate." He also acknowledged his connection with Gaddafi: "Gaddafi has greatly helped us up till now. He is a good man with whom we have solid links.

"We are joined to him by profound friendship and our relationship is based on mutual respect. We dream the same dream—of a united Arab nation. He is a bird singing outside the tribe, but one day the birds will flock towards him and sing his song in unison. His country is an unshakeable base for the struggle against imperialism and Zionism. He is our great support."

Abu Nidal went on to boast about the number of Palestinian moderates whose murder he had ordered: "You have only a modest list. Every Arab who is in contact with Mossad will end like them. We have executed hundreds . . . We warn, then liquidate, even Said Hammami, who was my nephew." He argued that it was not a question of what such killings achieved but that "traitors must be punished."

Abu Nidal is by no means the only freebooting warlord of terrorism operations in what he believes to be the Palestinian cause. Another sinister and secretive group, operating from Baghdad as the "15th May organization" has also made its impact on the terrorist scene. The title was chosen as a reminder of the date of Israel's independence day. Mohammed Omari—who prefers to be known as Abu Ibrahim—is the mastermind of this minuscule group. He is one of the most technically dangerous and cunning terrorists in the world. Like many before him, he graduated from the special operations group of the old PFLP when it split. Apart from that, all that is known about him is that he is a Palestinian and that his home was in Tripoli, Lebanon.

Abu Ibrahim's power to cause fear stems from his extraordinary expertise as a maker of clever bombs, and his callous lack of discrimination in using them against innocent people. His masterpiece was the creation of almost undetectable suitcase bombs. To fabricate such infernal machines he used thinly rolled explosive molded into the fabric of the case and built in a miniature detonating device hidden in the metal studs to shield it from detection by X-ray machines. Connecting wires and batteries are also cunningly hidden. To any airport security people not trained to watch out specially for it, such a suitcase bomb would pass unnoticed.

The device is designed to explode in the baggage hold of an airliner when triggered by a barometric detonator set to act at a preselected height. Such tricks have already been used by other terrorist bombers to blow up planes in flight. But Abu Ibrahim is known to have refined the technique by linking the barometric detonator to a timing device.

Combined linkage makes it possible to delay the explosion so that it does not necessarily destroy the first airliner aboard which it is placed. This means that, for example, a suitcase bomb put on a flight to Athens could arrive there safely, be transferred to another plane heading for Israel, and still not explode until that airliner flew in low over Tel Aviv. At that point, if the timing device and the barometric trigger were correctly set, the aircraft would blow up over the city causing a double catastrophe. Mercifully no such diabolical plan has ever succeeded, though bomb experts believe that theoretically it could work.

Abu Ibrahim was experimenting with the barometric detonator as long ago as 1972. Two good-looking Palestinians, Adnam Ali Hashem and Ahmed Zaid, pretending to be Iranians, picked up two English girls on vacation in Rome and began an affair. They all made plans to continue the vacation by flying to Israel, and tickets were provided for the girls. But at the last minute Adnam and Ahmed said there was a hitch because they had first to go to Tehran to get money. It was arranged that the girls should go on ahead and they would all meet later in Jerusalem. Before saying goodbye a farewell present was made of a tape recorder.

It had been fitted out with a bomb and a concealed barometric detonator which exploded on the aircraft heading for Tel Aviv, causing serious damage, but without destroying the plane. El Al, the Israeli airline, had taken the precaution after the earlier bomb scares of armor-plating their baggage holds. Fortunately for the girls, they had put the tape recorder inside a suitcase instead of carrying it on as hand baggage. The two Arabs were later arrested and questioned in Rome, though they were soon released on the grounds that their explosive charge had not been strong enough to destroy the plane.

The same method of persuading an unsuspecting traveler to carry a bomb aboard an aircraft was again employed by Abu Ibrahim's men in April 1980. Using a European middleman, they persuaded a German named Uwe Rabe to take a suitcase on a flight to Israel by leading him vaguely to believe it had something to do with diamonds. He was provided with a ticket and with a false passport. It was while she was examining this document that a woman official at Zurich airport became suspicious. It contained a recently used United States visa and she asked Herr Rabe how he liked America. "I have never been to America," he replied; a remark that led to strict examination of himself and his baggage and the discovery of an early model of the Abu Ibrahim suitcase bomb.

Four years later after a number of experiments, not all of them successful, including an attempt in San Francisco to place a device aboard a Pan-American flight to Tokyo, discovered by American security, Abu Ibrahim was ready to begin larger-scale operations. Six identical brown, soft-sided suitcases sold under the trademark Lastric were converted into deadly weapons in his Baghdad workshop. The plan was to place them in American and Israeli airliners in order to destroy them in mid-flight and create panic among airline passengers, especially those flying to and from Israel.

Muhammed Rashid, a Jordanian operative of the 15th May group, and his Moroccan wife, Khadija, were trained to prepare and arm the bomb. In spring they were sent to Athens—chosen because of the laxity of security procedures at this airport, and the well-known reluctance of Andreas Papandreou, the prime minister, to offend Arab interests by too much vigilance. In the Greek capital Muhammed Rashid was joined by another Jordanian, Fuad Shara, whose task was to provide a dupe who could be persuaded to carry the suitcase on to an aircraft. The person whom he selected was a wandering Englishwoman named Denise, who did some business in Greece and in Israel. She agreed to fly to Tel Aviv, collect Holy Land and folklore art objects and then take them on to London.

If the plot had worked she would have been killed when the bomb and the airliner exploded. In fact the device failed. Denise arrived safely, but finding no "business" contact to meet her, she simply returned to Athens with the suitcase.

Western antiterrorist agencies and the Israeli secret

service, Mossad, already knew something of the plot and by this time the trail led to Shara the Jordanian. His flat was raided and the famous suitcase was discovered, still intact. There is still a great deal of concealment about this clandestine operation carried out by British and American agents which led to a diplomatic incident. What is known for certain is that a CIA agent recovered the bomb and took a white-knuckle drive with it in a Land-Rover, so that it could be removed for careful examination.

The Greek government launched a vigorous protest about the Anglo-American operation, which it claimed had been carried out without official approval. This was followed by a great deal of recrimination in the course of which the Greeks further complained that information had been denied to them and that the only thing they had been given was a photograph of the suitcase. Eventually the CIA station chief in Athens (simply referred to as "Huey") was declared *persona non grata*. American diplomats blamed the Greek authorities for failing to raid the apartment themselves. They gave the impression that it was because of Greek negligence in following up a tip-off, that, exasperated and alarmed by the emergency, CIA men had taken independent action outside their jurisdiction. The quarrel was no doubt a factor in producing the climate of hostility and distrust which soured the U.S.-Greek dispute after the TWA aircraft was hijacked on take-off from Athens the following year.

Fuad Shara was arrested for his part in the affair. After holding him for five weeks, the Greeks released him for lack of evidence, thus implying that the foreign agents had been reluctant, or unable, to supply any. The Englishwoman, in danger of a revenge attack by Abu Ibrahim's friends, remained safely in Greece for a while and then returned home, no doubt still thoughtful about her narrow escape.

That episode took care of one of the half-dozen explosive suitcases believed to have been produced. But the immediate concern of Western security men was that five others might still be in circulation and ready to go off. A special security alert was ordered at international airports around the world and warning notices with pictures of the case were displayed. By 1985 the intelligence community felt satisfied, after the discovery of another four (one of them in Berlin), that the immediate danger was over. Of the original half-dozen, one remained unaccounted for, but it was believed that it might have been used up by Abu Ibrahim for testing.

Indications that the Iraqi government—by then more concerned with the war against Iran than with Palestinian fringe terrorists—considered that the Ibrahim group had gone too far, came in the form of indignant denials that its headquarters were located in Baghdad. "There is no such person known in Baghdad. The government of Iraq condemns terrorism," wrote Tarad Koubaissi, press counselor in London, to the *Daily Telegraph*.

In any case, Abu Ibrahim seems to have gone to ground. It is reassuring to know that however imaginative he is as a bomb constructor, his devices by no means always work. Four years ago a young Arab was blown to pieces preparing an infernal machine in his room at the Mount Royal Hotel in London. In Beirut they put out posters bearing the stamp of the May 15th organization, declaring him a martyr, a martyr perhaps to another mistake by Abu Ibrahim.

Nevertheless, the "Dupe" technique pioneered by the master bomber is still being used. In April 1986 El Al security staff at London's Heathrow airport found a sophisticated bomb in the luggage of a pregnant Irish woman. It had been given to her by her Arab lover, Nezar Narwas Mansur Hindawi. This highly dangerous device had already passed through the normal screening process and was discovered only by El Al's stringent hand search procedure.

Two months later, a small-time crook was conned into carrying a suitcase onto an El Al plane at Madrid's Barajas airport. He was told by Nasser Hassam el-Ali, the Palestinian who gave him the case, that it contained drugs. But when it was opened by security staff at the check-in counter it burst into flames and injured 14 people. These incidents show, once again, that the old snares of love and money remain powerful terrorist weapons.

19.

The Great Carlos

'I am the Great Carlos'

—Ilich Ramirez Sanchez

Another leftover from Wadi Haddad's Special Operations Group is Ilich Ramirez Sanchez, the Venezuelan assassin better known as Carlos. He comes from a revolutionary family; his grandfather was a guerrilla in the Venezuelan Revolution of 1899 and his father, José Allagracia Sanchez, is a Stalinist who named his three sons Vladimir, Ilich and Lenin after the leader of the Russian Revolution. But José Sanchez is not only a Stalinist, he is also a millionaire who made his money out of property deals.

Carlos, born on October 12, 1949 was and remains the darling of his plump, good-looking mother, Elba; he took after her, becoming so plump himself that he was called El Gordo, The Fat One. So Carlos, pampered by his loving mother, indulged by his rich father, grew up to be a fat, petulant revolutionary with a taste for luxury. But there was nothing soft about his education. His father's communist friends saw that he got a rigorous training as a terrorist, first on the streets of Caracas where in 1964 he joined the Communist Students movement and then in one of Fidel Castro's training camps for young revolutionaries run by the Cuban Secret Service, the Dirección de Inteligencia (DGI).

His training completed, he returned to Caracas, and by 1966 was in so much trouble with the authorities that his father sent him with his mother and two brothers to London so that the boys could complete their education in a calmer atmosphere. However, two years later, sponsored by the Venezuelan Communist party, he went to Moscow to enter Lumumba University for students from the Third World. Students at Lumumba are taught ordinary university subjects—with the usual Soviet slant—but if they show aptitude and willingness they are trained to serve the intenational cause of communism. A Russian defector who had taught there reported that 90 percent of the staff are KGB members and that all the Russian students sent there to leaven the Third World mixture are either agents or stooges of the KGB.

The great problem with Lumumba is that it is extremely worthy and devastatingly dull—especially for noisy, extrovert students from Africa and South America. Carlos got bored, and using his large allowance from his father, created his own *dolce vita* in Moscow. The Soviet authorities asked his father to send him less money, but that dedicated communist refused, saying: "My sons have never lacked for anything."

However, behind the *dolce vita* mask, Carlos was involved in more serious business. He made contact with the PFLP, many of whose members have been trained as "freedom fighters" in Soviet army camps, and on one of his vacations he went to a PFLP camp in Jordan where he received military training and indoctrination in the Palestinian cause.

He then returned to Lumumba, but soon fell foul of the authorities, taking part in an unauthorized student demonstration in July 1970 during which he threw an inkpot at the Libyan embassy—an unintentionally ironic gesture when seen in the light of his future relationship with Colonel Gaddafi. This, according to the official story, was too much for the Russians, and they expelled him. Another version, more believable in the light of future events, is that this was a cover for his recruitment by the KGB and his insertion into the PFLP. While he is known to have criticized communists as being corrupt, and defined himself as an international revolutionary rather than a Marxist, he has always maintained his connection with the DGI, turning to its agents for help whenever he got into serious trouble. And the DGI's international operations are controlled by the KGB. There are also reports that he returned to Russia in 1974 with a

PFLP group for special training at a Russian camp. These reports came from Palestinians captured by the Israelis who say they saw him in the camp.

What is known for certain is that when he was "sent down" from Lumumba he went to Jordan, where he joined the PFLP just in time to take part in the "Black September" war provoked by the PFLP's mass hijacking of jets to Dawson's Field. King Hussein's Bedouin soldiers drove the Palestinian groups out of Jordan, but Carlos had a good war. He was one of the few non-Arabs who took part, and he made his reputation with Wadi Haddad.

He spent the next year polishing his skills as a hit man at PFLP camps set up in Lebanon. Then, in February 1972, Wadi Haddad sent him back to London as a "sleeper." This was easy enough, for his mother had separated from her much older husband (although still sustained by his generous monthly checks) and had made a new life for herself in Latin American diplomatic circles. Carlos was welcomed on the diplomatic cocktail party circuit, where he built up his cover as an irresponsible, womanizing playboy. But someone must have had suspicions about him, for on one occasion the Special Branch searched his apartment. They found nothing; he had taken care to hide his weapons and other incriminating evidence in the homes of accommodating girlfriends. No reason has yet been given for the Special Branch's interest in Carlos, and no one will admit that the search actually took place, but a former senior officer of the Branch admitted that they had "made a terrible cock-up."

Carlos carried out his first known act of terrorism in London on Sunday evening, December 30, 1973, when he shot 'Teddy' Sieff, the president of Marks and Spencer and an ardent Zionist. Carlos knocked on the door of the Sieff house in St. John's Wood and forced the butler to take him to his victim, who was in the bathroom. The terrified butler knocked on the door and when Sieff opened it Carlos shot him immediately, but only once because his gun jammed. The single shot should have been enough, for it struck Sieff full in the face, but the bullet hit his front teeth, which stopped much of its power and deflected it so that it came to rest a fraction of an inch away from his jugular vein.

Even so, Sieff would have died if his wife had not come to his assistance. Carlos ran off into the night. At that time nobody knew who he was. Lord Sieff, as he later became, said: "I never saw him nor heard him speak, and I know nothing about him other than when I have read in the press." However, the PFLP claimed responsibility for the attack "because the British Zionist billionaire Joseph Sieff . . . gives every year millions of pounds to the Zionist usurper . . ."

A month later, Carlos made his second attack in London, throwing a bomb packed into a shoe box into the Israeli Hapoalim Bank in the City of London. His aim was hurried, the bomb bounced off a door and exploded in front of a counter, injuring a typist. The PFLP claimed responsibility for this attack also, but Carlos remained unsuspected by the British authorities despite the previous Special Branch interest in him.

Then the chain of events started which was to lead to his being able to announce to a potential victim: "I am the famous Carlos." The Israelis killed Mohammed Boudia, the PFLP's chief terrorist in Europe. They blew him up with a bomb hidden under the driver's seat of his car while he visited one of his mistresses in Paris. And Carlos was summoned to take Boudia's place in Paris and rebuild his international network. It was a job he accepted willingly, for it was Boudia who had been his link in Moscow with the PFLP. An important part in this network was played by his large number of girlfriends, both innocent and not so innocent. He used them in bed and to cache guns, ammunition and passports and to maintain safe houses in which he could hide.

He mounted his first operations in Paris in August 1974, when he was responsible for three car bombs in the heart of the city, one at the offices of the Jewish publication *L'Arche* and the others at the right-wing newspapers, *L'Aurore* and *Minute*. In September he helped the Japanese Red Army plan the occupation of the French embassy in The Hague in order to force the French to release an arrested member of their organization. On September 15, in support of the Japanese operation, he threw a hand grenade into Le Drugstore, a popular meeting place for young people in St. Germain-des-Prés. Two people died and a score were wounded. He threatened the police with more such bombings if the French did not give in to the demands of the Japanese Red Army. The French government capitulated. He was suspected of being involved in a couple of shootings following the bombing of Le Drugstore, but the next incident in which he was certainly involved was the attempt to destroy an El Al airliner in Orly airport on January 13, 1975 with a hand-held rocket. The rocket missed, but Carlos's gang made another, similar attempt a week later. This time the police saw the two-man team setting up the rocket. In the firefight that followed, the terrorists took 20 people hostage, and after a two-day siege in the toilets they bargained their way aboard an Air France plane which took them to the Middle East.

The French police had no idea of Carlos's identity. At that time, before the ramifications of the PFLP's international set-up had been exposed, they hardly thought it likely that a Venezuelan would be the European leader of a Palestinian organization fighting the Israelis.

However, the French had been tipped off by their friends in Beirut's Deuxiéme Bureau about the activities of a Lebanese interior decorator called Michael Moukharbel whom they suspected of acting as a courier for Wadi Haddad. What they did not know was that Moukharbel not only carried orders and money from Haddad to Carlos but was also the Carlos gang's accountant. It is from his surprisingly detailed notebook, in which he recorded Carlos's expenses even down to tram tickets, that they were able to piece together so much of Carlos's activities during this period.

The French decided to play a cat-and-mouse game with Moukharbel when he flew to Paris on June 13, 1975. They photographed Carlos arriving for a meeting with the Lebanese at an apartment at 26 avenue Claude Villefaux, and this was the first time the Venezuelan had appeared "in the frame." They also noted that the apartment was occupied by Wilfried Boese, who unknown to them was leader of the German Revolutionary Cells and had helped Black September set up the attack on the Israeli athletes at the Munich Olympics. A week later Moukharbel flew to London, where the Special Branch, alerted by their French colleagues, put him back on a plane for Paris. The French now tired of their game. They arrested and deported Boese, and on the morning of June 27 they picked up Moukharbel and prepared to deport him as well. But first they wanted to ask him about the plump young man with whom he had been photographed. He was forced to admit that he knew the young man, and while insisting he was of no importance, agreed to take them to meet him at a friend's apartment in the rue Toullier.

This flat belonged to Nancy Sanchez, one of Carlos's network of female lover-helpers who that evening was giving a farewell party for a few friends to mark her return to Venezuela. The three policemen whom Moukharbel led to the party, Chief Commissioner Jean Harranz, Divisional Inspector Raymond Doubs and Inspector Jean Donatini, were so unaware of the jackal's den into which they were walking that they first went to a retirement party for one of their colleagues, and when they knocked on Nancy Sanchez's door they were unarmed. There seemed to be no cause for apprehension. The sound of music came through the door. Carlos was playing his favorite song, *Give Thanks for Life*, on a guitar. Commissioner Herranz was invited in and offered a drink. He talked to Carlos for 10 minutes and found the young man interesting enough to wish to take him to headquarters for some more serious questioning. However, before doing that he decided to confront Carlos with Moukharbel, who had been kept hidden outside the flat by the two inspectors. As Herranz moved to call them in Carlos excused himself to go to the bathroom. When he returned he had a gun in his hand. He first shot and killed Moukharbel. Two more shots killed the inspectors, and another seriously wounded Commissioner Herranz.

Carlos made a run for it, spent the night with another of his female helpers and then, with the aid of two Cuban diplomats, disappeared to Algeria. And so the Carlos legend was born.

Then came the raid on OPEC's headquarters in Vienna on December 21, 1975 in which a mixed gang of German and Palestinian terrorists led by Carlos killed three people and kidnapped the OPEC oil ministers. Their plan was to demand a plane and then set out on a grand tour round the world, liberating the oil ministers one by one in their various capitals in return for declarations of support for the Palestinian cause. But two ministers, Sheikh Zaki Yamani of Saudi Arabia and Dr. Jamshid Amouzegar, the Shah's oil minister, were to be "executed as criminals." It did not work out that way, partly because one of the Germans in the raid, Hans Joachim Klein, was desperately wounded in the gunfight and would have died if the gang had proceeded with the grand tour. Carlos also, "on instructions from my bosses," stopped the killing of Yamani and Amouzegar. Even at the last moment, though, after they had flown to Algeria with Yamani and Amouzegar and surrendered to the Algerian authorities, Khalid, 'the Palestinian deputy commander of the gang, tried to kill Yamani with a gun concealed in a shoulder holster. Carlos settled for a huge ransom from the Saudis and Iranians instead.

Much is now known about this raid and Carlos's character through the confessions of Hans Joachim Klein, who had a change of heart after he recovered from his wound and fled from his terrorist companions, sending his pistol to the German magazine *Der Spiegel* to prove his renunciation of terrorism.

He confirmed that there were six terrorists in the actual operation: Carlos; three Arabs, Khalid, Jussif and Joseph; and the two Revolutionary Cell members from Germany, Klein and Gabriele Krocher-Tiedemann, the former sociology student who cold-bloodedly shot dead two men during the raid. Four other members of the Revolutionary Cells were involved. Their task had been to reconnoitre the building for Carlos. One of them was Wilfried 'Bonnie' Boese.

Klein makes it clear in his story that Carlos also had other help: "the idea had been suggested to Haddad by an Arab head of state and the inside information we had been promised came from the same source." He is careful not to name the Arab head of state, but there is no doubt that it was Colonel Gaddafi of Libya. It is ironic that the man Carlos killed during the raid was Yousef Ismirli, an economist on the Libyan delegation, who had not been let into the secret of his master's plot. According to his colleagues, he thought they were being attacked by Israeli commandos. Ismirli tried to wrench Carlos's Beretta machine pistol out of his grasp, and almost succeeded. But Carlos had another gun, and pumped five bullets into him. This pitiless behavior was in accordance with the tactics laid down by Carlos. According to Klein, they were that "anyone who resisted was to be killed. The same went for anyone who tried to escape or became hysterical. Also for any member of the commando who refused to obey an order and endangered the operation. . . . "

Klein points out, incidentally, that Carlos is not known by that name in terrorist circles. In Europe he calls himself Johnny, and in the Arab countries he is Salem.

According to Klein, it was Wilfried Boese who invented the Carlos name when he was picked up after meeting Moukharbel in Paris. He told the police the cover story that he had called to see someone called Carlos, and that this Carlos had instructed him to make contact with armed groups in the Basque country.

Klein's impressions of Carlos are important, because no

other terrorists who have worked with him have revealed what they think of him. Klein says:

> At first I'd taken him to be an Italian mafioso. He was really a very cool guy. . . . When he talked about his own way of life, he admitted readily that he had remained a bourgeois. . . . He always dressed very stylishly and stayed at luxury hotels. He said it was better for his own safety. . . . When he saw from the wanted posters in Germany that the price on his head was no larger than that on anyone else's, he said that he was going to write a letter of protest. . . . He did tend to go along with his press image a bit. He compares himself with the character of the Jackal in Forsyth's book. . . . He's a very anal type, a maniac about cleanliness, and washes himself all the time.

Klein also talked about Carlos's "perspective of massacre," the belief that "the more violent things get, the more people will respect you." On another occasion Carlos said: "To get anywhere, you have to walk over corpses."

The next, and last, operation in which Carlos was involved on behalf on Wadi Haddad became exceedingly violent, but it won respect not for the terrorists but for the Israeli army. It was the hijacking which culminated in the raid on Entebbe.

Flight 139, an Air France Airbus, which had stopped at Athens on its way from Tel Aviv to Paris, was hijacked on Sunday, June 27, 1976, by Wilfried Boese and Brigitte Kuhlmann along with two Palestinians. Carlos could play no part in the operation, for by now his description and fingerprints had been circulated by Interpol and the security services of the world were looking for him. He could not risk trying to evade even the notoriously lax security organization at Athens. But his hand can be seen throughout the incident.

Boese, his man in Europe, commanded the enterprise, and when the plane landed at Entebbe after having been refueled at Benghazi on Gaddafi's orders, his long-standing colleague in terror, Antonio Bouvier, appeared among the PFLP leaders at the airport to enjoy what they confidently expected would be a great triumph. Bouvier is a shadowy figure, a member of the Cuban DGI who was one of Carlos's instructors at his Cuban training camp and fulfilled the function of administrative officer to Carlos in London, just as Moukharbel had done in Paris.

Then, when the hijackers made their demands, threatening to murder their 103 Jewish and Israeli hostages unless 53 terrorists imprisoned in Israel, West Germany, Kenya, Switzerland and France were freed, it was seen that most of the prisoners were connected with Carlos. The story of the dramatic assault on Entebbe airport and the freeing of the hostages by the Sayaret Matkal, Israel's equivalent of the Special Air Service, is well known. Boese and Kuhlmann died along with seven senior members of the PFLP, including Fayez Abdul Rahmin Jaber, one of the founders. Antonio Bouvier, who according to Israelis "took command of the entire action at Entebee," escaped because he had left the old airport terminal to eat and rest before resuming his guard duty. Wadi Haddad, who had arrived in Entebbe from Mogadishu, Somalia (where the PFLP had set up a command headquarters) also escaped, leaving the airport a short time before the Israelis landed.

After Entebbe Carlos freely praised the Israelis for the way in which they had carried out their raid. He told Klein that when an enemy did something well you had to recognize the fact. Klein had in fact been selected by Haddad to take part in the Entebbe operation but he had pleaded the ill effects of the wounds he had suffered in Vienna and was excused. In fact he had already made up his mind to try to escape from terrorism. He found it very difficult, both psychologically and practically. Eventually he made a run for it from a terrorist "safe house" in Europe, disclosed plans to murder two prominent European Jews and has been on the run ever since, hiding from his own former colleagues as well as the authorities.

Carlos spent some months helping the Revolutionary Cells rebuild their organization after the loss of their leader, Wilfried Boese, and then left Wadi Haddad's team. He was bought up by Gaddafi and transferred rather like a star footballer to captain the Libyan's own terrorist team. As so often happens in such cases, Carlos was unhappy with his new team. He had already expressed his disapproval of Libyan inefficiency during the OPEC affair when he told Sheikh Yamani at Tripoli airport: "These people are not disciplined. It is impossible to work with them." Captain Manfred Pollak, the Austrian Airlines pilot who had volunteered to fly the plane containing Carlos, his gang and their hostages, reported similarly:

> He was very frustrated and dismayed that he could not get properly honored by the Libyan government because the aircraft had been parked away from the terminal. As I recall, he said something to the effect that he had spent a month preparing this attack and this

commanding action, and now he was not getting proper consideration from the Libyan government and that was not right.

Once Carlos was working for Gaddafi he ran up against not only Libyan inefficiency but Libyan pride, in the person of Gaddafi's kinsman, Sayed Gaddafadem, head of the "Green Brigades"—the hit teams sent to kill opponents of the Gaddafi regime living abroad. The two terrorist chiefs quarreled bitterly after Carlos had sneered at Gaddafadem that several assassination attempts which had failed would not have gone wrong if he had been in command. His problem was that he was too easily recognized, and had been relegated to the position of coach rather than captain, and he spent most of his time at the training camps in Libya, Lebanon and South Yemen. It is known that he ventured to Yugoslavia, where he was spotted by British intelligence. Representations were made to the Yugoslavs, but they refused to deport him to any of the countries that had him on their "wanted" lists and allowed him to fly back to the Middle East.

His problems with the Libyans came to a head in the summer of 1981. It is not certain if he was thrown out of Libya, but in September of that year he appeared first in Beirut and then moved on to Damascus, where he sold his services to President Assad. He worked under the command of Brigadier Ali Khader, controller of Syria's Special Services, and was used to mount sabotage operations against Iraq.

Then, in January 1982, Syrian exile groups in Paris and the Moslem Brotherhood working from Aachen in West Germany attempted to overthrow the Assad government by a coup d'état and an uprising of followers of the Moslem Brotherhood in the town of Hama. Assad sent the army into Hama and they put the revolt down with much bloodshed. Estimates of the dead range from 5,000 to 30,000. Even allowing for Middle Eastern exaggeration, a great number of people lost their lives while others fled to join the ranks of the dissidents living in Europe.

It was against these people that Carlos was then directed. Eight hit teams were sent to Europe to carry the war to the Moslem Brotherhood and the "National Front for the Liberation of Syria," the umbrella organization formed in Paris mainly from former members of Assad's own Baath Party. As these activities were inter-Arab and lacked the drama of his previous exploits, there was a tendency to write him off as a terrorist. What had not been realized was that he had kept together the basis of his European gang and was using members of the Revolutionary Cells and other urban terrorist groups to carry out his attacks on Assad's enemies.

On February 16, 1982, two night watchmen guarding an underground garage near the Champs Elysées in Paris came across a man and a woman acting suspiciously. The night watchmen thought they were thieves, and challenged them. The "thieves" then produced pistols and tried to open fire, but both guns jammed. When they were arrested they claimed to belong to the "International Revolutionary Organization," but refused to give evidence to an investigating magistrate.

Police who examined their car discovered it had false license plates and contained explosives, two tear-gas grenades and dozens of small propane gas cylinders (a favorite device for increasing the force of an explosion). Their pictures and fingerprints were taken, and it came as no surprise to the police to discover that they were both on record. He was Bruno Breguet, a 32-year-old Swiss who had been arrested in Haifa in April 1970 when attempting to smuggle explosives into Israel for a Palestinian bomb attack. The Israelis had sentenced him to 15 years' imprisonment but set him free after he had served seven years. He had since registered as a student of economics in Zurich. She was Magdalena Kaupp, a 34-year-old West German from Ulm who was known to have connections with the Revolutionary Cells.

But that was all that was known about them. They would not say whom they were about to attack, why or on whose behalf. Then, two weeks after their arrest, a letter was dropped into the mailbox of the French embassy at The Hague, the same embassy that Carlos's Japanese Red Army colleagues had occupied in September 1974. The letter was half a page long, written in Spanish, and demanded the release of Breguet and Kaupp.

It was a splendid example of Carlos's arrogance:

> You have arrested two members of my organization, who had received no orders to stage an attack on French territory for we have nothing against the Socialist government. I give you one month to release them—if not I will take up the matter personally with the French government and in particular with Interior Minister Gaston Deferre.

He went on to demand that Breguet and Kaupp be provided with a plane to "fly them to a destination of their choice."

The letter was signed "Ilitch Ramirez Sanchez" though it might still have been dismissed as a hoax but for the fact that it was authenticated by his thumbprints. These were checked against those he had left at the rue Toullier and were found to be genuine. It caused consternation, and although the French government had no intention of releasing the terrorists, they took elaborate precautions to protect members of the government. Carlos's reputation is such that few people take his threats lightly. It also emerged that he delivered a similar warning to the German authorities.

Shortly before his deadline expired a bomb exploded on the Paris-Toulouse "Capitol" express, killing five people. Jacques Chirac, a prominent opposition politician, had booked a seat in the compartment where the bomb exploded, but decided at the last moment to accept a friend's offer of a lift in a private aircraft instead of taking the train. A Spanish right-wing group made a vague claim to have planted the bomb, but the French authorities are convinced that Carlos was responsible.

Then, on New Year's Eve 1983, two bombs exploded, one in Marseilles' Saint Charles railway station and the other on the Paris-Marseilles express. The significance of Marseilles is that it is the fief of Gaston Deferre, who was mayor of Marseilles as well as being minister of the interior. Carlos had scores to settle with Deferre on both counts. He and Moukharbel had been arrested in Marseilles after, astonishingly, getting themselves mixed up in an anti-Algerian riot, and as Minister of the Interior Deferre was ultimately the jailer of Kaupp and Breguet. Five people died in the explosion and 50 were injured. An unknown group calling itself "The Children of Sheik Abdullah" claimed responsibility in telephone calls to international news agencies. However, the Agence France Presse bureau in Berlin received a letter claiming responsibility for the bombs, and when the handwriting was checked it proved to match that of Carlos.

Neither the warnings nor the bombs prevented the French from sentencing Breguet and Kaupp to five years in prison. They both earned full remission, and were freed in 1985. The French handed Magdalena Kaupp over to the German authorities when she finished her sentence in May but they had no evidence on which they could hold her. She left for Damascus by way of East Berlin.

There she married Carlos. Perhaps that explains why he was so keen to secure her release.

So Carlos is well, married and active. He has also retained the European links which he fostered on behalf of Wadi Haddad when the PFLP was committing its acts of international terror. An indication of these links is given by the new and rather grandiose name of his group: The International Faction of Revolutionary Cells. It is derived from Wilfried Boese's old Revolutionary Cells organization which was divided into two sometimes competing sections, one of which operated inside Germany and the other which operated internationally. It was the international section which Carlos helped rebuild after Boese was killed at Entebbe. However, while Carlos may indulge himself on the European scene, threatening ministers and carrying out *coups de théâtre*, he will always have to recognize that he can only guarantee his safety, finances and backup support by selling his services to a Middle Eastern government.

This fact will have been brought home to him in the bloodiest of ways in 1986 by the shoot-out between rival South Yemeni factions which started with an attempted massacre at a meeting of the ruling Politburo—an event described as a "liquidation that might have made a Don Corleone wince"—and ended with tank battles in the street and house-to-house murders. It is not known if Carlos lost his Yemeni headquarters in these battles but the affair is hardly likely to have brought joy to an aging terrorist with a rapidly shrinking number of countries where his presence is tolerated.

Part Six

THE
FARAWAYS

20.

Tamils Turn Terrorist (Sri Lanka)

The beautiful and gentle land of Sri Lanka, the "Island of Serendipity," would seem the most unlikely setting for a brutal terror war. Yet that is precisely what it has been since 1977, with the Tamil minority waging a campaign of shooting and bombing to force the Sinhalese government to give them their own state of Eelam.

The history of this struggle goes back some 2,000 years to the time when the Tamil and Sinhalese kings fought for mastery of the island, but the seeds of the present conflict were sown in 1948 when Britain gave Ceylon its independence. The Hindu Tamils, bright, well-educated and businesslike, had been favored by the British, but when colonial rule ended they found themselves dominated by the Buddhist Sinhalese who form the majority of the island's population and who, under the democratic process bequeathed them by the British, have controlled the government ever since.

Successive Sinhalese-dominated administrations passed laws, particularly the language law of 1956 making Sinhala the country's official language, which the Tamils regarded as part of a campaign to destroy their national identity. It was more a question of stupid chauvinism on the part of the Sinhalese than an attempt to destroy the Tamils, many of whom lived happily in Sinhalese districts and played a large part in the economic, political and social life of the country—as many still do.

257

However, in the northern and eastern provinces where most Tamils live they began to talk of the threat of "genocide" and to demand their own state, which they called Eelam. Their politicians seemed unable to win any concessions from the government, and in 1977 groups of discontented young men took over and turned to violence to win Eelam.

They did so with a singular brutality, tying opponents to lampposts and shooting them through the head, mining roads and railways, wiping out isolated police posts and shooting individual policemen in their homes. Twenty-seven policemen enjoying their after-lunch siesta in the police station at Chavakacheri were massacred in November 1984, when a well-trained group of Tamils rushed the station and shot them as they tried to hide under their bunks. The Tamils also struck at economic targets, setting off bombs in Colombo to harm the lucrative tourist trade.

The situation which developed had a number of similarities with that in Northern Ireland. The terrorists were drawn from a religious nationalist minority which complained—with some justice—of being treated as second-class citizens; their complaints were ignored by religious bigots; they had an over-the-border base in the Indian state Tamil Nadu, where 50 million Tamils live; and they were prepared to kill in horrific fashion to achieve their aims. They even, like the IRA, became known as "The Boys."

The Sinhalese security forces estimate that there are about 600 hard-core terrorists drawn from five main groups. These groups are the Liberation Tigers of Tamil Eelam (LTTE), the People's Liberation Movement of Tamil Eelam (PLOTE), the Tamil Eelam Liberation Organization (TELO), the Eelam Revolutionary Organization (EROS), and the Eelam People's Revolutionary Liberation Front (EPRLF).

As its name implies, the EPRLF is a Marxist organization. Its aim is not only to set up a Marxist-Leninist state of Eelam but also to spread Marxism through the Sinhalese community. Its Secretary-General, K. Pathmanabha, made his policies clear at the party's first congress, where he said: "Marxism-Leninism is our ideology and we shall apply it in accordance with a correct understanding of concrete realities prevailing in our land. Let us resolve to work towards the building of EPRLF as the vanguard of the Eelam National Liberation Struggle by mobilizing the workers, peasants, the radical intelligentsia and all working people and by forming a united front with other organizations within the liberation movement . . . "

The two most effective groups, the Tigers and PLOTE, are also admittedly Marxist. Dr. Anton Balasingham, a British national of Sri Lankan origin, who is the political theoretician of the Tigers, talks of the need for a socialist revolution among the Tamil people, while Rajan Nithian, a leader of PLOTE, says that his group is based on Marxist principles, "because the Marxist philosophy is the best to guide revolutionaries."

Nithian also talks of the help PLOTE has received from "all progressive sections of the world. We are working closely with the Popular Front for the Liberation of Palestine led by Dr. Habash. Our PFLP comrades have trained some of our fighters." The Israelis confirmed this claim when they captured documents in Beirut listing Tamils who had been trained by the PFLP.

The early training of the Tamil terrorists was not as sophisticated as that offered by the Palestinians. It was acquired in India for a few rupees at the private schools run by retired soldiers who normally teach the rudiments of drill and weapon handling to would-be recruits to the Indian army.

However, that all changed after the events of July 1983 which first brought the situation in Sri Lanka to the attention of the world. Thirteen soldiers were killed by a bomb in the Tamil heartland of Jaffna province, and their funerals sparked anti-Tamil riots and burnings in Colombo and other cities. Some 400 Tamils were massacred, many of them burnt to death under the horrified eyes of European and American tourists. The well-organized Tamil propaganda machine operating in Europe and America went into action, and the Sinhalese government was portrayed as deliberately instigating the riots. A month later Indira Gandhi, then India's prime minister, authorized the military training of the Tamils by the regular Indian army at bases near Delhi. She did this partly because of pressure from the Tamil population in India and partly because she thought that Sri Lanka's president, Junius Jayawardene, was planning to lease the former British naval base of Trincomalee to the United States, and wanted to demonstrate to Jayawardene that India was the real power in the area.

The Tigers' campaign then took off. Dedicated, better armed than the Sri Lanka security forces and supported by a propaganda machine which ran rings round that of the Sri Lankan government, the Tigers turned whole areas in the north and east into "no-go" areas. The Tamil city of Jaffna was run by the terrorists, not by the authorities. The Sri Lankan army put up a woeful display of ineptitude and cowardice and indulged in brutal acts of revenge which played into its enemies' hands. Trained to fight a war that could never happen, they were hit by a savage guerilla war for which they were untrained, unprepared and unequipped. The effect on these simple country lads of seeing the remains of their colleagues strewn about the road after being blown up by landmines has been catastrophic. They have replied in the only way they know how—by setting their weapons on automatic and blasting away at anything that moves. But in the awful logic of terrorism, by the time they open fire the terrorists are long gone and the only people left to be killed are the innocents.

Realizing the need for outside help, President Jayawardene turned first to Israel, which provided a Mossad secret service team. Then he called in the highly professional British company KMS (Keenie Meenie Services), run by Colonel James Johnson, former commander of the Special Air Service. Johnson decided that the army was best left to its own officers to sort out, and sent a team of former SAS officers and NCO's to train picked volunteers from the police force to fight the Tigers. The training is tough and expert, with instructors imparting years of knowledge gained in fighting terrorists in Ireland and Oman. The lesson which is constantly hammered home is self-discipline. The result has been impressive. Formed into a Special Task Force led by a Superintendent Zerney Vijesuria—the KMS instructors take no part in operations—the policemen began to strike back at the terrorists, working their way up the east coast towards the Tamils' northern strongholds.

At the same time Rajiv Gandhi, who had succeeded his assassinated mother as prime minister in India, stopped the training of Tamils at Indian army bases. No doubt he felt a genuine abhorrence for all aspects of terrorism following the murder of his mother by Sikh extremists. But he was also in the embarrassing position of complaining about other countries harboring Sikh terrorists while India was training Tamil terrorists. And so the camps were closed down.

The war dragged miserably on and everybody suffered—the Tamil population, fearful of both the army and the terrorists; the army and the police, who were constant targets; the hoteliers, whose tourist trade vanished; and the government, desperately seeking a way out of the war, but unable to make the concessions which would have appeased the Tamils.

Then, on May 14, 1985 there occurred one of those events which by their sheer horror change the course of terrorist campaigns. A group of Tigers dressed in army uniforms drove through the ancient Sinhalese capital of Anuradhapura, one of the holiest cities in Sri Lanka, and mowed down people with indiscriminate automatic fire. Over 150 people died, including nuns, Buddhist pilgrims and children. Some of them died beneath the revered Bo tree which was brought to Sri Lanka from India nearly 2,500 years ago. Reputed to be the oldest tree in the world, it is believed to have grown out of a branch from the tree under which Buddha attained enlightenment. Even the Tamil propaganda machine could not explain away this outrage, and the Tamils lost much support in the outside world.

The carnage also meant that President Jayawardene—who had always hoped for a political settlement giving the Tamils a measure of autonomy within the Sri Lankan nation, but had been frustrated as much by the right-wing Buddhist priesthood as by Tamil intransigence—was at last able to impress the seriousness of the situation on the Buddhist leadership. With their acceptance, if not their blessing, he was able to send emissaries to Rajiv Gandhi, and went to Delhi himself in June to ask for India's assistance in ending the war.

From these talks there emerged a truce, not always honored, while discreet talks between the government and the Tamils took place under Indian patronage in the Himalayan kingdom of Bhutan.

First attempts to find a solution broke down in August 1985 and terror raids started again. But in the autumn both sides agreed to resume negotiations. In face of Rajiv Gandhi's increasing exasperation, the Tamils and the Sri Lankan government were then confronted by a clear choice: either to make a settlement, or to allow a small and dirty little war to fester away. As he began to use air power against the rebels, President Jayawardene boasted that he would have a military solution to eliminate violence by the end of 1986.

However, as the year progressed, a military solution seemed to be as far away as ever. An army assault on rebel strongholds in the north was halted by fierce Tamil resistance. But at the same time the Tamils were wracked by rivalries which led to shoot-outs between the various groups in which a number of leading separatists died before the "Tigers" emerged as the most powerful of the groups.

In London in July 1986, Lalith Athulathmudali, Sri Lanka's national security minister, admitted that the Tamils could not be stopped by military means. "We have been improving our military position but at the end of the day there has to be a political settlement."

At that time the Sri Lankans were basing their hopes for such a settlement on a new package of proposals which had Rajiv Gandhi's blessing. This package entailed devolving power to the Tamils by setting up nine provincial assemblies, creating local police forces and introducing land reforms. It seemed to go a long way towards meeting the Tamils' aspirations, and Athulathmudali suggested that the government would consider further concessions if the Tamil leaders were prepared to talk. But there is the problem. Will the Tamils talk or, as in the case of the Basque separatists, have they gone so far down the road of violence they will refuse everything except the fulfillment of their most extreme demands?

21.

The Golden Temple India

There is a sad paradox in the fact that Indira Gandhi was shot to death by Sikhs prepared to kill for their religious-nationalistic beliefs while her army was training Tamils prepared to kill for their own religious-nationalistic beliefs. It was perhaps a lesson that all terrorism should be shunned, no matter how attractive its short-term political advantages.

The Sikhs belong to a schismatic Hindu sect which is less than 500 years old—young in Indian terms. In that time they have developed into a martial and devout people whose quarrel with the Indian government stems from their demands to be treated as a separate nation. The more extreme among them demand their own country of Khalistan. Modern-style terrorism in pursuance of this aim started in 1981 when five Sikh hijackers seized an Air India Boeing 737 on a domestic flight and forced the pilot to fly to Lahore in an attempt to free members of their group. However, they were armed only with traditional Sikh daggers, and were overpowered without bloodshed by Pakistani soldiers posing as cleaners.

A more traditional and more dangerous form of terrorism was festering in Amritsar, the Sikhs' holy city, where a gaunt, bearded holy man, Sant Jarnail Singh Bhindranwale, had set himself up as the high priest of Sikh extremism. His headquarters were in the Golden Temple, the most holy of Sikh religious places, and from there his followers waged a

263

war of terror against their opponents and people they thought not fervent enough in the cause of Khalistan. Politicians, policemen, local authorities, ordinary people were all cut down. Bhindranwale's followers even murdered within the Golden Temple itself, shooting Deputy Inspector General Atwal of the Amritsar police, a devout and turbanned Sikh, as he was leaving the temple gate after completing his devotions.

Bhindranwale would hold court on a roof-top in the temple complex, dressed in starched white pyjamas and wearing a bullet-filled bandolier, while lounging on a charpoy. He swore that he would leave the Temple only "when the chains of slavery are removed from the Sikh people." The buildings in the complex were filled with his followers and their arms: machine-guns, mortars, anti-tank rockets, mines and grenades. It was they who left the temple—to kill on his orders.

It was a situation which no government could allow to continue. In June 1984 Mrs. Gandhi ordered the army to storm the temple. It was a fateful decision. Bhindranwale and his men fought to the end. When his body was found in the Akal Takht, the center of Sikh religious authority, it was surrounded by those of Ahai Amrik Singh, president of the outlawed All-India Sikh Students Federation, and two former major-generals of the Indian Army, Shahbeg Singh and Narinder Singh Buller, who had commanded the terrorists, many of whom were former soldiers. In all, 712 extremists and their supporters died in the battle, while the army suffered 90 dead and 300 wounded. Many of the army's casualties were incurred because the soldiers had been ordered not to damage the gold-domed Harimandir Sahib, the *sanctum sanctorum* of the temple. It was a bloody battle by any standards, but its effects were even more dramatic. The assault on their holy temple roused Sikhs all over the world to fury, even those who recognized that Bhindranwale had to be stopped. There were mutinies among Sikh regiments previously renowned for their loyalty, and vengeance was sworn in blood.

Four months later Mrs. Gandhi was assassinated by Sikh members of her bodyguard in the garden of her home in Delhi. Her death was not sufficient to wipe out the shame of the Golden Temple or to bring about Khalistan; Bhindranwale's successors are carrying on the battle. However, with the army still in tight control of Amritsar they have no chance of building another military-style headquarters, and so they have turned once again to modern-style terrorism.

A number of groups are now operating, both in India and abroad. Among them are the Dashmesh Regiment—literally the Tenth Regiment, referring to the tenth guru of the religion, Gobind Singh, the leader who turned the Sikhs into warriors. The Dashmesh operates principally in America and Canada. In the Punjab the most active group is the Dal Khalsa, which is organized, in customary terrorist fashion, into cells. It is this group which is believed to have been responsible for the wave of carefully synchronized bombings in north Indian towns, especially New Delhi, in May 1985.

At first the devices, crude but powerful time-bombs disguised as transistor radios, seemed to have been set in no particular pattern, being left in buses, trains and the city slums. Later it was realized that bus drivers and railwaymen had been blamed for their part in the anti-Sikh riots which had followed the murder of Mrs. Gandhi. Sikh passengers had been dragged from trains and buses and butchered during the riots, while it was slum-dwellers who had looted and burnt Sikh homes.

The bombs killed 86 people and injured a hundred more. They also demonstrated to the Indians that the Sikh terrorists had not given up the struggle. Even while the bombs were exploding the FBI announced in America that it had foiled a plot to assassinate Rajiv Gandhi during his visit to Washington in June 1985.

FBI director William Webster announced that one of his agents had penetrated a Sikh terrorist cell. The agent was not named, but according to affidavits filed in the district court in New York he was a former member of the Seals, the U.S. Navy's commando frogman force, and had won the U.S. Congressional Medal of Honor in Vietnam. He had discovered that the Sikhs planned to kill Bhajan Lal, the chief minister of the state of Haryana, while according to Webster the group was plotting "guerrilla-type operations" against the government of India, "including the bombing of a nuclear power plant, bridges, government buildings and other strategic targets in India."

According to the affidavits, two of the group's members, Gurpartak Birk and Lal Singh, told the FBI undercover agent that their purpose was "to cause the revolutionary overthrow of the government of India."

A month later, on June 23, 1985, an Air India Boeing 747 Flight 182 disappeared off the radar screens as it headed towards the Irish coast on a flight from Montreal. It had disintegrated in midair and fallen into the sea, killing 329 passengers and crew. On the same day a bomb exploded after it had been unloaded in a suitcase from a Canadian Pacific flight at Narita airport, Tokyo. It killed two baggage handlers. The passengers had disembarked from the flight minutes earlier. No one has ever claimed responsibility for this bomb. A deep-water operation to recover the crashed Jumbo's black boxes from 6,000 feet down in the Atlantic, and detailed forensic examination of the bodies taken from the ocean, provided enough evidence to convince Indian investigators that the 747 was destroyed by a bomb.

The Indian government believes that Sikh extremists planned to destroy two Air-India jumbos on the same day, with bombs in the cargo holds. They succeeded with one and failed with the other because the suitcase bomb which was scheduled to be transferred to an Air India flight at Tokyo exploded prematurely. Many Sikhs, among them the pilot, lost their lives in the destruction of Flight 182, but it is thought that the terrorists would consider this a worthwhile sacrifice if their design was, as FBI Director William Webster reported, to "cause the revolutionary overthrow of the Government of India."

Suspicion centred on two men, Lal Singh and Amand Singh, who were both implicated in the plot to kill Mr. Gandhi, and it was believed that it was Lal Singh who put the suitcase bomb on the flight to Tokyo. It was later revealed that he had attended a "Reconnaissance Commando School," a private establishment run by Mr. Frank Camper, a former American soldier, who said that Lal Singh attended his school with three other Sikhs in November 1984. "Explosive ordnance and demolition training was part of the course they took. It teaches bomb recognition and handling of explosives. We use military mines and grenades but not time-bombs." There was no doubt, he said, that "they were going to take the training back to India to act as commandos for the Sikh separatist movement."

While all this was going on Rajiv Gandhi was trying to find a way to give the Sikhs a large measure of autonomy without agreeing to their demand for Khalistan. It was precisely the problem facing Junius Jayawardene. At the end of July 1985 Gandhi signed an agreement with the Sikh moderate leader

Sant Harchand Singh Longowal which conceded practically all the demands of the main Sikh political party, the Akali Dal. But still the extremists were not satisfied. They made repeated threats in the common language of terrorists that they would "punish" those responsible for signing the accord. And on August 20, 1985 they shot Sant Longowal dead as he was addressing a public meeting.

Sant Longowal once told an interviewer: "Extremism will end only when it has taken my life." Alas, even his life was not enough. Modern-style terrorism aimed at India demonstrates how swiftly international relations carefully nurtured over many years can be endangered by the acts of a few ruthless men.

In February 1984 Ravindra Mhatre, the assistant commissioner at the Indian High Commission in Birmingham, was bundled into a car near his home by men who later said they belonged to the Kashmiri Liberation Army, a little-known group dedicated to self-determination for Kashmir, one-third of which is occupied by Pakistan and the remainder by India. In a letter to Reuter's news agency and in telephone calls to Zuhair Ansari, secretary-general of the Kashmir Liberation Front, Mhatre's kidnappers demanded £1 million and the release of Kashmiri prisoners held by India. But they gave Ansari no time to negotiate. They killed their hostage within 48 hours of kidnapping him.

The Indian government and people were enraged not only by the murder of this mild-mannered family man, but also because his killers were part of a movement which was allowed to carry on its activities in Britain, where some 10,000 predominantly Moslem Kashmiris live. This anger was calmed only by the British government's profound expressions of regret and the promise that "enhanced protection" would be given to Indian diplomats. It also helped that the two members of the KLF who murdered Mhatre were quickly caught and sentenced to life imprisonment.

More Anglo-Indian troubles came about when Mrs. Gandhi was assassinated and British television showed pictures of Sikhs dancing with joy in British streets, and allowed Dr. Jagit Singh Chauhan (self-styled leader of the Khalistan "government in exile") to gloat over her death. Indian fury was such that trade and diplomatic relations were seriously affected. The Indians resented not only the tasteless gaffe of British television in allowing Chauhan his macabre celebration but also what they felt was the failure of the British authorities to crack down on Sikh extremists plotting against the Indian government.

This feeling was exacerbated when Flight 182 blew up and crashed into the Atlantic, and it was suspected that Sikh terrorists were responsible. The Indian government complained bitterly that Sikhs in the United States, Canada and Britain were allowed to collect money for terrorist purposes and to plot unhindered by the authorities.

Two days after the Air India disaster the authoritative Indian newspaper The *Statesman* argued: "New Delhi has so far taken a lenient view of the hospitality extended [to expatriate groups] by the governments of Britain, Canada and the USA. But the terrible price paid on Sunday is far too high for continued indulgence. . . . "

Britain was in a vulnerable position. Two large arms deals with India were endangered. It was the sort of situation in which British governments tend to grovel. What the Foreign Office calls "intense diplomatic activity" took place. Apologies and promises were made. Chauhan, the Sikh leader, was ostentatiously visited by the constabulary, and when Prime Minister Rajiv Gandhi made an official visit to London in October 1985 a demonstration planned by the Kashmir Liberation Front was banned by the Home Secretary, and three leading Kashmiris and nine Sikhs were detained under the Prevention of Terrorism Act.

The British government took no chances. Gandhi's arrival at Heathrow airport was protected by armed police, Scorpion light tanks, troops in armored personnel carriers and antiterrorist experts of the Special Air Service.

Nevertheless, Gandhi made it clear during his talks with the British prime minister that he believed Britain should take a still tougher line with his terrorist opponents living in the United Kingdom. At a dinner given in his honor by Prime Minister Thatcher, he insisted it was only "the sustenance provided by external supporters" that kept alive the illusions of the extremists fighting for Khalistan.

Later, at a press conference, he maintained that Britain "could do more" in combating extremism. He particularly wanted to see action taken against the "breeding grounds" in the United Kingdom of Sikh and Kashmiri militancy. He also said that he wanted extremist Sikhs and Kashmiris holding British nationality extradited to stand trial in India.

With her own narrow escape from death in the Brighton bombing only a year past, and with orders for Harrier jump-jets and Westland helicopters worth some £200 million at stake, Mrs. Thatcher listened sympathetically and told Mr. Gandhi that Britain was ready to extend the Suppression of Terrorism Act of 1978 to cover India. This would make it easier to extradite fugitive terrorists who had previously been able to claim immunity from extradition by pleading that their offenses were political. Alternatively, it would ensure that they could be brought to trial in the country where they were caught. Whitehall let it be known that teams of legal experts in Britain and India would study what arrangements should be made to ensure that violent crimes committed in one country would also be regarded as offenses in the other.

Thus terrorism, unwittingly in this case, once again brought about a diminution of individual liberty with the granting of powers which in undemocratic hands could be used to undermine the normal process of political opposition.

The need for special powers to fight terrorism was, however, grimly underlined when four of the Sikhs detained before Mr. Gandhi's arrival in Britain were charged with conspiring to murder him.

The effects of Sikh terrorism could be seen even more clearly at the Golden Temple and in the rich wheatland of the Punjab. Inside the Temple complex, warring Sikh factions clashed with drawn swords in a struggle for power and for possession of strategic buildings in the complex. The authorities were forced to send the army and police back into the Temple, thus upsetting Sikh sensibilities even further. Outside Amritsar in the farmland and the small towns the situation became even worse, with Sikh terrorists mowing down Hindus in indiscriminate fashion—usually with Sten gunfire from the back of a motor scooter—and, in Abu Nidal fashion, killing any fellow Sikh suspected of working for moderation.

Thus we see, once again, how terrorism follows the same path wherever it is adopted, for whatever cause. It leads, inevitably, to the murder of innocents and of anybody who might argue that there is a different path.

22.

Castro's Legacy
(Latin America)

It is one of the maxims of terrorism that if a government can be forced to overreact and impose antiterrorist measures which are so draconian that the lives of ordinary citizens are made impossible, then those citizens will rise against the government, which will thus bring about its own downfall. Nowhere has that maxim been more vigorously pursued than in Latin America, and nowhere has it failed so signally—despite the area's historical addiction to revolution and guerrilla warfare.

A number of movements sprang up in the early sixties, inspired by Fidel Castro's victory in Cuba and the exploits of Ché Guevara. Among them was the Movimiento de Liberación Nacional of Uruguay, better known as the Tupamaros. They took their name from the Inca chief Tupac Amaru, who rebelled against the Spanish conquistadores and was burned at the stake. Marxist in ideology, the Tupamaros started life as a rural guerrilla force in the early 1960s but soon changed to urban operations in the capital, Montevideo. This was a move whose wisdom was apparently confirmed by Guevara's disastrous failure and death among the Indians of Bolivia in 1967. Revolution, it seemed, could thrive only in the city streets, not in the huts and fields of the peasantry.

The Tupamaros specialized in the kidnapping of diplomats. It was they who held the British Ambassador, Sir

271

Geoffrey Jackson, in a "people's prison" for eight months in 1971 and murdered Dan Mitrione, the American antiterrorist adviser to the Uruguayan government. They also kidnapped government officials, robbed banks, and attacked the offices of foreign companies operating in Uruguay. What had once been an easy-going (albeit poor and corrupt) country gradually became a prison-state as the government retaliated. The press was strictly censored, free-lance right-wing groups bombed the homes of leading leftists and shoot-outs became everyday events on the streets of Montevideo.

On April 16, 1972 eight Tupamaros died after a wild day in which they ambushed and killed a police intelligence officer, shot dead a navy captain who was a leader of the hard-line military opposition to terrorism, and then murdered a former under-secretary of the interior. President Juan Maria Bordaberry went to parliament and demanded a "state of internal war" to last 30 days. Parliament, although heavily liberal, did not hesitate, and within hours of the decree's being passed 40,000 troops were combing Montevideo for the terrorists. Bordaberry's harsh reaction virtually destroyed the Tupamaros, but even that was not enough for the military, who deposed him in 1973. The generals clamped a dictatorial regime on the country as a result of which the prisons were filled with political prisoners, many were tortured and about a tenth of the population of three million fled the country. All democratic rights were suspended.

This would seem to be precisely what the terrorists wanted. The repression they had planned had been brought about. According to theory, the people would now rise up against the oppressors. But it was not so. So effective was the strong-arm rule of the generals that nobody dared raise a squeak of protest. The Tupamaros, bourgeois students fighting against what they described as Uruguay's "repressive tolerance," had succeeded only in bringing disaster upon themselves and their countrymen.

The same thing happened in Argentina. There the *Ejercito Revolucionario del Pueblo* (ERP), the armed branch of the Revolutionary Workers' Party, and the Montoneros, formed by left-wing supporters of Peron, waged such a vicious and effective terrorist campaign that it contributed heavily to the overthrow in 1976 of Peron's widow Isabel by the military. Once in power the generals instituted their "Dirty War" against the terrorists, in which thousands of people were arrested, tortured and killed. Not only were the terrorists destroyed but many innocent people were snatched from their homes or from the street and were never seen again. They became "the disappeared ones."

In 1985 the generals and the torturers were put on trial—not because the people had risen against their repression but because Britain had defeated Argentina in the Falklands, and the junta had fallen as the result of that military defeat.

Terrorist and guerrilla movements still thrive in other parts of Latin America. One of the most active in 1985 was Colombia's April 19 movement (M-19) whose name derives from the date of a much-disputed presidential election in 1970. The movement announced its birth in 1974 by raiding the Simon Bolivar museum outside Bogotá and making off with the sword, spurs and epaulettes of the man who is revered as "the Liberator" of Latin America.

After that theatrical entrance M-19 followed the normal terrorist course of bank robbings, raids on military armories, killings and kidnappings. It has, however, always had a touch of flamboyance about its activities, and in February 1980 seized no less than 14 ambassadors at a party in the Dominican embassy in Bogotá. The ambassadors were held in a stand-off siege which lasted nearly two months in order, according to M-19, to "bring attention to violations of human rights" under the Liberal government.

M-19 has connections with Cuba, where a number of its members have been trained in Castro's camps for "freedom fighters." Castro himself took part in the fighting in 1948 which swept Colombia following the murder of the populist politician Jorge Eliecer Gaitan and led to a decade of unrest which became known as "La Violencia." Castro once said, "I was blooded in revolution in Bogotá. . . . "

But in 1984 it had become evident that M-19 was involved not only with Castro but also with the powerful Colombian cocaine barons. It is a cynical involvement in which the gangsters give the terrorists weapons and money so that they keep the army busy and divert the soldiers from their campaign against drug racketeers. But they are dangerous people with whom to do business.

In August of 1984 Carlos Teledo Plata, the founder and leading ideologist of M-19, was shot down by an assassin believed to belong to a paramilitary death squad financed by the racketeers. The possible reason for his murder at their hands emerged in February 1985 when it became known that there was dissension within M-19 over the movement's involvement with the racketeers. The dissension came to light when Ivan Marino Ospina, a member of M-19's five-man central command, endorsed the drug gangsters' threat to kill five members of the American community in Colombia for every gangster extradited to the United States, to face trial under a U.S.-Colombia treaty designed to stamp out the drug traffic between the two countries.

Marino Ospina's comrades rejected his support for the gangsters and sacked him as senior leader, but he remained a member of the central command—it may be that they objected not so much to his support of the gangsters as to the fact that he made his views public—and he retained a considerable following within M-19. In August 1985, shortly after his return from a visit to Libya—that Mecca of terrorists—he was trapped by the army in an apartment in the town of Cali. In the ensuing gun battle he and his three bodyguards were shot dead.

M-19 was by then being written off as a failure, a movement with nothing new to say politically, compromised by its connections with the drug trade, and with its leadership being picked off by the army. The other main terrorist organization in Colombia, the Moscow-line communist Colombian Revolutionary Armed Forces (FARC), had accepted the government's proposals for a truce and a return to normal political life. And President Belisario Betancur had eroded M-19's support in the country by his campaign for peace, promise of amnesty and his maintenance of a high degree of civil liberty—despite a state of siege imposed following the murder by the drug barons of Rodrigo Lara Bonilla, the minister of justice.

It was in these circumstances that in November 1985 M-19 launched a bloody, suicidal assault on the Palace of Justice in the Central Plaza of Bogotá. Some 50 heavily armed terrorists seized the building and scores of hostages, among them the President of the Supreme Court, Alfonso Reyes Echandia, and 11 other senior judges. From the outset President Betancur refused to negotiate. He demanded the release of the hostages, and offered only one concession: the terrorists could be tried by civil courts and not by military tribunals.

The terrorists' reply was to kill all the judges. Dr. Reyes's body was thrown into the street with the warning that more would die if the army attacked the building. Twenty-four hours after the siege started an armored car battered down the huge carved doors of the Palace of Justice. In the battle that followed some 100 people died, including all the M-19 force, among them its leader Andres Almareles Manga. The building caught fire, and hostages burned to death tied to their desks. Some of the young terrorists who carried explosives strapped round their waists crowded into a lavatory and blew themselves up in an act of mass suicide.

When it was all over the minister of justice, Enrique Parejo Gonzalez, said the terrorists' actions proved the connection between M-19 and the drug barons. He pointed out that all the murdered judges had been involved in processing the extraditions of cocaine gangsters for trial in the United States, and he claimed that early in the siege the terrorists referred to the extradition treaty. One hostage was told he would be wise to find legal points on which to reject extraditions. "Either this is all a coincidence—which I discount"—said Dr. Parejo, "or clear evidence that behind the siege was a defensive action on behalf of the dark interests of the drug racketeers."

It was an appalling affair. It was carried out with M-19's customary flamboyance, but this time it was the flamboyance of desperation and it achieved nothing. Some 50 innocent people lost their lives, including brave supporters of democracy who were struggling to maintain Colombia's civil liberties in the face of death threats from the hit men of the drug barons. M-19, which could have accepted President Betancur's offer of amnesty months before, lost nearly a quarter of its strength. The only people who benefited were the drug gangs, whose records were burnt when the Palace of Justice went up in flames.

In July 1986 when the pope visited Colombia, representatives of M-19 tried to enlist his help in mediating with the government. But he would have none of it and in an impassioned address to hundreds of thousands of the faithful in a Bogotá park he urged the extremists to lay down their arms and give up a fight which had led only to "desolation and death."

Elsewhere in Latin America terrorism is in one of its periods of recession. There is murder from both the right and the left in Chile. Three communists were kidnapped and killed in March 1985 by unknown assailants generally thought to be members of a police "death squad." On the other side, the communist-linked Manuel Rodriguez

Partiotic Front has carried out a number of attacks against the police and public buildings; and in August 1983 General Carol Urzua, the chief administrator of Santiago, was shot dead by five men and a woman who riddled his car with bullets. But such is the ferment in Chile, with the military government of General Pinochet striving to keep the lid on a volcano of popular protest, that these incidents can hardly be regarded as part of terrorist campaigns but rather as lumps of molten lava thrown out before the volcano erupts.

It may be argued that the wars being fought in El Salvador and Nicaragua are terrorist wars. Certainly terror plays a large part in them, but we regard them as being traditional guerrilla wars with the added complication of the deep involvement of both the United States and the Soviet Union, and therefore outside the scope of this book. (It is worth noting in passing, however, that Nicaragua, now a base for Soviet subversion in Latin America, has become a haven for a cosmopolitan collection of international terrorists who have found life too hot for them in Europe and the Middle East, while the CIA, despite the disapproval of Congress and Senate, has hired men who can only be described as terrorists to try to overthrow the Nicaraguan regime.)

There is, however, one country in Latin America where modern terrorism is alive and flourishing, and that is Peru, where the Sendero Luminoso (Shining Path) organization is conducting an increasingly effective campaign against the government. Founded by Abimael Guzman, professor of philosophy at Ayacucho university in the Central Andes, the Sendero has an ideology which is a mixture of Mao Tse-Tung's military teachings, Pol Pot's Khmer Rouge ruthlessness and Inca mysticism.

Guzman, a plump man with kidney trouble, took his group's name and its guidelines from *Seven Essays For the Interpretation of the Peruvian Reality* written as long ago as 1928 by the Peruvian Marxist José Carlos Mariategui. In these essays Mariategui argued that because of the semifeudal nature of life in the countryside, revolution in Peru was likely to begin among the rural populace, and that therefore the revolution's character would be "a unique blend of Western technology and the ancient communal traditions of the Andean cultures." Despite Ché Guevara's disastrous attempt to rouse the peasants of Bolivia to revolution, and the failure of several previous attempts to make revolutionaries out of the Peruvian peasants, Guzman at first took his revolution to the countryside rather than the towns.

He prepared most carefully, recruiting the usual middle-class students who had become addicted to revolutionary violence and students from peasant families who under the left-wing military governments which ruled Peru between 1968 and 1980 were allowed into the universities for the first time. These peasant students were dismayed to find that their aspirations could not be realized, and the only path open to them led back to the harsh life of the high Andes. They preferred to return as revolutionaries rather than as peasants.

The authorities took little notice of Guzman's teachings in his remote university, but the followers who gathered round him called him the "Fourth Sword of Marxism," the others being Marx, Lenin and Mao Tse-tung. Their fanaticism for Guzman and his teachings acquired something of the character of a religious sect. In the early 1970s they began to disappear from the university. They started new lives among the peasants as schoolteachers, administrators, even laborers working in the fields alongside the peasants, and marrying into local families. They learned the Indian language, Quechua, and began to preach Guzman's message of revolution. In 1978 he followed them into the bleak Andes. Two years later, during Peru's first election for 11 years, the Shining Path announced its existence by blowing up ballot boxes in a remote town and hanging a number of dead dogs from lampposts in the center of Lima, the Peruvian capital.

From this curious beginning, Guzman's followers went on to destroy electricity pylons and blow up roads and bridges and wreck model farms. There was a double reason for this campaign. In the first place he wanted to further isolate the people of the highlands from government control, reasoning that as they had never derived any benefit from modern technology they would not object to its destruction. Secondly, he, too, was a believer in the maxim of causing the government to overreact.

But the government was very slow to react, even when its installations and police posts were attacked. President Fernando Belaúnde Terry publicly dismissed the group as "insignificant." How wrong he was. While the authorities did nothing the Sendero gradually took over large areas of the Ayacucho region.

Not all the Indian peasants welcomed the Senderistas. They led harsh and brutal lives and behaved in a harsh and brutal fashion, carrying a centuries-old hatred for the "Spaniards," the white people from the cities. In January

1983 the villagers of Uchuraccay lynched a group of Senderistas and then, when eight journalists from Lima on the track of the lynching story entered the village, the Indians, thinking they were Senderistas come to avenge their comrades, set on them with axes and killed them all.

This massacre at last focused attention on the Sendero Luminoso. President Belaúnde had initially sent in the Civil Guard to try to contain the situation but that ill-trained organization failed miserably, succeeding by their frightened brutality only in driving more peasants to join the terrorists.

Guzman's tactics became clear. He kept the army occupied with his own mobile columns in the highlands, baiting the generals into repression, at the same time striking at the authority of the government in the capital.

He lost many of his highly motivated followers in this campaign, dead or imprisoned in the formidable island prison of El Fronton and in Lurigancho prison outside Lima. However, the prisoners did not give up the struggle. They held Maoist indoctrination classes, raised their movement's flag every morning and behaved like a disciplined force inside the prisons. In July 1986, timed to concide with the meeting of the Socialist International in Lima, the Shining Path prisoners mutinied.

The security forces reacted swiftly and brutally. Within 24 hours the mutinies were suppressed and at least 156 prisoners were dead. Among them was Antonio Diaz Martinez, the Shining Path's leading ideologue. At first it was claimed that the prisoners died fighting pitched battles from fortified positions. But then President Alan Garcia, the young Social Democrat president of Peru, was forced to admit that about 100 prisoners had been taken out into the courtyard of Lurigancho, forced to lie face down and then shot through the back of the head.

President Garcia barely survived the consequent political crisis. He fired General Andres Maximo Martinez and the justice minister, Dr. Gonzalez Posada. The terrorist theory of overthrowing governments by forcing repression had come very close to succeeding, but it had done so by accident. Previous riots in the jails had always been settled by negotiation. The prisoners expected this riot would end the same way after they had succeeded in embarrassing the government before the assembled Socialist International. But this time the Republican Guard decided there would be no deal.

In reacting the way they did, they helped Guzman towards

his goal of destabilizing the government. The fact that the destabilizing process in this instance came about by bloody accident does not detract from the fact that the chubby professor of philosophy and his fanatic followers are the most efficient and dangerous exponents of terrorism in Latin America today.

Part Seven

THE WESTERN RESPONSE

23.

The Dilemma of the Democracies

After every major onslaught it is customary for the United States, echoed by its allies, to announce "we have declared war on terrorism." Such statements reveal a misconception about this never-ending, shadowy form of conflict, for it is impossible to declare war on war. Western democracies find terror difficult to comprehend and are therefore ill equipped politically and intellectually to fight it. It is a clash between two alien worlds in which language and ideas easily become deformed.

"Terrorism" and "terrorists" are both unsatisfactory words to describe a phenomenon which has never been appropriately defined, though we all know what it is when its ugly head is reared. Equally unsatisfactory are the words used by the practitioners. They hate to be called terrorists and euphemistically dignify themselves as "freedom fighters." But what sort of freedom are they fighting for? Certainly not the kind we enjoy. To be "liberated" by terrorists means to be given all the freedom of a Marxist prison camp, to do everything the commissar orders and never to question his authority. We are used to doing things in the open, whereas they are men of the shadows, plotting in secret. In our part of the world public opinion is always on the alert, ready and anxious to criticize those in power. That is the meaning of democratic life, but it does make it very difficult to combat those who interpret criticism as disloyalty and treason, punishable by summary death. Terrorists inhabit a tenebral world of clandestine meetings to plot brutal raids which ultimately serve no purpose at all.

In the United States and in Western Europe a government formulates policies which will be approved by the electorate and modified by the elected representatives of the people. In the terror war nothing is more of a handicap than a pre-stated policy attaching a government to a declared course of action. Simply because the other side has such a wide field of action available, where all the world's a target, the West needs to be as flexible as possible in responding to its actions. The response should imitate the tactics of the terrorists and try to keep them guessing how, and in what form, the reaction to their attacks will come. Every option should remain menacingly open.

To declare, for example, "we shall never negotiate with terrorists" is to tie a hand behind the back. On occasion the only way out of an appalling situation may indeed be to negotiate. The leaders and sponsors of terror war should be kept in doubt. To negotiate is not always to surrender. Sometimes the riposte must take the form of heavyweight military action such as the raid on Tripoli, just to surprise terrorists and make them uneasy next time their state planners get busy. Sometimes a similar effect can be obtained by the quick and effective intervention of special forces, as with the storming by the Special Air Services of the London embassy of Iran. Occasionally it is better for a government to talk its way out of an awkward situation as the Reagan administration did in the case of the TWA hijack to Beirut. On that occasion it used the tools of diplomacy with some cunning.

President Reagan was hindered at that time of high drama by commentators railing and ranting about terrorist propaganda victories which in fact were not worth the newsprint or the videotape on which they were proclaimed. Who remembers now the names of the principles in that hijack affair, far less the causes they represented? Where are they now? Terrorism may be melodramatic theater, but the audience soon forgets the drama and gets back to the business of real life.

Diplomacy should not be neglected as a useful means of countering terrorism. When backed by good information from friendly intelligence services there is a good deal of quiet bargaining to be done, though perhaps not with practitioners like Colonel Gaddafi. On the other hand President Assad of Syria, with troubles of his own at home, did show himself susceptible to this kind of approach on several occasions.

The cloak and the dagger are undoubtedly of great assistance in the delicate business of finding out precisely who the enemies are. The most reliable way of preventing an attack is to know about it in advance and to have information about the people planning it. Sound intelligence is the best protection against the terrorist. Surveillance and penetration of their cells is worth dozens of static guards and tons of concrete defenses. It would, of course, be foolish to dispense with those precautions, even though experts recognize that it is not possible to guard every possible target all the time.

More effort needs to be made in the use of espionage against the terror networks and their masters, not only by the CIA, but also by the Western services, which should strengthen their cooperation. One advantage available is Western superiority in the use of electronic surveillance. As was demonstrated by President Reagan's disclosure of the long-range monitoring of orders sent from Libya to the hit team in Berlin through Gaddafi's diplomatic mission, this is a powerful tool for pinning responsibility on the states which mastermind campaigns. The terrorists have advanced communications at their disposal and we must listen in to their cabalistic messages.

This raises the question of covert operations on the basis of information so garnered. There is every reason why such methods should be used against people whose normal working pattern is the covert operation.

How far should they go? The revelations about CIA misbehavior in the lengthy investigations of their activities demonstrated that a democratic state refused to allow its special services simply to adopt the methods of the people they are fighting against. Covert combat has to be limited and kept under tight control. Naked counterterrorism which involves revenge murder and elimination of the terror war enemy seldom pays off. Even the Israelis, after Mossad had murdered one innocent man by mistake, were forced to abandon their campaign of revenge killings of those responsible for the Munich massacre because of the outcry at home and abroad. It has to be recalled, though, that so long as they killed guilty persons that campaign was successful. Sectarian killings in Ireland have done little to diminish the terrorist zeal of either Protestant or Catholic groups; nor have the counter-killers of Spain helped to master the ETA movement. General de Gaulle's *barbouzes* failed to make any impact through assassination on the rebel French Secret Army in Algeria.

The most frequently asked question is: "Why doesn't somebody kill Gaddafi?" It has to be admitted that such simple solutions are indeed a tempting way to hit back at the tin-pot dictators who support and direct so many murderous attacks. It seems unjust that the leaders should get away with it. But who would do the deed? It was rumored that the French secret service did have a plot to rid the world of the troublesome Libyan, though when the government found out about it they forced the intelligence planners to resign. The CIA is expressly forbidden to go in for such assassination attempts, and so is the British Secret Intelligence Service. The truth is that despite the occasional exasperation of the man in the street, public feeling in Western states would not tolerate the use of assassination, even as a defense against terrorists. Countries which by and large have deprived even their judges and juries of the right to sentence murderers to death would not stand for it. A large body of opinion is hostile to the idea of making terrorist killers pay with their lives when caught. The only real advantage in imposing the death penalty is that it deprives the terrorist band of the opportunity to use a prisoner as an excuse to seize hostages so as to demand his release.

Yet some way has to be found of hurting known terrorists and making them count the cost of their deeds. All the evidence is that when they do take losses in action as when the raiders were killed or wounded by the Israelis at Entebbe, or by the West Germans at Mogadishu, or when the shores of Tripoli were bombed, it had a wonderfully discouraging effect upon would-be hijackers and terrorists. In spite of all the bold talk about suicide squads, those squads are made up of human beings and there are few such creatures who do not fear death. Military action which inflicts losses on the guilty undoubtedly has a powerful effect in deterring their comrades. When a suitable occasion arises it should most certainly be used. In the meantime it is a useful threatening shot to keep in the locker.

In general, large-operations against countries which organize and sponsor terrorist attacks are only sometimes likely to be completely successful. The shelling by warships of terrorist nests in Lebanon did not prevent new attacks. Precise air raids by Israeli jets have had their temporary effect on dampening terror activities, though many converts to the Palestinian cause have claimed that air raids persuaded them to join the ranks of the guerrillas. Air attack is a clumsy form of war even when the very latest technology is used. It has never yet succeeded in bringing a nation to its knees. The Tripoli raid certainly frightened Colonel Gaddafi and threw him off balance, for it is a terrifying business being attacked from the sky, but he survived as the arch patron of terror to fight another day. Even if he had been killed, was there any guarantee that those succeeding him would have been an easier to deal with?

The strategic targets for full-scale attacks are all fairly obvious. It would be perfectly possible to damage the economic interests of Iran by bombing oil and petroleum stores and refineries. The Iraqis have been launching such attacks for years without destroying either the revolution or its armed forces. It is an unrewarding mission to bomb a revolution. Were Americans to try that method they would take heavy casualties diplomatically. And if the ancient Ayotollah Khomeini lost his life in the process that would only make things worse. Of the strategic targets, the most tempting is the Bekaa valley of Lebanon, a nursery of terrorists in the no-man's-land of Lebanon. Great damage could be done there to a whole range of subversive movements. But the cost might be general war in the Middle East. The conclusion must be that although America and its allies have the right to strike back with the tools of war they know best how to handle, a great deal of thought, planning and intelligence preparation is needed beforehand if they are to make the right impact.

Other methods must be tried to find ways to punish and discourage the rulers behind the gunmen. It is tempting to believe that economic measures would do the trick, though historically such measures have rarely worked except when they were backed by a complete naval and military blockade. Whenever attempts are made to hit rogue countries with sanctions there are always persons of enterprise and countries willing to play the market and profit by breaking such sanctions. In any case we could not prevent the Libyans or the Syrians from getting their Soviet-made weapons unless it was possible to persuade the Russians that it was in their own interest not to provide them—an unlikely eventuality.

What the allies must learn to do is to emulate not the methods but the low cunning of terrorists. The way to hurt them is to probe weak spots in their organization and to hit them there. They should be encouraged to fight each other, as indeed the Palestinian factions are only too ready to do.

Intelligence work has revealed how dependent are hit teams, working far from their home base, on local support usually provided by friendly embassies. The missions of Libya, Syria and Iran, to mention only the principal Middle Eastern ones concerned, have served as communications centers, armories and false passport offices for terrorists. The United States and Britain wisely closed down Libyan embassies in their countries and severed diplomatic relations. After the alarms of the spring of '86 other states of the European Community cut down the excessive number of Libyan diplomats in their countries. There can be no doubt that these actions helped to reduce the number of incidents in Europe the following summer. Under American pressure and when its economy was suddenly short of half a million cash-paying American tourists because of the alarms of 1986, the Greek government found the courage to do what others had done already. Though Andreas Papandreou still feared to make a public announcement and did not close Gaddafi's embassy, he at least cut the size of the mission in Athens by one-third. Although only five names appeared on the diplomatic list, no less than 52 others enjoyed diplomatic privilege and were even allowed to carry guns.

But why stop at expulsions to cut down numbers? It would be better to go the whole way and shut down pretend missions which are simply terrorist service stations. The world of embassies is overpopulated anyway and many of the diplomats would not be greatly missed, either theirs in our countries, or even ours in theirs. A real operational blow against the hit teams could be struck simply by shutting down any foreign embassy known to have given aid to terrorists.

It may well be impossible completely to cut the flow of arms to countries supporting the terror bands, but the West could at least take firmer measures to prevent international terrorists from getting their hands on newly developed and specialized weapons and explosives from our part of the world. A case in point arose in 1986 when the main threat was that a new phase was about the start in the air war. The appearance of handguns like the Glock, which fire plastic bullets and are almost entirely constructed of plastic and therefore undetectable by airport scanners presently in use, greatly increased the risk of hijacking. Terror groups were able to procure supplies of new plastic and sheet explosives which are easy to conceal and to detonate. The availability of such new materials and the fact that hijacking had become a more perilous activity inspired them to plan a fresh campaign to blow up airliners in flight.

The tragedy is that such equipment and materials are the fruits of Western technology which are acquired for use by the terrorists to attack the society which produced them. They themselves, even the most skilled bomb makers, know little of technology. They are not inventive people and could not hope to produce such refined war materiál. The obvious moral is that the first line of defense is to do everything possible to prevent such dangerous toys from getting into the wrong hands. The law, the police and the intelligence services must concentrate on circumventing the activities of unscrupulous men like Edwin Wilson who, before he was caught, sold huge quantities of explosives to Colonel Gaddafi. That useful form of passive defense might ensure that capitalists do not continue to sell the rope which will otherwise ultimately hang them.

The threat to international air transport is growing and the defenses will have to be improved. That costs money, and investment in new technologies for producing scatter X-ray machines and other devices for sensing explosives. Airlines have begun to improve their own security measures and are passing on the cost to their customers. Tiresome though this is, few would quarrel with the necessity. Additional steps need to be taken at many airports, especially in "weaker brethren" countries. The best way to stop a hijack is before it starts.

Otherwise President Reagan and his fellow Western statesmen are bound to be faced again with the dread decision whether to ensure the lives and safety of hostages by giving in to their captors. The alternative is to counterattack, and possibly thereby to sacrifice the innocent, in order to achieve the strategic aim of declared policy. One thing they should not do is to declare in advance how they intend to cope with such circumstances, and they should beware of public utterances. Bargaining for hostages was once a regular form of warfare practiced and well understood by our ancestors fighting in the Crusades. They did not consider it demeaning to negotiate for the release of those captured by Saladin or even feel that loss of face was very important. Negotiating was looked on as an opportunity to practice guile.

The predicament has become more dramatic in recent times as the behavior of hijackers becomes wilder and less predictable. On at least two occasions, the TWA affair and the seizure of the Egyptair flight to Malta, highjackers behaved like screaming maniacs and took positive pleasure in picking out passengers and shooting them. That surely is the point of no return. Once they start killing to make their point, special forces must be used to mount a rescue attempt at all costs.

As most of these dramas are enacted around the Mediterranean, perhaps the time has come to consider international cooperation in rescue operations. Storming hijacked aircraft has become a manhood test of gung-ho chauvinism for any nation involved, and a principle is emerging that it must be done by the country whose airliner is at risk. This leads to time-wasting arguments about who shall advise, touchiness about outside help and, finally, to ill-timed action to forestall other units which might try to get in on the act. It is absurd that more effective arrangements have not been made to fight off the peril from the multiplying war bands.

One way to do this is to get an international gentleman's agreement to have one élite force at a time on call and ready for action. During its three month spell on alert, its task would be to deal with any aircraft hijack in Europe or the Middle East regardless of nationality of the airline or its passengers. To start with, the fire brigade role would fall to battle-proven special forces in this field, the British SAS and the West German GSG 9. Israel, of course, has its own special squad and effective arrangements, though it would be politically unwise to use their undoubted prowess in international fight-back operations. Their pinpoint intelligence about Arab groups would be nonetheless welcome as backup.

The United States has spent a great deal of effort on creating Delta force and U.S. Navy SEAL units, which could take their place on the roster and get a chance to display their abilities and crown them with tactical success. First reserves for the time being would be the Royal Netherlands Marines, who have proved themselves on home ground, and the

French special gendarmes, although it is a unit with a patchy action record. A bolder stroke, eventually, would be to draw in the Russians. Even though their attitude towards terrorism is *nuancé*, to say the least, they do not like hijacking, and might just be tempted to show off how clever their Spetsnaz special forces could be in the cause of international law and order against "bandits." The military function of these units is very similar to that of the SAS, and their deployment against Mediterranean terror would enable them to demonstrate peaceful intentions in that part of the world, which they always claim to have. And the Soviets might just remember that their diplomats too were taken hostage in Beirut and one was murdered. They cannot remain for ever immune to the modern scourge.

Robert McFarlane, an ex-Marines officer and former head of the National Security Council, put forward an original idea for using special forces when he suggested the creation of a joint American and allied unit. Its task would be to infiltrate terrorist movements and then make preemptive strikes. If such a unit acted on reliable intelligence that a group was about to go carry out a terrorist operation and attacked first on enemy ground that would be a good move. Well trained commandos have proved much more useful and accurate in attack than aircraft can ever be.

Terrorists from the Arab world are international in organization and the response should be also, though there is no point in setting up mixed NATO units as has been suggested. A rotating duty squad from one country at a time would be the most satisfactory way of showing the solidarity of the gendarme against these excessively dangerous people who, despite their political pretensions, are nothing more than armed criminals.

Not enough imagination has been applied to the task of hurting the terrorists and their backers. An American lawyer who believes that the majestic power of law can perform many miracles has suggested that victims of a hijack should sue, not the airline, but the state deemed responsible for the attack. He recognized, of course, that such states would not be likely to pay up. The course of action then would be to ask for administrative action in the United States to freeze holdings of that country. Such schemes are worth a try. As it is known that large funds are needed to support terror groups and that money is often invested in Western enterprises, it should be possible to hit them in the purse if only financial skills were turned to the task of separating the killers from their money. We are supposed to be the cunning capitalists, so why should those skills be ignored in the fight against people devoted to the overthrow of capitalist imperialists?

What is needed is courage, boldness and more ingenuity in fighting off the never-ending threat. The central paradox of the terror war is that it cannot be ended until political solutions can be found to at least a dozen world problems. Equally no such solutions are possible until terrorism has been mastered and controlled. There is no nostrum against the malady in all its diverse forms. The message must be that we have to learn to live with terrorism, keep cool in the battle against it and do everything possible to make life as difficult as possible for the hate-filled, avowed enemies of our way of life.

APPENDICES

Who's Who
Of Terror

ISLAMIC AND LEBANESE

Al Dawa *The Call*
Shi'ite group of religious inspiration, mostly Iraqis hostile to Assad regime and supporters of Khomeini. Claimed bomb attack on British Consul, Baghdad, March 1984. Also active in Gulf states. Their suicide truck-bomber Raad attacked the U.S. embassy, Kuwait.

Amal *Hope*
Shi'ite group founded by Imam Moussa al-Sadr as Movement of the Disinherited. Nabih Berri took over when al-Sadr disappeared in Libya in 1978. Has militia of 5,000. Connections with other Shi'ite groups.

Hizbollah *The Party of God*
Lebanese Shi'ites, part of Islamic Jihad responsible for the TWA hijack in Beirut June 14, 1985. The spiritual adviser is Sheikh Fadlallah. Founded in 1982, it has links with Islamic Hope, Amal and the Soldiers of God. Supported by Iran in attempts to establish an Islamic republic in Lebanon.

Iraqi Islamic Revolution
Tehran-based Supreme Council opposing President Saddam of Iraq. Helped dissident refugees, then recruited them for Islamic terror attacks. Runs active groups like Iraqi Dawa and Iraqi Mijahiddin.

Islamic Amal *Islamic Hope*
Lebanese Shi'ite group under the leadership of Hussein Mussawi hived off from Amal and set up its own organization in Baalbek. Involved in terrorist activities.

295

Islamic Jihad *Islamic Holy War*
The Shi'ite cover organization uniting under this title a host of Lebanese, Iranian and Iraqi terrorist groups to make war on the West and to install Shi'ite Islamic revolution throughout the Middle East. Responsible for suicide bombings against the U.S. embassies in Beirut and Kuwait, and U.S. Marines of the peacekeeping force. Has also taken hostages and murdered.

Islamic Resistance Movement
Active in south Lebanon against the Israelis and their allies. Connected with Shi'ite groups. Title is also used by guerrillas and terrorists of many denominations.

Islamic Unification Movement *Tawhid*
Sunni Moslem fundamentalists with their base in Tripoli, Lebanon. Led by Sheikh Shabon.

EUROPEAN

Basque and Spanish

ETA *Basque Homeland and Liberty*
Basque separatist organization founded in 1959. Operates anticapitalist autonomous commandos. Killed some 450 people. Despite attempts by the democratic Spanish government to find a political solution, they fight on. Leader believed to be Domingo Iturbo.

GAL *Anti-Terrorist Liberation Group*
Spanish counterterror group of soldiers and police against Basque terrorists in France and Spain. Some are mercenaries hired by Basque businessmen fed up with "revolutionary taxes."

GRAPO *First of October Anti-Fascist Resistance Group*
Spanish group whose leader was killed in a shoot-out with police in Barcelona in 1982. Responsible for many bombings, murders and plots, but now largely broken by police action.

Belgian

Communist Fighting Cells *Cellules communistes* combattantes
Anti-NATO, left-wing group which began bombing campaign October 1984. Allied to Action Directe and RAF. Suspected leader, Pierre Carette.

British

Angry Brigade
Sole native British group, active 1968-71. Planted bombs and machine-gunned public buildings. Mostly students. Leaders arrested, and movement ended.

French

Action Directe
Fringe left anti-NATO group led by Jean-Mark Rouillan and Nathalie Menigon. Claimed murder of General Rene Audran. Works with RAF and CCC. Joint communique with Germans announced formation of "Political-Military Front in Western Europe," January 1985.

Breton Revolutionary Army *ARB, Armée revolutionnaire bretonne*
Nationalist group started in 1963 as the Breton Liberation Front. Few in number, loud in words. Several times broken by police action, but with attack on the Rennes court in October 1983 it announced that it was back in business.

CLODO *Computer liquidation and hijack committee, Comite liquidant ou detournant les ordinateurs*
Bombed Phillips Data System at Toulouse in April 1980. They believe that computers are used "to control and repress."

Corsican National Liberation Front
Launched terrorism with 22 attacks on the island and on the French mainland in May 1976. They announced a truce in 1985, but their militants stayed in action.

Corsican National Liberation Army *ALNC, Armée de libération nationale corse*
Actions against France in cause of Corsican independence. Bomb attacks July 1983.

Corsican Renaissance Action *ARC, Action pour la renaissance de la corse*
Founded 1967 to promote regional identity of Corsica. Non-violent to begin with, but became more militant in the 1970s. Bomb attacks mainly in Corsica.

Corsican Revolutionary Brigades *BRC, Les brigades revolutionnaires corses*
Declared aim after its appearance in December 1982 was to combat French "colonialism" and the "forces of occupation."

NAPAP *Noyaux armés pour l'autonomie populaire*
Autonomist, individualist body using murder to overthrow "a rotten society."

Greek

November 17
So named in memory of date of student uprising in 1973 against colonels' regime. Group claims responsibility for bomb attacks in Athens. Involved in the murder of American and Greek officers and of an Athenian publisher in 1985.

Irish

INLA *Irish National Liberation Army*
Socialist breakaway from the IRA. Assassinated the British politician Airey Neave, and is responsible for many murders and bomb attacks. Planned fresh attacks in London in autumn 1985.

IRA *Irish Republican Army*
The traditional nationalist guerrilla and terrorist group fighting for the unification of Ireland. After declaring a cease-fire its leaders quarreled, and many left to form the powerful Provisional IRA. This new group, known as PIRA, has completely taken over, and now heads the terrorist campaign in Northern Ireland and the British Isles.

Ulster Defence Association *UDA*
Counter-terrorist group involved in sectarian murders and raids on Provisional IRA and Catholic population in Northern Ireland.

Italian

COLP *Communists for the Liberation of the Proletariat*
Formed by Barbara Balzarini of the Red Brigades. Active in Italy, and works in France with Action Directe.

Lotta Continua *Continuous Struggle*
One of the most active groups, favors mass violence in demonstrations and strikes.

NAR *Armed Revolutionary Nuclei*
Extreme right-wing group held responsible for the bombing of Bologna railway station in August 1980, and the death of 84 people.

Ordine Nuovo *New Order*
Right-wing Italian group implicated in bomb attacks and other outrages.

Prima Linea *Front Line*
Active left-wing group, anti-state.

Red Brigades
Best known leftist group, responsible for many outrages, including the kidnap and murder of Aldo Moro. Its historic leader Curcio first suggested a European terrorist alliance.

Portuguese

FP 25 *Forças Populares 25 de Abril*
Left-wing Portuguese group which carried out anti-NATO attacks, including one on warships in Lisbon harbor. Has killed 12, including industrialists, police and bystanders, during bank raids.

West German

Baader-Meinhof Gang
Urban guerrillas named after Andreas Baader and Ulrike Meinhof. After their capture and prison suicide, movement developed into Red Army Faction and June 2nd movement.

German Action Groups *Deutsche Aktionsgruppen*
Leader Manfred Roder was accused with three others of carrying out seven bomb attacks on Jewish targets and anti-Nazi memorials. Right-wing, killed two.

German People's Socialist Movement *USBD*
Suspected of machine-gunning Jewish establishments in Paris. Organization banned in 1983.

RAF *Red Army Faction*
West German successor group to Baader-Meinhof which then merged with 2nd June movement (so named after the date on which a student was shot during a West Berlin demonstration). Most active 1977, but movement reborn in 1980s with new leaders. Attempted murder of U.S. General Kroesen in 1981. Killed Ernst Zimmermann February 1985, and was responsible for numerous bomb attacks. Allied with Action Directe and CCC.

Revolutionäre Zellen *Revolutionary (or Red) Cells*
Started with one cell formed in 1976, spread throughout the country. Tight-structured units of three to five members. Anti-imperialist and anti-Zionist. Many are "weekend terrorists." Bombing and fire bombing. Also

connected with Red Zora, a similar women's movement which specializes in bombing installations considered to be antifeminist.

Wehrsportsgruppe *Military Sports Group*
Neo-Nazis who planted bombs in cars of U.S. servicemen in West Germany. Their leader, Karl-Heinz Hoffman, charged with murder of Jewish publisher Shlomo Levin in 1981.

PALESTINIAN

Abu Ibrahim Faction-Arab Organization of 15th May
Small group formed in 1979 based in Baghdad, led by Muhammad Omari, war name Abu Ibrahim, formerly PFLP. Special operations group. Specializes in barometric suitcase devices.

Abu Nidal Faction
Formed when Sabri al-Banna—Abu Nidal—quit Fatah to start corrective movement. Based in Iraq, then Syria in 1983, and Libya 1985. Responsible for attacks in Europe, including murder of Israeli ambassador to London. Claimed revenge killings of two British diplomats in Athens and Bombay. Other title: Moslem Socialist Organization, Black June and Fatah—the Revolutionary Council.

Black September
Cover name for Fatah, Palestinian terror group. It never existed as a separate organization. Responsible for the Munich Olympic Games massacre.

DFLP *Democratic Front for the Liberation of Palestine*
Extreme leftists from the PFLP, led by Naif Hawatmeh, a Greek Orthodox Christian. Politically active but was responsible for attack on Israeli town in May 1974 which killed 22 children.

FARL *Fractions armées révolutionnaires libanaises* Revolutionary Armed Faction
Christian Lebanese group with Marxist-Leninist ideology formed in 1980 to attack American and Zionist targets, mainly in Europe. Killed American and Israeli diplomats.

Force 17
Originally the bodyguard of the PLO leader Yassir Arafat. Expanded for terror operations, and in 1985 attempted seaborne raids on Israel and then murdered three Israelis on a yacht at Larnaca, Cyprus. Rival Arafat squad is Western Sector.

International Faction of Revolutionary Cells
The fancy name for the new organization run by Carlos, the international terrorist.

Lebanese National Resistance Front
Another of those blanket titles used by various groups carrying out terror and guerrilla attacks in south Lebanon, including (see below) the Syrian Social National Party. Title first used in 1982. Claims 1,200 attacks, including attempts to blow up an Israeli headquarters using a donkey with TNT stuffed into its panniers.

Palestine Liberation Organization
Fatah is Arafat's power base in the PLO, and is devoted to what it calls the "armed struggle." Since 1983, split between Arafat loyalists with headquarters in Tunis and Fatah rebels in Damascus led by Abu Moussa.

PFLP *Popular Front for the Liberation of Palestine*
Marxist movement founded by doctors George Habash and Wadi Haddad. International terrorism involvement with Haddad special operations group caused row which split the movement. It became the origin of many splinter groups. Habash still runs the original, mostly deployed in Lebanon. His cofounder is dead.

PFLP-GC *Popular Front for the Liberation of Palestine-General Command*
Captain Ahmed Jibril, formerly of the Syrian army, runs this totally terrorist organization which has no interest in politics. Now operates under Syrian government orders.

PFLP-SC *Popular Front for the Liberation of Palestine-Special Command*
There seems no end to the suffixes of the PFLP. This is a small group under Salim Salem (Abu Mohammed). It keeps international contacts, and occasionally tries a raid on Israel.

Palestine Liberation Front
This outfit cut away from the General Command and then itself split into three groups: pro-Syrian under Abdul Ghanem; pro-PFLP led by Talaat Yaqub; and pro-Arafat controlled by Abu Abbas. He organized the piracy aboard the *Achille Lauro* and became the most wanted man in the world after the United States issued an international arrest warrant.

Sa'iqa *Thunderbolt*
Palestinian group loyal to Syrian Baath party. Headquartered in Damascus, led by Issem al-Qadhi. Not to be confused with Egyptian antiterror squad using the same name.

Syrian Social National Party *SSNP*
Prewar fascist-inspired party, originally National Socialist, founded by Antoine Saadeh, who was later executed. Reactivated as terror group in

the 80s in the cause of Greater Syria. Copied Shi'ite suicide bombing, and used young Lebanese to make car-bomb attacks.

ARMENIAN

ASALA *Armenian Secret Army for the Liberation of Armenia*
Demands national identity and Turkish apology for First World War massacres. Main targets are Turkish diplomats. Active internationally. Linked to PLO factions.

Justice Commandos of Armenian Genocide
Similar in aims to ASALA. Terror actions to draw attention to the plight of Armenians, including bomb attacks in United States and Britain.

TURKISH

Grey Wolves
Nationalist and fascist, grew from Colonel Turkes's National Action Party. Named after the legendary wolf said to have led the Turks westward out of Central Asia. Ali Agca (who tried to kill the pope) was connected with it.

LIBYAN

Al-Borkan *The Volcano*
Terror arm of the National Front for the Salvation of Libya, anti-Gaddafi exiles. Attacked Gaddafi headquarters at Bab al Azizia, 1984. Shot Libyan ambassador to Rome January 1984, and killed another diplomat there January 1985. Numerous attacks.

Mutarabesun *Ever Ready*
March 1985 Gaddafi announced recruitment of new force of 150 specially trained men to seek out and destroy Libyan enemies of the regime.

AMERICAN

Armed Resistance Unit
Minor domestic group of protest against U.S. involvement in Latin America. Revolutionary Fighting Group is similar.

Alpha 66
Miami-based Cuban exile group. Leader: Umberto Alvarado. Responsible for sabotage, assassination and sending teams into Cuba. Other leaders Andres Nazario Sargan, secretary-general, and chief of operations, Humberto Perez.

Croatian Freedom Fighters *CFF*
Separatist group responsible for hijacking a TWA flight and taking it to Paris in 1976. Sporadic bomb attacks in United States—two in 1982.

FALN *Armed Forces of Puerto Rican National Liberation*
Nationalist group which raids and murders in the United States. Ten bomb attacks in 1982. Seven other similar groups occasionally operational.

Jewish Defense League
American counterterrorist group carrying out attacks on Arabs in the United States.

Omega 7
Anti-Castro Cuban crowd based in the United States. They murdered Cuban diplomat at UN in 1980. Omega's leader, Eduardo Arocena, sentenced to life imprisonment for murder in 1984. He was found guilty on 25 charges, including bomb attacks, and of the attempted murder of the Cuban ambassador to UN.

Weathermen *The Weather Underground Organization*
Formed in 1969. Preached solidarity with ethnic minorities; made 30 bomb attacks.

LATIN-AMERICAN

April 19 Movement *M19*
Colombian group founded by Carlos Teledo Plata, 51-year-old doctor, murdered August 1984.

FMLN *Farabunde Marti National Liberation Front*
Cover organization for different antigovernment groups in El Salvador. Shot dead 13 people, including four off-duty U.S. Marines in San Salvador café killings in June 1985.

Manuel Rodriguez Patriotic Front
Although its name does not sound like that of a terrorist body, this group has bombed electric pylons in Chile.

Montoneros
Argentine group which began life on the extreme right in 1969, then murdered and kidnapped in the left-wing cause before being wiped out in the "dirty war."

Sendero Luminoso *Shining Path*
Peruvian Maoist rural group inspired by Inca mysticism, founded by Abimael Guzman, known as the fourth sword of Marxism after Marx, Lenin and Mao.

Tupamaros
National liberation movement, the scourge of Uruguay in the 1960s, now almost defunct.

JAPANESE

JRA *Japanese Red Army*
Formerly active at home and abroad with Palestinian international groups. Few operations in recent years. One leader freed by Israel in prisoner bargaining. Those who fled to North Korea asked to return home with a pardon in 1985.

Other groups which have emerged recently are *Chokaua* (Middle Core), *Senki-Kyosando* (Battle Flag Communist League), *Kakurokyo Hazama* (Hazama group of the Revolutionary Workers' Council). They all specialize in firing rockets or homemade mortars—so far, ineffectually—and share an ideology which amounts to abolishing the state. They were much in evidence during the Tokyo summit.

SRI LANKAN

Liberation Tigers of Tamil Eelam *LTTE*
The biggest of the Tamil groups fighting against the Sri Lankan government in the hope of achieving their own breakaway state. All fighters in Sri Lanka are now known as "Tigers," even when they belong to rival groups such as: People's Liberation Movement of Tamil Eelam, Tamil Eelam Liberation Organization, Eelam Revolutionary Organization and Eelam People's Revolutionary Liberation Front.

ISRAELI

Terror Against Terror
Israel counterterrorist group which bombed Palestinian notables; also planned to blow up holy places of Islam in Jerusalem.

AFRICAN

ANC *African National Congress*
Began as political movement in 1912. Fights for freedom from white domination in South Africa. Military arm is Spear of the Nation. Imprisoned leader is Nelson Mandela. President is Oliver Tambo. Refuses to renounce violence.

INDIAN

All India Sikh Students Federation
Claimed destruction of Air India Jumbo over Atlantic in 1985. Followers of Sant Jarnail Singh Bhindranwale, killed in army assault on Golden Temple, Amritsar. Military arm is Dashmesh regiment (Tenth Regiment), named after the Sikh tenth guru.

Babbar Khalso
Sikh extremists led by Singh Parman, who lives in Vancouver and is held responsible for terrorist acts.

Dal Khalso *Party of the Poor*
Sikh organization campaigning for Khalistan. Founded in 1979 by Dr. Jagjit Singh, former Punjab finance minister. Members worldwide in active cells.

Kashmiri Liberation Army *KLA*
Kidnapped and murdered Indian diplomat in Birmingham in February 1984. They want self-determination for Kashmir. Mostly Kashmiris living in Britain.

The Chronology of Terror: 1968-1986

In the calendar of modern terrorism 1968 was the seminal year. Although the roots of many terrorist conflicts go far deeper, it was the seed sown in that year which has grown into the terrorism we know today. It was the year that the Arabs, despairing of beating Israel in the field following the Six Day War of 1967, adopted terrorism as their main weapon. They started with small-scale raids inside Israel, killing kibbutzniks and blowing up water pumps, but these actions brought immediate and often brutal retaliation, and so the Arabs took their terrorism abroad. They started their hijacking campaign, and international terrorism was born.

1968 was also the year when students of Europe rebelled against their universities and their governments, coming close to toppling President de Gaulle. The students failed to achieve their main objectives, principally because the workers of France and Germany refused to use their industrial muscle in support of a revolution which seemed to them essentially frivolous—and dangerous—when judged alongside their own objectives of better wages and better conditions. But while most of the students went back to the lecture halls and became bourgeois with a radical flavor, there were some who turned to urban terrorism to achieve the ends for which they had taken to the streets and fought pitched battles with authority. From now on they were to use the pistol and the bomb instead of cobblestones.

307

It was also the year that saw the emergence of the Provisional IRA, the militants who broke away from the Officials, and the start of the present round of "the Troubles" in Ireland. And it was the year in which the first links were forged between groups from different countries, with different aims and different enemies, linked only by their use of terrorism. It was the year of the birth of international terrorism.

It would, of course, be impossible to list every act of terrorism since 1968 in a book of this size. There have been so many, by so many different organizations, for so many different reasons, that they would take many volumes to tabulate. So what we have done is to list those we think have either set a trend in terrorism or influenced the way in which the antiterrorist forces have gone about their work. Among these incidents are some—like the assassination of President Anwar el-Sadat—which have affected the course of nations. These spectacular incidents are few, but what emerges from the chronology is the way in which a long-term campaign of many acts of violence can bring about quite unexpected results; for example, the Argentinian terrorists brought about not only their own destruction but the "dirty war" in which thousands of innocents perished at the hands of the military dictatorship, and how the Palestinian raids and rocket attacks across the Lebanese border gave the Israelis cause to invade Lebanon.

The Chronology is like the balance sheet of a multinational company in which a smart accountant can spot market trends, and especially areas of developing danger.

DATE	PLACE	INCIDENT	GROUP
7/22/68	Rome	First of the Palestinian hijackings. El Al Boeing 707 flying from Rome to Tel Aviv hijacked to Algiers, where the Israelis on board were imprisoned for two months.	PFLP
12/26/68	Athens	Two Palestinians attack El Al Boeing 707 with grenades and submachine gun fire as it takes off. One passenger killed. Attackers arrested but released when Greek airliner flying to Cairo hijacked July 22, 1970.	PFLP

DATE	PLACE	INCIDENT	GROUP
12/28/68	Beirut	First of the Israeli retaliatory attacks on Beirut. Commandos by helicopter take over Beirut Airport and destroy or damage 13 Arab-owned aircraft. Raid led by General Raphael Eitan, later a controversial chief of staff of the Israeli army.	Israeli army
2/2/69	Zurich	El Al Boeing 707 preparing to take off for Tel Aviv is machine-gunned. Copilot killed, five passengers wounded. One attacker killed by Israeli guard on plane. Surviving three terrorists sentenced to prison. Release when Swissair plane flying to Amman hijacked June 9, 1970.	PFLP
7/7/69	London	The Middle East war comes to London. Marks and Spencer store firebombed. George Habash threatens to bomb Jewish-owned stores all over the world.	PFLP
8/29/69	Rome-Tel Aviv	First of the hijacks involving a third party. TWA Boeing 707 taken to Damascus where all passengers released except Israelis, who are exchanged for two Syrian pilots. Henceforth Israelis adopt principle of not giving in to hijackers' demands. Plane destroyed.	PFLP
9/9/69	Rio de Janeiro	First of the diplomatic kidnappings. Charles Elbrick, U.S. ambassador to Brazil, is held until 15 prisoners released and flown to Mexico. Leads to 4,000 arrests and harsh repressive measures.	MR-8 and ALN
9/9/69	Brussels Bonn, The Hague	Hand-grenade attacks on Israeli offices.	PFLP
12/12/69	West Berlin	Bombs defused near the El Al office and America House office block. Third bomb explodes in U.S. Officer's Club.	Baader-Meinhof
2/2/70	Zurich-Tel Aviv	Swiss airliner destroyed by mid-air explosion. Forty-seven people die. Never "claimed." Possibly Abu Ibrahim's work.	PFLP

DATE	PLACE	INCIDENT	GROUP
3/3/70	Tokyo	First of the Japanese Red Army's international actions. Group led by Kozo Okamoto's older brother Takeshi, wielding a samurai sword, forces Japanese airliner to fly to North Korea.	JRA
7/31/70	Uruguay	Two diplomats kidnapped: Daniel Mitrione, U.S. public safety adviser, and Aloiso Gomide, Brazilian consul. Mitrione murdered when Uruguay government refuses to negotiate over terrorists' demands for freeing of 150 prisoners. Gomide released February 21, 1971. Attempts also made to kidnap Gordon Jones, second secretary at U.S. embassy, and Nathan Rosenfeld, cultural attaché. Both escape.	Tupamaros
9/6/70	Dawson's Field, Jordan	In a well-coordinated operation two airliners are hijacked over Europe and flown to Dawson's Field, a World War II airfield in the Jordanian desert. A third airliner is hijacked to Cairo, where it is destroyed, but a fourth, an El Al Boeing 707 flying from London to Amsterdam, escapes when Israeli "sky marshals" shoot dead Patrick Arguello, a Nicaraguan working for the PFLP, and capture Leila Khaled, who had already taken part in one successful hijack. A fifth plane, a BOAC VC10, is hijacked three days later and flown to Dawson's Field to provide hostages for her. The 300 hostages at the field are eventually released in exchange for Leila Khaled and other Palestinian terrorists imprisoned in Switzerland and West Germany. The incident leads King Hussein to drive the Palestinian groups from their base in Jordan to the formation of Black September and (because the strain of making peace between Hussein and Yassir Arafat was so great) to the death from heart attack of Egyptian President Nasser.	PFLP
10/5/70	Quebec	James Cross, British Trade Commissioner, kidnapped by French-Canadian separatists and held to ransom for the release of prisoners, publication of political manifesto and payment of $500,000 in gold. Canadian government rejects demands. Kidnappers release him December 3, 1970 in exchange for safe conduct to Cuba.	FLQ

DATE	PLACE	INCIDENT	GROUP
10/10/70	Quebec	Pierre LaPorte, minister of labor in Quebec government, kidnapped and strangled by chain of his crucifix because demands made by James Cross's kidnappers are turned down. Prime Minister Trudeau invokes emergency and breaks FLQ. LaPorte's kidnappers sentenced to life imprisonment. Royal Canadian Mounted Police later accused of exceeding their authority.	FLQ
12/12/70	San Sebastian	Basque nationalists kidnap Eugene Beihl, honorary West German consul, and force Franco government to commute death sentences passed on six members of ETA for murdering provincial police chief.	ETA
12/8/71	Montevideo	Geoffrey Jackson, British ambassador to Uruguay, is kidnapped and held in a "people's prison." Kidnappers demand release of 150 prisoners, but government refuses to negotiate. One hundred six prisoners escape, possibly by arrangement. Jackson later knighted for his courageous behavior, is released after spending eight months under degrading circumstances.	Tupamaros
3/14/71	Rotterdam	Palestinians helped by French sympathizers, blow up fuel tanks. This is the first coordinated attack mounted from Paris by Yassir Arafat's organization.	Fatah
5/5/71	Istanbul	Ephraim Elrom, Israeli consul-general, is kidnapped and murdered by gang which demands release of all guerrillas imprisoned by Turkish government. There is a Palestinian connection.	TPLA. Palestinian
6/14/71	Bab el Mandeb	Israeli tanker *Coral Sea* damaged by rockets fired from small boat. Terrorists escape to South Yemen.	PFL

DATE	PLACE	INCIDENT	GROUP
7/20/71	Rome	First of series of attacks mounted on Jordanian offices and aircraft in revenge for Black September. Initial attack made on Rome office of Alia, the Jordanian airline. Other attacks on Jordanian targets follow in Cairo and Paris.	Fatah/PFL
7/28/71	Tel Aviv	Terrorist gives suitcase bomb to innocent Dutch girl in attempt to blow up El Al airliner. Attempt fails. Dutch girl arrested but released, suitably chastened. Believed to be first of the "surrogate" bombings, although destruction of Swissair plane February 21, 1970 may also have been brought about in this fashion.	PFLP
9/1/71	London-Tel Aviv	Attempts to destroy El Al plane by terrorist who gives suitcase bomb to innocent Peruvian girl.	PFLP
10/20/71	New York	Jewish extremists fire rifle shots into apartment occupied by members of Soviet delegation to the United Nations.	JDL
11/28/71	Cairo	Wasfi Tell, Jordanian prime minister, assassinated by Black September gunmen. This is first acknowledged Black September operation, and is carried out against the man blamed for Palestinian defeat in Jordan, September 1970.	Black September
12/15/71	London	Zaid Rifai, Jordanian ambassador to London, wounded in car ambush.	Black September
12/26/72	New York	Offices of Sol Hurok, impresario who organized U.S. tour by Soviet performers, firebombed.	JDL
2/6/72	Cologne	Five Jordanian "guest-workers" said to be Israeli spies are shot to death.	Black September
2/18/72	Hamburg	Factory making electric generators for Israeli aircraft heavily damaged by bombs.	Black September

DATE	PLACE	INCIDENT	GROUP
2/22/72	Aldershot	Bomb at Parachute Regiment headquarters kills nine soldiers and civilians. Attack made in revenge for "Bloody Sunday" killing in Londonderry on January 1, 1972, when paratroopers shot 13 demonstrators.	Official IRA
2/22/72	New Delhi-Athens	Lufthansa airliner hijacked to Aden by five terrorists claiming to belong to Organization for Victims of Zionist Occupation—one of long list of PFLP cover names. Plane and passengers released after airline pays $5 million ransom. South Yemen government takes $1 million for "landing taxes."	PFLP
3/21/72	Buenos Aires	Oberdan Sallustro, president of Fiat in Argentina, is kidnapped. Fiat agrees to kidnappers' terms for $1 million ransom and the reinstatement of 250 fired workers, but government refuses to release 50 prisoners and launches attack on kidnappers' hideout. Kidnappers murder Sallustro.	ERP
5/8/72	Tel Aviv	Two men and two women hijack Sabena airliner and force it to land at Lod airport where they demand release of 317 Palestinians. In first successful assault on hijacked plane Israeli special forces disguised as mechanics kill both men and capture women. One passenger dies in the shooting.	Black September
5/11/72	Frankfurt	Series of bombs explode at Fifth U.S. Army Headquarters, killing Colonel Paul Bloomquist and wounding 13 others. Bombing is said to be in revenge for American bombing in North Vietnam.	Baader-Meinhof (RAF)
5/31/72	Tel Aviv	Three Japanese Red Army kamikaze killers working for PFLP attack passengers at Lod airport, killing 26 and wounding 76, mostly Latin-American pilgrims. Two terrorists killed; the other, Kozo Okomoto, sentenced to life imprisonment. This is the first of the transnational murder attacks.	JRA-PFLP

DATE	PLACE	INCIDENT	GROUP
6/1/72	Frankfurt	Andreas Baader and Holger Meins wounded and captured.	Baader-Meinhof
6/15/72	Hanover	Ulrike Meinhof betrayed and captured.	Baader-Meinhof
7/8/72	Beirut	Israelis strike back at PFLP in revenge for Lod massacre. Group's spokesman, Ghassan Kanafani, killed by a bomb hidden in his car. His successor, Bassam Abu Sharif, badly injured by a parcel bomb a month later.	Mossad
9/5/72	Munich	The Munich massacre. Seven terrorists take control of Israeli athletes' dormitory in Olympic village, killing two and taking nine hostage. Israel rejects gang's demand for release of 200 Palestinians, but West Germany agrees to give kidnappers safe passage to Egypt with their hostages. At Furstenfeldbrück airport West German sharpshooters open fire. In ensuing gunfight all the hostages, five terrorists and one policeman are killed. Incident staged before massed television cameras, brought Palestine issue before world.	Black September with help from European sympathizers
9/9/72	London	Dr. Ami Shachori, agricultural counselor at Israeli embassy, killed by letter bomb. In next few days some 50 letters are intercepted—all posted in Amsterdam, and all addressed to Israelis. Then second batch posted in Malaysia start to arrive, followed in November by more posted in India.	Black September
9/12/72	Jerusalem	Israeli Prime Minister Golda Meir declares war on Arab terrorists: "We have no alternative solution but to strike at the terrorist organizations wherever we can locate them."	
10/16/72	Rome	The Israelis strike back. Wael Zuaiter, Fatah's representative in Rome, shot dead outside his apartment.	Mossad

DATE	PLACE	INCIDENT	GROUP
10/24/72	Belgrade	Israelis post series of bombs in Belgrade addressed to Palestinian leaders in Lebanon, Egypt, Libya and Algeria.	Mossad
10/29/72	Beirut-Ankara	Lufthansa plane hijacked by two terrorists who threaten to blow it up in mid-air if the three surviving Munich massacre terrorists are not released. They are, and are given heroes' welcome in Libya.	Black September
12/8/72	Paris	Mahmoud Hamshari, PLO representative in Paris, is killed by an electronically triggered bomb attached to his telephone by a 'telephone engineer'.	Mossad
12/10/72	Buenos Aires	Donald Grove, managing director of the British industrial company Vestey, is kidnapped but released after nine days when Vestey pays $1 million ransom.	ERP
1/26/73	Madrid	War of kill and counterkill fought out in streets of Europe. Israeli intelligence officer Baruch Cohen is shot down in a café on the Grand Via. Palestinians claim he had played part in killing of Hamshari and Zuaiter.	Black September
2/9/73	Amman	Jordanians arrest hit team of 17 Palestinians headed by Black September leader Abu Daoud on mission to attack U.S. embassy and Jordanian government offices. King Hussein was probably one of targets. Abu Daoud talks freely under questioning, and makes first public admission that Black September is part of Fatah. He is sentenced to death, but later reprieved and released.	Black September
2/21/73	Sinai	Israeli Phantoms shoot down Libyan Boeing 727 airliner which has strayed over Sinai. Israelis fear it has been hijacked and is to be used as a flying bomb against Tel Aviv. One hundred six passengers and crew die.	

DATE	PLACE	INCIDENT	GROUP
3/1/73	Khartoum	Eight terrorists take over Saudi Arabian Embassy during party for U.S. diplomat George Curtis Moore. Moore and number of other diplomats seized. Terrorists demand release of Palestinian and Baader-Meinhof prisoners, Sirhan Sirhan (killer of Robert Kennedy) and Kozo Okamoto, surviving member of Lod hit-team. President Nixon refuses. Terrorists, on orders received from Lebanon, murder Moore, U.S. ambassador Cleo Noel and Belgian chargé d'affaires Guy Eid.	Black September
3/28/73	Ireland	Freighter *Claudia* arrested by Irish navy as it tries to run five tons of Libyan arms into County Waterford. *Claudia* has been shadowed by Royal Navy throughout its voyage. One of six men arrested is Joe Cahill, former PIRA commander in Belfast.	PIRA
4/10/73	Beirut	Israeli commandos attack PLO establishments and apartments of leading Palestinians. Seventeen people killed in fighting, including three high-ranking members of PLO. Israelis also seize large quantities of documents.	Mossad-Sayaret Matkal
6/28/73	Paris	Mohammed Boudia, the leading Arab terrorist in Europe, is killed by a bomb placed under his car seat. His death clears the way for Carlos, the Venezuelan assassin, to be called from London where he was "sleeping" to take over European operations and to build transnational terrorist network for PFLP incorporating West German, Dutch, Japanese and French terrorists.	Mossad
7/1/73	Washington D.C.	Colonel Yosef Alon, Israeli military attaché shot dead outside his home. Voice of Palestine broadcast says he has been executed in retaliation for the killing of Boudia. First such murder in the United States.	PFLP

DATE	PLACE	INCIDENT	GROUP
7/21/73	Lillehammer, Norway	Moroccan waiter killed in error by Israelis who thought they were on the trail of Ali Hassan Salameh, a Black September leader and one of the chief planners of the Munich Olympic affair. Several of hit teams are arrested and jailed by Norwegians. Incident severely embarrasses Israeli government, which calls a halt to such operations outside the Middle East.	Mossad
8/5/73	Athens	Five passengers killed and 55 wounded in machine-gun and grenade attack on TWA plane arriving from Tel Aviv. Killers claim to be members of Black September, but are disowned. Later identified as members of the Libyan-sponsored National Arab Youth for the Liberation of Palestine led by Fatah renegade Ahmed al-Ghafour.	NAYLP
8/18/73	United Kingdom	Fire and letter bomb campaign launched in London, Birmingham and Manchester. In six weeks some 30 people are injured by 40 bombs. Many others safely defused.	PIRA
9/5/73	Rome	Terrorism turns to electronic aerial warfare. Italian police arrest five Arabs armed with SAM 7 ground-to-air missiles supplied by the Russians to Libya. The terrorists had rented an apartment on the flight path to Rome airport and were planning to shoot down an El Al plane.	NAYLP
9/28/73	Vienna	Two Palestinians claiming to be members of the "Eagles of the Palestine revolution" seize a train and take three Jewish emigrants from Russia hostage. They are released after Chancellor Bruno Kreisky, 'an agnostic Jew,' promises to close the transit camp for Jewish emigrants at Schonau Castle. Terrorists prove to be members of Syrian-backed Sa'ika.	Sa'ika

DATE	PLACE	INCIDENT	GROUP
12/17/73	Rome	Five terrorists throw thermite bombs into Pan-Am airliner, burning 32 passengers to death and injuring 40. They then hijack Lufthansa plane to escape, cold-bloodedly murder airport worker and fly on to Damascus and Kuwait with hostages. They surrender to PLO officials, who say they will be tried for carrying out an "unauthorized operation."	NAYLP
12/18/73	London	Bombs left in two cars and parcel bomb injure 60 people. Reprisal for jailing of PIRA members who set off car bomb outside the Old Bailey in March 1973.	PIRA
12/20/73	Paris	Sabotage headquarters discovered in villa outside Paris. Used by international group comprising members of PFLP, Algerian and Turkish terrorist groups. Arms, propaganda and bomb-making equipment seized. Confirms international nature of terrorism in Europe and is setback to Carlos's plans for rebuilding Boudia network.	PFLP/ Carlos
12/20/73	Madrid	Prime Minister Luis Carrero Blanco assassinated by mine that blows his car over a church. Basque militants claim responsibility, saying it was revenge for killing nine of their comrades.	ETA
12/30/73	London	Leading British Zionist Teddy Seiff, president of Marks and Spencer, shot in his bath by Carlos. Bullet deflected by his teeth, and Carlos unable to fire second shot because pistol jams.	PFLP/ Carlos
1/24/74	London	Carlos throws a bomb into the Israeli Bank Hapoalim in City of London. One woman wounded.	PFLP/ Carlos
1/31/74	Singapore	Two Palestinians and two Japanese attack Shell fuel installations. Seize five hostages and hold out for a week on a boat until five more terrorists occupy Japanese embassy in Kuwait. Japanese government capitulates to their demands, and all nine are flown to South Yemen.	PFLP/JR

DATE	PLACE	INCIDENT	GROUP
2/3/74	M62 England	A 50 lb. suitcase bomb hidden in the luggage compartment of a bus carrying soldiers and their families kills nine soldiers, a woman and her two children.	PIRA
2/5/74	Berkeley, California	Heiress Patricia Hearst kidnapped. She later joins her kidnappers in bank raid.	SLA
4/11/74	Qiryat Shemona Israel	Three Palestinians storm block of apartments in this northern Israeli town. They kill 18 and wound 16 before being killed in turn by Israeli troops. First major operation by PFLP-General Command.	PFLP-GC
5/17/74	Los Angeles	Six suspects in Hearst kidnapping die in gun battle with police.	SLA
7/17/74	London	Bomb explodes in a Tower of London crowded with tourists, many of them from overseas. One woman killed, 41 people wounded.	PIRA
7/26/74	Paris	Yoshiaka Yamada arrested at Orly airport carrying Japanese Red Army's treasury—$10,000—to finance series of kidnappings. Most of the money proved to be poor counterfeits.	JRA
8/4/74	Bologna	Bomb planted on Rome to Munich express explodes just outside Bologna, killing 12 and injuring 48. This neo-fascist group is responsible for a number of bombings in Italy.	Ordine (Black Order)
9/7/74	Athens	TWA airliner that had landed in Greece from Israel is blown up in flight over the Ionian Sea as it flies to the United States. All 88 on board are killed.	NAYLP
9/12/74	Beirut	Ahmed al-Ghafour, code-named Abu Mahmoud, leader of NAYLP and responsible for series of murderous attacks on airliners, is shot dead by a Fatah execution squad because his activities were harmful to Fatah policies.	Fatah

DATE	PLACE	INCIDENT	GROUP
9/13/74	The Hague	In an operation partly planned and financed by Carlos, three Japanese take over French embassy and successfully demand release of their currency courier, Yoshiaka Yamada.	JRA/Carlos
9/15/74	Paris	Carlos throws hand grenade into Le Drugstore, killing two and wounding 34 in support of demands of Japanese occupiers of French embassy at The Hague.	Carlos
10/5/74	Guildford	Bombs planted in pubs frequented by British soldiers kill three men and two women and injure 54.	PIRA
10/11/74	Rabat	Abu-Iyad, second-in-command of Fatah, plots the assassination of King Hussein and other moderate Arab leaders at the Rabat summit. Plot is foiled by Moroccan authorities, who arrest 15 after Israeli tip-off.	Black September
11/21/74	Birmingham	Series of bombs, part of the Provisionals' campaign to take terror to the mainland of England, kill 21 and wound 168.	PIRA
12/13/75	Paris	Members of Carlos's gang try to destroy El Al plane at Orly using hand-held rocket. They miss target, hit Yugoslav airliner instead. No casualties.	PFLP/Carlos
12/19/75	Paris	Carlos's men, under the name of the "Muhammed Boudia Group," return to the attack at Orly, but are spotted before they can fire their rocket. In ensuing gunfight they wound 20 bystanders, seize hostages and bargain their way onto a flight to Iraq.	PFLP/Carlos
12/24/75	New York	Bomb at Fraunces Tavern in Wall Street area kills 4 and injures 51.	FALN
12/29/75	Washington, D.C.	Bomb causes extensive damage to U.S. State Department building. No casualties.	Weather Underground

DATE	PLACE	INCIDENT	GROUP
2/27/75	Berlin	German politician Peter Lorenz is kidnapped and held to ransom for freedom of five Baader-Meinhof terrorists. West German government capitulates, freeing the five and giving them DM 20,000.	Baader-Meinhof (RAF)
6/27/75	Paris	Carlos's identity revealed when French police are led to his apartment in the rue Toullier by Michael Moukharbel, his PFLP courier. Carlos kills Moukharbel and two police officers and wounds a third. Escapes to Algeria. From now on boasts: "I am the famous Carlos."	Carlos
12/6/75	Balcombe Street, London	An active service unit which has carried out an attack a week for a whole year machine-guns fashionable Scott's restaurant in the heart of London. Gunmen are chased to a flat in Balcombe Street where they take the occupants hostage. They surrender after a six-day siege under threat of assault by the SAS. The four men, Martin O'Connell, Eddie Butler, Harry Duggan and Hugh O'Doherty, are sentenced to over 30 years' imprisonment each. Among their victims was Ross McWhirter, joint founder and publisher with his brother of the *Guinness Book of Records*.	PIRA
12/21/75	Vienna	OPEC's headquarters seized by Carlos and a mixed gang of Arab and German terrorists. Three men are killed and 11 oil ministers kidnapped and held hostage.	PFLP/ Carlos
12/23/75	Athens	Richard Welch, long-serving CIA officer is murdered after being named as CIA station chief in Athens by anti-CIA publication *Counter Spy*.	
5/4/76	Stammheim	Gudrun Ensslin admits to the Baader-Meinhof gang's responsibility for three of the bombings with which they are charged.	Baader-Meinhof (RAF)

DATE	PLACE	INCIDENT	GROUP
5/8/76	Stammheim	Ulrike Meinhof hangs herself from the bars of her cell window.	Baader-Meinhof (RAF)
5/23/76	Assen, Netherlands	South Moluccans seize train at Assen and school at Bovinsmilde in pursuance of their hopeless cause to wrest an independent republic from Indonesia. The schoolchildren are released after four days, but train siege lasts 22 days. Captured by Dutch Marines in dawn assault in which two hostages and six terrorists die.	South Moluccans
6/27/76	Entebbe, Uganda	A mixed gang of West German and Palestinian terrorists hijack Air France Airbus to Entebbe, where they separate Jews from other passengers until their demands for release of jailed terrorists are met. At least three governments, Uganda, Somalia and Libya, involved with the terrorists. Hijacking brought to an end by spectacular assault on Entebbe airport by troops of Israel's élite Sayaret Matkal. They kill two West German terrorists, Brigitte Kuhlmann and Wilfried Boese (one of Carlos's Paris gang), and five members of the PFLP. It is the first great defeat of international terrorism.	PFLP/ Carlos/ RAF
7/19/76	Argentina	Robert Santucho, overall leader of the ERP, is killed in gunfight with the authorities.	ERP
7/31/76	Dublin	Christopher Ewart-Biggs, British ambassador to Ireland, assassinated by a culvert bomb.	PIRA
10/28/76	Belfast	Maire Drumm, violently anti-British Provisional IRA leader, is shot to death in hospital while recovering from an operation.	UDA
4/7/77	Karlsruhe	Siegfried Buback, West Germany's chief public prosecutor, is shot to death in revenge for Ulrike Meinhof's suicide.	Baader-Meinhof (RAF)

DATE	PLACE	INCIDENT	GROUP
4/10/77	London	Former Yemeni prime minister Abdullah al-Hejiri, his wife and the minister at Yemeni embassy are shot dead by the Palestinian assassin Zohair Akache. Akache, well known to London police for his violent pro-Palestinian behavior, had been deported but had sneaked back into the country. Hejiri's murder was ordered because he was working for the Saudis to form a Western-oriented alliance of Arab countries in southern Arabia and the horn of Africa.	PFLP
7/31/77	Frankfurt	Juergen Ponto, one of Germany's most influential bankers, murdered by terrorists who are let into his heavily protected home by his goddaughter, Susanne Albrecht.	Baader-Meinhof (RAF)
9/5/77	Cologne	Hans-Martin Schleyer, powerful West German businessman, ambushed by terrorists who kill his driver and three bodyguards. They kidnap him and demand the release of 11 Baader-Meinhof prisoners, who are to be given $50,000 each and flown to country of their choice. This kidnapping, following murders of Buback and Ponto, virtually brings governmental life to standstill.	Baader-Meinhof (RAF)
9/28/77	Bombay	Japan Air Lines plane hijacked and held to ransom for $6 million and the release of six IRA prisoners. Japanese government capitulates. Hijackers and released prisoners join international group being built up by Wadi Haddad of PFLP and Carlos.	JRA
10/13/77	Majorca-Frankfurt	Lufthansa airliner with 79 passengers is hijacked by Palestinians—two men and two women—in support of Schleyer operation. They demand release of Baader-Meinhof leaders and an $18 million ransom. German terrorists threaten to kill Schleyer, while Palestinians threaten to blow up plane with passengers and crew. After wild flight around the Middle East and the Horn of Africa (during which	PFLP/Baader-Meinhof

DATE	PLACE	INCIDENT	GROUP
		terrorist leader murders Jurgen Schumann, the plane's captain) they land at Mogadishu, Somalia. There the plane is stormed by West Germany's GSG9 commando unit and the passengers released. Two members of the British Special Air Service take part, using their "stun" grenades. Three of the terrorists are killed, the fourth, a woman is wounded. The terrorist leader is identified as Zohair Akache, killer of Abdullah al-Hejiri.	
10/19/77	Mulhouse, France	Schleyer's body is found in a trunk of a car. He has been shot through the head.	Baader-Meinhof (RAF)
10/20/77	Stammheim	Andreas Baader, Gudrun Ensslin and Jan-Carl Raspe, who had expected to be freed by the Schleyer kidnapping and the Mogadishu hijacking, commit suicide in their cells. This is the end of the Baader Meinhof gang.	Baader-Meinhof (RAF)
12/31/77	London	Two Syrian diplomats killed when a bomb they are taking to plant at an Egyptian office explodes in their car in Mayfair.	Syrian Intelligence
1/4/78	London	Said Hammami, PLO representative in London, is shot dead in his office. Killing causes furor in Arab world because Hammami, a moderate, was being used by Arafat to sound out Israeli liberals. It is the start of murder campaign by Abu Nidal against Arafat's moderate supporters.	Abu Nidal
2/18/78	Larnaca	Two gunmen murder Egyptian editor Yusuf Sebal, then seize Cypriot airliner. Egyptian commando attempt to "do an Entebbe" goes sadly wrong at airport where 15 of the commandos die in fight with Cyprus National Guard. Gunmen are captured, and sentenced to death, then reprieved and set free.	Abu Nidal
3/16/78	Rome	Aldo Moro, Italian elder statesman, ambushed in car. His five bodyguards are slaughtered, and he is kidnapped.	Red Brigades

DATE	PLACE	INCIDENT	GROUP
4/1/78	East Berlin	Wadi Haddad, operational commander of PFLP, dies of cancer. He is buried in Baghdad. When George Habash renounced terrorist operation in 1972, Haddad, co-founder of PFLP, defected to continue directing hijackings and other acts of terrorism from Baghdad. He formed his own PFLP-Special Operations Group, and maintained contacts with a number of international terror groups, including Carlos, JRA, PIRA, RAF and Red Brigades. He never fully recovered his prestige following defeat at Entebbe.	PFLP
5/10/78	Rome	Aldo Moro's body found in trunk of car in Rome side street. He had been shot by Skorpion machine pistol.	Red Brigades
6/15/78	Kuwait	PLO representative Aly Yasin is murdered.	Abu Nidal
6/23/78	Turin	Red Brigades leader Renato Curcio sentenced to 15 years. Another founding member of Red Brigade, Pietro Bassi, also gets 15 years.	Red Brigade
7/19/78	London	General al-Naif, former prime minister, assassinated outside Intercontinental Hotel	Iraqi Secret Service
7/31/78	Paris	Culmination of mini-war between Iraq and Fatah involving Iraqi support for Abu Nidal, who has been condemned to death by Fatah. Gunmen invade Iraqi embassy and take eight hostages. They then surrender to French police but are ambushed by Iraqi secret servicemen as they are taken from the building. In ensuing battle a French police inspector and an Iraqi diplomat are killed.	Fatah
8/3/78	Paris	PLO representative Izz Ad-Din Qalaq is assassinated.	Abu Nidal
9/7/78	London	Broadcaster Georgi Markov murdered by pellet containing ricin poison fired into his thigh through tip of "umbrella." His broadcasts to his	Bulgarian Secret Service

DATE	PLACE	INCIDENT	GROUP
		native Bulgaria had revealed too much about the workings of the regime. It was a straightforward assassination by a communist government. It is not known if the KGB was involved.	
9/24/78	Dortmund	Angelika Speitel alnd Michael Knoll are wounded and captured when surprised by German police as they are target-shooting in a forest. Speitel wanted for murders of Buback, Ponto and Schleyer.	Baader-Meinhof (RAF)
1/12/79	Rhodesia	Civilian airliner shot down by hand-held Russian Sam-7 missile.	ZAPU
1/22/79	Beirut	Ali Hassan Salameh, who planned the Munich massacre operation, is killed by a car bomb. It is the end of a seven-year chase by the Israelis. Six passers-by are also killed.	Mossad
3/22/79	The Hague	Sir Richard Sykes, British ambassador to the Netherlands, and his Dutch footman shot dead at front door of residence.	PIRA/Red Help
3/30/79	London	Wartime hero and member of parliament Airey Neave killed by highly sophisticated (mercury-fused) bomb attached to his car as he drives out of House of Commons underground car park.	INLA
6/29/79	Belgium	General Alexander Haig, then NATO commander, narrowly escapes death when bomb explodes under his car.	RAF
7/25/79	Cannes	Zuhair Mohsin, leader of the Syrian-controlled Sa'ika group, is shot dead outside his apartment. This is part of the underground war going on between Iraqi and Syrian secret services.	Abu Nidal for Iraqi Secret Service
8/8/79	Sligo, Ireland	Earl Mountbatten and three other people murdered by radio-detonated bomb planted in his fishing boat.	PIRA

DATE	PLACE	INCIDENT	GROUP
8/27/79	Warrenpoint	Eighteen British soldiers killed in double bomb ambush.	PIRA
11/5/79	Tehran	United States embassy seized by Revolutionary Guards at instigation of Ayatollah Khomeini's government. Leads to abortive raid by American Delta force. Fifty-two hostages eventually released January 20, 1981 in exchange for $6 billion of Iranian assets frozen by U.S. government.	Revolutionary Guards
3/6/80	Lisbon	Pirate whaler *Sierra* sinks at its moorings after explosion of bomb planted by conservationists.	Anon
4/30/80	London	Iranian embassy seized by Arab Iranians demanding autonomy for "Arabistan." Operation planned and controlled by Iraqis as part of war against Iran. Embassy stormed by Special Air Service May 5, 1980. Five terrorists killed. Two hostages murdered. Embassy gutted. Surviving terrorists sentenced to life imprisonment.	Group of the Martyr/Iraqi Secret Service
8/2/80	Bologna	Bomb at Bologna railway station kills 84 people and wounds 186. Most lethal of series of atrocities committed by right-wing groups attempting to destabilize government. Their activities have been obscured by those of left-wing Red Brigades.	Armed Revolutionary Nuclei (NAR)
9/26/80	Munich	Neo-Nazi plants bomb at Bierfest. Kills himself and 12 others, wounds 312. This, combined with Bologna bomb, leads to realization of danger of Nazi resurgence and right-wing terrorism.	Wehrsports-gruppe (Military Sports Group) Hoffman
3/10/80	Paris	Bomb on back seat of motorcycle explodes at entrance to synagogue in rue Copernic. Four people die. One of series of bombs planted by PFLP-SC formed by Salim Abu Salem to take over from the late Wadi Haddad.	PFLP-Special Command

DATE	PLACE	INCIDENT	GROUP
11/29/80	Tripoli	Colonel Gaddafi confirms to authors that his hit team will continue to eliminate the "stray dogs"—the opponents of his regime living in foreign countries.	
12/31/80	Nairobi	Norfolk Hotel, owned by Zionist supporters, is blown up. Sixteen people die. Seen as revenge for part Kenya played in helping Israel mount the Entebbe raid.	PFLP-SC
3/1/81	Maze Prison, Ulster	Republican prisoners convicted of terrorist crimes start hunger strike to gain political status. Ten die before strike collapses on March 10, 1981.	PIRA/ INLA
3/2/81	Kabul	Followers of executed Pakistan President Ali Bhutto hijack PLA airliner. Kill Pakistan official and take plane to Damascus. Threaten to kill foreign passengers. President Zia capitulates and frees 54 political prisoners.	Al Zulfiqah (The Sword)
3/30/81	Washington	President Reagan shot in chest. Press Secretary James Brady and two others wounded by 25-year old John Hinckley.	Loner
5/9/81	Sullum Voe, Shetlands	Bomb explodes while Queen tours North Sea oil terminal. Causes little damage, no casualties and is not near Queen, but much concern felt for royal safety.	PIRA
5/13/81	Vatican	Pope John Paul II severely wounded by Mehmet Ali Agca, known assassin and member of Turkish nationalist organization Grey Wolves. He is arrested and admits shooting, but gives confusing evidence. Italian courts charge Bulgarian Secret Service with complicity.	Loner/ Bulgarian Secret Service?
6/13/81	London	Queen fired on by 17-year-old Marcus Sarjeant using blank cartridges in replica gun as she rides at the head of a Sovereign's Escort of the Household Cavalry to the Trooping the Colour ceremony.	Loner

DATE	PLACE	INCIDENT	GROUP
8/5/81	Warsaw	Abu Daoud, leading member of PLO and Black September, wounded in coffee shop of Intercontinental Hotel. First such incident in Eastern Europe.	Abu Nidal
8/31/81	Ramstein	Car bomb at the headquarters of the USAF in Europe wounds 20.	RAF
9/15/81	Heidelberg	General Frederick J. Kroesen ambushed. RPG-7 rocket fired at his armored Mercedes. He escapes with scratches.	RAF
10/6/81	Cairo	President Anwar Sadat assassinated by Islamic zealots while reviewing army at celebrations marking the anniversary of the October war.	Al Takfir Wal Higra
10/10/81	Porton Down	Parcel of anthrax-infected soil from Hebridean isle of Gruinard, contaminated by wartime experiments, dumped at chemical warfare center.	'Dark Harvest' Commando
10/10/81	London	Provos start new bombing campaign following failure of hunger strike. Nail-bomb attack on bus carrying Irish Guards returning from ceremonial duty at the Tower of London kills two passers-by and wounds 35 soldiers and civilians.	PIRA
10/17/81	London	Sir Stuart Pringle, commandant-general Royal Marines, loses leg when bomb hidden in his car explodes as he drives off. Same type as that which killed Airey Neave.	PIRA
10/20/81	New York	Kathy Boudin, a fugitive for 10 years, arrested in shoot-out after murder of security-truck driver and two policemen in wages snatch.	Weather Underground
10/21/81	Milan	American ambassador to Italy, Maxwell Rabb, flown home in great haste following threatened assassination by Libyans in revenge for shooting down of two Libyan warplanes over Gulf of Sirte by U.S. carrier planes.	Libyan Secret Service

DATE	PLACE	INCIDENT	GROUP
10/26/81	London	Bomb-disposal expert Kenneth Howarth killed by booby-trapped bomb at Wimpey Bar in Oxford Street.	PIRA
11/13/81	London	Sir Michael Havers, British attorney general, and his wife escape bomb explosion which wrecks their Wimbledon home. Thomas Quigly and Paul Kavanagh later jailed for a minimum of 35 years each for the 1981 bombing campaign.	PIRA
11/14/81	Belfast	Robert Bradford, leading Ulster Unionist and MP for Belfast South, shot dead outside university.	PIRA
11/28/81	Damascus	Car bomb kills 64 in city's crowded middle-class district. Part of campaign mounted against Syrian government by Moslem Brotherhood operating from Jordan.	Moslem Brotherhood
1/18/82	Paris	Lt. Col. Charles Ray, U.S. assistant military attaché, killed by single shot in the head as he leaves his house in Passy district. Killing claimed by Fractions armées revolutionaires libanaises, a Christian Lebanese group formed in 1980 to strike at American and Israeli targets.	FARL
2/16/82	Paris	Bruno Brequet, a Swiss, and Magdalena Kaupp, a West German, arrested and charged with a number of terrorist offenses. They claim to belong to the "International Revolutionary Organization," a new name for Carlos's group.	Carlos
3/1/82	The Hague	The French embassy receives a letter in Spanish signed by Carlos and authenticated by his thumb-prints. In it he threatens to take action against members of government unless Kaupp and Brequet are released: "I give you one month."	Carlos

DATE	PLACE	INCIDENT	GROUP
3/30/82	Limoges	Exactly one month after Carlos made his threat to "take on members of the government" a bomb explodes on board the Paris-Toulouse "Capitol" express. Six people are killed and 15 wounded.	Carlos
4/3/82	Paris	Ya'acov Bar Simantov, second secretary in charge of liaison with French political parties at Israel embassy, is shot dead in hall of his apartment by a woman.	FARL
6/3/82	London	Shlomo Argov, Israeli ambassador to London, shot through the head by Abu Nidal hit team. Argov lives, although desperately wounded. Hit team captured and sentenced to long terms of imprisonment.	Abu Nidal
7/20/82	London	Bomb attacks on Household Cavalry in Hyde Park and the band of the Green Jackets in Regent's Park kill 11.	PIRA
8/18/82	Paris	President Mitterrand orders the dissolution and banning of Action Directe. Order made under 2936 law against private militias.	Action Directe
9/3/82	Palermo	General dalla Chiesa and his wife shot dead in their car. Chiesa, who had broken the Red Brigades, had been made Prefect of Palermo to tackle the Mafia. It was the Mafia who killed him, not the terrorists.	Mafia
9/14/82	Beirut	President-elect Bashir Gemayel killed by huge bomb planted in his office building. Bomb planted by Habib Shartouni, 26, member of the Syrian People's Party, but no one in Beirut had any doubt that the order to kill Gemayel came from Damascus.	Syrian Secret Service
11/4/82	Madrid	Lt. Gen. Victor Lago, commander of Spain's crack Brunete armoured division, shot dead by ETA's military wing in their continuing campaign for Basque independence.	ETA-M

DATE	PLACE	INCIDENT	GROUP
2/9/83	County Kildare	Shergar, winner of the Derby, is kidnapped from the Aga Khan's stables. Ransom negotiations break down. Horse is assumed to have been killed.	PIRA
4/10/83	Albufeira	Issam Sartawi, PLO moderate and adviser to Arafat, shot dead at Socialist International Congress.	Abu Nidal
7/15/83	Paris	Orly airport bombed by Armenians as part of their sporadic but unending campaign for nationhood. Seven die, 60 are injured.	ASALA
8/25/83	Ulster	In mass breakout from Maze prison 39 Republican prisoners escape. Prison officer James Ferris stabbed to death.	PIRA
10/9/83	Rangoon	North Korean army officers plant remote-controlled bombs in roof of the Martyrs' Memorial. Explosions kill 21, including 17 members of South Korean government delegation. Four cabinet ministers are among the dead, but bombers miss primary target, South Korean president Chun Doo Hwan. One member of hit team killed by Burmese forces, other two captured.	North Korean Secret Service
10/23/83	Beirut	Suicide lorry bombers attack headquarters of U.S. Marines and French troops serving with the multinational peacekeeping force. 241 Marines and 58 French soldiers die. Attack one of major factors in forcing U.S. troops out of Lebanon.	Islamic Jihad
11/15/83	Athens	U.S. Navy captain George Tsantes killed by leftist terror group. Same gun, a .45 Magnum, was used to kill Richard Welch, CIA station chief in Athens, on December 23, 1975.	
12/12/83	Kuwait	Suicide truck bomber attacks U.S. embassy. Other bombs—non-suicide— planted at French embassy and number of Kuwaiti offices. Four people die and 60 are injured.	Al-Dawa (The Call)

DATE	PLACE	INCIDENT	GROUP
12/17/83	London	Harrods, the exclusive store in London, is attacked by a car bomb when packed with people doing their Christmas shopping. Telephoned warning comes too late for police to find bomb. It kills 6 and wounds 94. Outrage caused such disgust around the world, especially in America, that PIRA leaders disclaim responsibility; say the Active Service Unit acted without permission.	PIRA
1/29/84	Paris	Bomb damages offices of Panhard-Levassor, makers of military equipment. Action Directe says it planted bomb in protest against French military operations in Chad.	Action Directe
1/29/84	Madrid	Lt. Gen. Guillermo Lacaci shot dead while walking home with his wife after attending Mass. He is the sixth Spanish general to be murdered since 1978.	ETA-M
3/10/84	London	Series of bombs explode in Arab establishments frequented by Gaddafi's opponents. Most serious incident at El Oberge club near Berkeley Sq., where 27 are injured.	Libyan Secret Service
3/14/84	Belfast	Gerry Adams, leader of Provisional Sinn Fein, shot and wounded several times.	Ulster Freedom Fighters
3/28/84	Athens	Kenneth Whitty, first secretary at British embassy, shot dead in his car on way to work. Killing is revenge for imprisonments of Abu Nidal's hit team who shot Shlomo Argov. One of imprisoned men is Nidal's cousin.	Abu Nidal
4/17/84	London	WPC Yvonne Fletcher killed by diplomatic gunman firing from "Libyan people's bureau" in St. James Sq. at demonstrating Libyan dissidents. Shooting and subsequent siege of bureau led to severing of relations between Libya and UK.	Libyan People's Bureau

DATE	PLACE	INCIDENT	GROUP
6/24/84	Brussels	An 1,800-pound cache of explosives is stolen from a quarry in Ecaussines village. This explosive is distributed among groups forming new Euro-terror international, and is used in a number of bombings.	CCC
7/8/84	London	Body of Libyan businessman found in rented flat in Bickenhall Street. He was due to stand trial for the Gaddafi bombings of dissident meeting places. It is assumed that he was murdered by Gaddafi's men to stop him talking.	Libyan Secret Service
7/31/84	Tehran	Air France Boeing 737 hijacked to Tehran on flight from Frankfurt to Paris. Demand release of terrorists jailed by French for attempted murder in 1980 of Chapour Bakhtiar, opponent of Iranian regime. Two people killed. Demands not met. Belief is that Iranian government colluded with hijackers.	Islamic Jihad
9/20/84	Beirut	Suicide bombing of U.S. embassy annex. Driver of truck shot by British Military Police bodyguard of Ambassador David Miers, who was visiting his American colleague. Truck swerves off course and misses target. Nine killed.	Islamic Jihad
9/29/84	Kerry	Trawler *Marita Ann* carrying cargo of arms for PIRA is captured by Irish patrol boat.	PIRA
10/12/84	Brighton	Long-delayed-action time bomb planted in the Grand Hotel almost wipes out Prime Minister Margaret Thatcher and entire British cabinet, who are attending Conservative party conference. Five people are killed, including Sir Anthony Berry, and many are seriously injured, among them Mr. Norman Tebbit, the industry minister, Mrs. Tebbit and Mr. John Wakeham, the Tory's chief whip, whose wife was among the dead. Bombing led to complete review of security procedures for the prime minister and cabinet ministers.	PIRA

DATE	PLACE	INCIDENT	GROUP
10/31/84	New Delhi	Indira Gandhi, prime minister of India, assassinated by Sikh members of her bodyguard in revenge for the army's assault on the Golden Temple of Amritsar, a Sikh holy place which had been turned into a fortress by Sikh nationalists.	Sikh Nationalists
11/17/84	London	Millions of Mars Bars taken from shops after claim that they have been contaminated with rat poison.	Animal Liberation Front
11/27/84	Bombay	Percy Morris, British Deputy High Commissioner, shot dead at a traffic light. This is another of Abu Nidal's revenge killings against a "soft" target.	Abu Nidal
12/3/84	Tehran	Shias hijack Kuwait jet on flight from Dubai to Karachi. Demand release of terrorists jailed in Kuwait for bombing of U.S. embassy and other targets. Hijackers brutally kill two U.S. officials of Agency for International Development. They surrender after six days at Tehran airport. Suspicion once again is that they acted with complicity of Iranian authorities.	Islamic Jihad
12/11/84	Belgium	Six bombs blow up valve chambers in sections of secret NATO oil pipeline at Verviers near Brussels and other areas. This heralds start of Christmas bombing campaign against NATO targets by new Euro-terrorists.	CCC/RAF/ Action Directe
12/25/84	Pensacola, Florida	Christmas Day chosen for bombing of three abortion clinics. There have been been 30 such attacks since 1981.	
1/15/85	Paris	The new Euro-terrorists send a long and verbose communiqué to a news agency spelling out their creation of "Political-Military Front in Western Europe" with NATO as its main target in its fight against the imperialist bourgeoisie.	Action Directe/ RAF

DATE	PLACE	INCIDENT	GROUP
1/25/85	Paris	The new alliance kills its first victim. General René Audran, head of France's international arms sales organization, is shot dead in his car outside his house.	Action Directe
1/30/85	Anglet	French move against Basques for first time, arresting eight, including Juan Mikilena, deputy head of ETA, in raid on ETA headquarters on French side of the border.	ETA-M
2/1/85	Munich	The new alliance kills its second victim. Ernst Zimmermann, president of the West German Aerospace and Armaments Association, is shot after being tied up in his home when woman tricks her way in. His wife identifies woman as Barbara Meyer and actual killer as RAF veteran Bernhard Lotze.	RAF
3/10/85	Metullah	Suicide bomber drives explosive-laden car into Israeli convoy before blowing himself up. Twelve men die. Sets a new fashion for suicide bombers.	Syrian National Socialist Party
3/26/85	Sofia	Seven killed by bomb on train from Burgos on Black Sea coast to Sofia. Follows bomb August 30, 1984 at Varna airport. Four other Bulgarian cities reported to have been attacked.	Turks
4/20/85	Brussels	Headquarters of North Atlantic Assembly bombed by new group: Revolutionary Front for Proletarian Action. Also claimed bombing on following day of AEG-Telefunken offices in Brussels.	FRAP
4/21/85	Haifa	Fatah makes its first attempt to mount major operation against Israel since Israeli invasion of Lebanon in 1982. A group of 28 guerrillas trained in Algeria is sent by ship to land on Israeli coast, split into three groups and carry out a number of missions. Ship is intercepted and sunk by Israeli navy. Twenty guerrillas and crew drown. Eight are captured.	Fatah

DATE	PLACE	INCIDENT	GROUP
5/20/85	Tel Aviv	Kozo Okamoto, the Lod killer, is among 1,154 mainly Palestinian prisoners released by Israelis in exchange for 3 Israeli soldiers held by Ahmed Jibril's PFLP-General Command. Release of so many convicted prisoners causes much controversy in Israel.	
6/14/85	Beirut	TWA Boeing 727 hijacked on flight from Athens to Rome. Becomes international incident involving prestige of President Reagan. For the full story see pages 37-51	Islamic Jihad
6/23/85	Toronto	Air India Boeing 747 on flight from Toronto to London disintegrates and crashes into the sea off Irish coast. 329 people die. At same time suitcase taken off Canadair flight from Vancouver to Tokyo explodes, killing two baggage handlers. Believed to have been planned for transshipment to Air India flight but exploded prematurely. Indian government convinced Sikh extremists responsible.	Sikh Extremists
8/8/85	Rhine-Main	Car bomb kills two Americans, a soldier and one woman civilian at U.S. Air Force base. This is the seventh attack on U.S. and NATO installations in West Germany so far this year. Terrorists gained entrance to the base by murdering a 20-year-old American soldier and using his documents.	RAF
9/25/85	Larnaca, Cyprus	Hit team from Force 17, Yassir Arafat's bodyguard, comprising two Arabs and an Englishman, Ian Davison, murder three Israelis on yacht in Larnaca harbor. Israelis retaliate by bombing PLO headquarters on October 1, 1985. Unrepentant hit team sentenced to life imprisonment.	PLO/ Force 17

DATE	PLACE	INCIDENT	GROUP
9/30/85	Beirut	Four Russian diplomats kidnapped by Sunnis demanding that Russia order Syria to lift siege of Tripoli, northern Lebanon, where Syrian-backed Shias were attacking Sunnis. One Russian, Arkady Kathov, murdered. Others released. First time Russians have been victims of terror in Lebanon.	Islamic Liberation Organization
10/7/85	Mediter-ranean	Italian cruise liner *Achille Lauro* hijacked. Crippled 69-year old American Leon Klinghoffer murdered. Pirates surrender to Egyptians. Plane to Tunis intercepted by American Tomcats, diverted to Italy, and terrorists arrested by Italians after confrontation between carabinieri and U.S. Delta Force who wanted to fly them to U.S. Italians allow mastermind Abu Abbas to go free.	PLF/PLO
11/6/85	Bogotá	Fifty terrorists seize Palace of Justice. Kill President of Supreme Court and 11 other judges. Hundred people, including all terrorists die when building is stormed and catches fire.	M-19
11/23/85	Luqa, Malta	Egyptair Boeing 737 hijacked on flight from Athens to Cairo. Security guard kills one hijacker, then is shot himself in midair battle. Plane forced to land at Luqa, where hijackers start to murder Jewish and Western passengers one by one. Plane stormed by Egypt's élite antiterrorist "Thunderbolt" force, which had successfully stormed this same plane before—when it was hijacked at Luxor in 1975. This time the plane caught fire, either from the hijackers' grenades or from explosives used by commandos to blow open cargo doors. Nine people died—mostly by fire and fumes—in the bloodiest hijack so far. President Mubarak blames Colonel Gaddafi and a PLO splinter group.	Libya/ Abu Nidal

DATE	PLACE	INCIDENT	GROUP
12/23/85	Durban	South Africa's racial strife moves into a new and more vicious phase with the bombings of a crowded shopping center at Amanzimoti. Five whites, three women and two boys, are killed and 48, all but three white, are wounded. Bombing follows land-mine explosion on northern Transvaal border with Zimbabwe which killed six whites, women and children from two families. South African whites prepare for war against the African National Congress.	ANC
12/27/85	Rome/ Vienna	Coordinated attacks on El Al check-in desks at airports kill 19 and wound more than 100. Three terrorists killed in shootout at Leonardo da Vinci airport, one wounded and captured. One killed in Austrian police ambush after fleeing airport, two wounded and captured. Document found on sole survivor of Rome hit team threatens a "river of blood."	Abu Nidal
1/26/86	Ireland	Three arms caches found, two in County Sligo and one in County Roscommon. Crates marked "Libyan Armed Forces" contain ammunition of a type made in Yugoslavia for Libya.	PIRA
2/6/86	Madrid	Vice Admiral Cristobal Colon, direct descendent of Christopher Colombus, assassinated in grenade attack on his car. He is 54th senior officer to be murdered since December 1973 when ETA blew up Admiral Luis Carrero Blanco, Franco's prime minister.	ETA
2/21/86	Paris	*Le Monde* reports that France has released two of Abu Nidal's convicted hit men in a "hands-off" deal with the terrorist. Assad Kayed and Husni Hatem who murdered two PLO representatives in Paris in 1978 are set free under law allowing conditional release in exceptional cases of prisoners who have served half their sentences.	Abu Nidal

DATE	PLACE	INCIDENT	GROUP
2/22/86	Rome	Antonio Da Empoli, economic advisor to Prime Minister Craxi wounded in classic Red Brigades assassination attempt. Driver killed gunwoman who carried proclamation signed by Union of Communist Fighters.	Red Brigades
3/22/86	Dublin	Evelyn Glenholmes, Britain's "most wanted woman" accused of number of bomb outrages, escapes extradition and is freed by court on grounds that Scotland Yard arrest warrant is incorrectly sworn.	PIRA
3/26/86	Amsterdam	Dutch court refuses to extradite PIRA bomber and Maze Prison escaper Gerard Kelly on grounds of his crimes being "political."	PIRA
3/29/86	London	Serena De Pisa, wanted in Italy for bank robbery, is extradited. She is a member of the right-wing Armed Revolutionary Nuclei held responsible for Bologna railway massacre.	NAR
4/2/86	Athens	Bomb blows hole in side of TWA Boeing 727 as it approaches Athens from Rome. Plane survives but four people, including 18-month-baby sucked out of plane and killed. May Mansur, Lebanese widow of Syrian Socialist National party fighter, is named as bomber. She admits she was on plane but denies planting bomb.	SSNP
4/5/86	West Berlin	Bomb in La Belle discotheque kills U.S. soldier and Turkish woman and wounds 204. Intercepted messages between Tripoli and Libyan people's bureau in East Berlin prove Libyan guilt. One of main reasons for U.S. bombing of Libya. Ahmed Nawat Mansur Hasi charged with being accessory. Arrest follows that of his brother, Nezar, in London for trying to smuggle bomb on El Al plane in baggage of his pregnant Irish mistress.	Syria/ Libya

DATE	PLACE	INCIDENT	GROUP
4/15/86	Libya	U.S. aircraft from carriers and British bases bomb terrorist targets in retaliation for Libyan-inspired attacks on Americans. Prime Minister Thatcher criticized for allowing F-111s to operate from British bases. Despite criticism of raid it appears to have accomplished objective of halting Gaddafi's summer terror campaign.	USAF
4/17/86	Lebanon	Two British hostages held by Abu Nidal murdered as reprisal for bombing of Libya. Sir Geoffrey Howe says British Government had good reason to believe they had been in Libyan hands "although we decided not to publicize it because of the risk to their lives. This was part of the evidence we had before us of Libyan state-directed terrorism."	Abu Nidal
4/17/86	London	El Al security staff at Heathrow find bomb in luggage of pregnant Irish woman, Anne-Marie Murphy, being used as innocent dupe by her Jordanian lover, Nezar Narwas Mansur Hindawi. His interrogation leads to Syrian ambassador's being called to Foreign Office and three Syrian diplomats' being expelled. Also leads to arrest of Hindawi's brother in West Berlin for being accessory to La Belle discotheque bombing.	Syria/ Libya
4/18/86	Ankara	Two Libyans arrested as they attempt to throw suitcase bomb and hand grenades into wedding party at American officers' club.	Libya
4/25/86	London	Twenty-two Libyan students deported "in the light of their involvement in Libyan student revolutionary activity in the UK." One of them, Adil Masood, a student pilot, had threatened "We, the revolutionary force, are prepared to become suicide squads against America and its oppression."	Libya

DATE	PLACE	INCIDENT	GROUP
5/3/86	Colombo	Bomb planted by Liberation Tigers of Tamil Eelam kills 17 people including three British tourists when it destroys Air Lanka Tristar. Attack seen as influencing Prime Minister Thatcher to provide support for Sri Lankan government.	LTTE
5/3/86	Ulster	Seamus McElwaine killed and Kevin Lynch wounded in army ambush as they plant 800 lb. boobytrap bomb. McElwaine had been serving life for two murders when he took part in mass breakout from Maze Prison. Armalite rifles carried by two men had been used to murder off-duty policeman and a barman in February 1986.	PIRA
5/7/86	Colombo	Bomb wrecks two floors of Central Telegraph Office in heart of capital opposite President's office. Fourteen die, 100 injured.	LTTE
5/7/86	Tokyo	Summit of leaders headed by President Reagan and Prime Minister Thatcher ends with declaration of determination to fight international terrorism.	
5/11/86	Rome	Brigadier General Ambrogio Viviani, former chief of Italian military counterespionage, discloses that Italy and Libya had worked out deal: Gaddafi would not conduct terrorist operations against Italians if they would turn blind eye to activities of his men and PLO. Viviani says Italy not only provided Gaddafi with help against his enemies but also showed Libyans how to set up a secret service. Irony is that deal was made by Aldo Moro, who was to be murdered by Red Brigades—allies of PLO.	
5/16/86	Washington	Secretary of State George Schulz tells American Jewish Committee that CIA should be given Congressional backing to wage secret war against terrorism. "We have to get rid of the idea that 'covert' is a dirty word."	

DATE	PLACE	INCIDENT	GROUP
6/18/86	Peru	At least 150 Sendero Luminoso prisoners shot in cold blood when they mutiny to coincide with meeting of Socialist International in Lima.	Peruvian Army
6/23/86	London	Patrick Magee sentenced to recommended minimum of 35 years in prison for Brighton bombing.	PIRA
6/26/86	Cuzco	Seven people, including an American, 2 West Germans and a Spaniard, killed, 39 wounded by bomb on tourist train to Inca ruins of Machu Pichu.	Sendero Luminoso
8/3/86	Cyprus	British base at Akrotiri attacked by RPG, mortar and automatic fire in two coordinated attacks. Wives of two NCO's wounded. Believed to be Libyan inspired.	Unified Nasserist Organisation
9/5/86	Karachi	Four men hijack Pan Am Boeing 747 but crew escapes, thus immobilizing plane. Hijackers panic when generator runs out of fuel and lights go out. Open fire on passengers. Twenty killed, hijackers captured. Operation claimed by "Libyan Revolutionary Cells."	Abu Nidal
9/6/86	Istanbul	Twenty-one Jewish worshippers in Neve Shalom synagogue killed when two men open fire with Kalashnikovs and grenades. Terrorists are trapped and blow themselves up with hand grenades.	Abu Nidal
9/17/86	Paris	In culmination of week of bombing in center of Paris bomb is thrown into crowded store, killing 5 and wounding 61. Campaign designed to force French government to release Georges Abdallah, leader of FARL.	FARL

Select Bibliography

Barril, Capitaine. *Missions Très Speciales*. Paris: Presses de la Cité, 1984.

Becker, Jillian. *Hitler's Children: The Story of the Baader-Meinhof Terrorist Gang*. London: Granada, 1978.

Beckwith, Col. Charlie. *Delta Force*. New York: Harcourt Brace, 1983.

Bell, J. Bowyer. *A Time of Terror: How Democratic Societies Respond to Revolutionary Violence*. New York: Basic Books, 1978.

Bulloch, John. *Final Conflict: The War in Lebanon*. London: Century, 1983.

Cline, Ray S., and Alexander, Yonah. *Terrorism: The Soviet Connection*. New York: Crane-Russak Co., 1984.

Dobson, Christopher and Payne, Ronald. *The Terrorists: Their Weapons, Leaders and Tactics*. rev. ed. New York: Facts On File, 1982.

———. *Counterattack: The West's Battles Against the Terrorists*. New York: Facts On File, 1982.

Hirst, David. *The Gun and the Olive Branch*. London: Faber, 1977.

Laqueur, Walter. *Terrorism*. New York: Little Brown, 1979.

Tophoven, Rolf. *GSG9 German Response to Terrorism*. Koblenz, W. Ger.: Bernard & Graefe, 1984.

Wilkinson, Paul, ed. *British Perspectives on Terrorism*. New York: Allen Unwin, 1981.

INDEX